Local and Urban Governance

Series Editor

Carlos Nunes Silva, LISBOA, Portugal

This series contains research studies with policy relevance in the field of sub-national territorial governance, at the micro, local and regional levels, as well as on its connections with national and supranational tiers. The series is multidisciplinary and brings together innovative research from different areas within the Social Sciences and Humanities. The series is open for theoretical, methodological and empirical ground breaking contributions. Books included in this series explore the new modes of territorial governance, new perspectives and new research methodologies. The aim is to present advances in Governance Studies to scholars and researchers in universities and research organizations, and to policy makers worldwide. The series includes monographs, edited volumes and textbooks. Book proposals and final manuscripts are peer-reviewed.

The areas covered in the series include but are not limited to the following subjects:

- Local and regional government
- Urban and metropolitan governance
- Multi-level territorial governance
- Post-colonial local governance
- Municipal merger reforms
- Inter-municipal cooperation
- Decentralized cooperation
- Governance of spatial planning
- Strategic spatial planning
- Citizen participation in local policies
- Local governance, spatial justice and the right to the city
- Local public services
- Local economic development policies
- Entrepreneurialism and municipal public enterprises
- Local government finance
- Local government and sustainable development
- Anthropocene and green local governance
- Climate change and local governance
- Smart local governance

The series is intended for geographers, planners, political scientists, sociologists, lawyers, historians, urban anthropologists and economists. **Local and Urban Governance—now indexed in Scopus**

Karl Kössler • Erika Schläppi
Editors

Citizen Participation in Local Governance

An Urban-Rural Perspective

Springer

Editors
Karl Kössler
Institute for Comparative Federalism
Eurac Research
Bolzano, Italy

Erika Schläppi
Ximpulse GmbH
Bern, Switzerland

ISSN 2524-5449 ISSN 2524-5457 (electronic)
Local and Urban Governance
ISBN 978-3-031-99823-2 ISBN 978-3-031-99824-9 (eBook)
https://doi.org/10.1007/978-3-031-99824-9

This Springer imprint is published by the registered company Springer Nature Switzerland AG
The registered company address is: Gewerbestrasse 11, 6330 Cham, Switzerland

Acknowledgement

This project has received funding from the European Union's Horizon 2020 research and innovation programme under grant agreement No 823961.

Contents

Chapter 1
Citizen Participation in Local Governance: Four Issues in Focus

Karl Kössler

Abstract This edited book assembles chapters that focus on how citizens are involved in the decision-making of local governments. Within this broad thematic area, our research within a Horizon 2020 project on "Local Government and the Changing Urban-Rural Interplay—LoGov", which brought together the expertise of 18 partner institutions from six continents, has revealed several issues as particularly salient and under-researched from a global comparative perspective, namely. These issues are participation in local development and planning, in large-scale projects, participatory budgeting and the promises and pitfalls of digital participation. This chapter first discusses to what extent local citizen participation can be a remedy for the current crisis of representative democracy, then provides short introductions to the four above-mentioned issues and concludes with an overview of the guiding questions for the case studies included in this volume.

Keywords Citizen participation · Local governance · Local development and planning · Large-scale projects · Participatory budgeting · Digital participation

1.1 Introduction

This edited book assembles chapters that focus on how citizens are involved in the decision-making of local governments. Within this broad thematic area, our research within a Horizon 2020 project on "Local Government and the Changing

K. Kössler (✉)
Institute for Comparative Federalism, Eurac Research, Bolzano/Bozen, Italy
e-mail: karl.koessler@eurac.edu

K. Kössler, E. Schläppi (eds.), *Citizen Participation in Local Governance*, Local and Urban Governance, https://doi.org/10.1007/978-3-031-99824-9_1

Urban-Rural Interplay—LoGov",[1] which brought together the expertise of 18 partner institutions from six continents, has revealed several issues as particularly salient and under-researched from a global comparative perspective. These issues are participation in local development and planning, in large-scale projects, participatory budgeting and the promises and pitfalls of digital participation.

The case studies included in this volume, conducted across multiple countries, underscore the extensive geographical breadth of the LoGov project. While some of the core themes explored have been previously addressed in scholarly literature, the distinct contribution of this edited collection lies in its global comparative scope. To expand the analytical horizon, it includes lesser-known cases which have so far been understudied in relation to classical European cases. Anchored in a comparative framework, the volume adopts a multiple case study design (Yin, 2003, 56). This enables a systematic cross-case analysis while preserving the integrity of intra-case specificity. The aim is to identify convergences and divergences in how comparable governance challenges are addressed across different institutional, legal, and socio-political contexts, and to assess the potential for policy transfer and contextual adaptation.

Methodologically, the chapters enhance the credibility and robustness of their findings by using, to the extent possible in each case, multiple data sources (Patton, 2002, 38). Each case study endeavors to integrate multiple sources of evidence, contingent upon contextual feasibility and data accessibility. The interdisciplinary character of the volume—drawing upon the expertise of scholars specialized in public law, political science, and public administration—facilitates a methodologically pluralistic approach. Data sources include but are not limited to statutory and constitutional texts, judicial decisions, statistical data, reports issued by governmental and non-governmental organizations, and peer-reviewed publications from the three above-mentioned disciplinary fields.

While desk research has played a key role, our authors have, to varying degrees, also engaged in original field research. This includes, in particular, semi-structured interviews with local government stakeholders, conducted within the framework of the LoGov project's country reports,[2] which are referenced in the chapters where analytically pertinent. The synthesis of data from these diverse sources enables each case study to deliver a multidimensional analysis, enhancing descriptive richness, mitigating single-source bias, and producing robust, triangulated findings concerning the four salient issues identified above. These four overarching topics and their respective research questions structure the chapters assembled in this edited book.

[1] This dualism is, of course, a simplification. Instead of a binary distinction implied by the thinking of an urban-rural divide, our point of departure is the recognition that it is more appropriate to speak of an urban-rural continuum and that local governments are located at different points of this continuum.

[2] https://www.logov-rise.eu/country-map/.

1.2 Local Citizen Participation as Potential Remedy for the Crisis of Representative Democracy

As one leading scholar put it, "[i]f democracy is a good thing … , then more democracy should presumably be an even better thing" (Dryzek, 1996, 475). But what is the actual meaning of "democracy" and how can we have "more of it"? For decades these questions about how people govern themselves have been the subject of political and scientific debates with regard to all levels of government, not least also the local one. Such debates have grown out of a certain dissatisfaction with representative democracy, as the latter came to be seen as providing insufficient opportunities for citizen participation.

Without doubt, indirect democracy through elected representatives is prevalent around the world, so that it has been regarded, from an empirical perspective, as the "proper form of democracy" (Böckenförde, 1982, 301–328). From a normative point of view, however, the question of whether the people *shall* make laws or only choose legislators to make laws has been answered differently. Whereas Rousseau famously quipped that the English people "is free only during the election of the members of Parliament" and "[a]s soon as they are elected, it is a slave" (Rousseau, 1978/1762, 102–103), fellow Enlightenment philosopher Montesquieu became a main proponent of representative democracy and the vast majority of political thinkers, from Madison (1961/1787, 77–84) to Dahl (1956, 51) followed suit. Especially as the extension of suffrage gave rise to complex mass democracies, many of them claimed that the representative approach was the only "realistic" form of democracy. Perhaps most famous is Schumpeter's minimalist characterization of the "democratic method" as a procedure through which "individuals acquire the power to decide by means of a competitive struggle for the people's vote" (Schumpeter, 1976/1942, 269). Thus, participation of the people is reduced to producing a government and nothing more. Typical arguments advanced in favor of indirect democracy are that direct popular legislation would be vulnerable to the influence of special interests (as if representatives were free from lobbying pressures) and that elected representatives, together with the free mandate and the separation of powers, would form cornerstones of a rational and transparent legislative process, thus ensuring "government of law and not of men" (Article 30 of the Constitution of the Commonwealth of Massachusetts 1780; Frankenberg, 2012, 254). In this way, liberal democracy has demonstrated from its outset a strong penchant towards representative government and has sometimes even been equated with it (Sartori, 1987, 383–398).

However, the 1960s witnessed the surge of a participatory conception of democracy among both a politically active citizenry and committed academics, which opposed the prevailing "realistic" democratic theory (Pateman, 2012, 7). They challenged arguments for the representative approach, such as Madison's point that political accountability would require a clear distinction between the "rulers, men who possess most wisdom to discern, and most virtue to pursue the common good of the society" (Madison, 1961b/1788) and those they represent. Since the 1960s, the above-mentioned conception of liberal democracy came to be criticized as "thin" democracy from whose "precarious foundation, no firm theory of citizenship, participation, public goods, or civic virtue can be expected to arise" (Barber, 1984, 4). These two opposing conceptions of democracy exhibit several differences (Michels, 2006, 326), but all these culminate in a specific role of citizen participation. The latter is an essential feature of a democracy for participationists and a rather marginal one for proponents of the representative approach.

Why is it then that the minimalist definition of aggregating from time to time people's votes in elections was no longer accepted as forming the "essence of democracy" (Dryzek, 2000, 2)? For one, this was the result of fundamental changes in the self-conception of citizens who, having benefitted from better access to education and information and increasingly espousing post-materialistic values, became more willing to have a direct say rather than leaving decisions entirely to elected representatives (Inglehart, 1977, 295–297; Inglehart & Welzel, 2005). Besides these societal transformations, it was also the inherent shortcomings of the representative approach itself which contributed to discontent and, as a consequence, to another conception of democracy (Held, 2006, 84–87). This is vividly reflected in critical perspectives characterizing the current state of affairs as "audience-democracy" (Manin, 1997, 223), that is, people being passive receivers of political messages, or "unpolitical democracy", which claims to identify two major trends: an expansion of non-partisan decisions and a focus primarily on output legitimacy. Both these trends would "tend to neutralize that which makes democratic politics so characteristically associated with dispute, disagreement, deliberation, and majority decisions that are open to change" (Urbinati, 2014, 81).

While the crisis of representative democracy is therefore a more general phenomenon, the situation obviously varies considerably from country to country, which makes a differentiated assessment of the state of democracy based on a number of factors all the more important (International IDEA, 2024). With regard to the local level, it has been argued that the dissatisfaction with representative government has become manifest in two varieties: first, political apathy, characterized by scarce knowledge about politics and little interest in it; secondly, political cynicism, which is marked by a gap between considerable knowledge and low satisfaction with both existing opportunities for participation (input-legitimacy) and the content of policies determined by elected representatives (output-legitimacy) (Kersting & Cronqvist, 2005, 28). As the argument goes, the result is then a disengagement from the formal political system and a decrease in voter turnout and party membership, on the one hand, and an increase in (sometimes violent) political protests, on the other. Thus, the question arises whether there are "any alternatives to the brick and the ballot" (Kersting, 2012, 15).

Whereas some governments reacted to this situation with repression, most responded by providing new spaces for citizen participation. Some of these new experiments were dominated by political parties and formal institutions, which often did not meet the expectations of people to raise their voices. Therefore, if formal channels for participation, generated top-down by the authorities, ("invited spaces") were either insufficient or completely absent, people have tended to create for themselves ad hoc informal channels to have their say ("invented spaces") (Cornwall, 2002, ii). Cases in point are protest marches, pickets, sit-ins, or flash mobs. These direct actions also challenge the reductionist view nurtured by representative democracy that state institutions like, above all, parliament are the exclusive public spheres of discourse. As parliament swallowed up other public spheres beyond that of a legislative assembly (Fraser, 1997, 91), a broader understanding of participation contends that it should be a guiding principle in various contexts, from schools and the workplace to civic associations (Morison & Harkens, 2018, 13).

A key question is then what we take "citizen participation" to mean, given that similar expressions exist with partly overlapping meanings. What is clear is that over several decades, participation has become a buzzword that is on everybody's lips. This is epitomized, for example, by the publication in 1996 of a widely disseminated World Bank participation sourcebook (World Bank, 1996) and, as one observer succinctly put it, by a status quo in which "[i]nstitutions as diverse as the World Bank, the United Nations, Brazil's leftist Workers' Party, and India's Communist Party currently promote the adoption of participatory institutions" (Wampler, 2008, 61). Moreover, the hype around participation is also reflected in numerous efforts to clarify it as a concept by means of adding several adjectives. *Public* participation was defined as being, at its core, concerned with information about governmental action and an opportunity to comment on them. It was thus seen as included by the more general concept of public engagement, whose central element is arguably assembling individuals to address an issue of public concern (Nabatchi & Amsler, 2014, 3). Others promote the term *political* participation, understood broadly as an act to influence political decision-making which can occur in four distinct spheres, that is, participation through representative democracy, through direct democracy, deliberative participation, and demonstrative participation (Kersting, 2013, 272). The latter sphere is probably the least obvious. Demonstrative participation is related to the above-mentioned "invented spaces" insofar as it refers to direct actions such as flash mobs that are addressed to policymakers "without invitation" (Kersting, 2013, 271). Such participation has been characterized as highly symbolic and expressivity-focused because primary goals are arguably to demonstrate political positions and the belonging to a certain political group (Kersting, 2013, 275). In reality, the four above-mentioned spheres evidently overlap and influence each other, as some tools combine, for instance, deliberative participation and direct democracy according to the motto "first talk, then vote" (Goodin, 2008, 108–24).

Yet another term, *citizen* participation, has been understood to encompass both deliberative and participatory democracy as two distinct forms (Pateman, 2012, 7). These notions of democracy clearly differ concerning several features like their origin, nature, and focus. The first push for participatory democracy in the 1960s was linked to popular movements expressing their discontent with representative democracy (Pateman, 1970), while the invention of the often-emulated participatory budgeting in the Brazilian City of Porto Alegre in the late 1980s[3] provided another boost. In both cases the starting point for participatory democracy have been concrete hands-on innovations based on which it was then conceptualized. Indeed, as has been pointed out, the significance of Porto Alegre's practice "for the theory of participatory democracy cannot be overstated" (Fung, 2011, 859). Deliberative democracy, by contrast, has been characterized as a rather "political theory-led enterprise" (Pateman, 2012, 8). As for its focus, participatory democracy is on "the engagement of citizens and the variety, breadth, and depth of democratic involvement" (Morison, 2017, 651). Deliberative democracy, on the other hand, is mainly concerned with the quality of "public reasoning" (Morison, 2017, 651), a deliberation process that is rational and impartial (Teorell, 2006, 8), as well as "oriented toward problem solving" with participants having "an adequate opportunity to speak, listen attentively and consider carefully the contributions of other participants" (Gastil, 2005, 164–173). As deliberative democracy has gained popularity since around 1990 in what has been called the "deliberative turn" (Dryzek, 2002), its relationship with participatory democracy has become a contentious issue. Whereas some assert that "deliberative democrats tend to be participatory democrats, too" (Goodin, 2008, 266), the latter have emphasized distinctiveness. As a leading participationist argues, deliberation is necessary for democracy but not sufficient. Moreover, she also criticizes the allegedly narrow focus of deliberationists on processes inside deliberative forums so that "democracy in the wider society and political system is outside of their purview" (Pateman, 2012, 10). What both do have in common, however, is that they can be considered forms of citizen participation.

Importantly, processes of citizen participation are often open to people beyond the formal category of passport-holders with the right to vote to include, for example, foreign residents and youth. To be sure, many scholars in public and international law adhere to the traditional static view of citizenship as a formal legal status, which reflects—most visibly through a passport—full membership in a state and entails, as a consequence, particular rights and obligations. From this point of view, citizens and foreigners are "correlative, mutually exclusive, exhaustive categories" (Brubaker, 1992, 46). More recently, however, another conception of citizenship has gained traction which is based on three dimensions, namely rights (not necessarily those flowing from formal citizenship) (Marshall, 1950),[4] participation, and a sense of belonging (Bellamy et al., 2004; Shaw, 2007). Compared to the formal conception above, which sees citizenship as something bestowed by states and separating individuals in a binary manner, this social science view is more open (Medda-Windischer & Kössler, 2024, 39–62) and thus better captures the various categories of people admitted to processes of citizen participation.

---

[3] See Sect. 1.4.

[4] Marshall proposed an evolutionary and rights-based concept of citizenship that starting with the conferral of civil rights, then political rights, and at last social rights.

A crucial issue is then how such participation relates to local government. The most obvious link is that opportunities for citizens to be involved are facilitated by small-scale settings. A case in point is assembly democracy in ancient Athens, whose combination of direct popular participation and a deliberative process focused on the local government level, that is, the *polis*. Regarding direct democracy in large territorial states, Madison used the above-mentioned argument of scale to claim that such democracy would be inferior to the representative approach because of "the greater number of citizens, and greater sphere of country, over which the latter may be extended" (Madison, 1961a). While Switzerland's extensive use of direct democracy at the national level appears to prove Madison wrong, this case remains an outlier and there is little doubt that people's involvement through referendums and popular initiatives is usually facilitated by small-scale settings. The same holds true for citizen participation, as defined above. While the exclusion of certain people due to social divisions may be at least as big a problem at the local level, the smaller scale seems to make this government level, in many ways, the most natural and feasible one for many participatory tools. Cases in point are "deliberative polls" (Fishkin, 2009, 25–32) or neighbourhood meetings on a "deliberation day" (Ackerman & Fishkin, 2002, 129–152). This is because territorial entities with larger populations aggravate Fishkin's famous trilemma, which says that three aims, that is, a large number of participants, equality concerning inclusiveness and quality of deliberation, cannot all be realized at once (Fishkin, 2009, 32–64). Moreover, there are also normative arguments for bolstering citizen participation, particularly, in municipalities. Dahl claimed, for example, that opportunities to influence local, small-scale politics might help bridge the growing gap between people's increasing expectations regarding participation, on the one hand, and their decreasing influence on decisions as a result of globalization (Dahl, 1994, 33). Indeed, the 1992 UN Conference on Environment and Development in Rio and local Agenda 21 stemming from it have been credited with providing an impulse for the establishment of participatory processes in a number of countries (Kersting et al., 2016, 329).

A key question is what the actual impact of these manifold novel instruments is. Initial research on citizen participation at the local level has "largely extolled the positive benefits" (Wampler, 2008, 61) of these tools for the quality of democracy, such as the generation of social capital, empowerment of citizens and increased transparency of governments. Theories of participatory democracy, deliberative democracy and social capital have often argued that citizen involvement has the potential to yield positive effects in several ambits (Michels & De Graaf, 2010, 480–481; Fung, 2015, 2). First, citizen participation would strengthen inclusiveness by making people feel part of their political community and thus also feel more personally responsible for public decisions, as their voices were heard. Secondly, it would have an educational function by improving civic skills, such as the ability to debate public issues and civic virtues, such as interest and active participation in public life. Thirdly, it would enhance the legitimacy of both the process and outcome of decision-making and, as a corollary of this, also the effectiveness of government decisions because being more legitimate they would face less resistance. Finally, another point that should be added is the quality of decisions, as participatory processes enable informed decisions by authorities based on the variety of interests expressed by citizens.

Some empirical research, however, has cast doubt on whether these aspired benefits actually materialize. As for inclusiveness, several studies have found that groups of people involved in participatory processes often lack diversity (Michels & De Graaf, 2017, 877). Those who are available for participation are frequently well-educated, older and already active in politics or civil society (O'Flynn & Sood, 2014, 41–81). Other factors determining whether people get involved are time resources and sufficient confidence that the final decision will really respond to their needs, something that people from marginalized and underprivileged groups often lack. In particular, it has been emphasized that better education makes the voice of some individuals stronger because it drives both political interest and enhances skills like the ability to gather information, organize and process information or debating skills (Bovens & Wille, 2017, 84). Thus, educational inequalities have been blamed for leading to what has been called "diploma democracy" (Bovens & Wille, 2017, 156). Overall, the observed participation bias appears to imply that "a sense of public engagement is a precondition for participation rather than a consequence" (Michels & De Graaf, 2017, 878) and is, quite obviously, a major obstacle for real inclusiveness. If the latter is compromised, this also has repercussions on the other two expected positive effects mentioned above, that is, the improvement of civic skills and the legitimacy of decision-making. An increase in civic skills is evidently limited when involvement, especially of people who are less educated and less civically active, is scarce. As for legitimacy, it is certainly diminished by a lack of inclusiveness and further reduced in case of weak responsiveness on the part of the government so that people have little incentive to participate. The need for any participatory process to be taken seriously and be effectively linked to the outcome of final decision-making in order to have an impact was already emphasized by a pioneer of citizen participation. For Arnstein, citizen participation was "a categorical term for citizen power" understood as "the real power needed to affect the outcome" (Arnstein, 1969, 216). Consequently, her famous "ladder of citizen participation (Arnstein, 1969, 217) had eight rungs ranging from "manipulation" up to full "citizen control". Unsurprisingly, therefore, the degree of power granted to a participatory mechanism is also one of Fung's famous institutional elements for participation to effectively deepen democracy, next to the eligibility criteria for individuals to be involved and the mode of decision-making (Fung, 2006, 67).

If such power is absent, participation will become an "empty and frustrating process for the powerless" (Arnstein, 1969, 216), something that has only recently received attention in empirical research. A phenomenon called "participatory frustration" (Fernández-Martínez et al., 2020, 718–748) has been attributed to four causes, namely, inflated expectations which are then easily disappointed, failures of process design, poor results, and abrupt discontinuations. Despite such innovative lines of empirical research, observers have highlighted that most of the literature focuses on the internal functioning of participatory processes (e.g., the quality of deliberation and satisfaction of people involved) (Michels & Binnema, 2019,

749–769) or "is still preoccupied with making a normative argument and with contesting the dominant focus on representative institutions"(Baiocchi et al., 2011, 1) at the cost of neglecting the link of participatory processes with these institutions and the outcomes of their decisions. Another scholar similarly highlights that studies on the impact are only starting to become more numerous and that "the results so far suggest mostly modest outcomes"(Piper, 2014, 52). One reason for this status quo is arguably the difficulty or even impossibility to isolate the impact of participatory processes and to ascertain why and how they actually make a difference (Baiocchi et al., 2011, 1). Against the existing body of research on citizen participation in local governance, the sections of this edited book seek to make a valuable contribution to the understanding of how participation works, by focusing on four specific issues.

1.3 Participation in Local Development and Planning

Local development and planning form an issue of particular relevance for citizens since decisions made in this area directly shape their living environment in a very concrete and tangible way. Yet, their participation in decision-making has not always been a given. Indeed, when planning emerged as a discipline after World War II, it was conceived as a rational process in which professionals derived alternatives from their scientific knowledge and elected politicians then made their choice. In such a setting, citizen participation had no place and decision-makers simply assumed what *they* saw as the needs and preferences of the local population. This only changed with a shift from blueprint planning to more collaborative processes (Lane, 2005, 283–299). The 1960s proved crucial for what has been called the "democratization of planning" (Sandercock, 2005), which was propelled by civil society pressure to be involved and scholars in introducing social justice perspectives into planning. Key among the latter were Arnstein's above-mentioned "ladder of citizen participation" (Arnstein, 1969, 217), arguing for participation as a tool to empower "the have-nots" vis-à-vis "the powerholders", and Lefebvre's "right to the city" (Lefebvre, 1968), defining (urban) space as a social construction that should be inclusive with a view to all inhabitants.

As a result of this shift towards collaborative processes, participation is widely practiced in manifold forms regarding both the formulation and implementation of local development and planning (Tippett & How, 2020, 109–132). Indeed, an increasing number of actors being involved and a more "consensus-oriented" process have been identified—at least for Europe—as key trends in planning (Reimer et al., 2014). Another indicator of the growing importance of participation is that it found its way into the very definition of spatial planning. In fact, the latter is today seen as referring to the management of land and property involving "active cooperation across government, market and civil society actors to coordinate decision-making", which has "an impact on the quality of places and their development"

(Nadin et al., 2018, 8). In a similar vein, others argue that what distinguishes the more novel concept of spatial planning from the "traditional idea of land-use planning" is, among other things, that it involves "community participation" (Tewdwr-Jones, 2004, 593). However, one should caution against assuming that there is a local community representing homogeneous interests. Particularly in planning processes, there is often a clash of interests, depending on whether the project in question is perceived as having a positive or negative impact by the relevant interest groups. Thus, tensions are possible between the different local stakeholders such as companies and local citizens.

Less clear is what participation in planning actually means, since the term is sometimes regarded as comprising any type of formal or informal public involvement and used interchangeably with such notions as co-creation, collaboration, consultation or deliberation (Hofer & Kaufmann, 2022, 2). Recently, an attempt has been made to conceptualize participation as a web of interacting elements (Hofer & Kaufmann, 2022, 1–23). The framework differentiates between three dimensions (actors, arenas and aims), which correspond to the well-established distinction of the who, how and why questions regarding participation (Fung, 2006, 67). Each of the three dimensions is again constituted by three elements, namely subjects, roles and recruitment (regarding actors), spaces, formats and rhythms (arenas) and issues, rationales and outcomes (aims).

The last dimension has attracted particular attention, as it is not always clear what aims participation in planning pursues and whether they are actually achieved. Some observers distinguish normative and pragmatic arguments for the involvement of citizens (Nadin et al., 2021, 794–795), which resembles that between "participation as an end" and "participation as a means" (Nelson & Wright, 1995, 1–18). Pragmatic aims are to improve the acceptance of planning decisions and thus facilitate their implementation or to harness the local knowledge and interests of stakeholders concerned, which has been increasingly recognized since the end of the twentieth century as a valuable complement to experts' professional knowledge (Sandercock, 1998, 258). Normative aims include the enhancement of equity, fairness, responsiveness, transparency, the quality of decision-making and democratic empowerment regarding planning processes.

A big question is then, for the chapters of this volume and more generally, whether participation in planning is able to achieve these aims. Leading experts in the field have acknowledged that "there is skepticism about whether it can deliver on its promises" (Nadin et al., 2021, 795). The then resulting gap between rhetoric and reality risks to reduce participation to a fig leaf. While its real impact regarding the specific aims above may be difficult to assess, some observers have cast doubt on whether it achieves considerable benefits concerning the democratization of local governance (Brownill & Parker, 2010, 275–282). A critical perspective towards participation in local development and planning is therefore just as much needed as more research on its impact.

1.4 Participation and Large-Scale Projects

There are obvious links between participation in local development and planning, on the one hand, and the involvement of citizens regarding large-scale projects, on the other. This is simply because the latter are also the object of a planning process, or even several planning processes. Still, participation concerning such projects is arguably different due to its focus on a single issue and the greater potential of mobilization around this issue, which also seems to have implications for how citizens get involved.

Importantly, "large-scale projects" or, as they are sometimes called, "megaprojects" (Esposito et al., 2023, 259–273) are not only related to what is known as "locally unwanted land uses" (LULUs) (Hubbard, 2009, 403) such as potentially hazardous facilities (e.g. incinerators, landfill sites or power plants). It may also be other projects that people associate with negative connotations (e.g. prisons) or even with, in principle, positive connotations (e.g. big apartment buildings, sports stadiums or supermarkets), but often do not want them in their vicinity. The term "Not in My Back Yard" (NIMBY) has become an often-used buzzword in public discourse to characterize this phenomenon. It is precisely such opposition, propelled by fears that facilities may create nuisances or have other negative local effects, which makes channels of participation regarding large-scale projects particularly important. This also holds true from the perspective of policymakers because pushing a large-scale project without participation often entails considerable risks of delay or even the failure of a project that could otherwise have been designed and approved in a way that is acceptable for a majority of local citizens. Opposition to a project needs to be taken seriously. After all, it is predictable that people will go to great lengths to protect their assets, most often their home, against unwanted projects that represent—unlike fire, flood, or theft—an uninsurable risk.

That is why participation regarding large-scale projects arguably has a specific nature. If policymakers fail to provide formal participatory channels that are provided by the authorities ("invited spaces"), it is a particular characteristic—given the high stakes—that people will create ad hoc informal channels to have their say ("invented spaces"). Direct actions in invented spaces are related to demonstrative participation mentioned above, insofar as they are addressed to policymakers "without invitation". If citizens, by contrast, are invited to participate through formal channels such as hearings and consultations regarding a large-scale project's impact on the environment, health, etc., this arguably forces them to adapt their strategy. Opposition to the project simply based on a NIMBY rationale is then not sufficient, but arguments about the concrete negative effects of increased traffic, noise, pollution, etc. are needed. One concern has been that such invited spaces favor, like instruments of citizen participation more generally,[5] well-educated, politically

[5] See Sect. 1.2.

articulate and resource-rich people who, as a consequence, could be in a position to enforce the displacement of unwanted large-scale projects onto other neighborhoods (Hubbard, 2009, 405). Even if it is widely acknowledged that participation regarding large-scale projects is still a rather under-researched issue, preliminary evidence appears to suggest that there indeed is a shift from "straightforward, linear, and rational decision-making processes" determined by a technical-economic logic to decision-making that employs tools of participation "as a valuable resource to address complexity, uncertainty, and conflict" (Esposito et al., 2022, 55–79). It seems important then that people are involved early enough and substantially, even if that requires going beyond legally mandated hearings, that transparency and access to information, especially via the internet, are recognized as cornerstones of participation in large-scale projects, that project developers are obliged to respond to the points raised by the public and that involvement is adequate to the project at stake. The latter issue of who shall (be allowed to) participate in invited spaces is crucial. Research on NIMBYism assumes that some projects (e.g. a major airport) have "a larger externality field" (Hubbard, 2009, 403) than others (e.g. a hospital) and the broader circle of the people affected often also implies that the circle of those involved is broader too. But then again, this is not the only possible rationale for delimiting the group of people allowed to participate. In fact, studies on NIMBYism also assume that, regarding large-scale projects, there is a conflict between local interests (however defined), and wider regional or even national interests. Indeed, a case could be made that the latter should also be represented in the decision-making process. But where to concretely draw the line of whom to include and exclude or how to give the views of those more (directly) affected more weight in a participatory process is anything but a straightforward issue.

1.5 Participatory Budgeting

There can be little doubt that participatory budgeting (PB) has been, in recent decades, one of the most popular forms of citizen participation. From its origins in the Brazilian City of Porto Alegre in 1989 (de Sousa Santos, 1998, 461–510; Baiocchi, 2003, 45–76), it has spread across the globe, which inevitably entailed a process of diversification with the initial idea being adapted to local contexts. Yet, despite this increasing variety, all these practices still have in common that they are all about deliberating and deciding collectively on allocating a portion of a public budget. Typically, this is done through a multi-stage process involving phases of information, consultation, prioritization/evaluation of proposed projects and, finally, accountability, as local authorities are obligated to inform the public about the implementation status of projects (Sintomer et al., 2010). Beyond the minimal definition of involving citizens in budgetary decision-making, PB has been conceptualized in different ways. Some have developed ideal types of PB, which makes it possible to classify single examples despite their stark differences (Sintomer et al., 2012, 16–28). Others contend that it is more expedient to conceptualize PB as a set of principles with a view to their potential to bring about social change. The principles suggested are (Wampler, 2012, 2–7): "voice" through the promotion of active citizen participation; "vote" by conferring on citizens the authority to make local decisions beyond mere consultative deliberation; "social justice" through the reallocation of resources to traditionally marginalized lower-income segments of the population, even if there seems to be a trend in Europe, for example, that this redistributive element is no longer at the forefront of PB (Kersting et al., 2016, 330); and "oversight" due to improved transparency of government spending. The purpose of these four core principles should then be to serve as both a starting point for local governments and civil society to develop the concrete rules for their individual participatory process and a standard against which citizens and researchers can assess PB (Wampler, 2012, 7).

Besides these various conceptualizations, empirical research on PB has grown immensely since the phenomenon emerged. There are comparative publications that identify similarities and dissimilarities in how the instrument is applied in different countries and equally serve as useful resources for policymakers (Sintomer et al., 2013, 9–24). The popularity of PB is further epitomized by the fact that there is a "World Atlas of Participatory Budgeting" which, among other things, aims to track the reach of the phenomenon and its main trends on a global scale (PB Network, 2019). Comparative publications with a more academic approach have demonstrated that spatial, temporal, economic and organizational factors tend to result in different PB programs *across* different parts of the world but similar programs *within* continents (Wampler, 2012; Sintomer et al., 2012, 6–16). Still other comparative studies have gone a step further by both mapping existing models of PB and then exploring under which contextual variables (financial autonomy, political culture, size of municipalities, etc.) these could be successfully applied and thus be advisable for local governments in other countries (Krenjova & Raudla, 2013, 18–46).

1.6 Promises and Pitfalls of Digital Participation

Given the extraordinary fast pace of the digital revolution that has fundamentally changed many parts of life, not least the political sphere, several publications from the late twentieth century, the starting point of this revolution, seem rather outdated today. And yet, it is worthwhile and useful from our "future" perspective to look back at how a pioneer of participatory democracy like Benjamin Barber envisaged the evolving relationship between the new technologies and democracy. He outlined a worst-case scenario of technological determinism, another scenario defined by complacency, and a third in which people acknowledge risks but actively seek to benefit from positive uses of the new technologies for modernizing democracy (Barber, 1998, 576–584). Whichever of Barber's three scenarios eventually materializes, technology has without doubt substantially affected democracy, something that scholars have attempted to grasp with new terminology. Some introduced the notion of "virtual democracy" (Norris & Jones, 1998, 1–4) and others "electronic democracy" (Kersting, 2012, 11–54). Still others prefer "digital democracy" (Hacker & Van Dijk, 2000, 1), as it arguably best encapsulates the new reliance on information and communication technology (ICT) and computer-mediated communication (CMC) for purposes of strengthening democracy.

The ways in which these technologies may affect democracy by potentially enhancing people's participation are manifold and range from online newspapers and blogs to deliberation forums. Attempts of categorization of these various tools are therefore very useful. One of these attempts categorizes online tools relevant to digital democracy according to their main function, depending on whether it is information, communication or participation (Kersting, 2012, 23–33). Even if the focus of the chapters in Section 4 of our book is on digital *participation*, this does not mean that the other two functions are irrelevant because all three are, quite obviously, interconnected. As Barber noted, "democracy is a form of government that depends on information and communication" (Barber, 1998, 582) and participation requires informed citizens able to communicate with each other. Thus, the effects of new technologies in these two spheres inevitably influence the quality of digital participation.

As for information, the Internet has immensely facilitated both the retrieval and exchange of information for all actors in democracies such as citizens, civil society organizations, governments, etc. In particular, the increasing access to an enormous number of sources through the Internet since the 1990s has certainly entailed a drastic weakening of the gate-keeping function of traditional media. The hope is then that "[i]dealistically, the emancipated citizen selects information and is not manipulated by a monopolized media in the hands of powerful politicians and traditional organizations" (Kersting, 2012, 24). Of course, the new situation does not mean that nobody has a gate-keeping function regarding information. It is just that others, for instance, private social media companies, now have this function so that the warning that "an overly restrictive filtering system is likely to impoverish a public sphere" (Benkler, 2006, 183) is quite a relevant one.

As for communication, Aristotle had famously remarked that the ideal size for a democratic polity would be such that people could traverse in a day, ensuring that all citizens could attend an assembly (Barber, 1998, 574). It is obvious that new technologies have enabled the creation of online publics and that they exchange views and mobilize to action across spatial boundaries with, for instance, the "hashtag" emerging as a coordination mechanism. This has been the result of the Internet's shift from one-to-many communication of its early stage to many-to-many communication so that "the Web is no longer about idly surfing and reading, listening or watching; it is about peering, sharing, socializing, collaborating and most of all creating within loosely connected communities" (Tapscott & Williams, 2010, 45).

Besides the areas of information and communication which are, as argued, functional to participation, the digital revolution has also affected participation more directly. Undoubtedly, the Internet has facilitated the creation of both "invited spaces" and "invented spaces". Regarding the latter, flash mobs and shit storms have been mentioned as phenomena that have primarily expressive demonstrative functions because they are focused on showing someone's position and belonging to a certain community (Kersting, 2013, 275–276). As for "invited spaces", most tools of online participation offered to citizens appear to relate to the agenda-setting stage of the policy cycle, the stage where the process is potentially still sufficiently open to integrate suggestions from citizens (Macintosh, 2003, 95–97). What seems clear by now, however, is that the simple shift of offline tools into the online world is not enough. At least as far as participatory budgeting is concerned, attempts in some countries to move these procedures online have led them to lose their deliberative nature and to degenerate into little more than an "electronic suggestion box" (Kersting et al., 2016, 329).

The digital revolution's overall impact on the three interrelated spheres of information, communication, and participation (Tsagarousianou, 1999, 189–208) is still not easy to gauge. However, an important piece of advice appears to be to adopt a differentiated and nuanced approach by moving "beyond the glory days rhetoric about new golden ages of democracy as well as the hell-in-a-handbasket predictions of contemporary Luddites" (Hacker & Van Dijk, 2000, 2). Instead of uncritically praising online tools as "a technical fix … to break particular limits of time, place and size" (Hacker & Van Dijk, 2000, 210) for people to participate simultaneously, this requires the chapters in our book to not only consider the advantages of tools of digital participation but also the challenges that they face.

One of these challenges certainly concerns the tendency of information and communication bubbles on the Internet. This inevitably creates problems of inclusiveness regarding people and arguments, with a more fragmented discourse ultimately risking the loss of a shared understanding of and trust in the political process. While bonding within these bubbles is strong, the frequent phenomenon of "outgroup hostility" severely complicates bridging to other communities, something that is arguably easier with tools of offline participation (Kersting, 2013, 278). The fact that self-affirmation often prevails over deliberation brings us to a second challenge for digital participation, that is, to ensure the quality of deliberation online (if it occurs). Hope was expressed at the early stages of the Internet that it might make it easier to engage people in deliberation (Coleman & Gøtze, 2001) and to facilitate deliberation across communities, thus rendering decision-making "less parochial" (Barber, 1998, 585). The more anonymous situation in online forums has been seen as increasing people's willingness to contribute their views, but also as decreasing their accountability for them (Nabatchi & Amsler, 2014, 17). Overall, it is difficult to say how digital participation tools fare concerning Fishkin's famous conditions for deliberation such as thoughtful discussion, mutual respect, active participation and an openness of the process to all groups (Fishkin, 1995, 142). While some claim that online tools are detrimental to important qualities like respect, reciprocity and reflexivity because aggressive dialogues or pure monologues are more frequent (Kersting, 2005; Kies, 2010; Kamlage & Nanz, 2017, 12), others emphasize that a persisting gap in empirical research concerning online deliberation quality makes a conclusive assessment exceedingly difficult (Strandberg & Grönlund, 2018, 365–377). A third recurrent key challenge relates to inequalities among people regarding their involvement in digital participatory processes. Some imbalances, such as those regarding education, interest, and resources in terms of time or income, certainly replicate those of offline tools and are not specific for online participation. Inequalities regarding digital skills and access to the Internet, however, are specific. While increasing information inequalities have been observed in Western democracies since the 1990s and sparked warnings about the rise of information elites (van Dijk, 2000, 166–183), the digital divide is still an issue for participation today (Hirst, 2015; Kamlage & Nanz, 2017, 12). A fourth and ultimate challenge is finding a balance between online and face-to-face tools of participation. As mentioned above, simply shifting traditional participatory processes like PB online does not seem to bode well for effective participation, so an outright replacement of offline tools is arguably neither realistic nor desirable. The latter also holds true because online tools have sometimes been used as fig leaves, as "cheap" instruments that allow the avoidance of cumbersome meetings in person (Kersting, 2013, 279). Thus, there are various reasons for digital participation to be perceived rather as a complement to face-to-face communication (Hacker & Van Dijk, 2000, 1) so that the following assessment from an early work on digital democracy still rings true: "The future relies on the interaction of virtual and organic politics. Hopefully, digital technology will shape conditions for a fruitful interplay between virtual and organic, online, and offline political activities" (Hacker & Van Dijk, 2000, 218). The same publication also suggests that the most suitable level for such an interplay to work well is the local one. This is because it seems easiest at this smaller scale to combine different tools of participation.

1.7 The Book's Guiding Questions

It is precisely regarding this local level that the chapters in this book explore the four key topics identified and set out above. The contributions from experts from different disciplines and a variety of contexts provide very diverse perspectives.

Our research within the above-mentioned LoGov project had revealed common key issues related to participation from a global comparative perspective, and a set of guiding questions was established to ensure the coherence of the chapters and to facilitate our comparative analysis. These questions delve into the core aspects that define the effectiveness and impact of participation and are closely interlinked.

Firstly, understanding the aim of participation helps to clarify the underlying intentions behind and expectations towards participatory processes. The aim often shapes other related issues such as who needs to take part in the participation process or what format is used. Secondly, identifying the broader policy areas or specific subjects addressed by participatory processes is important because it shows where citizen input is being sought and how it might influence public policy. This question helps to determine whether participatory processes are being applied to critical issues or remain limited to less impactful areas. It also sheds light on the alignment between citizen concerns and policy priorities. Thirdly, the question of who is participating, who is in-and excluded in the participation process is central in evaluating participation's inclusiveness, which ought to be one of the positive aspects of citizen's participation as mentioned above. The fourth question explores how local interests are organized and the influence of political parties and stakeholders. It is relevant because it reveals the dynamics of power and influence within participatory processes, including how regional and national interests might shape local decisions. The fifth question relates to the format of participatory processes. It asks whether they are "invited" or "invented" spaces, digital or face-to-face and how they directly affect the level and type of engagement. This question is important because it examines how the structure of participation influences outcomes, the behavior of local authorities, and the overall effectiveness of the process. The format can determine who participates, how decisions are made, and the quality of the engagement. The sixth question focuses on the specificities of the urban and rural contexts. This question is relevant to understanding how context influences the design and success of participatory processes, as urban and rural areas often have different resources, needs, and power structures. Finally, the question of the actual impact of participatory processes is important because it determines the real-world effectiveness of these processes. Without proper implementation and monitoring, participation risks being symbolic rather than substantive, failing to bring about tangible changes.

All chapters thus address the following set of guiding questions:

1. What are the aims of the analyzed participatory processes? Are they intended to put certain topics on the local agenda, to shape local policies and plans at different stages of decision-making, to add legitimacy to these decisions, to build trust in political institutions or among citizens or to serve still other purposes?
2. What are the broader policy areas or concrete subjects that the participatory processes are concerned with?
3. Who is invited to participate and who is excluded (e.g. politicians, civil servants and other potentially biased people)? Who are the actual participants and are otherwise marginalized people and groups among them?
4. How are (different) local interests organized? What role do political parties and other local stakeholders play? To what extent do regional and national interests influence participatory processes?
5. What is the format of the participatory processes? Are they characterized by "invited" or "invented" spaces of participation? Do they rely exclusively on participation in a digital manner or also on face-to-face meetings and how does the format affect people's engagement, as well as on the behavior of local authorities?
6. What are the specificities of the participatory processes in urban and rural contexts?
7. What is the actual impact of the participatory processes? Do local authorities effectively implement decisions made in a participatory manner and are there monitoring mechanisms to ensure they do? Are there broader societal impacts of the participatory processes?

References

Ackerman, B., & Fishkin, J. (2002). Deliberation day. *The Journal of Political Philosophy, 10*(2), 129–152. https://doi.org/10.1111/1467-9760.00146

Arnstein, S. (1969). A ladder of citizen participation. *Journal of the American Institute of Planners, 35*(4), 216–224. https://doi.org/10.1080/01944366908977225

Baiocchi, G. (2003). Participation, activism, and politics. The Porto Alegre experiment. In A. Fung & E. O. Wright (Eds.), *Deepening democracy. Institutional innovations in empowered participatory governance* (pp. 45–76). Verso.

Baiocchi, G., Heller, P., & Silva, M. K. (2011). *Bootstrapping democracy: Transforming local governance and civil society in Brazil*. Stanford University Press.

Barber, B. (1984). *Strong democracy: Participatory politics for a new age*. University of California Press.

Barber, B. (1998). Three scenarios for the future of technology and strong democracy. *Political Science Quarterly, 113*(4), 573–589. https://doi.org/10.2307/2658245

Bellamy, R., Castiglione, D., & Santoro, E. (2004). *Lineages of European citizenship: Rights, belonging and participation in eleven nation-states*. Palgrave Macmillan.

Benkler, Y. (2006). *The wealth of networks*. Yale University Press.

Böckenförde, E.-W. (1982). Mittelbare/repräsentative Demokratie als eigentliche Form der Demokratie. Bemerkungen zu Begriff und Verwirklichungsproblemen der Demokratie als Staats-und Regierungsfrom. In K. Eichenberger & G. Müller (Eds.), *Staatsorganisation und Staatsfunktion im Wandel. Festschrift Kurt Eichenberger zum 60. Geburtstag* (pp. 301–328). Helbing & Lichtenhahn.

Bovens, M., & Wille, A. (2017). *Diploma democracy: The rise of political meritocracy*. Oxford University Press.

Brownill, S., & Parker, G. (2010). Why bother with good works? The relevance of public participation(s) in planning in a post-collaborative era. *Planning Practice and Research, 25*(3), 275–282. https://doi.org/10.1080/02697459.2010.503407

Brubaker, R. (1992). *Citizenship and nationhood in France and Germany*. Harvard University Press.

Coleman, S., & Gøtze, J. (2001). *Bowling together: Online public engagement in policy deliberation*. Hansard Society and BT.

Constitution of the Commonwealth of Massachusetts. (1780).

Cornwall, A. (2002). *Making spaces, changing places: Situating participation in development*. Institute of Development Studies.

Dahl, R. (1956). *A preface to democratic theory*. The University of Chicago Press.

Dahl, R. (1994). A democratic dilemma: System effectiveness versus citizen participation. *Political Science Quarterly, 109*(1), 23–34. https://doi.org/10.2307/2151659

de Sousa Santos, B. (1998). Participatory budgeting in Porto Alegre: Toward a redistributive democracy. *Politics and Society, 26*(4), 461–510. https://doi.org/10.1177/0032329298026004003

Dryzek, J. (1996). Political inclusion and the dynamics of democratization. *American Political Science Review, 90*(3), 475–487.

Dryzek, J. (2000). *Deliberative democracy and beyond: Liberals, critics and contestations*. Oxford University Press.

Dryzek, J. (2002). *Deliberative democracy and beyond: Liberals, critics, contestations*. Oxford University Press.

Esposito, G., Terlizzi, A., & Crutzen, N. (2022). Policy narratives and megaprojects: The case of the Lyon-Turin high-speed railway. *Public Management Review, 24*(1), 55–79. https://doi.org/10.1080/14719037.2020.1795230

Esposito, G., Felicetti, A., & Terlizzi, A. (2023). Participatory governance in megaprojects: The Lyon–Turin high-speed railway among structure, agency, and democratic participation. *Policy and Society, 42*(2), 259–273. https://doi.org/10.1093/polsoc/puac029

Fernández-Martínez, J. L., García-Espín, P., & Jiménez-Sánchez, M. (2020). Participatory frustration: The unintended cultural effect of local democratic innovations. *Administration & Society, 52*(5), 718–748. https://doi.org/10.1177/0095399719833628

Fishkin, J. (1995). *The voice of the people: Public opinion and democracy*. Yale University Press.

Fishkin, J. (2009). *When the people speak: Deliberative democracy and public consultation*. Oxford University Press.

Frankenberg, G. (2012). Democracy. In M. Rosenfeld & A. Sajó (Eds.), *The Oxford handbook of comparative constitutional law* (pp. 250–268). Oxford University Press.

Fraser, N. (1997). *Justice interruptus: Critical reflections on the 'Postsocialist' condition*. Routledge.

Fung, A. (2006). Varieties of participation in complex governance. *Public Administration Review, 66*, 66–75.

Fung, A. (2011). Reinventing democracy in Latin America (review essay). *Perspectives on Politics, 9*(4), 857–871.

Fung, A. (2015). Putting the public back into governance: The challenges of citizen participation and its future. *Public Administration Review, 75*(4), 513–522. https://doi.org/10.1111/puar.12361

Gastil, J. (2005). Deliberation. In G. J. Shepherd, J. St. John, & T. G. Striphas (Eds.), *Communication as … : Perspectives on theory* (pp. 164–173). Sage.

Goodin, R. (2008). *Innovating democracy: Democratic theory and practice after the deliberative turn*. Oxford University Press.

Hacker, K., & Van Dijk, J. (2000). *Digital democracy: Issues of theory and practice*. Sage.

Held, D. (2006). *Models of democracy*. Polity Press.

Hirst, D. (2015). *Mind the gap: The digital divide and digital inclusion*. Retrieved February 13, 2024, from https://www.statslife.org.uk/science-technology/2445-mind-the-gap-the-digitaldivide-and-digital-inclusion

Hofer, K., & Kaufmann, D. (2022). Actors, arenas and aims: A conceptual framework for public participation. *Planning Theory, 22*(4), 357–379. https://doi.org/10.1177/14730952221139587

Hubbard, P. (2009). NIMBY. In A. Kobayashi (Ed.), *International encyclopedia of human geography* (2nd ed., pp. 403–407). Elsevier.

Inglehart, R. (1977). *The silent revolution: Changing values and political styles among Western publics*. Princeton University Press.

Inglehart, R., & Welzel, C. (2005). *Modernization, cultural change, and democracy: The human development sequence*. Cambridge University Press.

International IDEA. (2024). *Democracy assessment*. International IDEA. Retrieved February 24, 2024, from https://www.idea.int/theme/democracy-assessment

Kamlage, J.-H., & Nanz, P. (2017). *Public participation and democratic innovations: Assessing democratic institutions and processes for deepening and increased public participation in political decision-making*. World Forum for Democracy.

Kersting, N. (2005). The quality of political discourse: Can E-discussion be deliberative? In *Annual Conference of the British Political Studies Association, Leeds*.

Kersting, N. (2012). The future of electronic democracy. In N. Kersting, M. Stein, & J. Trent (Eds.), *Electronic democracy* (1st ed., pp. 11–54). Barbara Budrich Publishers.

Kersting, N. (2013). Online participation: From 'invited' to 'invented' spaces. *International Journal of Electronic Governance, 6*(4), 270–280.

Kersting, N., & Cronqvist, L. (2005). *Democratizaton and political culture in comperative perspective*. VS Verlag für Sozialwissenschaften.

Kersting, N., Gasparikova, J., Iglesias, A., & Krenjova, J. (2016). Local democratic renewal by deliberative participatory instruments: Participatory budgeting in comparative study. In S. Kuhlmann & G. Bouckaert (Eds.), *Local public sector reforms in times of crisis. Governance and public management* (pp. 317–331). Palgrave Macmillan.

Kies, R. (2010). *Promises and limits of web-deliberation*. Palgrave Macmillan.

Krenjova, J., & Raudla, R. (2013). Participatory budgeting at the local level: Challenges and opportunities for new democracies. *Halduskultuur—Administrative Culture, 14*(1), 18–46.
Lane, M. (2005). Public participation in planning: An intellectual history. *Australian Geographer, 36*(3), 283–299. https://doi.org/10.1080/00049180500325694
Lefebvre, H. (1968). *Le droit à la ville*. Anthropos.
Macintosh, A. (2003). Using information and communication technologies to enhance citizen engagement in the policy process. In J. Caddy & C. Vergez (Eds.), *Promise and problems of E-democracy: Challenges of online citizen engagement* (pp. 19–142). OECD.
Madison, J. (1961a/1787). Federalist No. 10. In C. Rossiter (Eds.), *The Federalist Papers,* (pp. 77–84). New American Library
Madison, J. (1961b/1788). Federalist No. 57. In C. Rossiter (Eds.) *The Federalist Papers* (pp. 350–356). New American Library.
Manin, B. (1997). *The principles of representative government*. Cambridge University Press.
Marshall, T. H. (1950). *Citizenship and social class*. Cambridge University Press.
Medda-Windischer, R., & Kössler, K. (2024). Integration of third-country nationals in subnational entities: Is regional citizenship a viable instrument? In G. Grote & A. Carlà (Eds.), *Changing borders and challenging changing borders and challenging belonging: Policy change and private experience* (pp. 39–62). Peter Lang.
Michels, A. (2006). Citizen participation and democracy in the Netherlands. *Democratization, 13*(2), 323–339. https://doi.org/10.1080/13510340500524067
Michels, A., & Binnema, H. (2019). Assessing the impact of deliberative democratic initiatives at the local level: A framework for analysis. *Administration & Society, 51*(5), 749–769. https://doi.org/10.1177/0095399718760588
Michels, A., & De Graaf, L. (2010). Examining citizen participation: Local participatory policy making and democracy. *Local Government Studies, 36*(4), 477–491. https://doi.org/10.1080/03003930.2010.494101
Michels, A., & De Graaf, L. (2017). Examining citizen participation: Local participatory policy-making and democracy revisited. *Local Government Studies, 43*, 875–881. https://doi.org/10.1080/03003930.2017.1365712
Morison, J. (2017). Citizen participation: A critical look at the democratic adequacy of government consultations. *Oxford Journal of Legal Studies, 37*(3), 636–659.
Morison, J., & Harkens, A. (2018). Principle of participation. In *The Max Planck Encyclopedia of Comparative Constitutional Law*.
Nabatchi, T., & Amsler, L. (2014). Direct public engagement in local government. *The American Review of Public Administration, 44*(4), 63S–88S. https://doi.org/10.1177/0275074013519702
Nadin, V., Maldonado, A. M. F., Zonneveld, W., Stead, D., Dąbrowski, M., Piskorek, K., Sarkar, A., Schmitt, P., Smas, L., Cotella, G., Rivolin, U. J., Solly, A., Berisha, E., Pede, E., Seardo, B. M., Komornicki, T., Goch, K., Bednarek-Szczepańska, M., Degórska, B., … Münter, A. (2018). *COMPASS: Comparative analysis of territorial governance and spatial planning systems in Europe*. ESPON EGTC.
Nadin, V., Stead, D., Dąbrowski, M., & Fernandez-Maldonado, A. M. (2021). Integrated, adaptive and participatory spatial planning: Trends across Europe. *Regional Studies, 55*(5), 791–803.
Nelson, N., & Wright, S. (1995). Participation and power. In N. Nelson & S. Wright (Eds.), *Power and participatory development: Theory and practice* (pp. 1–18). Intermediate Technology Publications.
Norris, P., & Jones, D. (1998). Editorial: Virtual democracy. *Harvard International Journal of Press/Politics, 3*(2), 1–4. https://doi.org/10.1177/1081180X98003002001
O'Flynn, I., & Sood, G. (2014). What would Dahl say? An appraisal of the democratic credentials of deliberative polls and other mini-publics. In K. Grönlund, A. Bächtiger, & M. Setälä (Eds.), *Deliberative mini-publics: Involving citizens in the democratic process* (pp. 41–81). ECPR Press.
Pateman, C. (1970). *Participation and democratic theory*. Cambridge University Press.
Pateman, C. (2012). Participatory democracy revisited. *Perspectives on Politics, 10*(1), 7–19. https://doi.org/10.1017/S1537592711004877

Patton, M. Q. (2002). *Qualitative evaluation and research methods*. Sage.
PB Network. (2019). *PB World Atlas list over 11,000 participatory budgeting experiences*. PB Network. Retrieved February 13, 2024, from https://pbnetwork.org.uk/pb-world-atlas-list-over-11000-participatory-budgeting-experiences/
Piper, L. (2014). How participatory institutions deepen democracy through broadening representation: The case of participatory budgeting in Porto Alegre, Brazil. *Theoria: A Journal of Social and Political Theory, 61*(139), 50–67. https://doi.org/10.3167/th.2014.6113903
Reimer, M., Getimis, P., & Blotevogel, H. (2014). *Spatial planning systems and practices in Europe: A comparative perspective on continuity and changes*. Routledge.
Rousseau, J. J. (1978/1762). *On the social contract*. St. Martin's Press.
Sandercock, L. (1998). *Toward cosmopolis: Planning for multicultural cities*. John Wiley.
Sandercock, L. (2005). The democratization of planning: Elusive, or illusory? *Planning Theory and Practice, 6*(4), 437–441. https://doi.org/10.1080/14649350500349607
Sartori, G. (1987). *The theory of democracy revisited*. CQ Press.
Schumpeter, J. (1976/1942). *Capitalism, socialism and democracy*. Harper & Row.
Shaw, J. (2007). *The transformation of citizenship in the European Union: Electoral rights and the restructuring of political space*. Cambridge University Press.
Sintomer, Y., Herzberg, C., & Röcke, A. (2010). Der Bürgerhaushalt. In *Europa—Eine realistische Utopie? Zwischen partizipativer Demokratie, Verwaltungsmodernisierung und sozialer Gerechtigkeit*. VS Verlag für Sozialwissenschaften.
Sintomer, Y., Herzberg, C., Röcke, A., & Allegretti, G. (2012). Transnational models of citizen participation: The case of participatory budgeting. *Journal of Public Deliberation, 8*(2), 16–28. https://doi.org/10.16997/jdd.141
Sintomer, Y., Herzberg, C., & Allegretti, G. (2013). *Participatory budgeting worldwide*. Engagement Global and Service Agency Communities in One World.
Strandberg, K., & Grönlund, K. (2018). Online deliberation. In A. Bächtiger, J. Dryzek, J. Mansbridge, & M. Warren (Eds.), *The Oxford handbook of deliberative democracy* (pp. 365–377). Oxford University Press.
Tapscott, D., & Williams, A. (2010). *Wikinomics: How mass collaboration changes everything*. Portfolio/Penguin.
Teorell, J. (2006). Political participation and three theories of democracy: A research inventory and agenda. *European Journal of Political Research, 45*(5), 787–810. https://doi.org/10.1111/j.1475-6765.2006.00636.x
Tewdwr-Jones, M. (2004). Spatial planning: Principles, practice and culture. *Journal of Planning and Environment Law, 57*(5), 560–569.
Tippett, J., & How, F. (2020). Where to lean the ladder of participation: A normative heuristic for effective coproduction processes. *Town Planning Review, 91*(2), 109–132. https://doi.org/10.3828/tpr.2020.7
Tsagarousianou, R. (1999). Electronic democracy: Rhetoric and reality. *European Journal of Communication Research, 24*(2), 189–208.
Urbinati, N. (2014). *Democracy disfigured—Opinion, truth, and the people*. Harvard University Press.
van Dijk, J. (2000). Widening information gaps and policies of prevention. In K. Hacker & J. van Dijk (Eds.), *Digital democracy, issues of theory and practice* (pp. 166–183). Sage.
Wampler, B. (2008). When does participatory democracy deepen the quality of democracy? Lessons from Brazil. *Comparative Politics, 41*(1), 61–81.
Wampler, B. (2012). Participatory budgeting: Core principles and key impacts. *Journal of Public Deliberation, 8*(2), 1–13.
World Bank. (1996). *The World Bank Participation Sourcebook*. World Bank. Retrieved February 24, 2024, from http://www.gtz.de/de/dokumente/en-SVMP-sourcebookworld-bank-intro-1997.pdf
Yin, R. K. (2003). *Case study research: Design and methods*. Sage.

Part I
Participation in Local Development and Planning

Chapter 2
People's Participation in Local Decision-Making: The Government Goals Plan in Cordoba/Argentina

Romina Del Tredici

Abstract This chapter examines the institutionalization of direct democracy mechanisms in Argentina, focusing on the City of Córdoba's implementation of the Government Goals Plan (Plan de Metas de Gobierno). Introduced in 2012, this plan was among the first in Argentina to enhance government transparency and citizen participation at the local level. The study investigates the plan's development and impact across three administrations, presenting the results of an analysis of citizen participation in 11 public hearings held thus far. It explores the topics addressed in these hearings, revealing the key concerns and demands of different sectors of the community. Despite its successes, the Government Goals Plan faces significant challenges, including the need for better training of public officials, improved goal presentation, and more effective coordination between urban and rural areas. Additionally, the plan struggles with limited citizen participation and insufficient responses from public officials to citizen proposals. While the Government Goals Plan has potential as a tool for urban planning and fostering public oversight, it must overcome these obstacles to achieve broader and more effective citizen involvement. The findings underscore the broader limitations of direct democracy mechanisms in Argentina.

Keywords Goals plan · Local government · People's participation · Direct democracy mechanisms · Public hearings

---

R. Del Tredici (✉)
Consejo Nacional de Investigaciones Científicas y Técnicas (CONICET) and Universidad Católica de Córdoba, Córdoba, Argentina
e-mail: romina.deltredici@ucc.edu.ar

K. Kössler, E. Schläppi (eds.), *Citizen Participation in Local Governance*, Local and Urban Governance, https://doi.org/10.1007/978-3-031-99824-9_2

2.1 Introduction

In Argentina, the incorporation of direct democracy mechanisms into the legal framework is recent and it is not attributable to a demand from society for greater involvement and transparency (Del Tredici, 2021a). Rather, it was included in a set of reforms promoted in 1994 by the nation's president, Carlos Saúl Menem, to convince the other parties to vote and allow presidential reelection (Welp, 2008, 127).[1] Two other processes have made participatory institutions occupy an important place on the political agenda in recent decades: the crisis of representative democracy, characterized by the increase of citizens' distrust in politics; and the decentralization of the national state, which transferred greater powers to subnational levels of government (provincial and municipal) (Welp, 2008, 118). The primary instruments of participation mentioned in the national Constitution are referendums and popular consultations, popular legislative initiatives, revocation of mandate, popular juries, public hearings, and participatory budgets. These mechanisms are mainly to make proposals, however, they can also be informative, consultative, and, in a few cases and depending on specific regulations, they can mandate a decision (Eberhardt, 2019).

Despite these common national processes, "the institutionalization of participatory democracy mechanisms shows uneven development in Argentina" (Del Tredici, 2021a, 74). This may be because it is a country with a large territorial area, in which each province was created in a different context. Furthermore, each of them has the autonomy to define many aspects, including participation mechanisms. The laws that formally established the direct democracy's processes were largely produced at the municipal level over the past three decades. In certain instances, they were regulated by municipalities in their organic charters, but in the majority of situations, they were formalized by provincial constitutions and provincial legislation for municipal regimes (municipal organic laws). The procedures of direct democracy are not included in the Province of Buenos Aires' municipal organic code; nonetheless, they are enshrined in the province's and the city's constitution. In certain instances, the constitutions specify the steps required to carry them out, while in others, they state that a statute setting particular conditions is essential (García, 2009, 88).

[1] During the presidency of Raúl Alfonsín (more precisely in 1985), a group close to him proposed a constitutional reform to limit the presidential term to four years and allow re-election. Many provinces supported this idea and 12 modified their constitutions accordingly. However, defeat in the legislative elections of 1987 stopped this momentum. Carlos Menem, as governor of the province of La Rioja, never hid his re-election desire and supported the reform contrary to the official will of his party (Justicialist Party). Upon assuming the presidency, he took up this project again. Without the possibility of achieving the necessary two-thirds of votes in the Chamber of Deputies, he met with Alfonsín, now head of the opposition party (*Unión Cívica Radical*), to negotiate what became known as the "Pact of Olivos". For his consent to reelection, Alfonsín asked to limit presidential powers so that the agreement included, among other issues, mechanisms for citizen participation. Despite this, the new constitution not only did not put limits on presidentialism but rather strengthened it (Natale, 2000).

These processes are hardly mentioned in the laws of the provinces of Catamarca, Entre Ríos, La Pampa, and Santiago del Estero. The three primary mechanisms—revocation of mandate, popular legislative initiative, and referendum—are not even mentioned in Santa Cruz, San Luis, Salta, or Tierra del Fuego. Nonetheless, a sizable portion of their municipalities—such as the capital towns of Salta, San Luis, and Ushuaia—have included provisions in their organic charters that are directly appealing to the populace (García, 2009, 88). Direct democracy processes are not included in the Mendoza and Santa Fe Constitutions or Municipal Organic Laws. Furthermore, these provinces' capital cities have not yet ratified their organic charters, which would allow them to incorporate these procedures in accordance with the 1994 National Constitution's principle of local autonomy (García, 2009, 88). At the other extreme, the provincial constitutions, organic laws, and organic charters of Córdoba, Chubut, Chaco, and Río Negro demonstrate a greater development of the processes of direct democracy. They are so thoroughly regulated that special ordinances are not required (García, 2009, 88).

Although some places are more developed than others, all direct democracy mechanisms have limitations (Del Tredici, 2021b). Many procedures need to be activated or mediated by state powers (García, 2009, 93) or require large investments in time and money from citizens (Eberhardt et al., 2008). "All these criticisms of the effectiveness of institutionalized forms of participation mechanisms correlate with the importance of other non-institutionalized or spontaneous forms of citizen participation in Argentina" (Del Tredici, 2021a, 75). However, this does not make it any less important to study formal mechanisms.

The objective of this chapter is to analyze a case of an institutionalized citizen participation mechanism in the City of Córdoba, which operated during the last three administrations. This case is important because Córdoba was one of the first four cities in Argentina to implement the Government Goals Plan (*Plan de Metas de Gobierno*) in 2012. Currently, this tool is being extended to other cities, such as the federal capital. The chapter is organized as follows. First, I describe the origin of the practice and its implementation during three government periods. Second, I carry out an analysis of participation, taking into account different positions towards the government, the institutional affiliation, and the main demands different sectors make. Third, I explore the topic of the interventions in the public hearings over time. Finally, I present some reflections that raise questions for further investigation.

2.2 What Is the Government Goals Plan?

The Government Goals Plan is a tool for governments to transform campaign proposals into clearly specified and measurable objectives, and concrete goals based on performance indicators that will be annually monitored and reported (Romanutti, 2012, 4). The Municipal Council of Córdoba unanimously approved it in 2011 (Ordinance 11,942/11), but it was a bottom-up initiative: "A network of citizens and organizations, the Red Ciudadana Nuestra Córdoba, endorsed the approval of the ordinance, inspired by other similar networks: the Red Nossa Sao Paulo and Cómo Vamos from Colombia. These organizations demanded an instrument to get information on the priorities and criteria of the public officials' decisions and to allow citizens to control them" (Del Tredici, 2021b, 83). The Government Goals Plan increased transparency, accountability, and participation, since it helped citizens to get the right information, which is a basis for holding authorities accountable.

Three contextual factors helped the approval of this mechanism (Del Tredici, 2021b). First, the support of several organizations and key local stakeholders was crucial, including the two most important universities in the province and 50 civil society organizations, which were members of the Red Ciudadana Nuestra Córdoba. Second, the demand got great publicity in the local media, "allowing the Goals Plan to be installed as an issue in the public agenda" (Romanutti, 2012, 4). Finally, the municipal council was divided into several factions and no party had the majority of the votes. Members of the Red Nuestra Córdoba stated that although this situation could have put the approval of the ordinance in danger, in practice, it forced local representatives to reach an agreement. In the context of local government's financial and legitimacy crisis, which was due to several problems inherited from previous administrations and having to face a project endorsed by civil society, the best strategy for local councilors was to reach a consensus (Del Tredici, 2021b). The local council raised the Goals Plan as "an instrument to rebuild dialogue and mutual trust between citizens and the municipal government" (Romanutti, 2012, 15).

According to the ordinance (11,942/11), the Government Goals Plan must be presented within a maximum of 120 calendar days of the mandate's start. Up to this point, three Plans were implemented, corresponding to the periods 2011–2015, 2015–2019, and 2019–2023. One more is currently active (2023–2027) and will not be analyzed. The four main focuses of the first two were sustainable development, competitiveness, equity and inclusion, and institutional development. These two periods were run by Mayor Ramón Mestre (Radical Civic Union) (Municipalidad de Córdoba, 2016). The third Plan, implemented by Martín Llaryora (Justicialist Party), was structured around five themes: innovation, opportunities and inclusiveness, sustainability, service quality, and a planned and appealing city. The local administration established objectives for each topic (Municipalidad de Córdoba, 2020).

Additionally, the legislation stipulates that by March 10 of every year, the municipal government must report to the public on the goals and their progress. The hearings are open to neighborhood groups, civil society organizations, and other city dwellers who choose to participate. Each registered individual has 5 min to speak once the mayor concludes their address, and they must register in advance (Ordinance 11,709/10). Informing the public on the Goals Plan's implementation, bringing specific issues to the local agenda, and giving municipal choices more legitimacy are the objectives of the participative process. Public hearings give citizens and civil organizations a chance to draw attention to issues that require government action.

In the period 2012–2023, the government concluded 11 public hearings. The first time that a government did not comply with presenting the Goals Plan around the period indicated in the ordinance (120 calendar days after taking office) was in 2020.

Public officials reported that it would be irresponsible to present a 4-year plan in the context of this uncertainty imposed during the COVID-19 pandemic. Civil society organizations and opposition councilors requested the local government to comply with the rules and democratic controls (Del Tredici, 2021b). The 2021 public hearing was not held because the government decided it was not worth holding two hearings in such a short time. In 2022 and 2023, public hearings took place normally.

2.3 Analysis of Citizen Participation in the Government Goals Plan

This section presents the results of an analysis that I carried out of citizen participation in the 11 public hearings held so far. 374 people participated in them between 2012 and 2023, which means an average of 34 people. The first public hearing registered the highest participation, with a total of 52 statements. Then, during the first term of government, participation declined until reaching its second lowest level in 2015, with 21 people. In the first hearing of the following government period, participation rose again, registering 40 people in 2016. During this government, participation increased, reaching 49 citizens in 2019. This hearing was the last of Mayor Ramón Mestre. In the last three hearings (late 2020, 2022, and 2023), participation was low and declining, reaching a historic low of 19 participants in the last one (see Fig. 2.1).

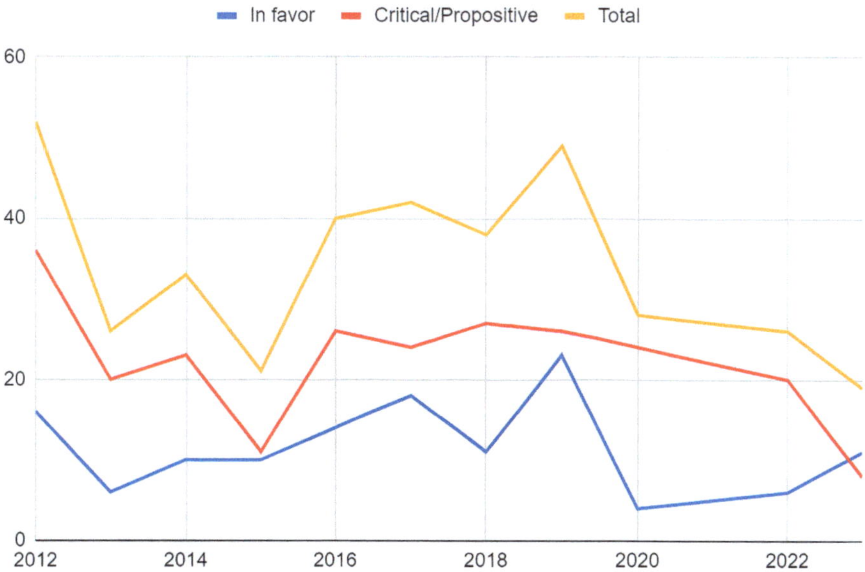

Fig. 2.1 Participation in public hearings by position regarding the goals plan and municipal management, 2012–2023. (Source: Own elaboration based on the official stenographic versions of the public hearings)

Some people registered to speak and then did not attend. Since a justification is not necessary, we cannot know the reasons behind these absences. Furthermore, we cannot know the exact number of people in this situation or to what sectors they belonged to, since the government did not report it in the stenographic versions of the public hearings. The number of participants without a request to speak (those who attended to listen but did not make a statement) is not reported either.

I classified the statements into two types, according to what they expressed about the Goals Plan and municipal management more generally. On the one hand, I recorded as "In favor" when those who spoke said only positive things about the government policies, mainly praising the implementation of public works in their neighborhoods and other public policies with territorial impact. On the other hand, I included in the "Critical/Propositive" category those interventions that referred to deficiencies in the formulation of the Goals Plan and the fulfillment of the objectives or to differences between what the plan says and what the government implemented. I also included those who made proposals on how to improve what is being done. This category also includes a few interventions with particular complaints from neighbors (not linked to the Goals Plan) such as problems with a particular administrative procedure.

Of the total interventions (374) made in the 11 hearings of the Goals Plan, 34.5% were classified as "In favor" and 65.5% as "Critical/Propositive." Public hearings seem to function as a space for citizens to make comments and proposals about the management of the city (see Fig. 2.2).

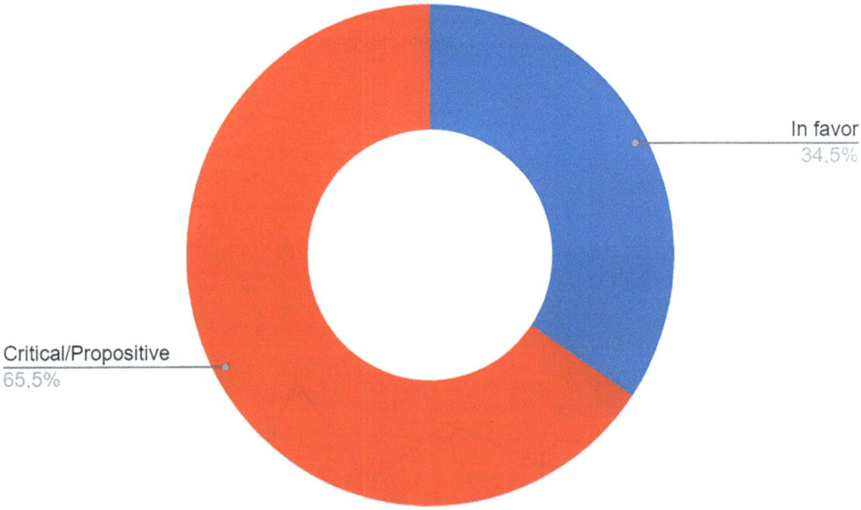

Fig. 2.2 Participation in public hearings by position regarding the goals plan and municipal management, average 2012–2023. (Source: Own elaboration based on the official stenographic versions of the public hearings)

When analyzing the evolution of each of the types of interventions, we can see that in all public hearings, more statements were "Critical/Propositive" than "In favor," except in the last one (2023). However, there are important differences over time. While in the first three hearings, both types of participation vary similarly, in the fourth, there is a significant drop in the "Critical/Propositive" type while the other remains stable. The "In favor" participation dropped in 2018, but it increased again in 2019 and fell sharply in 2020. The other type remained stable between 2016 and 2022. In 2023, "Critical/Propositive" statements had a significant drop (similar to the one in 2015). Both years coincide with the last of the municipal government's management.

Those persons in charge of organizing the hearing assign the order of presentation. The ordinance only establishes that the convening body must make it available to the participants and the general public 24 h before the hearing takes place. The graph below shows the participation for each year in the order they were presented, classified by their position concerning the Goals Plan and Municipal Management in "In Favor" (green) and "Critical/Propositive" (Red) (see Fig. 2.3). In many cases, there are "blocks" of statements favorable to and critical of the municipal government, and it seems to be more of the latter in the last part of the hearings (when participants are often tired, and the mayor and the media have departed). Despite this, it cannot be inferred that governments made political use of this order.

The statements encompass all the areas of local policy because they are about the entire government's plan. Nevertheless, people who participate in public hearings normally focus their presentations on a specific topic, such as public spaces, trash, or public transport. For example: "Our proposal, obviously, has to do with structuring the planning a little regarding transportation and urban mobility in Córdoba,

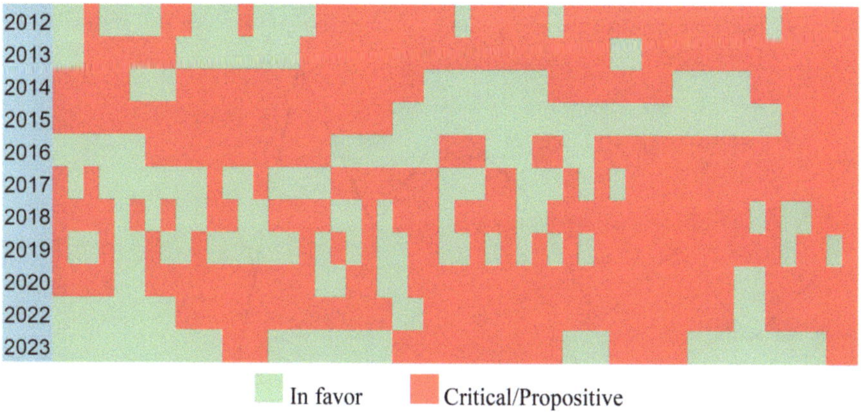

Fig. 2.3 Participation in each public hearing by position regarding the goals plan and municipal management, 2012–2023. (Source: Own elaboration based on the official stenographic versions of the public hearings)

which is a strategic factor" (Román Ballesteros in Deliberative Council of the City of Córdoba, 2017) or "Basically, I am going to talk about environmental management and urban hygiene" (Matías Emmanuel Roldán in Deliberative Council of the City of Córdoba, 2017).

Regarding the institutional affiliation of the participants in the public hearings, I classified each of the people into four groups: Non-Governmental Organizations (NGOs), Neighborhood Associations, and Others (this category includes representatives of professional associations, business chambers, and cooperatives, universities, public sector, political parties, clubs, and churches). I also included Independent Neighbors as a category for those who do not mention any institutional affiliation, since one does not need to be part of an organization to be registered to speak. According to Ordinance No 11,709/2010, each institution/organization can register only one representative. Sometimes, people register themselves as "Independent Neighbors" even though they belong to a collective space. In cases where this membership could be verified (either by what they said during the intervention or by their mention in journalistic articles as representatives of the organization), I included these people within the NGO or Neighborhood Associations categories, as appropriate.

The average participation of NGO representatives between 2012 and 2023 was 13 people per public hearing. The highest figures in participation are during the first year of each of the three municipal administrations that implemented the Goals Plan (2012, 2016, and 2020). In these hearings, the mayors presented the government's program that will serve as a guide for the 4 years of their mandate, and the organizations could comment and present agreements or disagreements about the goals and raise issues that were omitted. In the next public hearings, the participation of NGO representatives decreased, reaching its lowest values in 2015 and 2023 (the last year of the first Mestre government and the last year of the Llaryora government) (see Fig. 2.4).

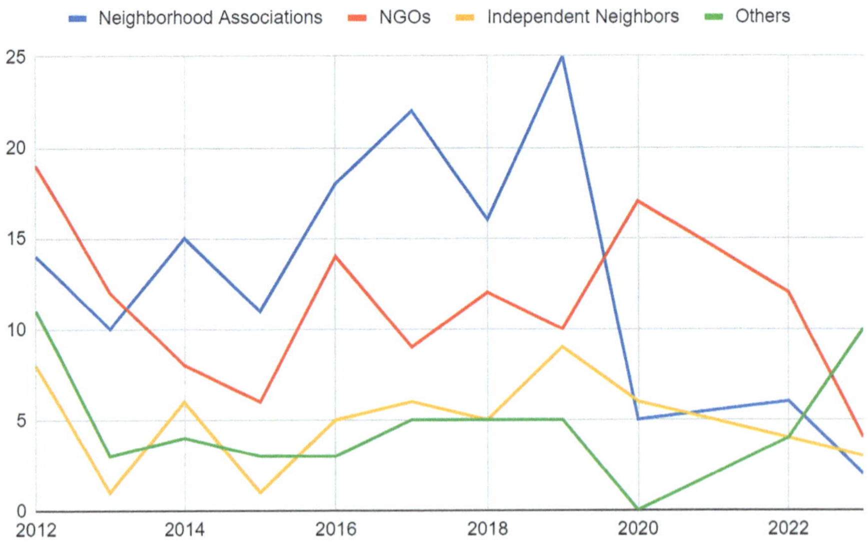

Fig. 2.4 Participation in public hearings by sector of belonging, 2012–2023. (Source: Own elaboration based on the official stenographic versions of the public hearings)

The participation of representatives of Neighborhood Associations is, on average, 11 people per public hearing and shows an increasing trend between 2012 and 2019 (the year in which it reached its historical maximum of 25 people). In 2020, there was a pronounced drop, which coincides with the change of government. As we can read in the stenographic records of the public hearings, the Mestre government invited the Neighborhood Associations to participate. It could be assumed that either the Llaryora team did not make this invitation, or the authorities of the Neighborhood Associations did not respond with the same effectiveness as they did before.

When comparing the nature of the statements between these two types of actors, I see important differences. The statements of the representatives of the Neighborhood Associations were mostly "In favor" of the municipal management (65%), while in the case of the representatives of NGOs, 84% were of the "Critical/Propositive" type.

Between 2012 and 2023, the number of statements "In favor" correlates with the number of participations by representatives of the Neighborhood Associations with a coefficient of 0.82. We might propose two hypotheses about this: first, the Neighborhood Associations that participate have a certain "affinity" with the government in power; secondly, they feel that they are not the ones holding accountable but (together with the municipal government) the ones being held accountable as elected intermediaries between neighbors and the administration. The representatives mention the government's achievements in their neighborhoods as a result of joint work with them. Therefore, there is a tendency to highlight the positive aspects. These two hypotheses are complementary and the increase in the participation of Neighborhood Associations throughout the 8 years of management can account for the construction of personal ties in the joint work between municipal administration and the authorities of the Neighborhood Associations. On the contrary, the pronounced drop in participation of these institutions in 2020 may be the result of the absence of an invitation from the government to the Neighborhood Associations and/or the difficulties of the incoming administration in building links with them.

The number of people who do not belong to any organization or who at least do not mention it in their presentation is low: less than five people[2] on average per public hearing in a city with more than a million inhabitants. In 2019, this category reached its highest peak of participation (nine statements), coinciding with a decrease in NGO statements and an increase in those of Neighborhood Associations. This may explain the importance of civil society organizations for the functioning of the Goals Plan. It is not a tool that has been used by citizens in general, which is perhaps related to its complexity as an instrument, but it seems to be important for some organized groups. These groups have similar characteristics: most of them are small social associations on a voluntary basis that are integrated by adults with

[2] In the 2023 elections the city of Cordoba had an electoral roll of more than a million of people. Although it is not necessary to be on the electoral roll to register for public hearings, this number can give us an idea of how many people could participate and do not.

professional degrees and a middle-class background. Furthermore, these organizations have political advocacy on particular issues among their objectives. "This is a common problem of mechanisms for semidirect democracy, in which people with less education and lower income often face more difficulties getting involved" (Del Tredici, 2021b, 85).

Only 22 people made more than a quarter (27.5%) of the 374 statements in the 11 public hearings. On average, each of these participants had almost five statements. Some of them participated as speakers in 10 of the 11 hearings of the Goals Plan that have been held to date. The majority of the presentations of these 22 people (85%) were classified as "Critical/Propositive." Half of these people belong to the Red Ciudadana Nuestra Córdoba, the network of associations that promoted the creation of the Goals Plan.

Of the 374 statements, 18 organizations accounted for 75 interventions, that is, 20% of the total. In addition, members of the Red Ciudadana Nuestra Córdoba made 18.7% of the participations. The ordinance establishes that "Neighborhood Associations, Neighborhood Participation Boards, and Non-Governmental Organizations designate one member from their ranks to represent them. In all cases, only one speaker is admitted to represent them." However, other representatives can register under the "Independent Neighbors" category and participate in the hearing. In the first hearing of 2012, the vice mayor pointed out: "As a comment, everyone will have the opportunity to express themselves, just like the man who a while ago asked me for the opportunity to do so instead of other registered people who did not come. But in the case of this organization, 11 people have already participated" (Marcelo Cossar in Deliberative Council of the City of Córdoba, 2012).

A recurring complaint among participants in public hearings is that the mayors never stay until the end to listen to all the registered speakers. Although in almost all cases the vice mayors remained in the room, a neighbor stated: "Actually, our request is addressed to the mayor ... we are very sorry that he is not there ... I would like you to convey that to the mayor. I would have very much liked to have him here and tell him, looking him in the eyes, as a person, as a human being, from heart to heart" (Cristina Verduro in Deliberative Council of the City of Córdoba, 2014). In the same way, another neighbor spoke: "It's a shame that Mestre had to leave just when the important thing comes" (Claudia Casas in Deliberative Council of the City of Córdoba, 2017). This may suggest that participants value face-to-face instances with the highest authorities of municipal government as something positive. The ordinance states that the mayor must participate in the hearings "as a reporting member". In all cases, the mayors fulfilled their role of reporting progress in the Goals Plan and then left the room, except for the first and second of the public hearings in 2012 and 2013, in which Mestre stayed until the end. Some hearings lasted more than 3 h and mayors excused themselves with the need to attend other activities.

Another recurring complaint participants made is that they received the Goals Plan and the call for the hearing without sufficient time to carry out a detailed analysis of such a complex document. In the words of one participant: "Also, we observed a late publication of the document, a call very close to this date, with the obligation to register in person, when before it could be done through remote systems; It exists like a fear that I don't know from whom or what" (Eduardo Ingaramo in Deliberative Council of the City of Córdoba, 2016). The ordinance establishes that the call must be "published for at least two days, in two widely distributed local newspapers, on the websites of the Municipality of Córdoba and the Deliberative Council and available mass audiovisual media at least two days in advance of the date of the hearing." Although these deadlines were met and even exceeded in many years, there are complaints from the city's residents: "We cannot fail to observe the public hearing as a typical participation mechanism, it was called from December 22 to 29, with four non-working days in between, which in our view greatly curtails the right to participation, not only in quantity but in quality to make a more in-depth and detailed analysis of the plan" (María Victoria Sibilla in Deliberative Council of the City of Córdoba, 2020).

Finally, a third recurring complaint refers to the fact that, in each administration, the mayor presents the Goals Plan as something "closed". There is no possibility of making modifications based on the comments received at the public hearing. In the words of one of the participants: "We request that this hearing be a first instance of opening and other periodic and thematic instances be established so that the contributions of citizens can be considered" (María Victoria Sibilla in Deliberative Council of the City of Córdoba, 2020). Legally, public hearings are not binding participation mechanisms and the municipal administration has no obligation to respond or incorporate the comments made into the Goals Plan. They can do it or not as a political decision.

2.4 Topical Issues Raised in the Public Hearings

In this section, I present the results of an analysis of the topics that people spoke about in the public hearings during the first three periods of the implementation of the Government Goals Plan in Córdoba. As I already mentioned, the participants in the public hearings have 5 min to make their statements. In addition to the positions for or against the policies of the current government, we can differentiate that some participants focus on a single issue, while others mention several issues.

Participation and accountability are the topics most addressed in the public hearings between 2012 and 2023. On the one hand, participants voiced their opinions about the functioning and results of citizen participation mechanisms (such as neighborhood meetings, participatory budgeting, and public hearings). On the other hand, they highlighted processes of municipal government accountability (such as aspects of the design of the goals and objectives in the Plan, progress reports, and requests for public information). Numerous interventions refer to the same Goals Plan and its implementation, a pattern likely explained by the fact that many of the audience participants are part of neighborhood centers or other types of organizations that are linked to the local government.

In these interventions, the speakers mentioned the challenges of the Government Goals Plan. First, for some people, "it is necessary to improve the presentation of the plan. The local government has to train public officials because many do not know how to define goals in the plan" (Del Tredici, 2021b, 84). Secondly, they also mentioned that it would be better if the government georeferenced each goal of the plan (by adding information on specific areas of the city where interventions would take place with each goal) so that decisions and their execution are more transparent: "We believe that the goals should be georeferenced to make it easier for residents to track their achievement" (María Virginia Romanutti in Deliberative Council of the City of Córdoba, 2018). Thirdly, participants said goals need to have a budget attached to them: "We believe that the goals should have an assigned budget or rather be directly related to the municipal budget" (María Virginia Romanutti in Deliberative Council of the City of Córdoba, 2018). Finally, they mentioned that, in the definition of the goals, the government should pay attention to the problems of the metropolitan area: "We regretted that there were no goals that included the metropolitan vision, despite its repeated mention in the speech" (María Beatriz Valencia in Deliberative Council of the City of Córdoba, 2022). Córdoba's metropolitan area has expanded significantly in recent years, yet there is still a lack of cooperation among municipal authorities and a lack of integration between rural and urban areas. Cooperation between local governments is neither encouraged by the Goals Plan in particular nor by participation mechanisms in general. The plan's goals are limited solely to the boundaries of its domain (Del Tredici, 2021b).

The environment is another often-mentioned topic that remained stable over the years, showing that it is a relevant issue for the city. It includes interventions regarding urban trees, green public spaces, urban solid waste, pollution, and animal protection.

There are also a lot of mentions about public works regarding urban infrastructure (roads, lights, sidewalks, ramps), mobility (public and private transportation in the city), access to land and housing, and land use. This gives relevance to the Goals Plan as a space for citizen participation in spatial planning. Being a mechanism for citizen participation at the local level and due to the powers that local governments have in Argentina (Cravacuore, 2016), public hearings for the Goals Plan have an important role in the discussion of the form it is taking. For example, within the land use category, one of the most-mentioned topics is the City Planning Agreements, "an instrument that enables public-private articulation for urban development projects with modifications to current regulations" (Valencia, 2021). These agreements are a way to introduce significant changes in urban spaces with high governmental discretion and low transparency. Some complaints refer to general urban planning (such as the decision of what types of constructions and uses are possible in the different territories of the city), as well as aspects related to the form of expansion of the urbanized territory (vertically, horizontally, with different types of neighborhoods).

There is a certain regularity in the presence of different themes in the statements over time. However some events increased the relevance of specific topics. For example, in February 2014 mayor Ramón Mestre presented a "new urban passenger transportation system" (Tránsito Córdoba, 2014) for the city, which caused mentions of the mobility issue to increase in the public hearing of the Goals Plan in April of that year. In 2020, perhaps due to the context of the pandemic and confinement in homes, requests for more and better instances of citizen participation increased. Some of the participants said: "We need more instances of participation in this Goals Plan so that the Government proposal is fair, serious and responsible" (Agustín Cerda in Deliberative Council of the City of Córdoba, 2020); "The end of our presentation only reaffirms the need to deepen these democratic instances" (Dante Martínez in Deliberative Council of the City of Córdoba, 2020).

In the last four hearings analyzed (2020–2023), three topics became increasingly prominent: gender, digitalization, and modernization. During this period, gender-related issues played a much greater role at all levels of government in Argentina. The president and 11 of the provincial governors created ministries dedicated to the issues of women and diversity (Lopreite & Gustá, 2021; Digón, 2023). For the first time, the Municipality of Córdoba had a Women, Gender and Diversity area with the rank of Secretariat (El Doce, 2021). The institutionalization and the increase in mentions may have been a result of the context of sustained massive mobilization of feminist groups in Argentina since 2015 (Buchara, 2020). Regarding modernization, although there are previous changes that have been taking place on the subject (Azumendi López et al., 2021), the conditions of the pandemic and virtuality may have generated a greater need and pressure from citizens for a more digitalized government.

Some of the least mentioned topics (such as security, education, and health) refer to functions that are the responsibility of the provincial government and that the municipality only carries out in a subsidiary manner.

2.5 Conclusions

This chapter has described and analyzed an example of participatory institutions of democracy and accountability in Córdoba, Argentina. The study of the 11 public hearings of the Goals Plan of the city of Córdoba between 2012 and 2023 reveals significant patterns in citizen participation and its relationship with municipal management. Throughout this period, 374 people participated in these hearings, with fluctuations in both the level of participation and the type of interventions carried out. These results allow us to draw relevant conclusions about the role of this participation mechanism and its impact on the interaction between citizens and local government.

One of the most notable findings is the role of public hearings as a space to express criticism and proposals towards municipal management. With 65.5% of the interventions classified as "Critical/Propositive", it is evident that these meetings have been used mostly to point out deficiencies, make suggestions and express concerns about the implementation of the Goals Plan. This contrasts with the 34.5% of "In Favor" interventions, which usually highlight government achievements on specific issues, mainly related to public works in specific neighborhoods. It is important to note that, with the exception of the 2023 hearing, critical interventions have predominated in all sessions, which underlines the relevance of this mechanism as a space for accountability from citizens towards the government.

In terms of participation by sector, the data show significant differences in the dynamics of interaction between the government and civil society organisations. Representatives of NGOs and Neighborhood Associations play a central role in the hearings, although with different approaches. While NGOs tend to make critical interventions (84%), Neighborhood Associations present a higher proportion of statements in favour of the government (65%). This phenomenon could be related to the links that Neighborhood Associations build with the municipal administration, which often translate into direct collaborations in works and projects. On the other hand, the participation of independent neighbors has been very low, which suggests that this mechanism has not yet managed to capture the interest of the general public, probably due to its technical complexity and the perception that it is a more accessible instrument for established organizations.

Regarding the topics addressed, accountability and citizen participation emerge as the most recurrent themes, reflecting the importance that citizens attach to transparency and inclusion in municipal decision-making. Other relevant issues include the environment, public works, and urban mobility, all of which are areas of direct competence of the local government. However, topics such as health, education, and security, which are mostly the responsibility of the provincial government, have had a lesser presence in the interventions. Due to the topics addressed by the Goals Plan and the interventions in its public hearings, this participatory mechanism becomes an important instrument for spatial planning in the city of Córdoba. In the absence of participation mechanisms in other instances of defining urban planning such as the "City-Planning Agreements" (Valencia, 2021), public hearings can become the space to influence the planning of the urban development of the city.

The temporal analysis shows significant variations in participation and in the topics discussed over the years. For example, the transition between governments has had a notable impact on the participation of certain sectors, such as Neighborhood Associations, whose presence decreased dramatically with the change of administration in 2020. In addition, external events, such as the COVID-19 pandemic, influenced citizens' priorities, increasing the demand for digitization and modernization of municipal administration.

Despite the richness of this participatory space, the analysis also identifies important limitations. Recurrent complaints about the lack of time to analyze the Goals Plan, the absence of the mayor during hearings, and the impossibility of modifying the Plan based on citizen input, reveal challenges in the implementation of this mechanism. The organizations that participated underscored the need for public officials to respond to their proposals. Although public hearings are not a binding mechanism, the municipality could justify the decisions that citizens objected to.

"Currently, the "control" that this tool allows consists of influencing the public agenda with the visibility of the urban problems or the inconsistencies between the plan, its reports, and the actions of the municipality. Sometimes what the organizations report is taken over by opposition parties, putting greater pressure on the government" (Del Tredici, 2021b, 85). These limitations undermine its potential as a tool for effective participation and open dialogue between government and citizens.

In summary, the public hearings of the Goals Plan have been a valuable space for citizen expression, especially for organized actors such as NGOs and Neighborhood Associations. However, to enhance their impact, it is necessary to strengthen aspects such as dissemination, the capacity of influence of participants and the government response to the proposals made. This mechanism has the potential to become a pillar for citizen participation and accountability in Córdoba, but its effectiveness will depend on political will and more inclusive and transparent management in the future. It is necessary to continue investigating some aspects such as its effectiveness in improving the provision of services that help to evaluate the tool more accurately.

References

Azumendi López, S., Facchina, M., Zapata, E. (2021). *Liderazgo público y participación privada y de ciudadanos: La transformación digital de la ciudad de Córdoba en Argentina*. Policy Brief #24. Nota de CAF-banco de desarrollo de América Latina. Retrieved November 25, 2024, from https://scioteca.caf.com/bitstream/handle/123456789/1699/Liderazgo_publico_y_participacion_privada_y_de_ciudadanos_la_transformacion_digital_de_la_ciudad_de_Cordoba_en_Argentina.pdf?sequence=1&isAllowed=y

Buchara, A. (2020). *Ni Una Menos: Cinco años del grito que cambió la historia de los feminismos argentinos*. El Ciudadano y la Región. Retrieved April 17, 2024, from https://www.elciudadanoweb.com/ni-una-menos-cinco-anos-del-grito-que-cambio-la-historia-de-los-feminismos-argentinos/

Cravacuore, D. (2016). Gobiernos locales en Argentina. In R. de la Fuente, J. Manuel, V. Cossani, & M. Camilo (Eds.), *Manual de Gobiernos Locales en Iberoamérica*. Retrieved April 17, 2024, from http://cdn-ua.hostingreactor.com/ua_ichem/wp-content/uploads/2016/12/MANUALgobLocalesCLAD-1.pdf

Del Tredici, R. (2021a). People's participation in local decision-making in Argentina: An introduction. In L. González & R. Del Tredici (Eds.), *The country report on local government in Argentina is a product of the LoGov-project: "Local government and the changing urban-rural interplay"* (pp. 74–76). Eurac Research.

Del Tredici, R. (2021b). Government goals plan: Citizen participation in the control of compliance of the mandates in Cordoba. In L. González & R. Del Tredici (Eds.), *The country report on local government in Argentina is a product of the LoGov-project: "Local government and the changing urban-rural interplay"* (pp. 83–86). Eurac Research.

Deliberative Council of the City of Córdoba. (2012). *Audiencia Pública*. Expediente municipal 368.323 Asunto: Plan de Metas del Gobierno de la Ciudad de Córdoba. 28 de junio de 2012. Stenographic version.

Deliberative Council of the City of Córdoba. (2014). *Audiencia Pública*. Asunto: Nota 6678, Exp. 011678/14 Plan de Metas Municipal, Presentación resultados al 31-12-13. 30 de abril de 2014. Stenographic version.

Deliberative Council of the City of Córdoba. (2016). *Audiencia Pública*. Notas N° 6790: informe anual y final del Plan de Metas 2011-2015, y N° 6819: Plan de Metas de Gobierno 2016–2019 1° de julio de 2016. Stenographic version.

Deliberative Council of the City of Córdoba. (2017). *Audiencia Pública*. Nota 6908: Informe anual del Plan de Metas de Gobierno. 28 de abril de 2017. Stenographic version.

Deliberative Council of the City of Córdoba. (2018). *Audiencia Pública*. Nota 7022: Informe anual del Plan de Metas de Gobierno. 27 de abril de 2018. Stenographic version.

Deliberative Council of the City of Córdoba. (2020). *Audiencia Pública*. Asunto: Nota 7306—Plan de Metas de Gobierno período 2020/2023. 29 de diciembre de 2020. Stenographic version.

Deliberative Council of the City of Córdoba. (2022). *Audiencia Pública*. Nota 7424. Asunto: Informe de Cumplimiento Anual del Plan de Metas de Gobierno 2019/2023. 5 de mayo de 2022 (reunión semipresencial). Stenographic version.

Digón, V. (2023). *Ministerios de Mujeres: ¿Cuántos y para qué?* La Voz. Retrieved April 17, 2024, from https://www.lavoz.com.ar/ciudadanos/ministerios-de-mujeres-cuantos-y-para-que/

Eberhardt, M. L. (2019). *Acerca de la participación y la protesta social en Argentina*. Diagonales (15 July 2019). Retrieved April 17, 2024, from https://diagonales.com/contenido/acerca-de-la-participacin-y-la-protesta-social-enargentina/15542

Eberhardt, M. L., Maurich, M., Triguboff, M., & Urdinez, M. V. (2008). Mecanismos de Participación y Control Ciudadano en la Argentina. In *Ponencia mecanismos de participación ciudadana* (p. 28). Buenos Aires, Argentina. Retrieved April 17, 2024, from http://www.catedras.fsoc.uba.ar/castiglioni/paper3.pdf

El Doce. (2021). *Cambios en la Municipalidad de Córdoba: Quiénes son y qué cargo ocuparán*. El Doce TV. Retrieved April 17, 2024, from https://eldoce.tv/politica/cambios-municipalidad-cordoba-quienes-son-que-cargo-ocuparan-nuevo-gabinete-intendente_123545/

García, J. G. (2009). Los mecanismos de democracia directa como procedimientos institucionales de participación ciudadana en Argentina. *RMCPS, 51*(205), 77–96.

Lopreite, D., & Gustá, A. L. R. (2021). Feminismo de Estado en la Argentina democrática (1983-2021): ¿Modelo aspiracional o realidad institucional? *Revista SAAP, 15*(2), 287–311. https://doi.org/10.46468/rsaap.15.2.A2

Municipalidad de Córdoba. (2016). *Plan de Metas de Gobierno 2016–2019*. Retrieved April 17, 2024, from https://documentos.cordoba.gob.ar/MUNCBA/AreasGob/Edu/DOCS/Seguimos%20con%20vos%20aprendiendo%20en%20casa/Plan%20de%20metas/Plan%20de%20metas%202016-2019/Plan_de_Metas_YMXExb9.pdf

Municipalidad de Córdoba. (2020). *Plan de Metas 2020–2023, Ciudad de Córdoba*. Retrieved April 9, 2024, from https://documentos.cordoba.gob.ar/MUNCBA/AreasGob/Mod/plan-de-metas.pdf

Natale, A. A. (2000). La reforma constitucional Argentina de 1994. *Cuestiones Constitucionales. Revista Mexicana De Derecho Constitucional, 1*(2). https://doi.org/10.22201/iij.24484881e.2000.2.5588

Romanutti, M. V. (2012). *Plan de metas: Una experiencia de incidencia colectiva*. Red Ciudadana Nuestra Córdoba. Retrieved April 17, 2024, from https://www.nuestracordoba.org.ar/sites/default/files/Sistematizacion_Plan_Metas_Cordoba.pdf

Tránsito Córdoba. (2014). *Reordenamiento del transporte público de la Ciudad de Córdoba*. Cómo y dónde consultar los nuevos recorridos de colectivos de Córdoba. Retrieved April 17, 2024, from https://transitocordoba.com/2014/02/como-consultar-los-nuevos-recorridos-de-colectivos-de-cordoba/

Valencia, M. B. (2021). City-planning agreements in Córdoba. In L. González & R. Del Tredici (Eds.), *Local government in Argentina: Responses to urban-rural challenges* (pp. 14–18). Zenodo. https://doi.org/10.5281/zenodo.5708950

Welp, Y. (2008). La participación ciudadana en la encrucijada. Los mecanismos de democracia directa en Ecuador, Perú y Argentina. *Icons—Revista De Ciencias Sociales, 31*, 117–130. https://doi.org/10.17141/iconos.31.2008.267

Chapter 3
Participation in Local Development and Planning in Germany

Philip Nedelcu

Abstract There are two main mechanisms through which the public can participate in local development and planning in Germany: statutory participation and citizens' petitions for referendum. The statutory participation process according to the Federal Building Code (*Baugesetzbuch*) takes place in the course of municipal planning, more precisely each time local governments adopt or amend a land-use plan. The two-stage process gives everyone the right to comment on the drafts presented. The local government is not obliged to pursue alternative proposals, but must consider each point raised during the participatory process. Individuals who are directly affected by the adopted plan may also challenge the plan in court, but not every violation of participatory rights leads to the invalidation of the plan.

Petitions for referendum are a general participatory mechanism at the municipal level, open only to citizens of the municipality who are eligible to vote. In the field of planning, citizens can use petitions to initiate planning processes or to terminate an ongoing planning process. However, petitions may not prescribe a specific planning outcome, as this would prejudge the balancing of interests to be carried out by the local government. While statutory participation is more inclusive, referenda can produce legally binding outcomes.

Keywords Public participation · Participatory mechanisms · Planning law · Statutory participation · Citizens' referendum · Local government

3.1 Introduction

The participation of citizens in local decision-making can occur in various forms, with varying levels of influence and potential outcomes (Kienast & Altrock, 2017, 5; Arnstein, 1969; Riek, 2011, 15). One of the most relevant participatory options at the local level is the possibility to participate in the process of municipal land-use

---

P. Nedelcu (✉)
Ludwig Maximilian University of Munich (LMU Munich), Munich, Germany

K. Kössler, E. Schläppi (eds.), *Citizen Participation in Local Governance*, Local and Urban Governance, https://doi.org/10.1007/978-3-031-99824-9_3

planning. Planning processes are prevalent in both urban and rural areas. Local governments willing to enable land development must often resort to planning. It has been argued that participation is particularly relevant in the context of large-scale infrastructure projects (Lieb, 2021; Sinning, 2018, 1659). However, even minor projects may substantially affect citizens, their interests and the environment they live in, especially in densely populated areas (Piek, 2019, 96; Kienast & Altrock, 2017, 15–16). Hence, planning can be a highly controversial affair regardless of the scale of the proposed development. Given its far-reaching impacts, participation in planning decisions appears particularly desirable in order to ensure the quality and acceptance and also the democratic legitimacy of these decisions (Schink & Bachmann, 2024, marginal nos 3-4b).

The applicable planning laws provide for a statutory right of the public to participate in most planning processes. However, the term "participation" as it is understood here encompasses not only the involvement of citizens in ongoing planning processes, but also their ability to initiate or terminate planning processes. Therefore, petitions for referendum are another important participatory mechanism pertaining to local planning. Citizens may use such petitions to call for a referendum on the initiation or termination of a planning process. These two modes of participation are regulated independently from one another. Citizens' petitions are a matter of the municipal laws of the *Länder*, while the statutory participation process is regulated in the Federal Building Code. Consequently, the two modes of participation are open to different groups of individuals and have different aims and potential outcomes.[1] While the statutory participation process revolves around contribution and information, the petition enables citizens to decide—with certain limits—on planning processes.

The second section of this chapter will describe the general framework for local development and planning. This is because the different possibilities of participation in the planning process cannot be properly understood without a basic understanding of Germany's development and planning process. The third section will outline the statutory participation process, whereas the fourth section will delve into citizens' petitions for referendum. The last section will compare these participatory processes and highlight the particularities of urban and rural contexts.

[1] Please note that there also exists a right to participation for third parties in the process of permitting specific projects, especially for owners of adjacent/neighboring land (e.g. Article 66 of the Bavarian Building Ordinance (*Bayerische Bauordnung*)). However, this right relates to their possibility to take legal action against building permits and does not give them a right to participate further in the decision by the planning authorities. Additionally, citizens can always resort to informal participation by holding assemblies or establishing associations advocating for certain planning decisions. See for further participatory mechanisms Burgi (2024, § 11 marginal no 35). For a practical example of additional participatory mechanisms see the following report: Bezirksamt Lichtenberg von Berlin (2017, 12–13).

3.2 The Planning Process in Germany

While regional spatial planning (*Raumplanung*) occurs on the level of the *Länder* under the Spatial Planning Code (*Raumordnungsgesetz, ROG*), the local land-use and development planning is assigned to municipal governments in accordance with Article 28 (2) of the Basic Law (BL), which i. a. enshrines the municipalities' planning authority (Dreier, 2015, marginal nos 130–131; Krönke, 2021). The planning process itself is foreseen and regulated in much detail in the Federal Building Code (*Baugesetzbuch, BauGB*) (Chapter 1, Section 1, Articles 1–13(b) of the Federal Building Code).

According to the regulatory framework, land-use planning is conducted as a two-step process: first, the local government has to pass a so-called preparatory land-use plan (*Flächennutzungsplan*) that contains the broad-brush planning for a municipality's entire territory. This plan needs to be approved by the higher administrative authority.[2] Under certain circumstances, adjacent municipalities can draw up a joint preparatory land-use plan (*Gemeinsamer Flächennutzungsplan*).[3] This model is exceptional for its deviation from the municipality's constitutionally enshrined planning authority and therefore plays only a marginal role in the planning practice (Hornmann, 2024, marginal no 4).

After having drawn up the preparatory land-use plan,[4] the local government may proceed with one or several so-called mandatory/legally binding land-use plans regulating the use of specific areas within its territory (*Bebauungsplan*). These plans are meant to add detail to the policies outlined in the preparatory land-use plan. Within these plans, the local government can determine in great detail what types of development should be permitted in the planning area (e.g. housing, industrial use) and set out highly specific requirements for buildings.[5]

The Federal Building Code does not specify which body of the local governmental structure is responsible for the planning process. Responsibility is therefore determined according to the applicable laws governing municipal affairs. An

[2] See Article 6(1) of the Federal Building Code. Please note that this applies also for bigger (urban) local governments that otherwise function as both a first- and second-tier local governments, which means that they can take certain planning decisions themselves instead of them being delegated to the respective second-tier local government.

[3] See Article 204(1) of the Federal Building Code. A joint plan should be drawn up under this article if the land development is determined by common factors and requirements or if the involvement of several communities enables a just balancing of the different interests involved. For further remarks and examples of such planning practices, see Hornmann (2024, marginal nos 6 et seq).

[4] There is also the possibility to merge the two processes and move forward with both plans at the same time, see Article 8(3) of the Federal Building Code.

[5] The potential regulations that can be included in the mandatory planning are set out in Article 9 of the Federal Building Code. The Federal Building Code and the Federal Land Utilization Ordinance (*Baunutzungsverordnung, BauNVO*) foresee various types of areas, see Articles 2–11 of the Federal Land Utilization Ordinance. The Ordinance determines which types of development are permissible in which area, e.g. no commercial buildings are permitted in purely residential areas.

indirect exception can be found in Article 10 of the Federal Building Code, which stipulates that the legally binding land-use plan must be adopted as a municipal statute (*Satzung*). In most cases, this will be the responsibility of the municipal council (Will, 2022, § 2 marginal no 97). As a general rule, major planning decisions are made by the municipal council, while planning authorities, which are part of the municipal administration, carry out the day-to-day business of planning including the administration of participatory processes.[6]

Once a legally binding land-use plan has become effective, building permits (*Baugenehmigungen*) may be issued. In general, such permits are required for construction projects. The permission process is covered by state laws[7] and is assigned to the second-tier local governments.[8] In that regard, most urban local governments decide themselves on permission requests, as they fulfill the roles of a second-tier local government in planning law. In contrast, smaller rural local governments do not have such competences. However, local governments that do not decide for themselves have a right to be heard and need to approve of the development project concerned.[9] According to Article 36(2)(1) of the Federal Building Code, local governments may lawfully refuse this approval only if they consider that the project does not comply with the applicable planning laws. In that regard, they have an independent right to assess the legality of the project (Hofmeister, 2024, marginal nos. 22–25). Consequently, local governments have a co-decision role.

While planning is a general precondition for lawful construction projects, permits can, under certain prerequisites, also be issued for development in (already developed) areas that are not covered by a legally binding land-use plan (*Bebauungsplan*).[10] This has important repercussions for the participatory processes described below, as they focus on the stage of planning.

[6] In big cities such as Munich or Cologne, there are also district councils that participate in the decision-making in the area of planning, see e.g. § 15 of the District Council Statute of the City of Munich, available online under https://stadt.muenchen.de/rathaus/stadtrecht/vorschrift/20.html. A general overview of the different municipal organs is given by Krönke (2021) and also Burgi (2024, § 10 marginal nos 2–7 and § 13 marginal no 10 regarding the municipal administration). See additionally OECD (2017) for the division of responsibilities regarding planning and an overview including other types of planning that go beyond the scope of this chapter.

[7] E.g. the Bavarian Building Ordinance or the Building Ordinance Berlin (*Bauordnung Berlin*).

[8] See for this varying allocation of competencies in various *Länder* e.g. Will (2022, § 2 marginal no 623). In Bavaria, for example, it is either the county authorities or independent towns/cities (bigger and more urban local governments). The specific terminology and also the structure of government vary between the different *Länder*. See Krönke (2021) for a more detailed explanation of the several layers of local government, elsewhere discussed e.g. by Burgi (2024, § 5 marginal nos 2–5).

[9] See Article 36(1) of the Federal Building Code. As big local governments decide for themselves on the permission, this process does not apply to them, see Hofmeister (2024, marginal nos 10–11).

[10] This possibility is foreseen in Article 34 of the Federal Building Code and requires that the proposed project is compatible with the existing development in the area. An area that is neither covered by a legally-binding land-use plan nor already developed in the sense of Article 34 is considered a so-called external area (*Außenbereich*). In external areas, development is generally prohibited; only certain types of constructions such as agricultural buildings may be permitted under the extensive prerequisites of Article 35 of the Federal Building Code.

Therefore, urban and rural local governments face mostly the same legal requirements for the planning process, aside from the necessity of approval for building permits, which is waived for bigger local governments, and certain technical differences.

3.3 The Statutory Participation Process

An important part of the planning process is the just balancing of public and private interests. This is stipulated in Article 1(7) of the Federal Building Code. Article 1(6) contains a (non-exhaustive) list of interests that (potentially) need to be considered. Article 1a of the Federal Building Code enshrines certain environmental considerations that are to be taken into account as well. Hence, the authorities have to identify all the interests at stake before taking a planning decision (Article 2(3) of the Federal Building Code). To that end, the public has a statutory right to participate in the planning process.[11] The participatory process will be outlined and assessed in the following sections.

3.3.1 Two-Level Participation

The purpose of the statutory participatory regime is reciprocal information (Article 4a(1) of the Federal Building Code; Schink & Bachmann, 2024, marginal no 3). It is meant to inform the public about a planning initiative and its potential outcomes and to give individuals the opportunity to submit information or concerns. Based on the statements submitted, the planning authority can identify and evaluate all relevant interests and concerns that are to be considered when making the final planning decision (Bayerisches Staatsministerium für Wohnen, Bau und Verkehr, 2019, 7 and 14–16). This should improve the quality of the decision-making. It is important to note that there is no fixed definition of who may participate in the planning process. For both stages, the applicable statute just refers to "the public". As there are no explicit limits, the right to participate is neither limited to people residing in the area covered by the respective plan or in the area of jurisdiction of the acting local government nor to citizens having the right to vote (Schink & Bachmann, 2024,

[11] A different mechanism is the voluntary early public participation process foreseen in Article 25(3) of the Administrative Procedures Act (*Verwaltungsverfahrensgesetz, VwVfG*). This norm encourages the competent authority to ask private developers to inform the public in accordance with the envisaged procedure before they request a permission for big infrastructure projects. However, there is no legal obligation for private developers to do so, see Herrmann (2024, marginal no 22). Besides the public, authorities and other public entities that might be affected by the planning process also have a right to participate according to Article 4 of the Federal Building Code.

marginal nos 17–19; Battis, 2022, marginal no 6).[12] Additionally, NGOs are also given the right to participate (Sinning, 2018, 1656). The law was amended in 2013 to make it explicit that the public also includes children and teenagers (Article 3(1)(2) of the Federal Building Code). This is meant to clarify their position and appeal to municipalities to enable children and teenagers to participate (Schink & Bachmann, 2024, marginal no 21a).

The statutory participation is regulated in Article 3 of the Federal Building Code, which applies equally to urban and rural local governments. It foresees two different stages of public participation that take place one after the other.[13] As a first step, the planning authority has to conduct a so-called early public participation (*frühzeitige Öffentlichkeitsbeteiligung*) (Article 3(1) of the Federal Building Code). The main aim of this part of the participatory process is to inform the public about the general concept of the proposed plan (Lüttgau, 2017, marginal no 42). Individuals have a right to comment on the proposed planning. Thereby, everyone can raise concerns or specific issues of the proposed planning. To ensure that concerns and interests are included in the decision-making process, the authority is required to begin with the participatory process as early as possible (Schink & Bachmann, 2024, marginal no 32).[14] The authority is obliged to publicly announce the aims and purposes of the planning, potential solutions and alternatives and a prognosis on the impact of the envisaged planning. Comments and concerns expressed must be debated publicly in a structured dialogue (Schink & Bachmann, 2024, marginal no 40). The law does not prescribe any specific modalities, such as the means of information to be used or the form of the debate. In practice, planning authorities inform the public through available means, such as the official municipal gazette, local newspapers, posters, flyers and also online through government websites (Will, 2022, § 2 marginal no 116). Most commonly, they upload a preliminary draft of the envisaged plan (Krumb, 2022, marginal no 8). Individuals may give comments or raise concerns by e-mail or orally during the structured dialogue, which may take place in the form of a public assembly, but also individually in dialogues between representatives of the local government and individuals or groups of people (Will, 2022, § 2 marginal no 117; Schink & Bachmann, 2024, marginal no 41). Article 3(1) allows the authority to proceed without an early public participation in case the envisaged planning decision constitutes only a minor change of an existing plan or in case public notification and dialogue have already taken place under a different legal framework. Despite initial skepticism regarding its precise purpose,

[12] However, this may be different under the simplified procedure according to Article 13(2)(2) of the Federal Building Code.

[13] The first step is not necessary under the so-called simplified procedure. This procedure applies to planning initiatives that do not alter the previous character of the area concerned, see Article 13 of the Federal Building Code.

[14] Schink and Bachmann point out that to actually fulfil its purpose, the process should also not commence too early. There needs to be a specific basis and idea of the consequences of the proposed planning.

early public participation became an important part of the participatory process due to the increased transparency and democratic control already at this early stage (Battis, 2022, marginal no 3; Federal Ministry of Transport and Digital Infrastructure, 2012, 12–15).

Once the authority has completed the final draft(s) of the proposed plan, this marks the beginning of the second (and main) stage of public participation (Schink & Bachmann, 2024, marginal no 56), the so-called formal public participation (*förmliche Öffentlichkeitsbeteiligung*) (Article 3(2) of the Federal Building Code). Usually, the municipal council makes a formal decision to commence the period of formal public participation, although this is not mandatory (Schink & Bachmann, 2024, marginal no 69). The statutory requirements for this part of the participatory process are more detailed and have been further specified by an extensive body of jurisprudence. The formal public participation consists of the publication of the final draft(s) of the proposed plan for at least 30 days, together with several additional reports pertaining to the environmental consequences of the suggested planning. The area covered by the proposed plan has to be clearly recognizable and the authority needs to provide references to all the types of environment-related information available (Schink & Bachmann, 2024, marginal nos 87–89). Following a recent amendment, the municipalities are required to make the documents available online and put them on easily accessible public display.[15] The municipality needs to publicly announce where, when and for how long it will publish the draft(s) and additional documents and that it is possible for everyone to submit observations and statements during the publication period (Article 3(2)(4) of the Federal Building Code). The public needs to be specifically made aware that—different from the early public participation period—statements that were not submitted during the publication period may be excluded from the final decision-making.[16] Individuals or groups of people may submit statements in various forms, in writing or by e-mail, but also orally (Schink & Bachmann, 2024, marginal nos 117). All statements duly submitted must be examined and considered before the final decision is made (Article 3(2)(6) of the Federal Building Code). The consideration forms part of the final balancing of the relevant interests foreseen in Article 1(7) of the Federal

[15] Previously, the only requirement was to put the plan on public display, which is typically done by posting the plan and additional documents in a publicly accessible government facility. The possibility to upload the documents online was introduced as a reaction to the COVID-19 pandemic, when the federal government enacted a law to enable municipalities to fulfill the legal requirements of participation by uploading the documents online (*Planungssicherstellungsgesetz*), see BT-Drs. 19/18965 and BGBl. 2020 I, 1041. The law only foresaw this mechanism temporarily but was already at the time seen as a pilot project for further digitalization of the participatory process. See Thiele and Dombert (2020) for further elaboration. The change towards an online publication as the primary way of conducting the public display was introduced in July 2023 by a law aimed at strengthening the digitalization in planning processes, Gesetz zur Stärkung der Digitalisierung im Bauleitplanverfahren und zur Änderung weiterer Vorschriften, BGBl. 2023 I No. 176.

[16] See for this consequence Article 4a(5)(1) of the Federal Building Code; the duty to inform about this is enshrined in Article 4a(5)(2).

Building Code and therefore falls within the competence of the municipal organ in charge of deciding on the planning itself, which is usually the municipal council (Higher Regional Court of Mannheim, Judgment of 13 February 2008, NVwZ-RR 2008, 676). However, the planning authority may conduct the examination and assist by preparing documents for the decision-making process within the municipal council (Battis, 2022, marginal no 19). Afterwards, the individuals that participated have to be notified of the outcome of the examination of their statements and proposals (Article 3(2)(6) of the Federal Building Code). The local government does not need to give reasons for its decision, although a reasoned decision seems preferrable (Schink & Bachmann, 2024, marginal no 127). A reasoned decisioned can serve as evidence of careful consideration and increase the acceptance of the decision taken (Bayerisches Staatsministerium für Wohnen, Bau und Verkehr, 2019, 7 and 16). In case more than 50 people submitted similar statements, the local government can refer them to publicly displayed documents outlining the decision-making instead of notifying them individually (Article 3(2)(7) of the Federal Building Code). If the final draft is changed in reaction to one or several statements, the formal public participation process needs to be repeated, at least for the changed part (Article 4a(3) of the Federal Building Code; Schink & Bachmann, 2024, marginal no 140). In case municipalities engage in the above-described possibility of drawing up a preparatory land-use plan together, each participating municipality is responsible for conducting the participatory process described above for "its" part of the joint plan, i.e. relating to the parts of the plan covering its territory (Hornmann, 2024, marginal nos 16–17). The participating communities then discuss the outcomes and decide whether to amend the draft plan (Hornmann, 2024, marginal nos 16–17).

3.3.2 Legal Protection Against Administrative Mistakes in the Participatory Process

Failures in the participation process can be invoked to challenge a plan's validity before the higher administrative courts. The sanction of invalidity due to failures in the participatory process is meant to safeguard a proper participatory process.

However, invoking the invalidity of a plan requires standing (i.e. an alleged interference with a protected right), which is only accepted for people directly affected by the plan (Giesberts, 2024, marginal nos 34–42). Consequently, there is a discrepancy between the group of potential plaintiffs and the people able to participate in the planning process. Additionally, not every participatory failure leads to the plan's invalidity. Article 214 of the Federal Building Code contains a complex and layered approach to planning mistakes. Its purpose is to avoid the invalidity of plans for minor and negligent mistakes (Heitzer & Kaufhold, 2022, marginal no 108). Flaws that merely concern the planning process or the early participatory process without having affected the outcome are generally not significant enough to lead to a plan's invalidity (Will, 2022, § 2 marginal no 212). On the contrary, flaws in the formal public participation can lead to the invalidity of a plan.[17] However, there are ways to mitigate previously committed errors in the planning process (Article 214(4) of the Federal Building Code). Thus, the potential invalidity of the plan is a somewhat unlikely sanction, which means that the judicial protection of participatory rights is not as strong as it might seem at first glance.

3.3.3 Assessment of the Mechanism and Its Impact

Citizens' participation increases both the legitimacy and the quality of the planning process as it enables citizens to express their concerns about a proposed land-use plan or suggest changes to it (Nedelcu, 2021; Schink & Bachmann, 2024, marginal nos 3-4b). Participating individuals and NGOs may highlight issues that would otherwise have gone unnoticed. A further advantage of statutory participation is the enhanced transparency and accountability of local decision-making (Nedelcu, 2021). While the extension of the right to participate to individuals not affected by the planning process might render the participatory process more complex for planning authorities, it is nevertheless another praiseworthy feature of the mechanism. It can often be challenging to identify and distinguish between those who are affected by a plan and those who are not, given that the consequences of planning can extend well beyond the boundaries of the area covered by the plan[18] (Nedelcu, 2021).

While the law envisages a broad range of participants, certain groups of citizens are more likely to participate: better educated people, mid-aged males and civil servants, as well as representatives of parties and NGOs. On the contrary, foreigners, women and people working in low-income sectors are less likely to participate (Walther, 2017; Kast, 2008, 2).

Furthermore, it is questionable if the participation procedure can fully mitigate disputes over controversial projects. Rather than enabling a true dialogue or making different voices effectively heard, the second stage of participation seems like a reactive process in which the local government simply needs to show that it has considered the statements of participating individuals. One potential consequence of this is that critics may feel that their arguments were not taken seriously. Consequently, they may move to less structured political foras to present their arguments. Once the actual debate takes place outside of a structured participation process, both supporters and critics of a project attempt to sway public opinion through media appearances, which has the potential to hamper and damage the actual planning process (Friedrich-Ebert-Stiftung, 2012, 16). Therefore, it is

[17] See Article 214(1)(1) no. 1 of the Federal Building Code. Any such flaw needs to be raised within one year according to Article 215 of the Federal Building Code.

[18] This is particularly clear in the context of economic consequences of planning, e.g. in the case of a shopping mall. While the plan pertains to the area designated for the mall, the construction of the mall could have a significant (economic) impact on businesses located in adjacent municipalities.

desirable to conduct a transparent and thorough participation process involving all relevant stakeholders (Federal Ministry of Transport and Digital Infrastructure, 2012, 9–17).

Another problematic aspect is the lack of participation in already developed areas. As described above, planning is not always necessary to enable the granting of building permits. Such permits may be granted without a previous planning process if the area in question is already developed. This is particularly the case in central parts of larger cities, for some parts of which no plans exist.[19] The law then does not require a plan but dictates that the existing building structure determines the character of the area and, consequently, the type(s) of permitted development (Article 34 of the Federal Building Code). As no planning takes place, the statutory rules about participation do not apply. There are also no alternative rules for participation. In case neighbors disagree with a development project, they can file an administrative suit against the building permit. This may result in the revocation of the permit. However, this course of action is more costly and open only to those directly affected, as only they are able to successfully claim a violation of building-related norms that specifically protect third parties.[20] A recent monograph focusing on various practical examples of developing projects in already developed areas describes the underlying political interests as well as the consequences and repercussions for the adjacent population (Piek, 2019). There is a rationale behind these different approaches: the scope of decision-making regarding permission decisions under Article 34 of the Federal Building Code is narrower than in the case of planning, hence the law itself provides sufficient democratic legitimacy for the permission decision (Piek, 2019, 98–99). Nonetheless, the lack of opportunities for affected residents to participate in a process comparable to the statutory participation process is potentially problematic in the case of controversial projects (Piek, 2019, 99).

3.4 Citizens' Petition for Referendum

The citizens' petition for referendum is not a planning-specific means of participation. However, a successful referendum can have far-reaching consequences for planning processes.

[19] For example, the overview of the land-use plans for the city of Berlin, available online under https://fbinter.stadt-berlin.de/fb/index.jsp?loginkey=showAreaSelection&mapId=bplan@senstadt&areaSelection=address.

[20] To avoid an *actio popularis*, individuals who are not directly addressed by an administrative action can only claim specific violations and need to prove that they are directly affected under the doctrine of *Drittschutz*, see extensively for the relevance of this doctrine in the field of planning and building law Heitzer/Kaufhold (2022, marginal nos 398–420).

3.4.1 Introduction of the System of Petition for Referendum

The right to initiate a petition and to eventually hold a referendum is enshrined in the municipal laws of the *Länder*.[21] The petition system aims to strengthen direct democracy by giving citizens the opportunity to shape public policy on the local level. A successful petition leads to a referendum, which—if successful—replaces a binding decision of the municipal council. The success of petitions and referenda hinges on the number of received signatures and votes. The respective necessary quotas are determined in relation to the number of inhabitants of the local government (Burgi, 2024, § 11 marginal no 41). While the rules on petitions differ among the different *Länder*, one commonality is that there are strict rules regarding the ability to initiate and partake in a petition. Firstly, only the residents of the respective municipality may initiate or participate in a petition. In most *Länder*, the participation rights are furthermore limited to citizens who can vote (e.g. Article 18a and 15 of the Bavarian Municipal Code; Article 26 of the Municipal Code for North Rhine-Westphalia (*Gemeindeordnung für das Land Nordrhein-Westfalen*)). This means that non-EU foreigners are generally excluded from initiating and signing a petition or voting in referenda.[22] Furthermore, citizens of adjacent municipalities cannot participate, even if the decision affects them (Lieb, 2021).

Other requirements pertain to the content of the petition. Inter alia, it needs to propose a clear yes/no question which may not have an illegal aim and may not concern matters which are not municipal competences (Burgi, 2024, § 11 marginal nos 37–39). There are also certain time-related requirements (Burgi, 2024, § 11 marginal no 43). Repetitive petitions concerning the same subject-matter are not allowed until a certain period of time has elapsed. Negative petitions that aim to repeal a previous council decision must be initiated in proximity to the targeted decision. The municipal council decides on the admissibility of a petition (i.a. Article 18a(8) of the Bavarian Municipal Code). A rejection of a petition as inadmissible can be challenged in court.[23]

Should the required number of signatures be obtained and is the petition deemed admissible, the municipal council may immediately decide to implement the proposed decision (Burgi, 2024, § 11 marginal no 44). This occurs in approximately 14% of cases (Mehr Demokratie e.V., 2020, 27). In the absence of such a decision, a referendum takes place. If the referendum is successful and a sufficient number of voters participated, the proposed decision takes effect as

---

[21] Therefore, there are certain differences regarding the technicalities of the petition process. Addressing all these differences would go beyond the scope of this chapter. It should be noted that in the city states of Berlin and Hamburg, petitions for referendum are regulated in the laws governing the municipal districts.

[22] See Article 28(1)(3) of the Basic Law which grants foreigners from EU countries the right to vote in municipal elections.

[23] See e.g. this recent decision by the Higher Administrative Court of Bavaria, Decision of 18 January 2019, Case No 4 CE 18.2578, especially marginal no 19.

if the municipal council had taken it.[24] Approximately half of all referenda result in the petitioners' demands being accepted (Mehr Demokratie e.V., 2020, 28–29). Overall, roughly 40% of petitions are successful, either through the decision of the municipal council or referendum (Mehr Demokratie e.V., 2020, 24).

Petitions are a traditional instrument of participation in certain *Länder*, while other *Länder* have only recently established the right to petition (Burgi, 2024, § 11 marginal no. 32). This has led to significant regional differences in the number of petitions filed: Bavaria saw the highest number of referenda between 1956 and 2019 (3157), with Baden-Wuerttemberg ranking second with 992 referenda. With a mere 11 referenda, Bremen had the fewest, followed by 16 in Saarland (Mehr Demokratie e.V., 2020, 7 and 13). When juxtaposed with the number of years in which petitions had been possible and the size of each *Land*, the city states of Hamburg, Berlin, and Bremen had the highest number of referenda, whereas Rhineland-Palatine ranks lowest (Mehr Demokratie e.V., 2020, 19–20). Quantitative differences also exist between urban and rural municipalities. Petitions occur more often in urban municipalities (Mehr Demokratie e.V., 2020, 18).

On average, 46.4% of citizens eligible to vote participate in referenda, with the number decreasing in proportion to the size of the municipality (Mehr Demokratie e.V., 2020, 30–31). A study conducted in Switzerland revealed that there is not one homogeneous group of citizens who constantly participate in referenda (Mehr Demokratie e.V., 2020, 31). Participants may come from different backgrounds, depending on the topic of the referendum.

3.4.2 Petitions for Referendum in the Field of Local Planning and Development

In the area of local planning, petitions for referendum are a way of influencing planning decisions. Petitions may initiate planning processes, as long as the proposed decision is lawful. However, there is a significant limit to the effectiveness of petitions for referenda on land-use planning as a participatory tool. A petition demanding a specific plan would prejudge the outcome of the balancing that the planning process is meant to safeguard (Brüning, 2018, 300). Therefore, only petitions that concern the initiation of a planning process and leave substantial room for the balancing process are permitted (Higher Administrative Court of Bavaria, Decision of 16 April 2012, Case No 4 CE 12.517, marginal nos 28–32, juris). On the contrary,

[24] With the exception of the *Land* Hamburg: Article 32(9) of the Borough Administration Act (*Bezirksverwaltungsgesetz*) does not prescribe a minimum number of voters necessary for a successful referendum.

petitions may lawfully pursue the termination of an ongoing planning process (Lieb, 2021). In certain *Länder*, the municipalities are even under a statutory obligation to await the outcome of a petition that has been found admissible before taking action that would marginalize the outcome of the petition (e.g. Article 18a(9) of the Bavarian Municipal Code). Hence, petitions for referendum have a limited, but very far-reaching potential for local interests to be expressed and implemented. One well-known example is the referendum on the construction of the *Waldschlösschenbrücke* in Dresden (Lieb, 2021), which ultimately led to the removal of the Dresden Elbe valley from the list of UNESCO World Heritage Sites. Another example is the referendum to have the former Tempelhof Airport in Berlin preserved and inscribed as national and world heritage which preceded the famous *Land*-wide referendum to ban construction on the Tempelhof Field in Berlin (Jürgens, 2009; Genz, 2015, 10–13).

3.5 Conclusion: Potential and Limitations of the Participatory Mechanisms

There are significant differences between the statutory participation process and the citizens' petition for referendum as mechanisms for public participation in local development and planning. Each mechanism possesses distinct advantages and weaknesses. The potential of the mechanisms varies depending on the context of urban or rural local government.

In terms of personal scope, the statutory participation process is more inclusive. The right to participate is not confined to individuals residing in the area covered by the plan, but extends to the general public, including NGOs. Consequently, *everyone* can participate in local decision-making without significant obstacles or thresholds barring participation, especially since the relevant planning documents have to be put online as well. The involvement of individuals residing in adjacent municipalities allows for the identification of issues that might otherwise be overlooked (Nedelcu, 2021). There are imbalances in which groups of people usually participate. Nevertheless, the statutory participation process is a valuable tool that can contribute to an interaction between neighboring communities and to inclusive participation. The petition process has no such effect, as it is limited to residents of the respective municipality (Lieb, 2021).

In terms of its potential to influence planning decisions, the statutory participation process is limited. While the participation of affected residents by planning decisions may increase the acceptance of far-reaching planning decisions (Nedelcu, 2021), even reasonable input may be disregarded without justification. Although judicial remedies against (alleged) violations of participatory rights exist, the review of planning decisions by administrative courts is limited. Only certain individuals have standing, and not every violation of participatory rights leads to the invalidation of the plan. Hence, statutory participation will only be effective in case the local government engages in a transparent and open manner with the statements and concerns brought forward. The petition for referendum is constrained by the requirements for permissible petitions and therefore of limited use in the field of planning. However, it provides citizens who have the right to vote with an actual decision-making tool, meaning it is the more powerful participatory mechanism in terms of potential impact.

The two mechanisms play different roles in urban and rural contexts. The applicable laws do not typically differentiate based on the size of the local government in question. However, there are practical differences between urban and rural local governments. Smaller, rural local governments might lack the expertise required to adequately address the rather complex legal requirements associated with the planning process including the processing of citizens' statements. This issue could be addressed through an increased level of intergovernmental cooperation in the area of statutory participation (Nedelcu, 2021). Second-tier local governments could provide assistance to improve the ability of smaller municipalities to conduct the participatory process and to guarantee the inclusivity of the planning process.[25]

Conversely, statutory participation holds less significance for residents in urban local governments (Nedelcu, 2021). As previously stated, building permits may be issued without prior planning when the area in question has already undergone sufficient development and the proposed project is considered to align with the existing development in the area. Urban areas are by definition comprised of developed areas. Consequently, urban local governments are oftentimes not required to engage in any kind of statutory participatory process prior to the issuance of building permits. In such circumstances, processes of "informal participation (e.g. public gatherings, district council meetings)" assume greater significance as they represent the primary means through which residents may express their opinions and concerns (Nedelcu, 2021). In addition, it seems less likely that a particular planning project in an urban area will receive sufficient public attention to meet the threshold for a successful petition for referendum. Nevertheless, successful referenda occur more often in urban environments, particularly regarding controversial infrastructure projects (Lieb, 2021).

[25] There are guidelines by the higher administrative authorities aimed at ensuring the quality of participation processes, e.g. Federal Ministry of Transport and Digital Infrastructure (2012).

References

Arnstein, S. (1969). A ladder of citizen participation. *Journal of the American Planning Association, 35*, 216–224.

Battis, U. (2022). BauGB § 3 Beteiligung der Öffentlichkeit. In U. Battis, S. Mitschang, & O. Reidt (Eds.), *Battis/Krautzberger/Löhr, Baugesetzbuch*. C.H.Beck.

Bayerisches Staatsministerium für Wohnen, Bau und Verkehr. (2019). *Bürgerbeteiligung im Städtebau—Ein Leitfaden*. Retrieved May 14, 2024, from https://www.buergerbeteiligung-staedtebau.bayern.de/assets/stmi/miniwebs/buergerbeteiligung/buergerbeteiligung_im_staedtebau_e-book.pdf

Bezirksamt Lichtenberg von Berlin. (2017). *Leitfaden zur Bürgerbeteiligung bei Bauvorhaben in Berlin-Lichtenberg*. Retrieved May 14, 2024, from https://www.berlin.de/bebauungsplan-lichtenberg/beteiligung/leitfaden/artikel.830092.php

Brüning, C. (2018). Bindungswirkung von Bürgerentscheiden in der Bauleitplanung. *NVwZ, 2018*, 299–302.

Burgi, M. (2024). *Kommunalrecht*. C.H.Beck.

Dreier, H. (2015). GG Art. 28. In H. Dreier (Ed.), *Grundgesetz-Kommentar*. Mohr Siebeck.

Federal Ministry of Transport and Digital Infrastructure. (2012). *Manual for good public participation*. Retrieved May 14, 2024, from https://bmdv.bund.de/SharedDocs/EN/publications/manual-for-good-public-participation.pdf?__blob=publicationFile

Friedrich-Ebert-Stiftung. (2012). *Frühzeitige Bürgerbeteiligung für eine effizientere Verkehrsinfrastrukturplanung*. WISO-Diskurs. Retrieved May 14, 2024, from https://library.fes.de/pdf-files/wiso/09424-20121119.pdf

Genz, C. (2015). The wide field of participation. An essay on the struggle for citizen participation and the future of the Tempelhof field. *Journal of Urban Life, 2015*, 6–17.

Giesberts, R. (2024). VwGO § 47 Sachliche Zuständigkeit des Oberverwaltungsgerichts bei der Normenkontrolle. In H. Posser, H. A. Wolff, & A. Decker (Eds.), *BeckOK VwGO*. C.H.Beck.

Heitzer, S., & Kaufhold, A.-K. (2022). Öffentliches Baurecht. In P. M. Huber & F. Wollenschläger (Eds.), *Landesrecht Bayern*. Nomos.

Herrmann, D. (2024). VwVfG § 25 Beratung, Auskunft, frühe Öffentlichkeitsbeteiligung. In J. Bader & M. Ronellenfitsch (Eds.), *BeckOKVwVfG*. C.H.Beck.

Hofmeister, A. (2024). BauGB § 36 Beteiligung der Gemeinde und der höheren Verwaltungsbehörde. In W. Spannowsky & M. Uechtritz (Eds.), *BeckOK BauGB*. C.H.Beck.

Hornmann, G. (2024). BauGB § 204 Gemeinsamer Flächennutzungsplan, Bauleitplanung bei Bildung von Planungsverbänden und bei Gebiets- und Bestandsänderung. In W. Spannowsky & M. Uechtritz (Eds.), *BeckOK BauGB*. C.H.Beck.

Jürgens, I. (2009). Bürgerentscheid zu Tempelhof erfolgreich. *Berliner Morgenpost*. Retrieved May 14, 2024, from https://www.morgenpost.de/berlin/article104237790/Buergerentscheid-zu-Tempelhof-erfolgreich.html

Kast, A. (2008). *Überfordert oder Übersehen? Partizipation von MigrantInnen im Quartier*. Newsletter Wegweiser Bürgergesellschaft 17/2008. Retrieved May 14, 2024, from https://www.buergergesellschaft.de/fileadmin/pdf/gastbeitrag_kast_080829.pdf

Kienast, G., & Altrock, U. (2017). *Bürgerbeteiligung in der Stadtentwicklung und im Wohnungsbau*. vhw-Schriftenreihe 8. Retrieved May 14, 2024, from https://www.vhw.de/fileadmin/user_upload/08_publikationen/vhw-schriftenreihe-tagungsband/PDFs/vhw_Schriftenreihe_Nr._8.pdf

Krönke, C. (2021). The system of local government in Germany. In M. Burgi, L. Hagen, & N. Lieb (Eds.), *Local government in Germany: Responses to urban-rural challenges* (pp. 1–4). Zenodo. https://doi.org/10.5281/zenodo.5205578

Krumb, J. (2022). § 3 BauGB Beteiligung der Öffentlichkeit. In F. Rixner, R. Biedermann, & J. Charlier (Eds.), *Systematischer Praxiskommentar BauGB/BauNVO*. Reguvis.

Lieb, N. (2021). Citizens' petitions for referendum against essential large-scale infrastructure projects in urban areas. In M. Burgi, L. Hagen, & N. Lieb (Eds.), *Local government in*

Germany: Responses to urban-rural challenges (pp. 79–82). Zenodo. https://doi.org/10.5281/zenodo.5236426
Lüttgau, T. (2017). Das Mandat im Bauplanungsrecht. In H. Johlen & M. Oerder (Eds.), *MAH Verwaltungsrecht*. C.H.Beck.
Mehr Demokratie e.V. (2020). *Bürgerbegehrensbericht 2020*. Retrieved May 14, 2024, from https://www.mehr-demokratie.de/fileadmin/pdf/2020-09-28_Bu__rgerbegehrensbericht_Web.pdf
Nedelcu, P. (2021). Citizens' participation in urban planning. In *Local government in Germany. Responses to urban-rural challenges*. Retrieved December 9, 2024, from https://www.logov-rise.eu/citizens-participation-in-urban-planning/
OECD. (2017). *The governance of land use—Country fact sheet Germany*. Retrieved May 14, 2024, from https://www.oecd.org/regional/regional-policy/land-use-Germany.pdf
Piek, S. (2019). *Pragmatische Stadtentwicklung nach § 34 Baugesetzbuch*. Nomos.
Riek, O. (2011). *Bürgerbegehren und Bürgerentscheide in der Bauleitplanung—Bürgerbeteiligung und Bürgerinteressen in stadtplanerischen Entscheidungsprozessen in den Hamburger Bezirken*. Retrieved May 14, 2024, from https://repos.hcu-hamburg.de/bitstream/hcu/208/1/Masterthesis_ohneInterviews_Riek_Oliver.pdf
Schink, A., & Bachmann, P. (2024). BauGB § 3 Beteiligung der Öffentlichkeit. In W. Spannowsky & M. Uechtritz (Eds.), *BeckOK BauGB*. C.H.Beck.
Sinning, H. (2018). Öffentlichkeitsbeteiligung. In *Handwörterbuch der Stadt- und Raumentwicklung*. ARL-Akademie für Raumforschung und Landesplanung. Retrieved May 14, 2024, from https://www.arl-net.de/system/files/media-shop/pdf/2023-01/%C3%96ffentlichkeitsbeteiligung.pdf
Thiele, J., & Dombert, M. (2020). *Öffentlichkeitsbeteiligung in Zukunft übers Internet?* Legal Tribune Online. Retrieved May 14, 2024, from https://www.lto.de/recht/hintergruende/h/bauprojekte-oeffentlichkeitsbeteiligung-online-planungssicherstellungsgesetz-oeffentliche-auslegung-digitalisierung/
Walther, B. (2017). *Soziale Selektivität in der Bürgerbeteiligung*. Berlin Institut für Partizipation. Retrieved May 14, 2024, from https://www.bipar.de/soziale-selektivitaet-in-der-buergerbeteiligung/
Will, M. (2022). *Öffentliches Baurecht*. C.H.Beck.

Chapter 4
Coupling Social Innovation and Italian Local Government: Shared Administration in Commons Governance

Elisabeth Alber and Chiara Salati

Abstract This chapter explores how the Italian organizational model of shared administration (MSA) has been institutionalizing forms of grassroots social innovation thanks to the constitutional principle of subsidiarity. Since the pioneering experience of Bologna in 2014, more than 300 local governments started supporting civic participation through the shared governance of the commons. All of this is still largely unknown at the international level. The main aim of the chapter is to present MSA as a new mode of participatory governance (or of democratic innovations) that could be used in both urban and rural contexts. This is done by adopting a perspective at the intersection of law and political science, combining the diverse research streams of constitutional and administrative law together with studies on democratic theory, social innovation, and the commons. Through an analysis of MSA and its constitutional and legal framework, the chapter argues that the Italian model forces us to work on the institutionalization of participatory processes already taking place within society, and not instead on the abstract question of their feasibility. This chapter is particularly relevant for all those local governments willing to deal with the commons from an institutional perspective and through a participatory-deliberative approach.

Keywords Local government · Commons governance · Democratic innovations · Italy · Social innovation · Shared administration

Although a product of joint effort, Elisabeth Alber primarily authored Sects. 4.1, 4.5 and 4.6, while Chiara Salati wrote Sects. 4.2 and 4.4. Section 4.3 was co-authored by both Elisabeth Alber and Chiara Salati. Whenever used, the term 'state' refers to the central level of government. The term 'local governments' refers to the various forms of territorial organization below the regional level of government.

E. Alber (✉) · C. Salati
Institute for Comparative Federalism, Eurac Research, Bolzano/Bozen, Italy
e-mail: elisabeth.alber@eurac.edu; chiara.salati@eurac.edu

K. Kössler, E. Schläppi (eds.), *Citizen Participation in Local Governance*, Local and Urban Governance, https://doi.org/10.1007/978-3-031-99824-9_4

4.1 Theoretical Framework: From Government to Governance

Participatory governance has become a buzzword. Indeed, in times when democracy is no longer on the rise (IDEA, 2023; V-Dem, 2023), academia increasingly discusses new modes of participatory governance. Scholars investigate to what extent the offer of new participation formats meets with the demand and whether it exerts an actual influence on traditional instruments of democratic participation (Gjaldbæk-Sverdrup et al., 2023; Bussu et al., 2022; Jacquet et al., 2023). These topics are under-researched in comparison to the design and the use of new participation formats (Reuchamps et al., 2023; Alber & Zwilling, 2021; OECD, 2020). Little is also known about citizens' motives for participating in such new governance arrangements. However, there are three generally agreed upon motives (Gustafson & Hertting, 2016). First, citizens might want to participate to protect and promote their own interests; thus, to articulate their interests in the political arena (interest-based logic). Second, citizens might want to participate to contribute to the establishment of a political arena for reasoning together; thus, to integrate the partial and place-based perspectives usually embraced by the public sector with their own points of view (deliberative-consultative logic). Third, citizens might want to participate to act; thus, to give leeway to their potential as co-planners and co-designers by entering a partnership with the public sector and producing tangible changes in their everyday lives (functional-transformative logic).

Regardless of the underlying logic inspiring new modes of participatory governance, they mainly seek to enhance the effectiveness and legitimacy of public agencies and policymaking through forms of public involvement and deliberation (Bua & Bussu, 2023; Geissel, 2022; Elstub & Escobar, 2019; Heinelt, 2018; Bächtiger et al., 2018; Ackerman, 2013). They refer to democratic mechanisms that are meant to complement instruments of direct and representative democracy by the creation of collaborative networks and of deliberative spaces. Their overall aim is to make societies resilient and institutions sustainable. Most recently, new modes of participatory governance are best known under the umbrella term of democratic innovations. Democratic innovations include all those processes and institutions that "are new to a policy issue, policy role, or level of governance, and developed to reimagine and deepen the role of citizens in governance processes by increasing opportunities for participation, deliberation, and influence" (Elstub & Escobar, 2019, 11).

When it comes to the distinguishing attributes of new modes in participatory governance, scholars vividly discuss the pros and cons of the many practices that inevitably are context-bound. Of course, the persistent lack of a comprehensive theory on new modes of participatory governance makes an analysis of practices descriptive rather than normative (Palermo, 2015, 504). But the point is that their use, independent of where and on which level of government they are deployed, mainly responds to two needs. First, the attenuation of the majority principle through the inclusion of participatory (consensus-based) practices prior to a majority decision, so that the plurality of interests is considered before a decision is reached.

Such practices normally are of consultative nature only. Second, the attenuation of tensions between the different demands of citizens, organized civil society, and the public sector by giving grassroots social innovation leeway to reclaim participatory methods, so that citizens and organized civil society work with, within, and beyond state institutions to democratize not just the political sphere but also the economic and social spheres, as richly described in the literature on governing the commons (Ostrom, 1990).

A common (good of public interest) is composed of a shared resource (public or private) spanning from natural material goods to intangible digital knowledge, for which a community decides to take responsibility. Governing the commons is thus oriented to public interest and open access and "involves establishing rules or protocols for access and use, taking care of and accepting responsibility for a resource, and distributing the benefits in ways that take into account the well-being of others" (Gibson-Graham et al., 2016, 195). In Italy, the Rodotà Commission (2007)—tasked by the Italian Ministry of Justice to reform the public goods in the Italian Civil Code—defined the commons as those goods that are of non-rival but exhaustible consumption, such as rivers, lakes, air, shores (but today also internet and energy), which—regardless of their public or private ownership—are functional to the exercise of fundamental rights and the free development of citizens. The Rodotà Commission also added an intergenerational component to the legal regime applicable to the commons, providing that the law must guarantee the direct and collective use of such goods in favor of future generations.

The aim of this chapter is to assess the Italian model of shared administration (MSA) as one of the latest and less known new modes of participatory governance at local level. The MSA, with its collaboration pacts between citizens and local governments, unfolds in a participatory practice that exemplifies two shifts in literature. First, the gradual shift from democratic government to participatory governance (Gbikpi & Grote, 2002). Second, the gradual shift from studying participatory and deliberative processes as isolated initiatives towards investigating them in terms of democratic systems and interactions across different spaces of representative, deliberative, participatory, or direct democracy, i.e. a systemic approach (Mansbridge et al., 2012).

Contrary to participatory practices that respond to either the interest-based or the deliberative-consultative logic, the MSA embodies the functional-transformative logic. It channels grassroots social innovation by adopting a commons governance model that can be defined as civic participation through the commons (CPC) (Salati, 2023a). The CPC, based on collaboration pacts, includes elements of different democratic spaces: direct and mediated actions through the support and commitment of a local government for place or issue-based citizens' local government collaborative actions. The MSA so manages to embed itself within the political and administrative system. Its legal manifestation, the collaboration pact, embodies rootedness (Bussu et al., 2022) and empowerment (Della Porta et al., 2014). In other words, the MSA and its collaboration pacts are participation practices characterized by a dynamic, active, and productive relationship between the actors involved in the participatory practice who, by adhering to the working rationale of the CPC, ultimately reach out to the maxi-public too. The MSA and its collaboration pacts are continually realized and reworked in a process of ongoing mutual learning, so that they succeed to couple participatory spaces and centers of powers to produce new arrangements in the decision-making process and in the governance structure at local level (Hendriks, 2016). They go beyond institutional design (the institutionalization of democratic innovations) because their processes and outcomes are hard to dismantle. The MSA and its collaboration pacts represent a new mode of participatory governance in which governance-driven democratization (GDD) and democracy-driven governance (DDG) meet. By GDD, Warren (2014) intends an elite-led form of participation, where the aim is, on the one hand, to address the legitimacy crisis of institutions and experts and, on the other hand, to improve policymaking by involving new voices and interests. In contrast, DDG (Bua & Bussu, 2021) emerges through popular mobilization. It attempts to bring social movements into the state and to reinvent democratic participation according to the functional-transformative logic.

Based on this theoretical framework, Sect. 4.2 of this chapter explains the origins and functioning of the MSA. Section 4.3 discusses how the MSA is constitutionally anchored in the principle of horizontal subsidiarity. In Italian constitutional law, horizontal subsidiarity draws a subsidiarity paradigm (Donati, 2014) in the relationship between the state and the society, with local governments having a frontline role in the promotion and support of citizens' autonomous initiatives. Section 4.4 of this chapter provides empirical insights on different MSA regulations, on collaboration pacts, and on the CPC's subject areas. Although the MSA has its greatest prevalence in urban settings, rural areas also benefit from this new mode of participatory governance. Section 4.5 showcases the BRIGHT project that aimed at improving the awareness and exercise of EU citizenship rights among (foreign) female workers in the agricultural sector in Southern Italy. Section 4.6 offers concluding remarks.

Overall, in this chapter, we argue that the MSA has the potential to deepen democracy and increase administrative efficiency, but that such an endeavor must align with that of a decentralized and place-based territorial governance. However, for now, local governments in Italy are in search of role-clarity amidst generally unstable politics and several seasons of unfinished (federal) reforms (Alber et al., 2024).

4.2 The Model of Shared Administration (MSA)

The MSA (in Italian *amministrazione condivisa*) consists of a participatory process in which citizens collaborate with local governments to develop, manage, and reuse goods of general interest. The main aim of the MSA is threefold. First, it aims to improve the quality of life. Second, it aims to reuse abandoned public spaces. Third, it aims to tap grassroots social innovation in view of resilient societies and sustainable institutions. Institutions are considered sustainable when they aptly contemplate, balance, and support the concerns and interests of their peoples and territories;

when their functioning is grounded in a clear institutional vision that considers how formal and informal actors from various levels of government affect expectations in service delivery, so that their capacity to perform their functions lasts over the long term (Pfahl, 2005; Fedeli, 2017).

Broadly speaking, one can ascribe the MSA to the concept of democratic innovations (DIs) in so far as this seeks to rebuild the broken (or lost) relationship between the state and society. Indeed, shared administration renews local governance according to the bottom-up logic. In practice, it manifests itself through the collaboration pact, which institutionalizes an action of civic participation through the commons.[1] In relation to the two different participatory governance approaches—GDD and DDG—shared administration is ascribable to the one of DDG (democracy-driven governance), mainly for three reasons. First, it attempts to bring grassroots social innovation into the state. Second, it tries to reclaim and reinvent participatory governance that succeeds in embedding itself within political and administrative systems. Third, it pursues transformative aspirations in view of social inclusion and a thick form of democracy centered around localized practices of cooperative action. The notion of thick democracy builds on the seminal work of Barber (1984, 2004) who raised pivotal questions on the relevance of liberal democracy. His work discusses the tension between individualism and the rights of all citizens and suggests that participatory governance demands that every member of the community participates in self-governance. The MSA aims to thicken democracy by deepening it. It does so by providing a legal framework that facilitates the CPC, which either already occurs or ought to occur because of grassroots social innovation. In other words, through the MSA local governments not only recognize and support the CPC, but they also have a (mediating) role that enables the CPC.

Originally not connected to the topic of the commons, the MSA was first conceived in 1997 (Arena, 1997; later also referred to as "collaborative governance" by Iaione, 2016, 427), and it constitutes an organizational model which foresees an alliance between two sides: the one of citizens and the one of the state. Originally rooted in administrative law, its primary goal was to examine and challenge the traditional bipolar framework, which emphasizes the (frequently contentious) divide between administrators and the administered (Cassese, 2001). As demonstrated throughout years by the research collective *Labsus-Laboratorio per la sussidiarietà*, the MSA has transcended academic debates in administrative law. It has evolved into a new subsidiarity paradigm (Donati, 2014), redefining the relationship between citizens and the state, with local governments serving as catalysts for social innovation—a concept introduced by Osborne and Gaebler (1992)—to promote and support citizens' autonomous initiatives in managing the commons.

The MSA was first implemented in Bologna in 2014. Following 2 years of work and research, two tools were designed: (1) the Bologna regulation, governing the collaboration between citizens and public administration for the care and regeneration of urban commons; (2) the collaboration pact enabling the CPC. A municipal

[1] See Sect. 4.4.2 below.

regulation implementing horizontal subsidiarity[2] was chosen for its simplicity, flexibility, and adaptability. Leveraging their regulatory autonomy (Article 117(6) of the Constitution), other local governments have replicated the Bologna Regulation—albeit with varying success.[3] Since Bologna's pilot, over 300 local governments, including municipalities, provinces, metropolitan cities, unions of municipalities, and a mountain community, have adopted it, resulting in thousands of collaboration pacts. A prototype regulation is also available as open access (Labsus, 2022). The regulation prototype essentially determines seven attributes:

1. general provisions and definitions (e.g., urban commons, active citizens, shared administration, collaboration pact);
2. procedural provisions based on the type of cooperation: ordinary collaboration pacts (smaller actions) and complex ones (involving greater resources and planning);
3. actions of care, regeneration and shared governance;
4. forms of state's support for citizens' initiatives: for example, insurances for participants, economic benefits (e.g., free public asset use, expense coverage, material support, tax exemptions), procedural and bureaucratic simplification, and facilitation of self-funding;
5. communication, transparency and initiative evaluation;
6. responsibility;
7. final and transitional provisions.

4.3 The Principle of Subsidiarity as the Constitutional Anchorage of the MSA

The MSA in the city of Bologna has been deeply rooted in the constitutional principle of subsidiarity. In 1990, at national level, the first general law on local government was enacted (Law 142/1990) and throughout the 1990s additional measures were adopted that enabled municipal governments to become more active and autonomous (Alber et al., 2024). These reforms included increased financial autonomy, a reduction of the preventive control over the legitimacy of administrative acts, and the introduction of the direct election of mayors and presidents of provinces (a district type of local authority between the region and municipalities with a larger geographical scope). In addition, several changes to the regime of administrative functions were pivotal in empowering local governments, with the most significant being Law 59/1997. This law, along with its implementing legislation, introduced the principle of subsidiarity, later constitutionalized with the 2001 constitutional reform that altered the distribution of legislative powers by listing the exclusive

[2] See Sect. 4.3.

[3] See Sect. 4.4.4.

legislative powers of the central level of government as well as subject-matters that relate to concurrent legislation in the Constitution, with regions retaining residual powers.

Most importantly, Italian constitutional law distinguishes between two dimensions of subsidiarity: vertical and horizontal subsidiarity. The relevant article is Article 118 of the Constitution. Vertical subsidiarity concerns the distribution of powers among governmental levels, assigning administrative functions to those institutions (municipalities) closest to citizens, unless already allocated to higher levels (provinces, metropolitan cities, regions, or the state). Horizontal subsidiarity pertains to participatory governance between the public sector and the citizens. Its origins lie in Christian social doctrine, which adopted it from social philosophy (Luther, 2020). Pope Pius XI (1931) refined subsidiarity as the guiding principle for organizing society, addressing concerns about the expanding power of states over individuals' lives (including the Church). His concept emphasized individuals as capable, responsible societal actors and the state's role in supporting their actions when serving the general interest. In Italian constitutional law, horizontal subsidiarity is a doctrinal category introduced by D'Atena (1997). Its meaning has been made explicit in the Italian Constitution and as such is quite unique in the European legal space: however, we can say that its meaning is implicit in the European constitutional tradition, and it has been forgotten in the European legal context (Salati, 2023b; Giordano, 2022). The MSA with its practical manifestation, the CPC, reflect this principle, as expressed in Article 118(4) of the Constitution: "The state, regions, metropolitan cities, provinces, and municipalities shall promote the autonomous initiatives of citizens, both as individuals and as members of associations, relating to activities of general interest, on the basis of the principle of subsidiarity".

Accordingly, citizens are viewed not only as recipients of needs and demands but as contributors, alongside the state, to managing a community's general interest, both individually and in groups. Unlike the traditional view of citizens as volunteers or members of associations, horizontal subsidiarity extends beyond third-sector organization activities to include individual or informal group actions. In other words, civic forms of participation through the commons embody the principle of horizontal subsidiarity and shared administration. The collaboration pacts constitute the concrete organizational model for that. The MSA—characterized by "co-planning" and "co-design"–expresses a different and renewed collaboration between the public sector and the private social sectors that is not simply based on a synallagmatic relationship but has transformative aspirations too (Constitutional Court Judgment 131/2020).

Up to date, no comprehensive national legislation on the MSA has been passed. However, the MSA benefits from existing legislation in three fields (Salati, 2023a). First, from the third-sector national level legislation (Article 5 of Legislative Decree 117/2017), which refers to the procedures of co-planning and co-design, and a list of activities of general interest. Second, from four regional laws that expand the concepts of shared administration, commons, and horizontal subsidiarity: Regional Law 10/2019 (Lazio), Regional Law 71/2020 (Tuscany), Regional Law 3/2023 (Emilia-Romagna), and Regional Law 2/2023 (Umbria). Third, the MSA benefits from the law on local authorities (Law 267/2000) which outlines in Article 3(4) that municipalities and provinces may perform their functions through activities that can be exercised by the autonomous initiatives of citizens and social groups.

4.4 Some Insights on MSA Regulations, Collaboration Pacts, and Policy Areas

4.4.1 The MSA Regulations

A comparative analysis of some MSA regulations—Trento, Genova, Lucca, Gubbio, Viterbo, Palmi, Livorno, Ferrara, Latina, Bari, Empoli, Milano, Potenza, Torino, Bologna, Roma, Padova—demonstrates that they rarely deviate from the Bologna Regulation and from the seven attributes regarding the CPC described in Sect. 4.2 above. What changes are some specific elements on which a certain regulation may focus. For example, in relation to the field of local development and planning, the MSA regulations may contain more specific provisions for the promotion of social innovation and collaborative services (Trento); generative welfare (Livorno); urban creativity as one of the key tools for the re-development of urban areas (Latina); the specific use of the MSA for educational, re-educational, inclusive, and community-building purposes (Milano); the recognition of not only shared governance between citizens and public authorities, but also self-governing forms of government, such as civic and collective urban uses, where groups of citizens are managing certain public goods or services without institutional support (Torino); the requalification of public properties (Bologna); the recognition of initiatives by companies in the area of their corporate social responsibility (Roma); and the acceptance of the performance of economic activities within collaboration pacts aimed at self-financing (Padova). These specificities reflect the diversity of debates, backgrounds, and priorities of each local government that decides to adopt a MSA regulation.

Regarding the use of the MSA across Italy, a 2021 quantitative and qualitative survey demonstrates that 34% of the MSA regulations have been adopted in municipalities with a population between 5000 and 19,999, 27% in municipalities with 20,000–59,000 inhabitants, and 26% in municipalities with a population of 60,000–249,000 (Labsus Annual Report, 2021). When looking at the numbers of collaboration pacts signed following an adopted MSA, the same report demonstrates that the largest municipalities are the ones that have the most: 53% of collaboration pacts are signed in municipalities with more than 250,000 inhabitants; and 27% of them in municipalities between 60,000 and 249,999. Together, these two ranges of municipalities constitute 80% of the total number of signed collaboration pacts. These numbers were calculated in a survey based on a total amount of 1001 on-going collaboration pacts up until September 30, 2021. This means that the MSA has its greatest prevalence in urban settings, rather than in rural ones.

With regard to the actors involved, the MSA regulation must be adopted by the local council insofar as it constitutes an administrative act that is the result of a political will. The initiative for the adoption of a MSA either comes from the public side (politicians or civil servants) or from the civic side (individual or associated citizens) who invite the local council to act.

4.4.2 The Collaboration Pacts

The core of the MSA are the collaboration pacts and the actions taken by CPC. Both sides—the state and the citizen(s)—determine the rules of governing the commons in a collaboration pact that essentially consists of four stages (Salati, 2023a).

First, the proposal of an action of general interest. As a rule, the citizens autonomously propose how and when to act. However, sometimes politicians or the public sector acts too through public calls and manifestations of interest. According to the 2021 Labsus annual report, on the citizenry side, the signatory subjects are: associations (40%), individual citizens (20.97%), informal groups (13.3%), schools (6.96%), for profit enterprises (6.08%), social enterprises (3.44%), other (3.17%), more subjects among the ones mentioned here (1.94%), church entities (1.32%), foundations (1.06%), other public institutions (0.97%), professionals (0.53%), universities (0.26%). On the public side, signatories are usually civil servants with a managerial role (70%), who sometimes need prior political permission (22%). Politicians become signatories only rarely (8%).

Second, the co-design phase in which the citizen(s) and the local government negotiate the details of the CPC. To this end, each collaboration pact includes several specificities: (1) the signatory parties; (2) the aim of the collaboration by pointing to the general interest; (3) the object (commons) of the action(s) of care, regeneration, and shared governance; (4) tasks, resources, and responsibilities of each side; (5) the supportive measures provided by the public side; (6) the place where the activities are taking place; (7) possible insurances; and (8) the duration of the collaboration. Depending on the availability and needs emerging during the negotiation, the local government can provide various measures to support and commit to the collaboration pact. According to the 2021 Labsus annual report, support measures include materials supply (23%), initiatives promotion (19.34%), tax benefits (10.53%), technical support (10.35%), symbolic economic contributions (8.75%), insurance coverage (8.69%), bureaucratic simplification (3.67%), and free use of spaces (1.83%). Often several concessions are given at the same time (10.17%).

Third, the signing of the collaboration pact by all involved parties on both the civic and the public sides. Important to mention is the fact that the collaboration pact remains constantly "open". This means that other individuals or associated citizens can enter this agreement also at a later stage, both by adding new tasks on their own sides or questioning what has been agreed and contributing to a new co-design phase.

Fourth, the monitoring phase. All parties involved agree on the details of how the CPC shall be monitored. As a rule, in case of any dispute arising among the sides involved or among them and a third party, a reconciliation committee composed of three members is appointed. One is nominated by the public sector, one by the citizens, and the third one by the two sides together. They do not adopt a legally binding decision but submit to the parties a proposal of conciliation which aims at settling the dispute.

4.4.3 Policy Areas

The MSA targets various policy areas, where CPC materializes. They include social and welfare issues, health, cultural initiatives, sport activities, innovation, education, agriculture, environment, inclusion, spatial planning, and urban regeneration. Collaboration pact signatories determine the focus area and define the general interest. These areas align with the concept of commons, legally defined in the 2014 Bologna Regulation after being linked to general interest in the 2004 Charter of Subsidiarity (Labsus, 2004). The definition contained in the Bologna regulation started spreading also in other local governments through the regulation prototype and it outlines that the commons are tangible, intangible, or digital goods deemed essential for individual and collective well-being, fundamental rights, and future generations, with shared responsibility between citizens and public authorities for their care or regeneration. Although there is no exhaustive list of commons, examples of CPC include the management of public squares and streets, green areas, buildings, schools, cultural centers, sport events, and actions targeting social inclusion, education, historical memory, and data use. According to the 2021 Labsus annual report, most collaboration pacts are designed on tangible goods (63.14%). Thus, the commons include green areas (42.76%), streets and public squares (17.58%), buildings (8.59%), schools (6.09%), and in minor percentages, cultural spaces, libraries, brownfields, and others. The CPC also reshapes local governance by requiring collaboration across various government offices, fostering inter- and intra-organizational renewal.

4.4.4 Preliminary Conclusions

For now, due to the recent introduction of the MSA as a mode of participatory governance, no generalizations are possible on its concrete impact on democracy. Further empirical data needs to be collected, systematically mapped, and evaluated. Based on the experience of Labsus, the research collective and association that accompanies most practices, local governments also need to better understand the purpose of the MSA and be trained in supporting and committing to collaboration pacts. For example, there have been cases of misapplication and misunderstanding of the model which occurred because the regulation prototype was simply copied and not critically adopted (Foster & Iaione, 2019). This is reflected in the wide discrepancy between adopted MSA regulations and actual collaboration pacts: from the 2021 national survey, out of a sample of 252 municipalities with an MSA regulation only 62 had signed collaboration pacts which were freely accessible online (Labsus Annual Report, 2021). In addition to that, the collaboration pact is sometimes misused by citizens seeking to advance private interests, bypassing traditional competitive procedures and disregarding its functional-transformative logic for commons governance. Such cases highlight the critical role of public authorities in co-designing collaboration pacts to ensure the general interest is protected. Another critical aspect of this model lies in the lack of a state law on shared administration of the commons, which could provide for greater clarity. Despite these limitations, evidence shows that collaboration pacts are effective for governing the commons and for engaging citizens previously not involved in civic participation (Iaione et al., 2020). They are a valid tool to widen the democratic arena and augment administrative efficiency (Salati, 2023a).

4.5 Collaboration Pacts: An Example of Application in Rural Areas

Population decline is one of the biggest challenges that rural areas are facing, in Italy and elsewhere (Alber, 2025). It manifests itself in many ways and impacts on, among others, labor productivity and the amount of utilized agricultural areas. Foreign migrant workers (farm hands) may be a welcomed remedy, but their presence needs rural municipal government to act, in that it needs to facilitate migratory flows and to advance the integration of farm hands.

Against this backdrop, the current debate in agriculture is polarized, on the one hand, around the issue of the denial of rights and exploitative practices of workers and, on the other, around the idea that farm hands are a necessity for the agricultural sector. This awareness urges local governments in rural areas to develop policies in favor of the integration of farm hands in the respective communities. BRIGHT (2019–2022)—Building RIGHTs-based and Innovative Governance for EU women farm hands—was a project funded by the Rights, Equality and Citizenship Programme of the European Union (Labsus-Bright, 2022; Valentino et al., 2022). It focused on the Ionian Arc in Southern Italy, an area that is characterized by several agricultural sectors of great national importance in which the labor component, including that of women is fundamental. Women actually account for more than 50% of the population living in Italy's rural areas (21 million). The BRIGHT project was carried out by a partner consortium composed of ActionAID (Italy); Labsus (Italy); the Council for Research in Agriculture of the Italian Ministry of Agriculture, Food Sovereignty and Forests; the Fundatia Centrul Parteneriat Pentru Egalitate

(Romania); the Foundation Gender Project for Bulgaria (Bulgaria); and ALDA—European Association for Local Democracy (France).

The activities within BRIGHT included women's leadership and rights' awareness raising workshops. Relevant for the purpose of our chapter is the fact that many actions in the BRIGHT project were realized and reworked through the MSA. Three collaboration pacts laid down the details regarding the co-development of gender-sensitive public services that address women's needs. Although with different success, they created collaborative networks comprising local governments, citizens, farm hands, employers, unions, and third-sector associations. At the start of the BRIGHT project, a phase of listening, needs identification and co-planning was launched to prepare the content of the collaboration pacts that involved the municipalities of Corigliano-Rossano, Ginosa, Grottaglie. Due to the restrictions imposed by the Covid-19 pandemic and the succession of local political and administrative events (municipal elections; the merger of the municipalities of Corigliano and Rossano and the legal actions against it), this phase proved to be more difficult and lengthier than foreseen. Finally, the collaboration pact of Corigliano-Rossano with 12 signatories was realized. This pact not only contains a series of actions in favor of female farm hands (22 out of 33 activities), but it also foresaw the creation of a physical space, the Citadel of Sharing (*Cittadella della Condivisione*), a place for "discussion, experimentation, and the development of local policies, in which women play a leading role alongside businesses, the third sector, institutions and agricultural enterprises" (Bonasora, 2022, 39). In other words, the Citadel of Sharing serves as "the fulcrum of a system of relations to accompany and support in order to make the actions undertaken at local level increasingly effective and coordinated" (Bonasora, 2022, 39), and it includes the wider public too. Three are the main lessons learned from the evaluation of this pact. First, the participatory methodology used from the very beginning was key to unite the community of Corigliano-Rossano to manage in terms of an articulate debate with the wider public. Second, municipalities are the pivot subjects of any successful CPC. Third, the signing of a collaboration pact and its practical implementation by means of CPC becomes difficult in the absence of suitable (internal) organization and human and financial resources, even in presence of an adopted MSA regulation.

4.6 Conclusions: From Participation to Empowered Participation

By referring to different research strands—the literature on participatory governance, the literature on deliberative democracy and the literature on local government—and considering both a political science and a constitutional law perspective, this chapter has discussed the expectations, the legal foundation, and the empirical evidence regarding the MSA and its commons governance model. It has shown that the CPC is grounded in the concept of empowered participation (Della Porta et al.,

2014), with empowerment referring to the expectation that citizens' participation directly affects public policy and complements the (service delivery of the) public sector.

While many democratic innovations—consultative practices based on deliberative reflection—often may have no tangible, immediate influence, the model of shared administration does have such an influence in a number of municipalities. Indeed, its regulatory and practical manifestations—the prototype regulation, the collaboration pacts, and CPC—require actions by empowered citizens. They lay forth the terms on which the local government transfers commons governance provisionally to individuals, groups, or associations, with a view to regenerate tangible and intangible assets, and deepen democracy. This collaborative governance approach facilitates closer collaboration between local government and (civil) society. It not only helps to create more inclusive and embedded democratic spaces, but it also has the potential to bridge the gap between institutions and social movements. It can help us move beyond the dichotomy of invented/invited spaces (Bussu, 2019), in which initiatives are either top-down or bottom-up, because it requires different actors to collaborate and develop commons governance through interaction and co-operation. In short, it can sustainably transform democratic participation by exerting an actual influence on public policymaking through the joint governance of the commons.

Both institutional support and commitment are crucial for the success of the MSA, mainly for two reasons that are mutually dependent. First, public professionals might feel frustrated by the citizens' lack of understanding of administrative procedures or the limited scope a local government has, with citizens or social movements regularly trying to submit proposals that cannot legally be implemented or that do not fall within the local government's scope. Second, the rejection of many initiatives of collaboration exacerbates citizens' feelings of distrust and disengagement; thus, it weakens local government that per se is in a privileged position to tap the potential of grassroots social innovation in view of rebuilding broken (or lost) collaborative networks. According to Hendriks et al. (2020), connections across democratic systems are thin and neglected, which is problematic because weak connections impact on how groups are included and represented in democratic processes, as well as on democratic legitimacy and, consequently, administrative efficiency. Similarly, Gaventa already 20 years ago (Gaventa, 2004) made an important case for (re)building relationships between citizens and local governments through civil society-based, state-based and intersecting public political or institutional spaces for participation. The MSA with its collaboration pacts serves this purpose. If put into place effectively, it represents an important opportunity for local governments to strengthen their role of steering and scrutiny and to re-engage with the local community and social movements. Councilors and civil servants may become orchestrators and facilitators. Indeed, collaboration pacts require politicians and civil servants who listen and connect with individuals and associations to align and support participatory processes outside and inside the municipal institutions. In other words, as councilors and civil servants in local government are increasingly expected to engage and collaborate with citizens and stakeholders, their work becomes relational through and through (Blijleven & van Hulst, 2021; Bynner et al.,

2023). In a mutual learning process, they may help to develop strategies that enable individuals and community groups to build the skills, capacities and confidence required to make the most of their situated knowledge, so that grassroots social innovation finds its way to make societies resilient and institutions sustainable, in the sense of being responsive to the needs and ideas of citizens. Of course, revolutionary changes that dramatically alter the political or social environment are unlikely. But the local government may act as a catalyzer, in that it creates an environment conducive to citizen participation that better links citizens to the institutions and to each other, and that produces incremental change (across levels of government). In the end, the MSA and its collaboration pacts forge a new form of civic engagement and participation.

For all these reasons, this chapter represents a call for cautious optimism about the wave of democratic innovations sweeping the world. As argued by Pateman (2012), the question is no longer whether participatory democracy is feasible, but how to institutionalize and embed its various forms. The MSA with its collaboration pacts harness grassroots social innovation at the local level, where society can most effectively reimagine the connection between territorial belonging and the responsibility and knowledge needed to address local governance challenges.

References

Ackerman, J. M. (2013). From co-production to co-governance. In V. Pestoff, T. Brandsen, & B. Verschuere (Eds.), *New public governance, the third sector, and co-production* (pp. 101–128). Routledge.

Alber, E. (2025, forthcoming). Rural areas and institutional sustainability: Assessing the nexus between population decline and rescaling of municipal government in Italy. In K. Kössler & E. M. Belser (Eds.), *Local government structure and intergovernmental relations: An urban-rural perspective*. Palgrave Macmillan.

Alber, E., & Zwilling, C. (2021). (Eds.) *Von Government zu Governance. Direkte und deliberative Demokratie in europäischen Mehrebenensystemen*. Nomos.

Alber, E., Valdesalici, A., & Klotz, G. (2024). Italy. In N. Steytler (Ed.), *The Forum of Federations' handbook on local government in federal systems* (pp. 281–311). Palgrave Macmillan.

Arena, G. (1997). Introduzione all'amministrazione condivisa. In *Studi parlamentari e di politica costituzionale* (pp. 29–65).

Bächtiger, A., Dryzek, J. S., Mansbridge, J., & Warren, M. (2018). *The Oxford handbook of deliberative democracy*. Oxford University Press.

Barber, B. R. (1984). *Strong democracy: Participatory politics for a new age*. University of California Press.

Barber, B. R. (2004). *Strong democracy: Participatory politics for a new age (Twentieth-anniversary edition)*. University of California Press.

Blijleven, W., & van Hulst, M. (2021). How Do Frontline Civil Servants Engage the Public? Practices, Embedded Agency, and Bricolage. The American Review of Public Administration, 51(4), 278–292.

Bonasora, P. (2022). The BRIGHT project and the shared administration model. In Labsus (Ed.), *Rethinking horizontal subsidiarity in the European Union* (pp. 37–41).

Bua, A., & Bussu, S. (2021). Between governance-driven democratization and democracy-driven governance: Explaining changes in participatory governance in the case of Barcelona. *European Journal of Political Research, 60*(3), 716–737.

Bua, A., & Bussu, S. (2023). *Reclaiming participatory governance: Social movements and the reinvention of democratic innovation* (1st ed.). Routledge.

Bussu, S. (2019). Collaborative governance: Between invited and invented spaces. In S. Elstub & O. Escobar (Eds.), *Handbook of democratic innovation and governance* (pp. 60–76). Edward Elgar.

Bussu, S., Bua, A., Dean, R., & Smith, G. (2022). Introduction: Embedding participatory governance. *Critical Policy Studies, 16*(2), 133–145.

Bynner, C., Escobar, O., & Weakley, S. (2023). Facilitators as culture change workers: Advancing public participation and deliberation in local governance. *Local Government Studies, 49*(4), 738–758.

Cassese, S. (2001). L'arena Pubblica. Nuovi Paradigmi per Lo Stato. *Rivista trimestrale di diritto pubblico, 3*, 601–650.

D'Atena, A. (1997). Il Principio Di Sussidiarietà Nella Costituzione Italiana. *Rivista Italiana di Diritto Pubblico Comunitario, 7*(3/4), 603–627.

Della Porta, D., Reiter, H., & Alarcón, P. (2014). Institutional participatory initiatives and democratic qualities. In J. Font, D. Della Porta, & Y. Sintomer (Eds.), *Participatory democracy in Southern Europe* (pp. 71–114). Rowman & Littlefield.

Donati, D. (2014). *Il paradigma sussidiario. Interpretazioni, estensione, garanzie*. Il Mulino.

Elstub, S., & Escobar, O. (2019). *Handbook of democratic innovation and governance*. Edward Elgar.

Fedeli, V. (2017). Institutions matter: Governance and citizenship in a post-metropolitan perspective. In A. Balducci, V. Fedeli, & F. Curci (Eds.), *Post-metropolitan territories. Looking for a new urbanity* (pp. 266–273). Routledge.

Foster, S. R., & Iaione, C. (2019). Ostrom in the city. Design principles and practices for the urban commons. In B. Hudson, J. Rosenbloom, & D. Cole (Eds.), *Routledge handbook of the study of the commons* (pp. 235–255). Routledge.

Gaventa, J. (2004). Strengthening participatory approaches to local governance: Learning the lessons from abroad. *National Civic Review, 93*, 16–27.

Gbikpi, B., & Grote, J. R. (2002). From democratic government to participatory governance. In J. R. Grote & B. Gbikpi (Eds.), *Participatory governance* (pp. 17–34). Springer.

Geissel, B. (2022). *The future of self-governing, thriving democracies: Democratic innovations by, with and for the people* (1st ed.). Routledge.

Gibson-Graham, J. K., Cameron, J., & Healy, S. (2016). Commoning as a postcapitalist politics. In *Releasing the commons. Rethinking the futures of the commons* (pp. 192–212). Routledge.

Giordano, M. F. (2022). Subsidiarity, a transformative principle for the future of European democracy. In Labsus (Ed.), *Rethinking horizontal subsidiarity in the European Union* (pp. 6–17).

Gjaldbæk-Sverdrup, E., Nicolaïdis, K., & Hernández, N. P. (2023). "Technocratic democratization": What can we learn from the European Commission's new generation european citizens' panels? *RSC 2023/65* Robert Schuman Centre for Advanced Studies.

Gustafson, P., & Hertting, N. (2016). Understanding participatory governance: An analysis of participants' motives for participation. *The American Review of Public Administration, 47*(5), 538–549.

Heinelt, H. (2018). *Handbook on participatory governance*. Edward Elgar.

Hendriks, M. C. (2016). Coupling citizens and elites in deliberative systems: The role of institutional design. *European Journal of Political Research, 55*(1), 43–60.

Hendriks, M. C., Ercan, S. A., & Boswell, J. (2020). *Mending democracy: Democratic repair in disconnected times*. Oxford University Press.

Iaione, C. (2016). The CO-City: Sharing, collaborating, cooperating, and commoning in the city. *American Journal of Economics and Sociology, 75*(2), 415–455.

Iaione, C., Pais, I., & de Nictolis, E. (2020). Valutare: La Valutazione Dei Patti Di Collaborazione. In R. Paltrinieri (Ed.), *Culture e Pratiche Di Partecipazione* (pp. 67–99). FrancoAngeli.
IDEA. (2023). *The global state of democracy 2023*.
Jacquet, V., Ryan, M., & van der Does, R. (2023). *The impact of democratic innovations*. ECPR Press.
Labsus. (2004). *Carta della sussidiarietà*. https://www.labsus.org/la-carta-della-sussidiarieta/
Labsus. (2022). *Prototipo di regolamento sulla collaborazione tra cittadini e amministrazioni per la cura, la rigenerazione e la gestione condivisa dei beni comuni urbani*. https://www.labsus.org/wp-content/uploads/2017/04/Regolamento-Prototiopo-Labsus.2022.pdf
Labsus Annual Report. (2021). *Rapporto 2021 sull'amministrazione condivisa dei beni comuni*. https://www.labsus.org/wp-content/uploads/2022/03/LABSUS_Rapporto-2021-22_LOW.pdf
Labsus-Bright. (2022). *Rethinking horizontal subsidiarity in the European Union. New instruments for community welfare in the Italian experience: The Collaboration Pacts*. https://www.labsus.org/wp-content/uploads/2022/12/Bright_Documento_ENG.pdf
Luther, J. (2020). La Sussidiarietà Come Principio Sussidiario Del Diritto Pubblico Comune Europeo. In D. Ciaffi & F. M. Giordano (Eds.), *Storia, percorsi e politiche della sussidiarietà. Le nuove prospettive in Italia e in Europa* (pp. 209–225). Il Mulino.
Mansbridge, J., Bohman, J., Chambers, S., Christiano, T., Fung, A., Parkinson, J., Thompson, D. F., & Warren, M. E. (2012). A systemic approach to deliberative democracy. In J. Parkinson & J. Mansbridge (Eds.), *Deliberative systems: Deliberative democracy at the large scale* (pp. 1–26). Cambridge University Press.
OECD. (2020). *Innovative citizen participation and new democratic institutions: Catching the deliberative wave*. OECD Publishing.
Osborne, D., & Gaebler, T. (1992). *Reinventing government*. Addison-Wesley.
Ostrom, E. (1990). *Governing the commons: The evolution of institutions for collective action*. Cambridge University Press.
Palermo, F. (2015). Regulating pluralism: Federalism as decision-making and new challenges for federal studies. In F. Palermo & E. Alber (Eds.), *Federalism as decision-making* (pp. 497–513). Brill.
Pateman, C. (2012). Participatory democracy revisited. *Perspectives on Politics, 10*(1), 7–11.
Pfahl, S. (2005). Institutional sustainability. *International Journal of Sustainable Development, 8*(1/2), 80–96.
Pope Pius XI. (1931). *Littera Encyclica Quadragesimo Anno* (point 80).
Reuchamps, M., Vrydagh, J., & Welp, Y. (Eds.). (2023). *De Gruyter handbook of citizens' assemblies*. De Gruyter.
Rodotà Commission. (2007). *Report*. https://www.giustizia.it/giustizia/it/mg_1_12_1.wp?facetNode_1=0_10&facetNode_2=0_10_21&previsiousPage=mg_1_12&contentId=SPS47617#
Salati, C. (2023a). *Towards a theoretical framework for civic participation through the commons in EU cities: The contribution of horizontal subsidiarity in Italian cities*. PhD thesis, Università degli Studi di Macerata. Defended August 23, 2023.
Salati, C. (2023b). The forgotten meaning of the EU principle of subsidiarity. Horizontal subsidiarity in Italian local governments. *Diversity Governance Papers* 2.
Valentino, G., Forcina, B., & Zumpano, C. (2022). *I Patti di collaborazione e la nuova politica di sviluppo rurale e territoriale: Alcune indicazioni di metodo*. https://www.reterurale.it/flex/cm/pages/ServeAttachment.php/L/IT/D/9%252F3%252F7%252FD.4fdf030b2cb6da38be40/P/BLOB%3AID%3D24117/E/pdf
V-Dem. (2023). *Democracy report 2023: Defiance in the face of autocratization*.
Warren, M. (2014). Governance-driven democratization. In S. Griggs, A. J. Norval, & H. Wagenaar (Eds.), *Practices of freedom: Decentered governance, conflict and democratic participation* (pp. 38–60). Cambridge University Press.

Chapter 5
Public Participation in the Spanish Urban Planning System: A Model Between Legal Formality and Governance

Juan Antonio Chinchilla Peinado

Abstract Public participation in the elaboration of planning was already formalized in the first Spanish urban planning law of 1956. To this moment, the same general features have been maintained which means that participation is conceived as an instrument for the defense of the rights and interests of landowners. However, the concept of governance and deliberative democracy require us to rethink this model of participation. The aim should be to make the involvement of citizens in the shaping of the city model real and effective. It should be ensured that the choice of this model is not top-down but made jointly with the citizens.

Keywords Urbanism · Participation · Public consultations · Governance · Planning · Local government

5.1 Introduction: Participatory Planning in the Urban Agenda and the SDGs

The right to the city is defined as the individual and collective right to remake urban life from a socially and ecologically sustainable perspective (Ponce Solé, 2019, 25; Vaquer Caballería, 2015, 123; Pisarello Prados, 2011, 289). It requires democratic management of urban space, understood as a collective creation, as well as the establishment of the social and environmental function of both urban property and the city. From this perspective, among the Sustainable Development Goals (SDGs) incorporated into the 2030 Agenda, the aim is to "increase inclusive and sustainable urbanization and capacity for participatory, integrated and sustainable planning and management" (Goal 3, SDG 11, Sustainable Cities and Communities). This is a demand that has long been advocated by European policy. Within the framework of Local Agenda 21, the Charter of European Cities for Sustainability (Aalborg Charter

J. A. Chinchilla Peinado (✉)
Institute of Local Government Law, Autonomous University of Madrid, Madrid, Spain
e-mail: juanantonio.chinchilla@uam.es

K. Kössler, E. Schläppi (eds.), *Citizen Participation in Local Governance*, Local and Urban Governance, https://doi.org/10.1007/978-3-031-99824-9_5

of 1994), or the Aalborg+10 commitment, already demand "access to information for all citizens and interested groups ... so that they can participate in local decision-making processes" and the enhancement of the strategic role in urban design and planning, orienting it towards the common benefit. The 2030 Agenda demands that the SDGs be implemented through the alignment of all public policies that are exercised for the joint achievement of all the SDGs.

This is also the tenth Strategic Objective of the 2019 Spanish Urban Agenda, which aims at "improving intervention instruments and governance". Its objective 10.2 aims to "ensure citizen participation, transparency and promote multilevel governance". This objective is specified in three lines of action to be adopted by the public authorities:

1. Guarantee a participatory procedure open to all citizens prior to the formal procedure for the preparation of land and urban planning instruments as a way of ensuring true citizen participation;
2. Encourage participation in the design, monitoring and evaluation of public policies by the people; and
3. Integrate participation in planning in a real and effective way throughout the process and beyond the mandatory procedures of public information and allegations. It is necessary to seek co-responsibility in the adoption of decisions, promote networking and permanent social innovation.

The effective participation and governance of citizens in the design of the city is not pursued as an end in itself, but as an instrument to achieve the realization of the principle of sustainable development and the reality of people's right to the city and housing (Articles 3 and 4(2)(c) of Royal Legislative Decree 7/2015, of October 30, approving the consolidated text of the Law on Land and Urban Rehabilitation—hereinafter TRLSRU).

5.2 Participation in Urban Planning

5.2.1 Provisions on Participation in State Legislation

The TRLSRU regulates citizen participation from different perspectives. On the one hand, Article 4(2)I TRLSRU asserts that legislation on land use and urban planning must guarantee "the right to information for citizens and entities representing the interests affected by urban planning processes, as well as citizen participation in urban planning and management". On the other hand, Articl(e) TRLSRU recognizes the right of citizens to "effectively participate in the procedures for the preparation and approval of any land use planning or urban planning and execution instruments and their environmental assessment by means of the formulation of allegations, observations, proposals, claims and complaints and to obtain a reasoned response from the administration, in accordance with the legislation regulating the legal regime of said administration and the procedure in question".

This right is qualified as the right to real participation, and not just formal participation (Menéndez Rexach, 2008, 150; Chinchilla Peinado, 2016, 248). In terms of minimums imposed on the regional legislation, this right is specified in the obligation to submit the planning instrument to public information, per Article 25(1) TRLSRU. This procedure must at least include an executive summary of (1) the delimitation of the areas in which the projected planning alters the existing one, with a plan of its location, and the scope of such alteration; and (2) the areas in which the planning or the procedures of execution or urban development intervention are suspended and the duration of such suspension, in accordance with article 25(3) TRLSRU. Finally, public participation can involves a public action to demand before the administrative bodies and the contentious-administrative courts the observance of the legislation and other instruments of territorial and urban planning, under the terms of article 62(1) TRLSRU.[1] In turn, Articles 21, 22, and 30 of Law 21/2013 on environmental assessment—hereinafter LEA—require that the initial version of the planning instrument, together with the strategic environmental study, be submitted for public information and consultation (hearing) of interested persons within the ordinary procedure of strategic environmental assessment, and only for consultation within the simplified procedure of strategic environmental assessment. For this purpose, the documentation submitted for public information must include a non-technical document of the strategic environmental study.

5.2.2 *The Specification of Participation in Regional Planning Legislation*

The provisions of the TRLSRU have the character of basic norms, configured with the basic conditions to guarantee the equality of all citizens per Article 149(1)(1) of the Spanish Constitution. Based on the structural elements established by state legislation, it is up to each regional law, on the basis of its exclusive competence in matters of urban planning (Article 148(3) of the Constitution), to specify the regime of public participation in the preparation of planning instruments. The 17 regional laws, with different terminological variants, guarantee the promotion of citizen (social) participation in the formulation, management, and execution of urban planning activity, recognizing the right of individuals to access to the documents that make up the planning and execution, during the drafting process and after its approval.

[1] This linking of the recognition of public action with participation is affirmed by Menéndez Rexach (2008, 152) and Llorens Ferrer (2013, 162). The defense of urban planning legality does not require standing based on the ownership of a subjective right or legitimate interest (Article 4 of Law 39/2015 on Common Administrative Procedure, hereinafter LPAC, or Article 19 of Law 29/1998 regulating the Contentious-Administrative Jurisdiction), but rather, since Article 223 of the Land Law of 1956, public action has been recognized.

Participation in urban planning is specified in regional legislation in two ways. Firstly, there may be a phase of prior participation in the formulation of the general planning instrument (but not in the case of derived planning instruments). This participation may involve consultations or public information campaigns on the preliminary draft of the planning instrument (Chinchilla Peinado, 2017, 60). Generally, this participation is carried out either prior to the draft's formulation or, more usually, after the formulation of the preliminary draft by the city council. The decision to open such a process is made by the local administration. However, in certain regional laws, this is not an option but a mandatory procedure. All regional laws outline a minimum period in which the document is subject to a public consultation/information process, either expressly or implicitly by linking it to the strategic environmental assessment. In any case, the regional legislation specifies the possibility for citizens to formulate suggestions or other planning alternatives. Therefore, the approval of the preliminary draft must express the expected results of the participation phase.

Regional legislation foresees a second moment of participation once the planning instrument has been drawn up and preliminarily approved. In summary, such information is articulated by configuring a process of allegations open to the public. This procedure consists of the publication of the plan in the corresponding official gazette and in the electronic headquarters of the administration, opening a not very long period for the presentation of observations and comments. In this respect, it is required that such public information be made in a manner and under conditions that favor greater effective participation of the holders of affected rights and of the citizens in general. To this purpose, all the documentation required for the approval of the planning instrument, including the strategic environmental assessment, must be made available to the public.In addition, the initial approval must specify the elements incorporated that deviate from the model established in the in the draft plan.

Regional legislation also obliges the municipal administration to send an individualized notification to landowners included in the scope of the development planning instruments so that they are made aware of the hearing process. There are two models: (1) those regulations that require such notification regardless of whether the initiative for the formulation and approval of the development planning instrument is public or private; (2) those regulations that only require notification when the initiative for the formulation is private. In all these cases, a hearing is held for the affected owners, choosing to identify those who appear as such in the cadastre. When, as a consequence of the public information, substantive changes in the zoning are introduced in the initially approved document, the new document must again be submitted to the public information process. In this respect, some regional laws positivize the concept of substantial modification, circumscribing it to those cases involving the adoption of new criteria with respect to the classification and qualification of the land, or in relation to the general and organic structure of the territory. This public information procedure is configured as an essential procedure, whose absence (or its merely formal compliance without responding to the allegations presented) determines the nullity of the planning instrument.[2] The specific public

[2] See Supreme Court Ruling of May 5, 2015 (ECLI:ES:TS:2015:1839).

information process for the plan is carried out simultaneously with the public information process required by the strategic environmental assessment regulations. Therefore, the public information is open for both purposes.

5.3 Systematic Interpretation of Participation in Urban Planning

Certainly, legislation and jurisprudence recognize a wide margin of discretion for the planner when drawing up urban planning choosing what he considers to be the optimal model of management and growth in accordance with the guidelines and objectives set by him.

The plan report is the element that sets the dominant context in which a decision is made and is the basis for the justification of the choice of the model and the establishment of the determinations of the plan. The determinations of the plan must be a logical consequence of the concurrent factual circumstances. But the shaping of the decision on the city model must necessarily consider the interests and conceptions expressed by the citizens through their participation in the planning process. Essentially, the planning instrument is presented as the result of a balancing process. The balancing act is between the private interests of the owners, who seek to materialize more lucrative urban uses (e.g., residential uses for vacation tourism) and public interests, which seek to realize the principles of sustainability, access to housing, etc. (e.g., striving for a balance between residential uses for affordable housing and residential uses for vacation rentals). The regulations require that a certain percentage of the residential land (between 20% and 40%) be destined to affordable residential use, but the municipal administration decides on the rest depending on its public policies and the lobbying capacity of the owners.

5.3.1 The Advance of Planning as a Figure of Participatory Democracy

Participation in the advance phase is linked to the general mandate established by Article 9(2) of the Spanish Constitution directed at the constituted powers to promote citizen participation in the political, economic, social, and cultural spheres, and which is specified in Article 133(1) LPAC and the regional regulations. It is intended to achieve the formulation of urban planning regulations with the widest possible citizen participation prior to their adoption. It should be configured as a manifestation of participatory democracy and, therefore, directly connected to the democratic principle.[3] The purpose of this procedure is to obtain the opinion of the

[3] In the terms outlined in Constitutional Court Judgments 31/2015, FJ. 4. This modality does not constitute an expression of the right to participation guaranteed by Article 23(1) of the Constitution, nor can it be configured as a case of representative democracy or direct democracy.

citizens on a matter of public interest. Its aim is not to question the specific determination of the property right that the plan makes on a particular plot, but to help shape a prior decision: what is the model that will be adopted and that will condition the lives of citizens. This phase helps the planner's decision to find more and better contrasted elements of judgment and analysis, allowing a heterogeneous vision of all those individuals or groups of individuals who, representing their own or collective interests, can facilitate a decision-making process that is not only more transparent, but also more logical and accurate.[4] In some regions, the specific articulation of this participation in the advance phase of the General Plan or other derived plans are called "Citizen Participation Programs", "Citizen Participation Plans", or similar. Such programs or processes culminate in a report summarizing the development of the participatory process (material means, subjects in charge of promoting and dynamizing this figure, activities carried out, etc.), specifying the answers or suggestions offered (Rando Burgos, 2020, 82). Participation here can be done through multiple ways. Presenting formal written observations through established channels or participating in questionnaires or meetings articulated by the technical managers of the plan.

Citizen participation thus endows planning with a plus of democratic legitimacy, which is necessary given the intense and direct impact of the plan on the physical and environmental surroundings and, above all, on the quality of life of citizens. This participation helps to shape the adopted decision. However, it does not replace the decision-making power of the representative body that must approve the planning instrument.[5] Normatively, this participation phase only has internal administrative effects. It is not binding on the administration.

Public participation in the advance phase should occur when the planner has not yet shown a preference for any of the possible options, enriching the preparatory work with the suggestions that citizens can contribute. Therefore, what is relevant here is that all alternatives are open. It is required that citizens have the necessary information (transparency) and that this information is understandable for an "ordinary" citizen.[6] Based on such information, any citizen may make suggestions on the abstract city model to be adopted. Given the possible contradictory positions of citizens, the administration must decide on the total or partial incorporation of some of them. The criteria for this are legal ones in the first place and then of a technical and political nature. The content of such suggestions is the concretion of the general

---

[4] See Supreme Court Ruling of July 22, 2015 (ECLI:ES:TS:2015:3587).

[5] Article 69(2) Law 7/1985, of April 2, 1985, Regulating the Bases of the Local Regime, hereinafter LBRL.

[6] The White Paper on sustainability in Spanish urban planning (2010, 29) concludes that it is "essential that it be transmitted to non-technical people in a way that can be understood... (thus requiring) an interactive educational process between technicians and citizens without specific knowledge of urban planning. The bodies (or the body) in charge of drafting, monitoring the plan and observing the territory should also assume the task of education and dissemination of the aspects related to urban planning... (through) conferences, courses, forums, or information pages on the internet".

interest, and not so much the defense of a specific legitimate interest or a subjective right. The aim is to achieve more efficient, transparent, and co-responsible planning. This is where a deficit can be seen in most of the autonomous community legislations. Participation is often limited, on many occasions, to the simple opening of a public information procedure on the document already prepared by the administration. That is, once the local administration has agreed on the content of the plan, it simply proceeds to articulate a participation that can be described as "cosmetic" or referring to specific issues. Here, citizens have limited capacity to question the model already adopted. They will only be able to impose a subsequent judicial control. On the contrary, this public participation requires consulting and obtaining the opinion of citizens on the objectives and general proposals of the future planning instrument; that is, on its most relevant elements: the basic lines of intended development in terms of population growth and housing stock, mode of occupation and consumption of the territory, preservation of natural elements and biodiversity, among many others—or on specific aspects that are conflicting, such as the destination of a previous public endowment that has now been abandoned. Such general lines submitted to citizen participation may be predetermined by the city council, or the opinion of the citizens may be sought beforehand.

Today, all possible and effective channels of communication and participation should be used, and the use of ICT alone is not admissible (Castel Gayán, 2011, 308). Other participation must always be allowed with various instruments being possible. The competence to regulate the different forms of participation rooted in participatory or deliberative democracy (citizen hearings, consultation forums, citizen panels, citizen juries, assemblies, question and answer sessions, hearings, questionnaires, polls, consultations, etc.) corresponds to the regions.[7] All these methods guarantee the rights of all potential participants, although they are characterized by flexibility and informality. The data on participation in these models is variable and quite unclear, as it is limited in most cases to simple numbers. Data protection legislation appears as a limit in this regard. In practice, the most used instrument are questionnaires to be filled in by citizens during an extended period, where they are asked about previously selected issues, allowing them to express their opinion on such relevant issues. The administration is obliged to respond and does so in a generic reference in the Plan Report. Given the functionality of this procedure, when it is legally required, its omission determines the nullity of the procedure. The possible submission of allegations by citizens during the subsequent public information period does not remedy the omission of public scrutiny of the preparatory work.[8]

[7] All these mechanisms must be differentiated from the referendum. As Carrasco Durán (2013, 19) points out, while the referendum is an instrument of direct participation of citizens in public affairs, exercising here the fundamental right recognized in Article 23(1) of the Constitution, in the other instruments it is a matter of gathering the opinion of any collective on any matters of public interest through any procedures as a manifestation of the participatory democracy recognized in article 9(2) of the Constitution.

[8] See Supreme Court Rulings of September 30, 2008 (ECLI:ES:TS:2008:5395); January 23, 2003 (ECLI:ES:TS:2003:324); January 15, 2000 (ECLI:ES:TS:2000:74).

5.3.2 *The Figure of the Public Information as a Phase of Hearing in the Procedure of Elaboration of the Planning*

Participation through the public information phase is linked to the hearing process in the preparation of general administrative provisions regulated by Article 105(a) of the Constitution, developed in Article 133(2) LPAC and regional regulations. It is the realization of the principle of the rule of law and the guarantee of the right of defense in the procedure. The public information procedure is based on an initially approved plan, where the city model has already been adopted and specified. Therefore, in practice, it operates more as a criticism of the specific solution adopted than as a way to formulate alternative proposals based on a new model or design (Llorens Ferrer, 2013, 162). In short, its main purpose is to defend the legitimate interests and rights of affected individuals. Public participation thus helps to shape the adopted decision but does not replace the decision-making power of the representative body that must approve the planning instrument.[9]

This is a procedure that goes beyond the mere formal aspect. It presents a material dimension since the correctness and legality of the planner's decision depends on the effective consideration of this citizen participation. The ultimate decision corresponds to the planner in all aspects that do not have a prescribed content. This does not mean that the administration cannot impose a different arrangement. However, an explicit and sufficient motivation is required after the concerns have been accepted.

The documentation submitted to the public information process, once the planning instrument has been initially approved, is no longer reduced to a non-technical summary of the contents of the plan or of the strategic environment al study but must be comprehensive of all the actions carried out.[10] Therefore, in the public information process, the plan must be made publicly available with all the written and graphic documentation required by the regional legislation, including the executive summary.[11] Regional legislation also establishes that the documentation will be available to the public by telematic channels.

---

[9] See Article 69(2) LBRL.

[10] See Articles 25 TRLSRU, 21.3, and 30(1) LEA, with respect to information in the strategic environmental assessment procedure.

[11] Constitutional Court Ruling 141/2014, FJ 8(b) states with respect to such a provision of the State legislation that "the provision of this document constitutes a guarantee that is expressed in the availability to the citizen of information, selective and easy to understand, on the aspects of special relevance of the plan (changes in planning that it introduces and suspensive effects), favoring not only transparency, but also, and fundamentally, access to urban planning information and civic participation in the procedures for approval or alteration of urban planning instruments.... Nor is the procedure for the preparation and approval of urban plans regulated in its entirety, not even the executive summary itself, to which the Autonomous Communities could incorporate additional content if this does not distort the purpose of the same".

Only a decisive change in the planning model that served as the basis for provisional approval justifies the need for a new public information procedure. However, a second public information procedure is not necessary in three cases: firstly, when the modifications introduced respond to the allegations presented; secondly, when such modifications derive from legal issues; thirdly, when the modifications incorporated are minor so that they do not clearly affect the territorial and planning model accepted at the time. The consequence is that public participation in the planning process is not guaranteed when the urban planning legislation establishes a procedure that excludes the second public information, even when the initially approved document has undergone substantial modifications. However, the competence of the regional legislation to introduce quantitative variables to determine when such a substantive modification is present is recognized. What is not admissible is that the regional regulation directly excludes such a procedure. Participation is not guaranteed either when such legislation or administrative practice only requires the communication of such modifications to those interested parties who are present in the proceedings, which leaves all those affected who were not present in the procedure (who may not have been present, nor made allegations, because they were in agreement with the initially approved document) unaware of the modifications made during the processing.[12] If this information is partial and gives rise to an insufficient knowledge of the document finally approved, it entails the nullity of the urban plan.[13] Here, the determining criterion is whether the practical implementation of the participation procedure generates a lack of knowledge or an insufficient and biased knowledge of the essential content of the plan. In such an assumption, the concurrence of a cause of radical nullity must be affirmed, which is not susceptible to validation or subsequent rectification by the mere filing of the contentious-administrative appeal and the obtaining of the aspects previously not communicated. But if the report or the rest of the documentation allows the required information to be discovered, there will be no problem of legality. But if the report or the rest of the documentation provides the required information, no defenselessness is generated in any way.[14] What happens if the participation or public information process does not respect the term established by the regional regulations? If the allegations submitted after the deadline are processed, such formal defect will have no relevance.

---

[12] Therefore, a new public information process is only necessary when there are modifications or alternations between the initial and final approval of the planning instruments, being limited to cases of change, modification, or alteration of the territorial model. And here it must be considered that the determination of whether or not the modifications introduced in the document deserve to be considered substantial is a question that has a factual aspect, that relating to the content and entity of the variations whose entity can be quantified and verified. But it also incorporates a value judgment on the facts, which consists of determining whether the modifications are legally relevant, which allows their review in cassation. In this sense, cf. Supreme Court Ruling of January 8, 2013 (ECLI:ES:TS:2013:152); October 11, 2012 (ECLI:ES:TS:2012:6589); or December 9, 2008 (ECLI:ES:TS:2008:6902).

[13] See Supreme Court Ruling of January 18, 2013 (ECLI:ES:TS:2013:152).

[14] See Supreme Court Ruling of February 21, 2011 (ECLI:ES:TS:2011:795).

The perception of this modality of procedural participation is clear. The information obtained in this process has little relevance for the politicians and technicians responsible for the elaboration of the plan. It does not allow for the establishment of true public decision-making networks (Bono et al., 2021, 70).

5.3.3 *The Use of Direct Consultations with Citizens as a Tool to Strengthen Deliberative Democracy*

Today, new participation mechanisms are demanded that provide social legitimacy to the urban solutions adopted and make them resistant to erosion by increasing the citizens' sense of belonging. This is a requirement of the notion of governance. They do not replace representative democracy but reinforce it.[15] This makes bottom-up planning possible. But there are obvious risks here. Citizen participation through the various forms of consultation contributes to the evaluation process followed by the urban planning administration to draw up the plan that establishes the new urban planning ordinance. Therefore, such consultation mechanisms must be designed and assessed in such a way as to avoid easy confusion between individual and collective interests (Bermejo Latre 2013, 410), and must guarantee rigor in obtaining information on the interests involved on the part of the administration. In this sense, in recent years numerous citizen consultations have been held on urban planning matters. The municipal governments have assumed the political (but not legal) commitment to respect citizens' decisions, but in some cases, only if a certain number of participants exceeded a certain level of participation. Some were held under the traditional formula of voting in a ballot box with regard to on one or two specific and closed questions, aimed at determining the specific direction of a particular action; others, articulated online (where prior electronic registration was required), responding to more complex questionnaires on possible specific urban planning solutions in small spatial areas. The different forms of consultation are all addressed to the residents. These consultations are regulated by the urban planning laws of the various regions or by local ordinances on participation.

Regardless of the type of consultation, these procedures embody administrative participation in a material sense.[16] The scope in which they are raised is that of

[15] In the sense established by STC 119/1995, FJ 6.

[16] The Citizen Participation Guide for Urban Planning Projects (2022, 25) distinguishes, on the one hand, between a consultative model, where the promoter of the consultation requires the opinion of citizens on a topic or action of collective interest, either openly or on a previous proposal. On the other hand, there is a cooperative model, where the promoter convenes the citizens to identify the problems, needs, demands and expectations regarding a matter of collective interest and to elaborate together the appropriate public policies. The design of these participatory processes is built in different phases, as designed in the guide. In practice, however, the cooperation model does not play a role so that the focus of this chapter is on consultation.

municipal competences. The limits of these consultations, from a legal perspective,[17] are therefore determined by local competences. Consultations, whatever their modality, may consist of one question, which is submitted for acceptance or rejection, or of several questions to be chosen. There are three key elements. First, the question (or questions) must be clear (they must be unambiguously worded so that voters can pronounce themselves in the affirmative or negative based on their correct understanding). Secondly, it must be neutral (balanced and non-directed, without bias), allowing the citizen to take a position against the position defended by the local authorities. The lack of neutrality questions the voter's freedom. The neutrality of the question is the only element that guarantees an objective response from the citizen and, therefore, can validly contribute to forming the administrative decision. However, neutrality does not mean that the government that formulates the question does not show its preference for a certain solution, as an expression of its political program. Third, what must be avoided is that it prevents considering all the options or interests at stake. In addition, the consultation must have relevant "content", and not merely rhetorical questions, which can be assumed without question by most citizens.[18]

The consultation as a mechanism of participatory democracy cannot undermine the decision-making powers that correspond to the representative bodies of the municipality (Article 69(2) LBRL). Therefore, the consultation is not legally binding, either because it is expressly so determined, or because of the prevalence of the representative principle in the face of legal silence. However, the consultation is politically binding for the government that promotes the consultation (or that must process it when it is promoted by a certain number of citizens). The question is reduced to specifying what minimum participation must be required and what majority must be achieved in the absence of regulatory provisions in this regard.

The constitutional principle of democracy requires that, after the holding of the consultation, the mayor must appear before the municipal plenary and set out the legal position that the city council adopts on the result of the popular consultation. It is necessary for the local administration to get back to the citizens as a means of guaranteeing political and administrative responsibility, and to avoid its transformation into a merely formal procedure. As well as expressing this feedback in other channels, it should be reflected in the report of the planning instrument that is finally formulated. Both the total or partial assumption of the results of the participatory process and its rejection must be justified there. The result thus provides the local administration with elements of judgment to carry out the balancing of the interests at stake that are required to adopt the specific urban planning instrument. The relevance is political rather than legal. When the municipal authority considers it necessary or convenient, it submits an issue to the scrutiny of citizens to provide greater legitimacy and consensus to the result to be adopted. Only in certain cases do

[17] See STC 138/2015, FJ 3; 31/2015, FJ 6; 31/2010, FJ 69.

[18] It does not seem an optimal question to ask, for example, whether to stop the urban growth of the municipality. It is evident that today, most citizens are aware that uncontrolled and expansive growth is no longer possible.

municipal regulations impose consultation if enough citizens demand it. The choice of one or the other is also a political decision, depending on whether a more or less formalized voting procedure is to be adopted, giving greater or lesser legitimacy to the result. How can it be avoided that such informal consultations are only used by the urban planning administration as a placebo, to achieve an apparent legitimacy of its imposed decision? The aim of consultation is to convert citizens into relevant active agents in urban planning, so that consultation constitutes a more open and collaborative negotiation scenario in which all agents have a meaningful impact on decision-making. The use of consultations is not a guarantee of the choice of the best possible option. But it is a tool that generates spaces for awareness-raising, information, debate, and proposal of urban alternatives, allowing citizens to become involved in the construction of the city, incorporating their real needs. This tool also contributes to the accountability of urban planning authorities.

5.4 Conclusions

The regulation of participation in urban planning is not entirely satisfactory. The notion of governance, of building the city model from the bottom up, in a more horizontal and less vertical perspective, is not yet fully established in administrative practice. The city model is a collective decision that must be adopted once adequate information is available. However, participation should not only be a mechanism for obtaining information for the administration. It should also be a means to build consensus on the model to be adopted. For this reason, participation must occur before the choosing of a specific model. Participation must give rise to a space for co-decision, without prejudice to the fact that the final responsibility for the adoption of the specific solution lies with the administrations. Practical experience in Spain shows that the most successful experiences of participation are fundamentally articulated through citizen consultation as a governance mechanism. The advance phase in the approval procedure of urban plans shows reduced participation levels when the personal interest of the claimant is confused with the general interest in the construction of the city.

The primary objective is to achieve the construction of a city model in a collaborative manner, ensuring greater consensus. But in many cases, it is simply a top-down process. There is a broad social perception, reflected in the media, of the irrelevance of participation in urban planning procedures. For citizens, the urban planning solutions adopted are far removed from their real interests. They are perceived as solutions imposed from above, for the benefit of interests of certain property owners or developers, and are, therefore, seen as hardly democratic. The perception is that it is only when citizens organize themselves, and question the proposed urban planning, that they are effectively listened to by the urban planning authorities.

Participation is formally open to any citizen, whether or not they own land or buildings. In practice, if there is no active process promoted by the city council, those who participate are landowners interested in improving the urban use attributed by the plan, or environmental associations. There is no specific space for the participation of political parties. Regional and national interests are considered through the issuance of mandatory reports required by various sectoral laws (roads, water, coasts, telecommunications, etc.) which are issued by the different sectoral authorities of the national and regional governments depending on their sectoral competence.

The most successful participatory processes are those promoted by the city council, through the creation of face-to-face workshops with neighbors in small areas, identifying their problems and interests. Also successful are the consultations, in many cases held digitally, where the entire population is asked about specific and determined measures.

In this light, a key question is to what extent people's involvement has an actual impact. Local authorities must provide an express and written response to the suggestions made in the public participation processes. The results of the consultations convened are not binding from a legal perspective, although they may be binding from a political perspective.

As for urban and rural local governments, legal regulations are identical in both contexts. In practice, in urban settings it is easier to adopt participatory processes through consultations and workshops due to the greater economic capacity of the municipality, which allows it to provide funds for these activities, as well as the greater training of the population. However, when these processes are articulated in rural areas, the results tend to be more interesting, as they do not refer only to individual interests.

References

Bono, G., Juan, J. P. C., & Dasí, J. F. (2021). Marco General y narrativas predominantes que explican la forma en que se desarrollan los procesos: Una aproximación a la OT en España y las posibilidades de conexión con la política del desarrollo económico regional. In J. F. Dasí, E. P. Sánchez-Manjavacas, & E. R. Burgos (Eds.), *Evaluación de procesos: Una mirada crítica y propositiva de la situación de la política e instrumentos de ordenación del territorio en España* (pp. 45–82). Editorial Aranzadi.

Carrasco Durán, M. (2013). Referéndum "versus" consulta. *Revista Estudios Políticos, 160*, 13–41.

Castel Gayán, S. (2011). Descentralización política, participación ciudadana y renovación jurídica: ¿Hacia una democracia participativa? *Revista Catalana de Dret públic, 43*, 279–316.

Latre, B., & Luis, J. (2013). La información administrativa y la participación del público en materia de urbanismo. *Revista Aragon Administración Pública, 14*, 405–431.

Llorens Ferrer, M. (2013). La consulta popular como mecanismo para revitalizar el urbanismo democrático. *Revista catalana de dret públic, 46*, 160–181.

Menéndez Rexach, Á. (2008). El fomento de las buenas prácticas administrativas en la nueva Ley del Suelo y otras normas estatales recientes. *Anuario de la Facultad de Derecho de la Universidad Autónoma de Madrid, 12*, 135–168.

Peinado, C., & Antonio, J. (2016). La participación ciudadana en el urbanismo. ¿Mito o realidad? In J. G. Font, M. B. Coma, & Á. M. Rexach (Eds.), *El derecho de la ciudad y el territorio: Estudios en homenaje a Manuel Ballbé Prunés* (pp. 247–266). INAP.

Peinado, C., & Antonio, J. (2017). Las consultas a la ciudadanía como instrumento de legitimación social de concretas ordenaciones urbanísticas. *Revista Urban y Medio Ambiente, 311*, 57–78.

Pisarello Prados, G. (2011). Del derecho a la vivienda al derecho a la ciudad: Elementos para la democratización del espacio urbano. In Ararteko (Ed.), *Los retos de las políticas públicas en una democracia avanzada* (pp. 285–318). Ararteko.

Ponce Solé, J. (2019). El derecho de la Unión Europea y la vivienda. Análisis de experiencias nacionales e internacionales. *Basque Journal Public Administration, 2019*, 546–552.

Rando Burgos, E. (2020). Participación ciudadana. De los principios a la implementación. *Revista Española de la Transparencia, 20*, 65–96.

Vaquer Caballería, M. (2015). El derecho a la vivienda en su relación con los derechos a la ciudad y al medio ambiente. *Asamblea: Revista Parlamentaria de la Asamblea de Madrid, 32*, 121–154.

Part II
Participation and Large-Scale Projects

Chapter 6
Community Participation in Large-Scale Extractive Projects: How Communities Influence the Terms of Lithium Mining in the Argentine Puna

Lucas González and Richard Snyder

Abstract Argentina is a relevant global lithium producer, a key mineral for the global transition to renewable energies. Three Northwestern provinces concentrate most lithium mining: Catamarca, Jujuy, and Salta. They share a similar geography, cultural backgrounds, economic profiles, and, being subnational units in a federal system, the same political institutions. Nevertheless, there is enormous variation in indigenous communities' participation and engagement in defining the conditions under which mining companies can extract lithium. In some cases, there was a lack of community involvement, and companies operated without major restrictions. This occurred in Salar de Rincón in Salta and Salar del Hombre Muerto in Catamarca. In others, there was social organization from local communities, but conflict has been averted and companies could continue extracting lithium, such as in Salar de Olaroz in Jujuy. Still in other cases there was strong resistance and conflict escalated, resulting in aborted mining projects. That occurred in Salinas Grandes and Laguna Guayatayoc, also in Jujuy. In spite of the similarities, why is there variation in local participation, mobilization, and conflict? This chapter describes variation in community engagement and proposes explanations to account for strengths and weaknesses of communities in establishing the conditions of lithium extraction.

Keywords Green energy transition · Lithium mining · Federalism · Political institutions · Local indigenous communities' participation · Argentina

---

L. González (✉)
National Scientific and Technical Research Council (CONICET), National University of San Martín (UNSAM), Argentine Pontifical Catholic University (UCA), Buenos Aires, Argentina
e-mail: lgonzalez@unsam.edu.ar; lucas_gonzalez@uca.edu.ar

R. Snyder
Department of Political Science, Brown University, Providence, RI, USA
e-mail: richard_snyder@brown.edu

K. Kössler, E. Schläppi (eds.), *Citizen Participation in Local Governance*, Local and Urban Governance, https://doi.org/10.1007/978-3-031-99824-9_6

6.1 Introduction: Mitigation, Extraction, and Local Communities

Lithium is a strategic resource for mitigating climate change. About 60% of lithium reserves in the world are concentrated in the "lithium triangle," in the deserts of Northwestern Argentina, Northern Chile, and Southern Bolivia (US Geological Survey, 2022). Argentina is a key exporter of lithium carbonate, and soon will reach Chile, one of the world's leading producers (Fornillo, 2015, 12).

Production in Argentina began a few years ago, but it is expanding rapidly. Lithium in Argentina is located in salt flats (*salares*) of Catamarca, Jujuy, and Salta. Most lithium is extracted from subterranean brine deposits using pumping and evaporation techniques. On average, for every ton of lithium carbonate, 400,000 L of brine are evaporated. The evaporation process takes place in high-altitude deserts that are among the most arid places on earth (Díaz Nieto et al., 2020, 2), potentially affecting freshwater aquifers with negative consequences for nearby indigenous communities.

Mitigating the impacts of climate change requires extraction. This extractive underside of the global transition to a "green" economy can be seen vividly in communities where the lithium mining boom is occurring, often producing very harmful local effects (González & Snyder, 2021; González & Snyder, 2023). Previous works on lithium mining in Argentina indicate it has sizeable negative consequences on local productive activities, such as cattle raising, small-scale agriculture, and traditional production of salt. It also has substantial environmental impacts, because extraction requires large quantities of water to separate lithium from the brine pumped under the *salares* (Fornillo, 2015; Puente & Argento, 2015; Slipak, 2015; Argento & Zícari, 2017). Moreover, many communities complain that they do not get sufficient socioeconomic benefits in exchange for the lithium extracted from their territories. Still, other research underscore that extraction has positive outcomes (Brunnschweiler, 2008; Lederman & Maloney, 2008), because it generates innovation and enhances productivity (González, Snyder & Orihuela, 2025; López et al., 2018; Montenegro Bravo, 2018; Barandiarán, 2019).

Argentina has signed international agreements that provide safeguards for the rights of indigenous communities to prior, free, and informed consultation if companies (or governments) want to extract mineral resources in the territories they occupy. This includes International Labor Organization (ILO) Convention 169, signed in 1992. As indicated in other chapters on Argentina (Del Tredici in this volume), these mechanisms of direct democracy and citizen consultation have several limitations. First, these consultative mechanisms have to be initiated or intermediated by state authorities. As we will see, national and provincial governments do not always initiate these procedures, even when they should. Moreover, even when these processes are initiated by decisions of local communities, governments do not always accept them as legitimate.

Second, these instruments require community organization. Despite strong similarities among lithium extraction sites in Northern Argentina, in some cases a lack of community involvement allowed companies to operate without major restrictions. This occurred in Salar de Rincón in Salta and was also the case in Salar del Hombre Muerto in Catamarca until 2019, when protests erupted because of the drying up of a local river, which community members attributed to the expansion of Livent, the mining company. Instead of activating consultation, these protests were met with repression, as demonstrators were beaten and arrested by the provincial police, who were reportedly transported in mining company vehicles.

In other instances, such as in the Salar de Olaroz, although local communities were well-organized, lithium extraction proceeded and conflict has largely been avoided. There, the Sales de Jujuy mining project met great opposition from a local indigenous organization at the beginning. The company subsequently reached agreements with indigenous communities in a case-by-case manner, guaranteeing jobs, modest cash compensations, and some public infrastructure works. As a result of these negotiations, the company was able to start mining in 2015. By contrast, in other cases, such as Salinas Grandes and Laguna Guayatayoc, resistance and conflict resulted in the termination of mining projects.

Why, despite regional similarities and the same federal legal regulations, is there variation in local engagement, participation, mobilization, resistance, and conflict? This chapter describes variation in community participation and identifies some possible explanations for the strengths and weaknesses of local communities in establishing the conditions of mining. We explore, first, the role of federal and provincial legal frameworks, including those recognizing local indigenous communities and their right to free, informed, prior consultation. Second, we consider the role of geographic location and the availability of alternative economic activities to communities residing in the vicinity of lithium projects, and third, we assess how governments and mining companies can influence the outcomes. The fourth section focuses on how the organizational capacity of local communities affects their involvement and stance towards mining. A concluding section discusses some general trends and comparative implications.

6.2 Federal and Provincial Mining Regulations

Some scholars argue that community participation and mobilization depend on individual determinants, such as level of income or education, or societal factors, including economic needs, social cohesion and networks, or political resources and windows of opportunity (see, for instance, Tarrow, 2022). Without denying the relevance of these and other well-studied factors, this chapter claims that institutions may also play a role, especially if politico-institutional frameworks allow for community consultation and participation.

A series of treaties, laws, and regulations to safeguard the natural environment as well as indigenous communities regulates mining activities in many countries, including Argentina. Relevant international treaties include the UN Declaration on the Rights of Indigenous Peoples, ILO Convention 169, and the UN Convention on Biological Diversity (CBD). Most governments issue additional regulations at the national level, including setting tax and royalty rates on mining companies. Some studies find that more redistributive (federal and provincial) revenue-sharing institutions (Díaz-Rioseco, 2016; González & Lodola, 2019) are key to boost the socioeconomic impact of mineral rents and, hence, in reducing local conflicts.

At the federal level, the national mining regime of Argentina (Law 24,196 of 1993) granted mining companies "tariff exemptions, tax relief schemes, 30 years of fiscal stability, and low provincial royalties" (Puente & Argento, 2015, 122). It also abolished municipal taxes, setting a 3% mining royalty for subnational units (Marchegiani et al., 2019, 10). The national government kept a minimal authority in the areas of environmental protection and rights of indigenous peoples in deciding how mineral resources should be extracted in their land (Puente & Argento, 2015, 123).

The national constitution in Argentina grants provinces the domain over natural resources and the power to establish the conditions to extract and process oil and minerals (Article 124). Private companies are in charge of mining operations in Catamarca and Salta. In Jujuy, the provincial government declared lithium as a "strategic resource" (Decree-Agreement 7592) and established a public company in 2011, Jujuy Energy and Mining State Society (Jujuy Energía y Minería Sociedad del Estado, JEMSE). This state company has a minor share of the production sites, while the bulk of shares are in the hands of private transnational companies. Private firms are also in charge of exploration and extraction in Jujuy.

The legal framework at the federal level, which encompasses the whole country, cannot explain variation in citizen engagement, from participation, mobilization, resistance, to open conflict. In addition, similar provincial regulations, all providing for a leading role of private companies, cannot account for local variation, especially across extractive projects in the case of Jujuy. Moreover, static legal frameworks cannot account for temporal variation in community participation, as seen in Catamarca, where resistance to mining increased notably over time. We thus need to explore the relevance of other subnational factors.

6.3 Recognition of Indigenous Communities and Prior Consultation

Several indigenous communities demanded their rights to be respected once they got them recognized at the federal level. But not all communities have achieved that. The federal legal framework also requires provinces to legally recognize indigenous communities and grant them the possibility of informed free and prior consultation, following the regulations of the ILO Convention 169. There are relevant differences among lithium-producing provinces. The province of Jujuy granted indigenous peoples living near lithium extraction sites the rights to communal property and of being legally recognized as indigenous groups. They are now legal actors who have to be consulted if there is going to be extraction of minerals in their land. By contrast, Catamarca and Salta denied those rights to indigenous groups. These two provinces have not implemented these laws in their territories, challenging international and federal regulations on the matter. As a result, the Jujuy government has consulted indigenous groups, while the governments of Salta and Catamarca have not.

Different provincial regulations can partially account for variation in levels of mobilization, participation, and conflict across provinces. In Jujuy, within the same province and without variation in the role of the provincial state, there are quite conflictive sites with strong local involvement (Salinas Grandes and Laguna Guayatayoc) together with less conflictive ones where significant portions of communities have expressed support for lithium mining (Salar de Olaroz-Cauchari). Salta has seen minimal conflicts, and only recently have some mobilizations and protests taken place in Catamarca. This mostly static provincial legal framework can explain neither variation changes in the amount of protest participation and protests within the same province, as in Jujuy, nor across time, as in Catamarca.

Cross-province variation in the recognition of the rights of indigenous communities near extraction projects may partially explain differences in the nature of community participation. Still, we need to explore other local factors that may account for conflict and community negotiations with lithium companies within and across provinces.

6.4 Location and Challenges That Lithium Extraction Poses to Other Economic Activities

The geographical location of lithium extraction sites is one local-level factor that helps explain variation in local mobilization, participation, resistance, and conflict. Mobilization is less likely if lithium extraction takes place in a secluded site without important highways exposed to blockades by local communities. The 33 Communities in Salinas Grandes, Jujuy, are near a major international road linking the northern parts of Argentina and Chile. When they blocked it, they caused heavy damage not only to the lithium industry but to other economic activities. They could use the threat of blocking the road to negotiate with the company and the provincial government.

Salar del Rincón in Salta is a typical enclave. It is situated in a very isolated and sparsely populated portion of the province, very high above the sea level (3900 m.), and far away (150 km.) from San Antonio de los Cobres, the nearest town. Furthermore, very few roads connect it with other cities in the province, including the capital and the socially mobilized Salinas Grandes region (Puente & Argento, 2015, 126).

Although it may help account for some differences across cases, the problem with this static (or time invariant) factor is that it cannot explain changes in participation within the same location, as occurred in the Salar de Hombre Muerto,

Catamarca, where the local community went from demobilization and partial acceptance of lithium mining to increasing participation and growing resistance to it.

A second geography-related factor is whether lithium mining competes with other economic activities. Because it requires vast quantities of water, the construction of large evaporation ponds and the installation of many dozens of pumping stations across salares, lithium mining can impinge on traditional occupations, such as cattle raising, small-scale agriculture, and traditional salt extraction, as well as non-traditional economic alternatives such as eco-tourism. In Catamarca, Livent depleted the Trapiche River, its most prominent source of the freshwater used in the extraction of lithium concentrate, from brine. The company demanded more water for processing lithium carbonate and Los Patos River was one possible source in the arid landscape. With the backing of the provincial government, Livent began constructing a 30 km-long aqueduct. After more than two decades of silence, indigenous communities awakened and organized resistance against this decision. They claimed that water depletion driven by lithium extraction had affected their main sources of income: small-scale agriculture and cattle husbandry. Similarly, in the Salinas Grande region, local salt cooperatives considered lithium mining as a hazard to their sources of income and traditions (Argento & Zícari, 2018, 13–14). Lithium mining in neighboring Salta did not appear to be affecting other existing productive activities (Slipak, 2015).

These geographic and economic factors can partially account for variation in local community engagement, from quiescence to mobilization, resistance, and conflict.

6.5 The Roles of Mining Companies and Governments in Shaping Community Engagement

Another critical factor in shaping community engagement is the power of mining companies to coopt and demobilize local leaders and members of organizations, particularly under conditions of disagreements among them on whether and how mining should proceed. Some mining companies were very skilled in accentuating these tensions and disagreements, insulating vocal leaders who were against mining.

Mining companies can offer cash payments, employment, and public works (such as public buildings or bridges) to communities and key members (as well as to local politicians) in exchange for agreement to extraction or to certain conditions to extract set by the company. The capacity of mining companies to affect negotiations is conditional on several factors, including the size of their sunk costs in the project and the amount of other fixed investments. Companies have more leverage in negotiations when they have lower sunk costs and anticipate limited profits.

Negotiations among local communities, subnational governments, and mining companies take place both in formal and in informal arenas. Sometimes agreements among them may become more or less institutionalized. That is particularly the case when a governments, either municipal or provincial, take part in negotiations. In other circumstances, community leaders may directly negotiate with mining companies and reach ad hoc informal agreements.

Local and provincial governments play a key role. They can prevent and manage conflict, promoting consensus between companies and communities and among factions in the latter, or they can decide to be absent. In a simplified way, local and provincial governments can either be more pro-market (i.e., "laissez-faire"), or they can be more pro-State intervention (i.e., "interventionist"). Laissez-faire governments tend to support the idea that countries with abundant natural resources should make use of their comparative advantage and export raw materials to industrial nations. These countries have capacity to add economic value. They also claim that foreign direct investment (FDI) from richer and more developed countries should create more jobs in the mining sector. Interventionist governments, on the contrary, endorse the notion that the state should have a stronger role in the economy, including the mining sector. States should regulate this activity and impose high taxes to collect more revenue. Governments should use this revenue, in turn, to create industrial capacity to manufacture goods and add value to raw materials. The archetypical example of this type of goods are lithium batteries.

Provincial governments can also have a demobilizing role, using the police to repress mobilized community members or the judiciary to detain, prosecute, or incarcerate activists. This occurred in Catamarca in October 2019. In Antofagasta de la Sierra, near the Salar del Hombre Muerto, the local indigenous communities got organized and rallied against the construction of the aqueduct from the Río Los Patos to the plant of the US lithium company Livent. This company needed fresh water to process lithium in the salt flat. The indigenous communities claimed local authorities violated ILO's Convention 169 because they had not consulted them and had not asked for their approval to build the aqueduct. The provincial police responded by beating and arresting protestors. The police detained some members of an indigenous family resisting the decision of the provincial government to remove a livestock fence on the land they and their ancestors claimed was theirs. The fence was removed to let Livent's vehicles cross their land to build the aqueduct. Livent used its pick-up trucks to transport provincial police forces to safeguard the personnel in charge of building the aqueduct (Aranda, 2020). Both the provincial and the local governments sided with Livent by proclaiming that the indigenous family had no rights over the disputed land.

Both the previous (Lucía Corpacci, 2011–19) and current governors (Raúl Jalil, 2019–) are affiliated with the Frente para la Victoria (FPV), a populist, more interventionist faction of the Justicialist Party (PJ). But the government, the judiciary, and the police in this province have taken a laissez-faire stance, at least in mining. The provincial Judge (called Electoral and Mines Judge, or Juez Electoral y de Minas) and the Minister of Mines did not respond to petitions from indigenous communities to stop the construction of the aqueduct (González & Snyder, 2021; González & Snyder, 2023).

Several social organizations, such as *Pucará: Pueblos Catamarqueños en Resistencia y Autodeterminación* and *Antofagasta Resiste*, support the claims of communities near the salt flat in Catamarca. But these communities have not reached the visibility, organization level, and mobilization power of communities in Salinas Grandes. One of the possible reasons is the secluded location of lithium projects in Catamarca, located more than 10 hours away from the provincial capital by car. Another reason could be that the locals faced Livent, a well-established US company that started doing business in the province more than 20 years ago. The company has large sunk costs in the salt flat and has built enduring connections with both the local and provincial governments.

By contrast, interventionist governments are more likely to negotiate with mining companies using their legal and regulatory power. Eduardo Fellner (2011–15), the PJ governor of Jujuy, passed a law declaring lithium a strategic resource, created the state-owned company JEMSE, and negotiated with representatives of local communities. But the governor who replaced Fellner, Gerardo Morales (2015–2023), had a market-friendly stance. Morales took 3 years to decide on a protocol for extraction created by local communities and finally rejected it in 2018. This, together with an attempt to modify the constitution in order to limit protests, spurred a wave of citizens' demonstrations on the streets in 2023, which were met with strong repression by the provincial police.

6.6 Local Communities' Organizational Capacity

A final key factor for explaining varied local responses to lithium mining concerns communities' organizational capacity and their power to create linkages with provincial, national, and international actors and legal organizations. Communities differ in their capacity to protect their interests depending on their internal cohesion, mobilizational capacity, and links to government authorities, agencies, and other critical supporters at the local, national, or international level. They may leverage international, national, and provincial laws to support their efforts. When local communities can seek help and legal assistance, they may also be able to file legal cases with the judiciary, being at the provincial, national, or international levels.

The urban and rural divide has an influence over the organizational capacity of local communities. Citizens are more likely to get organized when they live in larger and denser urban centers. Hence, more organization is likely when mining sites are near larger localities. When communities are able to organize, they are more likely to protest, block highways, and occupy salt flats.

Communities often have to decide between negative environmental and human health impacts of mining, on one hand, and potential benefits in terms of jobs, local economic expansion, and better infrastructure, on the other. In relation to these tensions, two strategic groups can be identified: *maximalists*, who tend to categorically oppose any form of mining, and *moderates*, who are more willing to accept mining if it operates under a "social license" with terms that are clearly acceptable (González and Snyder 2023).

The maximalist stance against lithium mining is exemplified by a statement of an indigenous leader from the community of *Santuario Tres Pozos* in Salinas Grandes, who said: "For us, Salinas Grandes is like a sacred mother. We must respect her because she takes care of me, my family, and my children. … There is no place for lithium mining"[1].

By contrast, moderates tend to express a form of conditional support for mining, provided the terms of extraction are fair for them and agreed upon. This perspective is reflected in statements from leaders of the indigenous community *El Angosto*, also in Salinas Grandes, who claimed: "We are not opposed to mining, but we want our voice to be respected," and "we say no to lithium if a prior, free and informed consultation is not made" (Flores, 2017; Roth, 2019; González and Snyder, 2021; González and Snyder, 2023).

Indigenous communities mounted strong resistance against lithium mining companies in Salinas Grandes. Mobilizations successfully halted their projects. Indigenous Kolla and Atacama settlements were geographically dispersed, loosely connected, and sparsely populated before the companies' arrival in 2010. However, the arrival of mining companies spurred a wave of local coordination and organization that led to the formation of a confederation representing 33 indigenous communities (*33 Comunidades de la Cuenca de las Salinas Grandes y la Laguna de Guayatayoc*). The 33 Communities were not entirely opposed to lithium mining, but they insisted it could only proceed with their consent and under their terms.

Having organized effectively, the 33 indigenous communities gained support from local environmental lawyers and the national NGO *Fundación Ambiente y Recursos Naturales* (FARN). With this assistance, they were able to formed a Transnational Action Network (TAN) (Keck & Sikkink, 1999). This strategic collaboration enabled them to take legal action in 2010, filing an injunction against the provincial governments of Jujuy and Salta. They demanded that their right to prior, free, and informed consultation had to be respected, as mandated by ILO Convention 169. Their legal battle succeeded in advancing the case to the Argentine Supreme Court, where it was reviewed by the Inter-American Court of Human Rights (CIDH) (Roth, 2019). Additionally, their cause gained international visibility when the UN Special Rapporteur for Indigenous Rights, James Anaya, visited the region and publicly endorsed their fight (González & Snyder, 2021). This international attention added weight to their efforts and highlighted their struggle.

The 33 Communities conducted a deliberative process that culminated in the creation of a document called *Kachi Yupi* (Footsteps in the Salt) (Comunidades Indígenas de las Salinas Grandes y Laguna de Guayatayoc, 2015). This document is a protocol, developed and approved by the communities, outlining the conditions mining companies have to follow to obtain their consent to extract minerals in their

[1] https://www.bbc.com/mundo/noticias-50082466

land. The communities formally submitted the protocol to the provincial government and demanded its adoption into law. However, the Morales government ultimately refused to ratify Kachi Yupi, breaking down negotiations on the fair terms for resource extraction that the communities requested.

Following the rejection of the *Kachi Yupi* protocol, A.I.S., a Canadian mining company, decided to finish the 8-year lithium mining standstill in Salinas Grandes with the approval of the Jujuy government. The company began exploratory drilling without community consent in 2019. In February of that year, the 33 Communities began protests and highway blockades against this unilateral decision from the company and the government, abandoning negotiations and adopting a maximalist stance by opposing any form of extraction rather than accepting unnegotiated projects. In response, mining companies targeted individual leaders or groups in the communities, trying to undermine the unified anti-extraction position. The Jujuy government exacerbated tensions by issuing tenders for new lithium projects in Salinas Grandes in early 2019 and 2023, disregarding indigenous claims.

The indigenous groups shifted from a moderate stance to outright hostility to mining because of their unsuccessful attempt to negotiate extraction terms, the government's failure to grant their right to consultation, and the efforts of the company to try to divide their communities. This change was embodied in their new protest slogan: "No al litio, sí al agua y la vida" ("No to lithium, yes to water and life") (González & Snyder, 2021). No lithium had been extracted from the Salinas Grandes and Laguna de Guayatayoc region as of 2025.

The approach to lithium extraction and community participation unfolded differently on the western side of the Puna Jujeña, just 50 miles from Salinas Grandes. In Olaroz, *La Apacheta*, an indigenous organization, initially strongly opposed and resisted all mining by the Australian-led consortium *Sales de Jujuy*, headed by Orocobre. This resistance highlighted the need for the company to negotiate and garner local community support, avoiding extraction halts that had occurred in Salinas Grandes-Guayatayoc. Orocobre offered employment, cash compensations, and minor public infrastructure projects, including a school and an Internet connection center, to pursue individual agreements with the indigenous communities in Olaroz.

Local residents met with representatives from Orocobre in the local council, where they were informed about the company's intended operations and discussed the conditions under which they would permit the mining project. Environmental organizations raised concerns, alleging that the consultation process was manipulated and lacked transparency. They claimed that companies provided unclear information and rigged decisions, creating divisions among local residents (Marchegiani et al., 2019).

La Apacheta was significantly weaker, had a more limited territorial scope, and lacked the transnational connections and support that the 33 Communities enjoyed. These differences in organizational strength and external backing played a key role in shaping the outcomes of the negotiations in both regions. Orocobre was able to begin mining operations in Olaroz in 2015, becoming the second company to extract lithium in the country.

The provincial government in Salta has neither recognized indigenous communities living close to the salt flats nor granted them formal land titles. Coupled with the weak, scattered, and demobilized nature of indigenous groups, the lack of indigenous recognition and land titles has resulted the absence of protests or resistance to lithium mining from the communities in this province.

6.7 Conclusions

The main aim of the participatory processes explored in this chapter is to decide the conditions under which lithium extraction may or may not take place. These participatory processes sought to set the conditions under which extraction could take place, including not only the economic benefits and infrastructure mining companies needed to provide local communities but also, crucially, how to preserve local aquifers, minimize environmental damage, and prevent harmful impacts on other economic activities, such as small-scale agriculture, livestock husbandry, and traditional production of salt. In some cases, communities produced documents, such as *Kachi Yupi*, formalizing the conditions under which extraction could take place. In others, they acquiesced and permitted companies to operate without major restrictions.

Local organizations, such as the 33 Communities or La Apacheta in Jujuy, and the local indigenous and anti-mining activists affiliated with the NGO "*Pucará: Pueblos Catamarqueños en Resistencia y Autodeterminación*" in Catamarca, played a fundamental role initiating the participatory processes that took place in the Argentine Puna. These indigenous organizations, usually diverse, sometimes divided across different local cleavages, and many times questioned in their capacity to represent the whole community, were crucial for organizing local interests, getting state recognition as indigenous groups, initiating a prior consultation participation process, filing legal injunctions against provincial governments requesting that the mining companies recognize their right to prior, free, and informed consultation, and setting the terms of extraction in their localities.

Provincial governments responded in varied ways to local mobilization around mining projects. In some cases, they delayed decisions, in others, they ignored them, and in still others, they repressed local mobilizations. When local communities were well-organized and reached provincial, national, and in some cases even international visibility, provincial and local governments were more likely to engage and negotiate with them.

In sum, these large-scale lithium mining projects suggest that community participation and engagement are critical to influence the socioeconomic and environmental terms of extraction. Moreover, community participation is also important for helping legitimize the decisions governments make about exploiting natural resources which are critical for the global energy transition yet also have harmful consequences for people who reside in the areas where extraction takes place.

References

Aranda, D. (2020, March 23)."Litio: Denuncia contra una minera en Antofagasta de la Sierra. *Página 12*.

Argento, M., & Zícari, J. (2017). Las Disputas por el Litio en la Argentina: ¿Materia Prima, Recurso Estratégico o Bien Común? *Prácticas de Oficio, 1*(19), 36–48.

Argento, M., & Zícari, J. (2018). Políticas Públicas y Conflictos Territoriales en torno a la Explotación del Litio en Salta: El Caso de Salinas Grandes. *Andes, Antropología e Historia, 1*(29), 1–36.

Barandiarán, J. (2019). Lithium and development imaginaries in Chile, Argentina, and Bolivia. *World Development, 113*, 381–391.

Brunnschweiler, C. N. (2008). Cursing the blessings? Natural resource abundance, institutions, and economic growth. *World Development, 36*(3), 399–419.

Comunidades Indígenas de las Salinas Grandes y Laguna de Guyatayoc. (2015). *Kachi Yupi. Huellas en la Sal. Procedimiento de Consulta y Consentimiento Previo, Libre e Informado para las Comunidades Indígenas de la Cuenca de Salinas Grandes y Laguna de Guayatayoc*.

Díaz-Rioseco, D. (2016). Blessing and curse. Oil and subnational politics in the Argentine provinces. *Comparative Political Studies, 49*(14), 1930–1964.

Flores, C. (2017). Entre el litio y la vida: Comunidades originarias y la lucha por la conservación del agua y de su cultural. In *Informe Ambiental 2017*. Fundación Ambiente y Recursos Naturales (FARN).

Fornillo, B. (2015). *Geopolítica del litio, Industria, Ciencia y Energía en Argentina*. CLACSO, El Colectivo.

González, L., & Lodola, G. (2019). The impact of oil rents on subnational development: Evidence from Argentina. *Studies in Comparative International Development, 54*(4), 550–570.

González, L., & Snyder, R. (2021). Modes of lithium extraction in Argentina: Mining politics in Catamarca, Jujuy and Salta. In G. França, D. Freire, & U. Mignozzetti (Eds.), *Natural resources and policy choices in Latin America*. Konrad Adenauer Stiftung.

González, L., & Snyder, R. (2023). Modes of extraction in Latin America's lithium triangle: Explaining negotiated, unnegotiated and aborted mining projects. *Latin American Politics and Society, 65*(1), 47–73.

González, L., Snyder, R., & Orihuela, J. C. (2025). Developmental extraction and the global energy transition: Lessons from South America's Lithium Triangle. *Journal of Globalization and Development*. In press.

Keck, M. E., & Sikkink, K. (1999). Transnational advocacy networks in international and regional politics. *International Social Science Journal, 51*(159), 89–101.

Lederman, D., & Maloney, W. (2008). In search of the resource curse [with Comments]. *Economía, 9*(1), 1–58.

López, A., Obaya, M., & Pascuini, P. (2018, December). Las Oportunidades del Litio: Más Allá de la Batería. *Alquimias Económicas*.

Marchegiani, P., Hellgren, J. H., & Gómez, L. (2019). *Lithium extraction in Argentina: A case study on the social and environmental impacts*. FARN.

Montenegro Bravo, J. C. (2018). El Modelo de Industrialización del Litio en Bolivia. *Revista de Ciencias Sociales, 10*(34), 69–82.

Nieto, D., César, K. R., & Flexer, V. (2020). Membrane electrolysis for the removal of Na^+ from brines for the T subsequent recovery of lithium salts. *Separation and Purification Technology, 252*, 1–10.

Puente, F., & Argento, M. (2015). Conflictos territoriales y construcción identitaria en los salares del noroeste argentino. In B. Fornillo (Ed.), *Geopolítica del litio, Industria, Ciencia y Energía en Argentina*. CLACSO, El Colectivo.

Roth, S. (2019, March). Communities challenge lithium production in Argentina. *Diálogo Chino*.

Slipak, A. (2015). La extracción del litio en la Argentina y el debate sobre la riqueza natural. In B. Fornillo (Ed.), *Geopolítica del litio, Industria, Ciencia y Energía en Argentina*. CLACSO, El Colectivo.
Tarrow, S. (2022). *Power in movement*. Cambridge University Press.
US Geological Survey. (2022). *Mineral commodity summaries*. US Department of the Interior.

Chapter 7
Participation and Large-Scale Projects in Germany: Procedures, Impacts and Developments

Patrick Zimmermann

Abstract Large-scale projects are needed to meet some of the most important challenges of the present and the future, such as securing economic prosperity and dealing with climate change. However, they raise many political, social and legal questions that are expressed through protests and citizen participation. This chapter examines what forms of citizen participation exist in the case of Germany, what effects they have, and how a constitutionally and democratically satisfactory implementation of large-scale projects with citizen participation can be achieved.

Keywords Citizens' petition and referendum · Large-scale projects · NIMBY · German administrative and municipal law · Stuttgart 21

7.1 Introduction

7.1.1 Definition and Necessity of Large-Scale Projects

From a project management perspective, large-scale projects have the following characteristics (Flyvbjerg, 2005, 1–2): "[1] Such projects are inherently risky due to long planning horizons and complex interfaces. [2] Technology is often not standard. [3] Decision making and planning are often multi-actor processes with conflicting interests. [4] Often the project scope or ambition level will change significantly over time. [5] Statistical evidence shows that such unplanned events are often unaccounted for, leaving budget contingencies sorely inadequate. [6] As a consequence, misinformation about costs, benefits, and risks is the norm. [7] The result is cost overruns and/or benefit shortfalls with a majority of projects." Depending on the project size, various other designations are sometimes used: "megaprojects" (> 1 billion USD), "major projects" (> 100 million USD) and

P. Zimmermann (✉)
Chair of Public Law, Business Administrative Law, Environmental and Social Security Law, Ludwig-Maximilians-Universität München, Munich, Germany
e-mail: Patrick.Zimmermann@jura.uni-muenchen.de

K. Kössler, E. Schläppi (eds.), *Citizen Participation in Local Governance*, Local and Urban Governance, https://doi.org/10.1007/978-3-031-99824-9_7

"projects" (> one million USD) (Flyvbjerg, 2014, 6). These characteristics also have repercussions for legal, political and social questions. This chapter addresses these issues with a particular focus on participation.

However, in order to meet big challenges major investments are required worldwide, in Europe and Germany. This captures small-scale, mid-scale, but also large-scale projects, namely when it comes to expanding renewable energies, including the grid infrastructure, and the transport infrastructure, especially railways (Bertrams, 2012, 289). The most important regulatory regimes from recent years are the Infrastructure Investment and Jobs Act (IIJA) of 2021 (Public Law 117–58, NOV. 15, 2021, 135 STAT. 429) and the Inflation Reduction Act (IRA) of 2022 (Public Law 117–169, AUG. 16, 2022, 136 STAT. 1818) in the United States of America and NextGenerationEU in the European Union (established by Council Regulation [EU] 2020/2094, L 433 I, 23). Within these regulatory regimes, numerous (large-scale) projects will be launched.

It should be borne in mind that, in addition to the justified and unjustified criticisms of large-scale projects, which are often the subject of citizen participation in terms of "whether" (not only "how"), another perspective can also be adopted. For example, citizens' acceptance of parliamentary, government and administrative action can also suffer because even agreed upon projects are implemented with long delays and cost increases (Schnieder, 2020, 142).

7.1.2 Participation

Citizen participation is often connoted with project rejection: "Saint Florian / Spare my house, set others on fire!"—This so-called Saint-Florian-Principle or the better known "Not in my backyard" (NIMBY) are classic terms for citizens who oppose infrastructure projects in their community (Holtkamp & Brockmann, 2016, 46–47; Brettschneider, 2019, 204). Beyond this catchy image, it is about the distribution of benefits, risks and costs. While a larger group of the population typically benefits, a smaller group—the residents in the immediate vicinity of the project—endures the most of costs and risks. Particularly controversial are the mentioned large-scale projects.

However, all projects (in the scope of administrative law) must also be sufficiently legitimized in terms of democracy and the rule of law, regardless of their economic, environmental or social necessity. In principle, democratic participation can occur through elections or referenda (Korioth & Müller, 2024, paras 117–122). Consequently, the federal constitution of Germany, the Basic Law (*Grundgesetz*), also refers to these two possibilities in Article 20(2); this similarly applies to the German states (*Länder*) according to Article 28(1) Basic Law (the so-called homogeneity imperative). However, on the federal level direct democratic participation is the exception rather than the rule since the Basic Law assigns the majority of the decisions to the democratically legitimized legislator and the indirectly democratically legitimized executive instead of directly leaving it to the people with notable exceptions in Articles 29, 118, 118a of the Basic Law (Sachs, in Sachs (ed.), 2024. Article 20 para 31–34). On the other hand, at the state level there is greater leeway for direct democracy (Burgi & Wolff, 2021, 67). Burgi and Wolff point out that to preserve the functioning of the municipal or county council, the leeway for the municipalities or counties is even narrower. As with all procedures of direct democracy, it is necessary to examine to what extent they are used in addition to, or instead of, the means of representative democracy and administrative procedures bound by the rule of law. Calls for more elements of direct democracy must therefore be carefully examined (Burgi & Wolff, 2021, 65–66).

In this chapter, I will examine the legal framework of participation in Germany (Sect. 7.2) and what that means for participation and large-scale projects in urban areas (Sect. 7.3) as well as in rural areas (Sect. 7.4). Based on these observations, I will make several proposals for amendments before I conclude (Sect. 7.5).

7.2 The Legal Framework and Practice of Participation in Germany

The Federal Republic of Germany is a democratic and social federal state (Article 20(1) Basic Law). The states have—just like the federation—their own constitutions, institutions (state parliaments, state governments, state administrations and courts), their own officials and their own competences (Articles 30, 70–72 and 83–85 of the Basic Law), insofar as the Basic Law, especially its Article 28, permits this. As the following three sub-sections point out, public participation in the administrative procedure is predominantly regulated by federal laws, while individual state constitutions and/or state laws exclusively regulate direct democratic participation at the municipal and state level.

7.2.1 Public Participation in the Administrative Procedure

In some administrative procedures, in particular planning and licensing procedures in construction law and environmental law, public involvement is mandatory. This concerns, for example, the planning approval (Sections 72–78 Administrative Procedure Act), construction planning (Section 3 Building Code) and immission control approvals (Section 10 Federal Immission Control Act). Since 2013 in response to the acceptance crisis with the project "Stuttgart 21", which is analyzed in Sect. 7.3 below, there is a general legal rule of (early) public participation in large-scale projects (Section 25(3) Administrative Procedure Act)[1] (Stender-Vorwachs, 2015, 154–156). This public sphere is broader than direct democratically

[1] English translation: "The authority shall work to ensure that, when planning projects which may have more than insignificant effects on the interests of a large number of third parties, the sponsor informs the public concerned at an early stage of the objectives of the project, the means of implementing it and the likely effects of the project (early public participation). If possible, early public participation should take place before an application is submitted. The public concerned should be given the opportunity to comment and to discuss the matter. [...]."

rooted citizen participation, as it also includes interest groups, associations and non-EU foreigners (Fraenkel-Haeberle, 2016, 551). According to the dominant opinion, EU foreigners are also entitled to vote in citizens' petitions and referenda at the municipal level pursuant to Article 28(1) Basic Law (see only BVerfG, NVwZ-RR 2016, 521 (524–525) with further references; from the literature Hellermann, in Epping & Hillgruber (ed.), 2023, Article 28 para 18 with further references).

It is often assumed that more intensive (early) public participation can increase the acceptance of a project (Stüer, 2013, 701; Schink, 2013, 1354–1355), even if some scholars are more skeptical (Hien, 2014, 495–496). However, public participation under administrative law—unlike citizens' or people's initiatives and referenda—does not fulfill a democratic function, but one concerning the rule of law (Gärditz, 2011, 274–275). This is is due to the fact that here, the decision is to be made by the administration, which has been authorized to do so by law and therefore been sufficiently democratically legitimized.[2]

Two other principles deriving from the rule of law spelled out in Article 20(3) Basic Law are relevant in this context: According to the reservation of the law (*Vorbehalt des Gesetzes*), the administration may not act in certain areas without a parliamentary act. According to the primacy of the law (*Vorrang des Gesetzes*), the administration is bound by the parliamentary statutes. Insofar as this legal obligation exists, citizens cannot use participatory elements to get the administration to make a different decision (on the constitutional limits for public participation based on these principles, see Knauff, 2012, 3). Moreover, this form of public participation has a strong connection to judicial legal protection (Fraenkel-Haeberle, 2016, 549 and 551–553).

The legislature, especially the federal parliament (*Deutscher Bundestag*) traces its democratic legitimacy back to the election by the people (Article 20(2) and Article 38(1) of the Basic Law). Improving the quality of justification of decisions, the transparency or the acceptance of projects are important (communicative) functions of public participation; however, they do not contribute to the democratic legitimacy (Article 20(2) Basic Law), which is to be justified formally only. This means that it is about the process, not the result of democracy (Gärditz, 2011, 274–275). Some even ask whether more citizen participation can mean less democracy because of the danger of pursuing particular interests rather than those of the common good (Hien, 2012; Hien, 2014, 497). Of course, the parliamentary procedure is not perfect either, but it does have some structural elements such as multiple readings and committee meetings to include a variety of interests (Wolff & Zimmermann, 2022, 20).

---

[2] In German constitutional law doctrine, there is the idea "that the constitutionally necessary democratic legitimation [...] requires an unbroken chain of legitimation [*Legitimationskette*] from the people to the organs and officials entrusted with state tasks. However, legitimation does not have to take place in every case through direct popular election. As a rule, it is sufficient that it can be indirectly traced back to the people as bearers of state power." English translation of BVerfGE 77, 1 (40)—Neue Heimat, with further references.

However, in today's practice, the legitimacy concept of parliamentary democracy and the indirectly democratically legitimized administration in some cases can no longer, by themselves, generate sufficient acceptance among citizens (Parthe, 2015, 201). Thus, elements of direct democracy come into play. It should also be examined to what extent they not only contribute to procedural input legitimacy, but also promote substantive output legitimacy.

7.2.2 Citizens' Petition and Referendum at the Municipal Level

The right to enact municipal codes (*Gemeindeordnungen*)[3] is part of the exclusive legislative competence of the states (Articles 70(1) and 71–74 of the Basic Law e contrario) (Burgi, 2024, Section 1 para 12).[4]

In the Federal Republic of Germany, 13 of the 16 states are so-called territorial states. They consist of different administrative levels, particularly municipalities and counties, and each state has its own municipal and county code. Other systems exist in the three so-called city-states (Berlin, Bremen and Hamburg). The following treatise, therefore, concerns the territorial states, with a particular focus on the three most populous ones: North Rhine-Westphalia, Bavaria and Baden-Württemberg, which comprise slightly more than half of the population in Germany (42.8 million residents of 84.4 million residents or 50.7%; Statistisches Bundesamt, 2023). When it comes to the overall number of citizens' petitions, their share is even larger, at 61.7%[5] (Rehmet et al., 2023, 14 and 17) so that their importance justifies their selection as case studies.

In the following, I will deal with the admissibility of citizens' petitions for the implementation of a referendum.[6] Today, citizens' petitions and referenda have found their way into all of the municipal codes. The "whether" of participation is no longer in dispute, but only the "how" (Burgi & Wolff, 2021, 65). The different municipal codes have similar rules of admissibility but differ as to the details (Schoch, 2014, 1474–1480; Lieb, 2021, 80; Burgi, 2024, Section 11 paras 37–43). The scope of a citizens' petitions is limited to local community affairs, as defined by the Federal Constitutional Court in *BVerfGE 79, 127 (151–152)—Rastede* (Ernst,

[3] As there are generally no official translations for the municipal codes, the German legal designations are used below (GO or GemO = Gemeindeordnung = municipal code).

[4] The same applies for the county codes (*Landkreisordnungen*). At this second-tier of local governments, there are also citizens' petitions and referenda. The following explanations of the municipal level can be largely transferred to the county level.

[5] Bavaria: 38.9%; Baden-Württemberg: 12.3%; North Rhine-Westphalia: 10.5%

[6] In some states, a decision of the municipal council can also initiate a referendum (*Ratsbürgerentscheid*). See e.g., Section 21(1) GemO BW; Article 18a(2) BayGO; Section 26(1)(2) GO NRW. In this respect, the referendum is an instrument of the defeated opposition factions in the municpal council (about this phenomenon Burgi & Wolff, 2021, 69). Of course, political parties, their council factions or individual party members in all states are free to initiate or support a citizens' petition.

2021, Article 28 paras 92–116).[7] Conversely, there are catalogues comprised of affairs that cannot be the subject of citizens' petitions. This can include e.g., budget, levies, personnel, organization of the municipal administration, etc.[8] There are major differences, which are significant in practice, for example, in the question of whether and to what extent land use planning may be the subject of citizens' petitions (Schoch, 2014, 1476). In any case, the local government must have the decision-making authority—i.e., the decision has to be a local community affair—and the municipal council (not the mayor) must be competent in accordance with the local government's internal rules of competence because the referendum replaces the decision of the municipal council.[9] Of course, the subject of citizens' petitions must also comply with the principle of legality (Schoch, 2014, 1476). Moreover, and related to the subject matter, there is the requirement that the question to be posed to the public must be sufficiently determinate: it must be possible to answer it with "yes" or "no".

The next requirement is that a certain number of citizens (quorum) sign the citizens' petition. Usually, the smaller the municipality the higher the quorum measured in terms of population share, typically ranging between 3% and 10% of all citizens eligible to vote.[10] Moreover, the petition must meet further conditions: It must be made in writing, must be justified, must contain a proposal for cost recovery and must name representatives (Schoch, 2014, 1478–1479). The final condition is the deadline. Previous citizens' petitions or referenda preclude new ones over the same item in some states for a certain period (up to three[11] years). For the rest, a distinction is made. So-called "cassatory" citizens' petitions may only be made for a certain period[12] after the council decision they are challenging has been made. "Initiating" citizens' petitions that raise a concern themselves are not bound by deadlines.

The municipal council decides on the admissibility of the citizens' petition. If approved, a referendum will take place unless the municipal council decides on the measure itself (in the spirit of the petition). If the petition is inadmissible, administrative legal protection may be sought against the council's decision (Burgi, 2024, Section 11 paras 45).

If the majority of the votes cast are in the affirmative and their number reaches a certain quorum for approval among all of those entitled to vote, the referendum is accepted. Here again, the smaller the municipality the higher is usually the quorum

[7] See e.g., Section 21(3)(1) GemO BW; Article 18a(1) BayGO; Section 26(1)(1) GO NRW.

[8] See e.g., Section 21(2) GemO BW; Article 18a(3) BayGO; Section 26(5) GO NRW.

[9] See e.g., Section 21(3)(1) GemO BW; Article 18a(3) BayGO; Section 26(1)(1) GO NRW.

[10] E.g., Article 18a(6) BayGO; Section 26(4) GO NRW; Section 25(1)(2) SächsGemO.

[11] E.g., Section 21(3)(2) GemO BW; Section 25(1)(3) SächsGemO.

[12] See e.g., Section 21(3)(3)(2) GemO BW: 3 months; Section 26(3)(1) GO NRW: 6 weeks.

measured in terms of population share.[13] This reflects the fact that voter participation is significantly higher in small municipalities than larger cities (Rehmet et al., 2023, 8, 28–29).[14] Nevertheless, one in eight referenda (12%) reaches a majority in favor of the petitioners but then fails due to the required quorum for approval. The general failure rate—rejection of the petition—is 36%, the success rate thus 52% (Rehmet et al., 2023, 8, 23, 27–28, 30–31).

7.2.3 *Practice at the Municipal Level: Political and Social Analysis*

This section deals with the practice of citizens' petitions and referenda in Germany. First of all, the objects should be considered. Of all the citizens' petitions filed in the history of the Federal Republic of Germany, 20.1% concerned economic projects (e.g., construction projects for commercial purposes or wind turbines), 16.0% transportation projects and 12.6% public infrastructure and utility services (e.g., public buildings and public electricity supply) (Rehmet et al., 2023, 22). According to another classification, almost 40% of the subjects in the period between 2007 and 2014 are classified as "infrastructure projects" (Sturm & Winkelmann, 2014, 27–28). Within this group, large-scale projects naturally attract particular attention: large-scale projects are a significant topic of citizens' petitions and referenda.

A variety of reasons can be considered as causes of protest and participation: They include criticism of the projects' costs and purposes, direct concern (NIMBY), rebellion against a (at least perceived) lack of transparency, a loss of trust in political institutions, or first-time or renewed political interest (Bertrams, 2012, 290).

But who carries the protests and the participation itself? Protests can generally stand for itself or prepare a formal participation process. For example, the typical activist against projects related to the transition towards renewable energy in Germany is male, 55 years old, still working, homeowner, has a university degree (in sciences or engineering) and is socially active for the first time (Marg et al., 2013, 98–102). It should be noted that petitions require a certain amount of organization and resources to collect the signatures and run the campaign. This tends to

[13] E.g., Article 18a(12)(1) BayGO and Section 26(7)(1) GO NRW: up to 50,000 citizens the quorum is 20% of all citizens eligible to vote, up to 100,000 citizens the quorum is 15% of all citizens eligible to vote, and above 100,000 citizens the quorum is 10% of all citizens eligible to vote. In Baden-Württemberg, by contrast, the quorum is always 20% of all citizens eligible to vote, Section 21(7)(1) GemO BW.

[14] Average turnout: 50.9%. Municipalities up to 5000 inhabitants: 61.9% average turnout; municipalities with more than 500,000 inhabitants: 27.4% average turnout.

favor existing networks and organizations and groups that can invest time and resources. An organization that is weak at the beginning can grow into this task by investing time and resources.

A strong orientation towards the status quo dominates. On the one hand, this can be explained by the age and class of the participants—they individually benefit less from investments in the future than younger people, socially ambitious people, etc. (Holtkamp & Brockmann, 2016, 47). On the other hand, this is also partly due to the nature of the instrument of citizens' petitions itself: If people (tacitly) support a project that is being planned anyway, there is less need to engage themselves than if they want to prevent its realization. After all, citizens tend to have less technical capacity than the developer and the administration for independent positive planning. This is one of the reasons why (destructively) preventing a project is easier than (constructively) offering design alternatives. For legal reasons, citizens themselves are not authorized to plan anyway; that is the task of the democratically legitimized administration, as demonstrated by the following example of the limits of voluntary civic engagement and the necessity of administrative action (Knobloch, 2022, 117).

Regarding the role of political parties, it should be noted that their importance in the context of citizens' petitions depends on one major factor: the shaping of the democratic system. Depending on the respective municipal code (legal) and administrative practice (political and social), there are two models: concordance democracy (low party polarization in the municipal council and vis-à-vis the mayor; strong role of the mayor) and competitive democracy (strong party polarization in the municipal council; rather weak role of the mayor) (Burgi & Wolff, 2021, 67). In competitive democracy municipalities, there are many more citizens' petitions and referenda, which are then often co-initiated or supported by the (opposition) parties, i.e. council factions (Brockmann et al., 2016, 208–211). The strategy is to transform political defeats in the municipal council into victories in referenda (Burgi & Wolff, 2021, 68).

This also raises the question of the impact. According to some empirical studies, direct democratic procedures can generally lead to higher public acceptance (Towfigh et al., 2016, 53–63). They can, therefore, be of value not only in terms of procedural input legitimacy, but also concerning substantive outcome legitimacy.

However, the social composition of the participants could also lead to or reinforce discrimination against underprivileged neighborhoods and their residents (Holtkamp & Brockmann, 2016, 50–51). This corresponds to the fact that middle- and upper-class citizens are generally overrepresented in local politics. This concerns the average turnout of 50.9% in referenda,[15] but in particular the membership in the municipal council (Holtkamp & Brockmann, 2016, 40–41; Burgi & Wolff, 2021, 67–68). In contrast, the highest voter turnout is seen in the federal elections, with values between 70.8% (2009) and 91.1% (1972) (Bundeswahlleiterin, 2021). Depending on one's point of view, citizens' petitions only replicate or reinforce existing differences on the local level.

[15] See footnote 14.

7.2.4 People's Initiative and Referendum at the State Level

Like at the local level, there are also a people's initiative and referendum at the state level throughout the country. Unlike citizens' initiatives and referenda at the municipal and county level, they have their legal basis in a code and in the individual state constitution (Lindner, 2019, paras 254–270; on their potentials and limits Lindner, 2020, 429–430). The subject of the people's initiative must be a draft law.[16] The procedure shares many similarities with citizens' initiative and referendum at the municipal or county level. However, the leeway, for example, with regard to the objects at the state level is greater, from a legal point of view. This is also the subject of the next section.

7.3 Participation and Large-Scale Projects in Urban Areas: The Case of the Railway and Urban Development Project "Stuttgart 21"

7.3.1 Introduction to the Project

"Stuttgart 21" has become a symbol in Germany for both: large-scale projects and citizens' protest against them (Bertrams, 2012, 289; Butzlaff et al., 2013, 52–53). The Stuttgart 21 railway project consists of two parts: the new construction of Stuttgart's main station (Stuttgart 21) and the new construction of the high-speed line Wendlingen–Ulm. The new construction of the main station includes the construction of an underground through station with eight tracks. On the vacated track areas behind the current terminus station, a new urban district with residential and commercial development is being developed. The completion of both parts will produce considerable time savings for train passengers[17] and expand the range of regional and long-distance services (DB Projekt Stuttgart–Ulm GmbH, 2023; Ministerium für Verkehr Baden-Württemberg, 2023).

The project was presented to the public in 1994. Due to numerous political, legal, administrative and business management issues and an interim project stop, construction work did not start until 2010. Projected construction costs increased from 2.5 billion EUR (4.9 billion DM) in 1995 (Land Baden-Württemberg et al., 1995, Section 3) to 4.5 billion EUR in 2009 (Land Baden-Württemberg et al., 2009, Sections 5, 6 and 8) to 9.8 billion EUR in 2022 (Deutsche Bahn, 2023, 134–135) to 11.5 billion EUR in 2024 (Deutsche Bahn AG, quoted from Kümmerer, 2024). The planned completion and opening was postponed from year 2008 (Deutsche Bahn,

[16] See e.g., Article 59(1–3) BWVerf; Article 71 BV; Article 68 (1) Verf NRW.

[17] In long-distance service, the travel time on the Stuttgart–Ulm route in particular is to be halved from 1 h to 30 min.

1995, 40–41) to year 2019 and then (Land Baden-Württemberg et al., 2009, Section 2 para 3) to 2025/2026 (DB Projekt Stuttgart–Ulm GmbH, 2023).

7.3.2 Protests and Participation Procedure

Shortly after the project was unveiled, Stuttgart 21 provoked opponents. They expressed their constructive criticism or even complete rejection in various formats such as signature collections, the founding of associations, demonstrations, publications, etc. The Stuttgart municipal council did not admit the first citizens' petition in 2007 to a referendum. It was maintained that the citizens' petition was inadmissible. Firstly, the relevant decisions had already been made in 1995 and 2001, which meant that the citizens' petition was overdue. Secondly, the citizens' petition pursued an inadmissible objective: the violation of a contractual obligation. In particular, concerning the second reason, the Administrative Court of Stuttgart confirmed the unlawfulness of the citizens' petition (VG Stuttgart, Judgement of July 17, 2009–7 K 3229/08, juris, paras 79–129). However, that was not the end of the protest.

Highly politicized protests against Stuttgart 21 continued and from 2009 onwards focused on the main station and the Palace Gardens, two sites listed as cultural heritage (Butzlaff et al., 2013, 66). The conflicts culminated in 2010, when the first trees in the Palace Gardens were to be cut down. To make this possible despite the expected protests, the police were deployed. In the course of the clashes, the police also used water cannons, tear gas and truncheons. The official number of people injured was more than 164, including 34 injured police officers (LT BW-Drs. 15/8008, 407). The opponents of Stuttgart 21 spoke of over 400 injured (quoted from Kutzer, 2020). This day went on to be called "Black Thursday" by the protest movement (Glenewinkel, 2012, 47; Staden, 2020, 89–110).

This had serious political and legal consequences (von Staden, 2020). The ongoing protests and their—from the protesters' point of view—unsatisfactory handling by the state government led to the following results: mediation, two committees of inquiry in the Baden-Württemberg state parliament, the ouster of the state government and the formation of a new state government in 2011. In its coalition agreement, the new state government agreed to call a referendum on Stuttgart 21 at the state level. In the meantime, another citizens' petition was once again denied admission to the referendum by the Stuttgart municipal council in June 2011 (VG Stuttgart, Judgement of July 17, 2013–7 K 4182/11, juris). The state government and the state parliament then implemented the referendum at the state level. There were some doubts about the legal admissibility of a referendum (Kirchhof, 2010). However, a constitutional complaint to the Federal Constitutional Court (*Bundesverfassungsgericht*) was unsuccessful due to lack of jurisdiction (BVerfG, Decision of November 21, 2011, 2 BvR 2333/11, juris). Further legal protection was not required later due to the referendum's defeat.

The question was "Do you vote in favor of the bill 'Act on the Exercise of Termination Rights in the Contractual Agreements for the Stuttgart 21 Railway Project (Stuttgart 21 Termination Act)'?" As a result, a "yes" meant the termination and a "no" meant the continuation of the project. The referendum was held on November 27, 2011. A majority of 58.9% of the valid votes were against the bill. The overall voter turnout was 48.3%. Even in the most affected state capital Stuttgart, with a turnout of 67.8%—the highest turnout in the entire state—52.9% voted against the termination bill (Landesabstimmungsleiterin Baden-Württemberg, 2011). As a result, funding from the state was maintained and the project was able to proceed and is expected to be completed this decade (2025/2026 at the earliest).

7.3.3 *Participants*

Who carried the protest in Stuttgart? Participants were better educated (university degree) and wealthier than average, in their middle adulthood or retirement and had a history of civic activism, especially in the anti-nuclear movement (Butzlaff et al., 2013, 67, 73 and 76). In this respect, there is a remarkable overlap with the participants of protests against renewable energy projects. The term "angry citizen" (*"Wutbürger"*) was coined in the media in connection with Stuttgart 21 (Kurbjuweit, 2010, 26–27). This picture also expresses the bottom-up approach of the protests and the (failed) citizens' petitions, while the governing parties in the state of Baden-Württemberg at the time, CDU and FDP, were precisely in favor of the project. The former opposition faction of the SPD was initially also in favor of the project, but with the change of government, together with its coalition partner from the Green party (as opponents of the project), who provided the new prime minister, nevertheless cleared the way for a referendum at the state level.

7.3.4 *Impacts*

Given that the legislative bodies, the administrative bodies like the Stuttgart municipal council and the people (in the referendum) voted in favor of the project, democratic pacification (no new people's initiative, electoral promises to stop the project after all, etc.) was expected afterwards (Jung, 2012, 13–14).

In the camp of protests, there were not only resigned but also sore losers who did not want to acknowledge the defeat in the vote. As the project progressed, however, this group became smaller and smaller (Henzler, 2020, 2).

As already seen above, Stuttgart 21 is also understood as a symbol. On the one hand, it is emblematic for the protest against a large-scale transport and urban development project. On the other hand, it exemplifies the political demand for and the scientific discussion about participation both substantively and procedurally

(Glenewinkel, 2012, 47). Section 25(3) Administrative Procedure Act, which was adopted thereafter,[18] can be understood as a result in this regard. The political, legal, and sociological discussion of whether and how citizen participation should be improved thus points beyond the Stuttgart train station.

7.4 Participation and Large-Scale Projects in Rural Areas

Stuttgart 21 was particularly suitable as an example for protests and participation in urban areas because of its symbolic character for politics and research. In the following, therefore, I will not engage in singling out one example. Instead, I will use some broader brush strokes to show what citizens' participation in rural areas in Germany has in common with the one in urban areas and what distinguishes them significantly.

Not necessary in relative terms, but in absolute terms citizens' petitions and referenda are more frequent in urban areas. In absolute figures, the number of referenda increases with the number of inhabitants. Thus, municipalities with fewer than 5000 inhabitants (share of all municipalities: 70.7%) account for 36.9% of all procedures, while municipalities with more than 50,000 inhabitants (share of all municipalities: 4.4%) account for 17.6% of all procedures (to the whole Rehmet et al., 2023, 18–19). It can also be observed that, in any case, large-scale (transport) projects tend to occur in urban areas, whereas they (and related citizens' petitions and referenda) are rarer in rural areas (Lieb, 2021, 79). Booming cities regularly have a greater need for large-scale transport or construction projects—and at the same time greater financial strength to fund them (Butzlaff et al., 2013, 49). Another typical effect of a region's economic strength is the greater self-confidence of its citizens. This can be the case in booming cities in particular and can increase the willingness to participate (Butzlaff et al., 2013, 49–50, 77). Another possible reason is that as the population of the municipality increases, party politicization in the municipal council also tends to increase. This also favors the initiation and/or support of citizens' petitions by opposition factions.[19]

The expansion of renewable energies, including the grid infrastructure, which is more likely to occur in rural areas (especially wind turbines, transmission grids or pipelines), will possibly shift that. Abstracted from general definitions,[20] even smaller projects can thus be "relatively large" in relation to the number of community citizens, the area or the community's budget respectively at least be perceived as such. Because of their size, small municipalities also have a greater proportion of

[18] See Sect. 7.2.1 above.

[19] See Sect. 7.2.3 above.

[20] See Sect. 7.1.1 above.

"backyards" affected by projects that take place there.[21] This is another reason why the relative citizen petition-to-inhabitant ratio can be higher in smaller municipalities.

7.5 Conclusions

Large-scale projects are indispensable to meet some of the most pressing challenges of the future. Furthermore, the acceleration of planning, licensing and public procurement is necessary for managing the green transformation of the economy and society (Burgi et al., 2022, 1321; Schlacke et al., 2022, 1577). A constructive form of citizen participation (measured against the legal basis and political practice) is not the only instrument here.

Another interesting strategy to effect projects consists of financial incentives or compensation for losses suffered (Scheele, 2012, 247–250; Kneuper & von Kaler, 2012, 251–253; van Wijk et al., 2021, 5–11; Hübner & Pohl, 2015, 11, 15, 20 and 23). For example, the State of Mecklenburg-Western Pomerania has enacted a law on the financial participation of citizens and municipalities in wind farms. This can be achieved, for example, through financial participation in the equity of a project-related company.

With regard to public participation, there are different approaches in the debate on acceleration. Depending on the point of view, acceleration impulses can be achieved by several measures: (1) Existing instruments could be made more effective, for example, through digitization of public participation (Burgi et al., 2022, 1325–1326; Wulfhorst, 2011, 587–590). (2) Existing instruments could be expanded (Stender-Vorwachs, 2015, 157–158), for instance, mediation (Parthe, 2015, 202–204) or a needs assessment process that already starts at the level of *whether* a project is needed and not only *how* it shall be implemented (Burgi, 2012, 277–280). (3) Third, – conversely—the participation measures could also be dismantled (e.g., the environmental impact assessment for liquefied natural gas projects since 2022). Discussions on this subject are still open, as are empirical findings.

Evaluation under democracy, the rule of law standards and political perception must be distinguished from the project-enabling perspective just described. However, empirical studies show that attitudes towards democracy often depend strongly on whether a referendum ends in a "victory" or a "defeat" (Butzlaff et al., 2013, 52, 66, 83–84; Towfigh et al., 2016, 55). Likewise, it is hardly possible to create acceptance among those directly affected by the project which is due to the aforementioned NIMBY phenomenon (Bertrams, 2012, 293). Finally, the protagonists of protests and citizens' petitions against large-scale projects are not a representative cross-section of the population.

---

[21] On the higher turnout in small municipalities, see Sect. 7.2.2 above.

Various positive effects offset this. Most important is that instruments such as citizens' petitions and referenda can complement representative democracy and contribute to the balancing of interests (Glenewinkel, 2012, 50). Especially in crises of representation, it appears as a way out. However, the desire for direct democratic participation could potentially decline if parliamentarians and those in power were to better anticipate deficits in representation in terms of procedure and content.

Finally, it is rightly pointed out that the positive or negative effects of participation instruments are always embedded in the respective political and legal culture (Schnieder, 2020, 145). Thus, the question of whether and to what extent the instruments of direct democracy from other countries, in particular Switzerland, can be transferred to Germany is a topic of German politics and constitutional law doctrine (Rapp, 2016, 582–590). When analyzing public participation in large-scale projects in one country, it is therefore always necessary to examine the extent to which these findings are transferable to other contexts.

References

Bertrams, M. (2012). Bürgerbeteiligung bei Großprojekten. *NWVBl, 26*, 289–293.

Brettschneider, F. (2019). Bau-und Infrastrukturprojekte—Mit dialogorientierter Kommunikation Konflikten vorbeugen. *ZKM, 22*, 204–208.

Brockmann, N. A., Holtkamp, L., & Noe, T. (2016). Direktdemokratische Hochburgen in Deutschland. In L. Holtkamp (Ed.), *Direktdemokratische Hochburgen in Deutschland. Zur Vereinbarkeit von Konkurrenz-und Direktdemokratie* (pp. 63–205). Springer VS.

Bundesamt, S. (2023). *Bevölkerung nach Nationalität und Bundesländern*. Retrieved May 10, 2024, from https://www.destatis.de/DE/Themen/Gesellschaft-Umwelt/Bevoelkerung/Bevoelkerungsstand/Tabellen/bevoelkerung-nichtdeutsch-laender.html

Bundeswahlleiterin. (2021). *Wahlbeteiligung*. Retrieved May 10, 2024, from https://www.bundeswahlleiterin.de/service/glossar/w/wahlbeteiligung.html

Burgi, M. (2012). Das Bedarfserörterungsverfahren: Eine Reformoption für die Bürgerbeteiligung bei Großprojekten. *NVwZ, 31*, 277–280.

Burgi, M. (2024). *Kommunalrecht* (7th ed.). C.H.Beck.

Burgi, M., & Wolff, D. (2021). Repräsentative und plebiszitäre Demokratie auf Kommunalebene: Ordnungsbedarf im Konkurrenzverhältnis. *NdsVBl, 28*, 65–70.

Burgi, M., Nischwitz, M., & Zimmermann, P. (2022). Beschleunigung bei Planung, Genehmigung und Vergabe. Zehn Thesen für ein ambitionierteres Sofortprogramm—Klima-Infrastruktur und Bundeswehr. *NVwZ, 41*, 1321–1329.

Butzlaff, F., Hoeft, C., & Kopp, J. (2013). "Wir lassen nicht mehr alles mit uns machen!" Bürgerproteste an und um den öffentlichen Raum, Infrastruktur und Stadtentwicklung. In S. Marg, L. Geiges, F. Butzlaff, & F. Walter (Eds.), *Die neue Macht der Bürger. Was motiviert Protestbewegungen?* (pp. 48–93). Rowohlt.

DB Projekt Stuttgart–Ulm GmbH. (2023). *Bahnprojekt Stuttgart–Ulm*. Retrieved May 10, 2024, from https://www.bahnprojekt-stuttgart-ulm.de/aktuell/

Deutsche Bahn, A. G. (1995). *Das Synergiekonzept Stuttgart 21. Die Ergebnisse des Vorprojekts*. Stuttgart.

Deutsche Bahn, AG. (2023). *Integrierter Bericht 2022*. Berlin.

Epping, V., & Hillgruber, C. (2023, May 15). *BeckOK Grundgesetz* (55th ed.). C.H.Beck. (Cited as: N. N., in Epping and Hillgruber (Eds.), 2023).

Ernst, C. (2021). Artikel 28. In I. von Münch & P. Kunig (Eds.), *Grundgesetz: Kommentar* (7th ed.). C.H.Beck.

Flyvbjerg, B. (2005). Policy and planning for large infrastructure projects: Problems, causes, cures. *World Bank Policy Research Working Paper 3781*.

Flyvbjerg, B. (2014). What you should know about megaprojects and why: An overview. *Project Management Journal, 45(2)*, 6–19.

Fraenkel-Haeberle, C. (2016). Zur Multifunktionalität der Partizipation bei großen Infrastrukturvorhaben. *DÖV, 69*, 548–555.

Gärditz, K. F. (2011). Angemessene Öffentlichkeitsbeteiligung bei Infrastrukturplanungen als Herausforderung an das Verwaltungsrecht im demokratischen Rechtsstaat. *GewArch, 57*, 273–279.

Glenewinkel, W. (2012). Die Protestbewegung gegen Stuttgart 21—Erfolg oder Misserfolg? *ZKM, 15*, 47–51.

Henzler, C. (2020, February 1). Umsturz auf schwäbisch. *Süddeutsche Zeitung*, 2.

Hien, E. (2012). Partizipation im Planungsverfahren. *UPR, 32*, 128–132.

Hien, E. (2014). Bürgerbeteiligung im Spannungsfeld der Gewaltenteilung. *DVBl, 129*, 495–498.

Holtkamp, L., & Brockmann, N. A. (2016). Direkte Demokratie. In L. Holtkamp (Ed.), *Direktdemokratische Hochburgen in Deutschland. Zur Vereinbarkeit von Konkurrenz-und Direktdemokratie* (pp. 11–55). Springer VS.

Hübner, G., & Pohl, J. (2015). *Mehr Abstand—Mehr Akzeptanz? Ein umweltpsychologischer Studienvergleich*. Fachagentur Windenergie an Land.

Jung, O. (2012). Stuttgart 21 und die Direkte Demokratie. Kritische Anmerkungen zum Umgang mit dem Ergebnis der Volksabstimmung. *RuP, 48*, 11–17.

Kirchhof, P. (2010). *Gutachtliche Stellungnahme zum Antrag der Fraktion der SPD im Landtag von Baden-Württemberg für eine Volksabstimmung über Stuttgart 21 und die Neubaustrecke Wendlingen—Ulm*. Heidelberg.

Knauff, M. (2012). Öffentlichkeitsbeteiligung im Verwaltungsverfahren. *DÖV, 65*, 1–8.

Kneuper, F., & von Kaler, M. (2012). Bürgerbeteiligung als Geschäftsmodell für Stadtwerke. *IR, 9*, 250–254.

Knobloch, V. (2022). Bürger-und Akteursbeteiligung im ländlichen Raum. In J. Abt, L. Blecken, S. Bock, J. Diringer, & K. Fahrenkrug (Eds.), *Von Beteiligung zur Koproduktion. Wege der Zusammenarbeit von Kommune und Bürgerschaft für eine zukunftsfähige kommunale Entwicklung* (pp. 103–125). Springer VS.

Korioth, S., & Müller, M. W. (2024). *Staatsrecht I: Staatsorganisationsrecht unter Berücksichtigung europäischer und internationaler Bezüge* (7th ed.). W. Kohlhammer.

Kümmerer, F. (2024). Urteil: Bahn muss Mehrkosten von Stuttgart 21 alleine tragen. Retrieved May 10, 2024, from https://www.swr.de/swraktuell/baden-wuerttemberg/stuttgart/entscheidung-stuttgart21-verwaltungsgericht-100.html

Kurbjuweit, D. (2010). Der Wutbürger. *Der Spiegel, 41*, 26–27.

Kutzer, C. (2020, September 30). Hunderte demonstrieren am Stuttgarter Bahnhof. *Stuttgarter Nachrichten*.

Land Baden-Württemberg, Landeshauptstadt Stuttgart, Verband Region Stuttgart, Bundesrepublik Deutschland, & Deutsche Bahn AG. (1995, November 7). *Rahmenvereinbarung zum Projekt Stuttgart 21*. Stuttgart.

Land Baden-Württemberg, Landeshauptstadt Stuttgart, Verband Region Stuttgart, Flughafen Stuttgart GmbH, DB Netz Aktiengesellschaft, DB Station&Service Aktiengesellschaft, DB Energie GmbH, & Deutsche Bahn Aktiengesellschaft. (2009, March 30). *Finanzierungsvertrag zu Stuttgart 21 als Teil des Gesamtprojekts Stuttgart 21 und Neubaustrecke Wendlingen—Ulm*. Stuttgart.

Landesabstimmungsleiterin Baden-Württemberg. (2011). *Endgültiges Ergebnis der Volksabstimmung über die Gesetzesvorlage des S 21-Kündigungsgesetzes am 27*. Stuttgart.

Lieb, N. (2021). Citizens' petitions for referendum against essential large-scale infrastructure projects in urban areas. In M. Burgi, L. Hagen, & N. Lieb (Eds.), *Local government in Germany: Responses to urban-rural challenges* (pp. 79–82). Zenodo. https://doi.org/10.5281/zenodo.5236426

Lindner, J. F. (2019). *Bayerisches Staatsrecht* (2nd ed.). Boorberg.

Lindner, J. F. (2020). Nachhaltigkeit und Innovation durch Volksgesetzgebung. *EurUP, 18*, 427–439.

Marg, S., Hermann, C., Hambauer, V., & Becké, A. B. (2013). "Wenn man was für die Natur machen will, stellt man da keine Masten hin". Bürgerproteste gegen Bauprojekte im Zuge der Energiewende. In S. Marg, L. Geiges, F. Butzlaff, & F. Walter (Eds.), *Die neue Macht der Bürger. Was motiviert Protestbewegungen?* (pp. 94–138). Rowohlt.

Ministerium für Verkehr Baden-Württemberg. (2023). *Stuttgart 21*. Retrieved May 10, 2024, from https://vm.baden-wuerttemberg.de/de/mobilitaet-verkehr/schiene/ausbau-der-schiene-in-baden-wuerttemberg/ausbauprojekte/stuttgart-21

Parthe, R. (2015). Mediation und direkte Demokratie. *RuP, 51*, 200–204.

Rapp, S. (2016). *Direkte Demokratie in der Schweiz. Ein Vergleich zu der Rechtslage in Deutschland*. Nomos.

Rehmet, F., Johannsen, L., Krenzer, S., Mittendorf, V., Müller, J., & Kroll, S. (2023). *Bürgerbegehrensbericht 2023* (2nd ed.). Mehr Demokratie e.V.

Sachs, M. (2024). *Grundgesetz* (10th ed.). C.H.Beck. (Cited as: N. N., in Sachs (Ed.), 2024).

Scheele, U. (2012). Stromnetze als NIMBY-Güter? Kompensationslösungen zur Verbesserung der Akzeptanz von Energieinfrastrukturen. *IR, 9*, 247–250.

Schink, A. (2013). Verstärkung der Öffentlichkeitsbeteiligung und neue UVP-Anforderungen für Unternehmen. *DVBl, 128*, 1347–1355.

Schlacke, S., Wentzien, H., & Römling, D. (2022). Beschleunigung der Energiewende: Ein gesetzgeberischer Paradigmenwechsel durch das Osterpaket? *NVwZ, 41*, 1577–1586.

Schnieder, P. (2020). Großprojekte und Bürgerbeteiligung—Ein Resumé. *RuP, 56*, 142–148.

Schoch, F. (2014). Bürgerbegehren und Bürgerentscheid im Spiegel der Rechtsprechung. *NVwZ, 33*, 1473–1482.

Stender-Vorwachs, J. (2015). Stärkung der Bürgerbeteiligung bei der Vorhabenplanung. *NdsVBl, 22*, 153–158.

Stüer, B. (2013). Das Planvereinheitlichungsgesetz. *DVBl, 128*, 700–707.

Sturm, R., & Winkelmann, T. (2014). Contested infrastructures: Citizen protest and the response of political parties in Germany. In R. Cordenillo & S. van der Staak (Eds.), *Political parties and citizen movements in Asia and Europe* (pp. 23–37). International IDEA.

Towfigh, E. V., Goerg, S. J., Glöckner, A., Leifeld, P., Llorente-Saguer, A., Bade, S., & Kurschilgen, C. (2016). Do direct-democratic procedures lead to higher acceptance than political representation? Experimental survey evidence from Germany. *Public Choice, 167*, 47–65.

van Wijk, J., Fischhendler, I., Rosen, G., & Herman, L. (2021). Penny wise or pound foolish? Compensation schemes and the attainment of community acceptance in renewable energy. *Energy Research & Social Science, 81*(102260), 1–14.

von Staden, J. (2020). *Stuttgart 21—Eine Rekonstruktion der Proteste. Soziale Bewegungen in Zeiten der Postdemokratie*. Transcript.

Wolff, D., & Zimmermann, P. (2022). Der Parlamentsvorbehalt in der COVID-19-Pandemie—Teil 1. *JURA, 44*, 18–31.

Wulfhorst, R. (2011). Konsequenzen aus "Stuttgart 21": Vorschläge zur Verbesserung der Bürgerbeteiligung. *DÖV, 64*, 581–590.

Chapter 8
Large-Scale Projects in Italy: Non-participation and the Case of a Nuclear Waste Deposit

Giulio Citroni

Abstract The chapter analyses the thirty-year long—and still unaccomplished—decision-making process over the siting of a deposit for high-level nuclear waste in Italy. Over decades, this issue has been at the centre of the nuclear power strategy of Italy and all other EU and industrialised countries, and is now prominent on the EU agenda in order to close the nuclear power cycle and determine its sustainability in the energy transition. The chapter describes the failed attempts to solve the problem of siting an unwanted infrastructure through authority and technical expertise, and analyses the very timid approach to deliberative democracy that is unsuccessfully being tested as we write. Comparison with other, more successful, experiences shows that coordinated, inclusive processes that challenge problem definition and manage expectations have higher chances of reaching some degree of consensus over time. Italy's inability to design inclusive processes for the planning and implementation of infrastructure is further argued in the chapter with a reconstruction of the recent dismantling of the Débat public that was briefly experimented between 2021 and 2023.

Keywords Nuclear waste · Italy · Deliberative democracy · Débat public

> If an agreement is not reached within the sixty days that follow, said agreement shall be reached by decree of the President of the Republic. (Italian government's Legislative Decree 31/2010).

8.1 Introduction

This chapter discusses the case of the failed attempt to establish a nuclear waste repository in the small southern town of Scanzano Jonico in 2003, in order to shed light on the difficulties that Italian governments have undergone in adopting effective tools of citizen participation and in implementing strategic infrastructural

G. Citroni (✉)
Department of Political and Social Sciences, Università della Calabria, Rende, Italy
e-mail: giulio.citroni@unical.it

K. Kössler, E. Schläppi (eds.), *Citizen Participation in Local Governance*, Local and Urban Governance, https://doi.org/10.1007/978-3-031-99824-9_8

decisions. The case described remains highly relevant after two decades in two main respects: first, it touches upon a key issue of energy transition policies, insofar as the management of nuclear waste and the siting of its repositories is a controversial point that defines whether nuclear power can be deemed "sustainable" and included as part of the energy transition; secondly, a recent attempt to introduce the French-style *débat public* in large-scale projects in Italy has substantially failed, showing that the inability to negotiate and debate with local communities is a structural problem in Italy. Therefore, the Scanzano Jonico story is paradigmatic of stark present difficulties, at a time when the country is engaged in an unprecedented effort to build strategic infrastructure under the European Green Deal and the Next Generation EU program. The planning of infrastructure for renewables is particularly problematic because it raises concerns with local communities and even environmentalists, and may give rise to factual, procedural, identity and value conflicts (Kühne et al., 2022) that span class, territorial, and intergenerational cleavages within and across national political systems (Brown & Spiegel, 2019). Such conflicts must be addressed with appropriate stakeholder engagement tools to guarantee the success of the energy transition.

8.2 The (Socio-political) Issue of HLW Disposal in the Framework of the Energy Transition

High-level nuclear waste (HLW) is the waste resulting from the production of nuclear power. The storage and disposal of HLW is a very controversial issue in most developed countries, and has been for several decades (Brunnengräber et al., 2015; Brunnengräber et al., 2018; Brunnengräber & Di Nucci, 2019). As required by directive 2011/70/Euratom, all EU countries are devising plans, and the prevailing tendency is that while most national authorities have planned some infrastructure, they are still in a design phase and construction will not be terminated before 2050–2070, depending on individual cases (European Commission, 2017). The design of decision-making processes and the analysis of conflicts which arise in the process is, therefore, a poignant issue, also because hardly any country has yet solved the problem in what seems to be a stable and socially accepted way—the Onkalo plant in Finland being the only one ready for operation (El-Showk, 2022). For reasons we will clarify shortly, the solution to this problem is central to the debate on the energy transition, and the conflicts over the disposal of HLW add one more piece to the intricate puzzle of social, political and economic conflicts arising from transition policies around the world (Sovacool, 2021).

Ever since the establishment of nuclear programs in industrialized economies in the early 1950s, it was widely acknowledged that HLW needed to be managed and regulated, as witnessed by Article 37 of the EURATOM Treaty in 1957. Most importantly, it is now estimated that the planning of disposal sites should guarantee safety for extremely long periods of time, on the order of a hundred thousand years according to the United Nations Economic Commission for Europe (UNECE, 2020, 98), or even a million years according to the German Federal Office for the Safety of Nuclear Waste Management (BASE, 2021).

The defining characteristic of the HLW problem is that the dangers of exposure to radioactive waste span such long periods of time that there is no guarantee that a human-made infrastructure, the social institutions entrusted with its maintenance, and even the memory of the danger it poses, will last long enough. No existing institution has lasted a hundred thousand or a million years, nor even a comprehensible language that may be used to leave messages to future generations at such distance. At present, therefore, there is general technical consensus that the most effective way to dispose of HLW are deep geological repositories (DGR), i.e. deposits in very stable geological environments where barrels can be buried deep and sealed in concrete forever: as the OECD Nuclear Energy Agency puts it, "deep rock is more stable than society" (NEA and OECD, 2017, 15).

The dangers posed by HLW over such long time-frames contribute to making the problem of storage and disposal a paradigmatic example of a "wicked" policy problem as defined by the seminal work of Rittel and Webber (Rittel & Webber, 1973; see also Citroni, 2024a; Lippi & Tsekos, 2024). Among the characteristics of the wicked problem identified by Rittel and Webber, several appear befitting:

1. "There is no definitive formulation of a wicked problem": unknown technical problems, or solutions that were unavailable at the time of design may (and most likely will) arise over the hundred thousand or million years of implementation, making past solutions suboptimal, ineffective, or harmful.
2. "There is no immediate and no ultimate test of a solution to a wicked problem": the full consequences of a solution cannot be appraised until all outputs and outcomes have developed their complex effects, which in the case of HLW is innumerable generations away.
3. "Because there is no opportunity to learn by trial-and-error, every attempt counts significantly": the long process of design and construction, and even more so the final act of sealing the waste in concrete, make the solution, in the words of Rittel and Weber, "a one-shot operation".
4. "Every wicked problem can be considered to be a symptom of another problem": the DGR solution can be expected to be challenged by opposers on the basis of a *montée en généralité* that calls into question nuclear energy altogether, or even the growth-based capitalist model, leading to heightened conflict and the intractability of the specific issue.

The relevance of the issue is demonstrated by the heated controversy that was raised by the inclusion of nuclear power in the so-called Taxonomy Regulation, which the EU Commission drew up to define the scope of investments that may benefit from subsidies oriented to sustainability such as the Green Deal (Citroni, 2024a). The Commission's Technical Expert Group (TEG) published its first report stating that nuclear energy generation has "near to zero greenhouse gas emissions *in the energy generation phase*", noting that it was not calculating the impacts of nuclear waste because it is impossible to estimate in the absence of proven, tested solutions (EU-TEG, 2020; EU-TEG., 2020). Similar conclusions were reached by the Commission's Joint Research Centre (JRC, 2021, 182) which also excluded the radiological dangers of nuclear waste from the calculation of impacts. Several countries, as well as other EU institutions, contested the exclusion of HLW storage and management from the calculation of risks connected to nuclear power, and called for a more cautionary approach (BASE, 2021; Stagl, 2020; SCHEER, 2021; Fouquet, 2022). The issue of nuclear waste thus becomes central to legitimizing the inclusion or exclusion of nuclear power from the energy transition policy, and governments across the world are seeking credible ways to tackle it.

While cautious about viewing it as a panacea that will cure all conflict and lead to fast and effective solutions, the most recent literature on wicked problems (Alford & Head, 2017; Head, 2019; Zeigermann & Ettelt, 2023) concedes that the wide debate on democratic innovation, deliberation and stakeholder inclusion has useful indications for political strategies: "[T]he 'wicked' problem perspective in public policy entails a call for governments to embrace stakeholder pluralism, acknowledge the limits of current knowledge, foster learning processes and develop procedural reforms to make policy-making more open and transparent" (Head, 2019, 192). Central to this debate are the contributions made since the 1990s by authors pointing to the need for a democratization of expertise and participatory research (Fischer, 1993, 1999) for frame-critical policy analysis and inclusive, frame-reflective policy practices, whereby analysts and practitioners engage in public deliberation over the framing processes that underlie policy controversies (Rein & Schön, 1996), and for network management in governance settings (van Bueren et al., 2003; Koppenjan & Klijn, 2004).

The relationship between wicked problems and deliberative, inclusive policy-making processes is also key to the debate on policy design and policy capacity (Howlett et al., 2015, 300) at a time when environmental policy and energy transition policies pose such hugely complex technical problems and new articulations of values and interests as to be defined as "super-wicked" (Levin et al., 2012).

8.3 The Siting Process: Decide, Announce, Give Up (1996–2003)

The nuclear program in Italy started relatively early and played a pioneering role in several respects (Nucci & Rosaria, 2006; Curli, 2022): by 1965, three plants were in operation and produced 13.8% of the (non-socialist) world capacity as opposed to France's 3% and Germany's 0.5% (Nucci & Rosaria, 2006). Further investments stalled for several years, until national plans in 1975 foresaw intense growth in nuclear power production in a hasty response to the oil crisis (Nucci & Rosaria, 2006). However, implementation lagged, and by the time the Chernobyl accident occurred, public opinion was ready to mobilize against nuclear energy. The *Partito*

Radicale proposed three referenda that effectively demanded a stop to the nuclear program; they were held in November 1987, and gained a large majority of votes.

The decommissioning of the existing nuclear plants and the disposal of the nuclear waste was long ignored by national authorities and the media; scandals on nuclear waste were frequently in the media, but mostly pertained to international trafficking and illegal disposal—no significant attention was paid to the fact that HLW was being held in inactive power plants in structures that were not designed for long-term storage (Risoluti, 2014). However, in 1996, a technical commission was established within the Civil Protection Authority to deal with the "great risks" and debate the problem of nuclear waste; the National Energy Agency (ENEA) followed suit, and they both soon set up a working group and a task force respectively (Risoluti, 2014). A first report was published in February 1999, establishing a strategy for the construction of a temporary surface deposit for HLW. However, no indication was given concerning the siting or even the procedures to define it. Meanwhile, at the political level, a National Conference on Energy and the Environment was organized in November 1998 by ENEA and the Ministries of the Environment, of Industry and of Research. In the concluding document, a "participatory process defined with the regions" was envisaged to deal with nuclear decommissioning. At the legislative level, a wide-ranging reform of the energy market was approved in 1999. To liberalize the market, the incumbent national company ENEL was subjected to a profound process of "unbundling", whereby generation capacity and network infrastructures were excluded from its perimeter. SOGIN, a new state-owned company, was established to take over the power plants and manage their decommissioning.

In 2001, new elections determined a change in government leadership; Bersani, the left-wing minister for industry who had led the reform of the energy market and initiated a dialogue with the regions over the design and siting of the deposit for nuclear waste, was no longer in charge in the implementation phase. The new Berlusconi cabinet was keen to promote public investment in "great public works" (*grandi opere*), and soon approved a piece of legislation intended to expedite the planning and execution of strategic infrastructure; the *Legge Obiettivo* (decree n. 443/2001) included norms that radically simplified decision-making procedures, centralizing executive powers in planning and contracting and dispensing central authorities from *ex-ante* evaluation and the search of inter-institutional cooperation whenever an infrastructure was defined as "strategic". In this political context, the government appointed a general of the army, Carlo Jean, as the head of SOGIN, and granted him full authority under the *Legge Obiettivo* to plan and execute the construction of a disposal site for nuclear waste.

Over the summer of 2003, SOGIN drew up plans for a DGR in Scanzano Jonico, a small town in the rural southern region of Basilicata (SOGIN, 2003). As per the government's instructions, the plan included infrastructure for the final storage of low- and medium-level waste and for the temporary storage of high-level waste; however, the SOGIN plan went much further, and included the possibility of a geological repository for HLW.

As soon as the plan was approved through a decree and made public on November 13th, protests broke out at both institutional and civic levels in Scanzano and the Basilicata region. The president of the region, leading a left-wing coalition, contributed to raising signatures for a popular petition, formally contested the legality of the plan, and even updated the seismic classification of the territory of Scanzano to a higher level that would prevent the establishment of sensitive infrastructure; several municipalities passed anti-nuclear motions; the Mayor of Scanzano—albeit a member of the governing right-wing coalition, and despite press revelations that he had informally known and approved of SOGIN's plan before it was announced—declared his disapproval (Zinn, 2007a). At the civic level, protests were also immediate and significant (Zinn, 2007b). It crossed paths with, and thrived on, the rather lively anti-globalization movement of the time, as well as the more diffuse opposition to the Berlusconi government (de Ruggieri, 2004): starting with the occupation of institutional buildings and with spontaneous road blocks, it culminated in the march of an estimated one hundred thousand people on November 23rd. The protest reached the national level the following day with a sit-in in Rome and the approval of a motion by the Conference of Regional Presidents asking for the repeal of the decree (Zinn, 2007b).

Within a few days, the national government receded and announced that the plans would be revised and a new siting process would occur. In a new round of legislation which evolved between November 2003 and August 2004, a new procedure was defined, a new commission was set up, and a new site was expected to be identified in just 12 months (Nucci & Rosaria, 2015). However, this time the process stopped again, and no new site was selected or announced.

8.4 The Rhetoric of Deliberation in Slow-Motion (2010–2023)

After a short-lived left-wing government (2006–2008) the center-right coalition led by Berlusconi won again in 2008, and this time they planned a full re-establishment of a nuclear program. In 2009, legislation was passed that circumvented the decision made through the 1987 referendum, and the national company ENEL was ready to build at least four reactors (Nucci & Rosaria, 2015, 301). Law 99/2009 delegated to the cabinet the power to define the procedures to construct nuclear power plants, plants for the production of nuclear fuel, and plants for the storage of spent fuel. A whole new process was thus defined by Legislative decree 31/2010 for the siting of the HLW repository, largely intended to accompany the new nuclear program—and legitimize it, in the terms expressed above in the case of the EU Taxonomy. However, soon after the approval of the delegated decrees in 2010, a referendum was called to repeal the norms allowing for a new nuclear program; the anti-nuclear campaign quickly gained momentum, building on more general anti-government opposition, the widespread consensus for a concomitant referendum against the privatization of water, and the global scare generated by the accident at Fukushima. In June 2011, exactly 2 months after said accident, the referendum was held and passed, and the nuclear program was halted again. However, the legislation concerning the disposal site for HLW remains to this day and is still in the process of implementation.

This new legislation sets out the complete procedure for the selection of a nuclear waste deposit site and redefines the infrastructure as a "national repository and technological park". Within six months of the decree's approval, SOGIN is expected to publish a "map of potentially suitable areas" (CNAPI) based on geographical and geological data—anthropic characteristics were missing from the original text and added hastily soon after. The map must also indicate potential local employment and compensation opportunities to make it more palatable for affected communities.

After the publication of the map of potentially suitable areas, the legislation states that a negotiation process is set in motion between stakeholders and central and local institutions. First, SOGIN must publish the map and a preliminary plan of the infrastructure on its website and in at least five major newspapers to make it publicly accessible and raise awareness; over the following three months, regional and local administrations, as well as unspecified "qualified stakeholders" may raise observations and technical proposals for improvement to SOGIN "in written, non-anonymous form" via an email address. Evidently, this procedure implies no collective discussion or deliberation, and resembles traditional one-way observations that are common in Italian land management legislation.

An opportunity for more deliberative dialogue is envisaged in a "national seminar" where relevant ministries, the Nuclear Safety Agency, affected local authorities, the Association of Municipalities, industrial associations, trade unions and universities are invited—clearly a strictly institutional forum that only includes public authorities and major interest organizations while excluding individual citizens or grassroot organizations. During the seminar, "all the technical aspects related to the technology park are thoroughly examined, […] as well as the aspects related to the safety of workers, the population, and the environment. Possible economic and territorial development benefits connected to the implementation of such projects and compensatory measures are also outlined."

Based on the results of the email consultation and of the national seminar, SOGIN then draws up a final map of suitable areas and sends it to the Ministry of Economic Development within 30 days; the Ministry, in accordance with the Nuclear Safety Agency and other ministries, will approve the map and SOGIN will publish it—all within another 60 days. Once the final map is published, regional and local administrations included in the map are expected to rush and declare their willingness to host the nuclear deposit within 60 days and start a negotiation—in case they do not volunteer, SOGIN will start negotiations with all of them. An inter-institutional committee is set up if an agreement is not reached directly. Finally, "if an agreement is not reached within the sixty days that follow, said agreement shall be reached by decree of the President of the Republic, following a decision of the

Council of Ministers, which includes the participation of the president of the relevant region" (Article 27(8) of the Legislative Decree 31/2010).

This somewhat lengthy description of the procedure envisaged by Legislative Decree 31/2010, and this final clause about the "agreement by decree", shows how a rhetoric of deliberation and negotiation is used (through words like observations, seminar, discussion, negotiations, agreement). However, the underlying logic is one of unidirectional persuasion (as testified by the continuous reference to the benefits to be outlined at every step), of strictly institutional engagement, and of the ultimate recourse to authority whenever an (evidently rather unlikely) agreement is not reached within the draconian time-limits. Overall, the procedure does not seem to allow a thorough investigation and composition of conflicting positions, needs, interests and values before authority comes into play with an ultimate verdict.

The implementation of this procedure has proven even more problematic than the formulation: the publication of the map of potentially suitable areas took 11 years—as opposed to the six months stated by law. Surely, the pressure posed by the nuclear program has vanished, and the issue of HLW has lost its momentum since the referendum of 2011. However, the procedure still stands, and HLW is still unsafely stored in former nuclear power plants: SOGIN and its political counterparts in ministries are evidently wary of conflict and buy time in classical NIMTOO ("Not In My Term Of Office") fashion. Indeed, when SOGIN first submitted a map to the Ministry of the Environment in 2015, it lay unattended by successive ministers before it was approved for publication in 2021 (Giliberto, 2021).

In addition, the observation of the implementation process further demonstrates that the deliberative and inclusive aspects of the procedure are weak and do not form a core part of the process. The publication of the map and its annexes, for example, is done through a set of zip files that amount to over 1GB of technical data, hardly accessible to civic organizations and small or medium municipalities that have limited technical staff and capability. Also, the national seminar is held online through a series of one-way YouTube webinars, with no Q&A or comment available on the platform.

In March 2022, SOGIN sent a final version of the map to the Ministry of the Environment, which has not taken any further action. The list, which includes 51 viable sites, was published by the Ministry in December 2023 (taking 21 months to do so, instead of the two set forth by the law). To increase the chance that local authorities will propose to host the deposit, the government contextually approved a norm to allow all municipalities to do so, even those which are not in the list. Nonetheless, no candidacy came by the March 2024 deadline, and the process is again halted.

8.5 Lessons Not Learned: Val di Susa, Scanzano, and the Failure of the *Dibattito Pubblico*

The case of Scanzano, and the failure to decide on a deposit for nuclear waste since, are symptomatic of a difficulty in the Italian administrative and political system to design effective decision-making processes that combine technical and political complexities. What is striking in international comparison (Citroni, 2024a) is not simply the inability to come to a final decision on the siting of the nuclear waste repository—an inability that is common to most developed countries—but rather the difficulties encountered in even structuring a decision-making process that may enable the build-up of the policy capacity required to define goals and negotiate solutions. Countries that have reached a more advanced stage in the strategy for the siting of HLW repositories have done so (Citroni, 2024a) through a combination of:

1. limited challenges to problem definition: most notably, a stable strategy in the nuclear program (be it an atomic consensus or a phase-out plan) helps isolate the problem of nuclear waste from the problem of nuclear energy production and stabilize the problem pressure that keeps the issue on the agenda;
2. multilevel coordination: joint committees, credible systems of local candidacies, political negotiation and coordinated planning have proved to be key to the build-up of consensus and the internalization of conflict;
3. time management: the politics of time is exemplified in Italy by the "NIMTOO (Not In My Term Of Office) syndrome", but other countries have experimented with more effective strategies like 1) clearly defined moratoriums—which separate decision-making from implementation and thus help deciding in a more abstract and less conflictual way - or 2) technical solutions which guarantee reversibility, and thus let stakeholders perceive the decision as provisional and increase acceptability;
4. finally, and most importantly for the purposes of our discussion, community engagement and public scientific engagement: albeit with relevant difficulties and partly undecisive results, France has resorted effectively to the use of *débat public*, a deliberative procedure that guarantees the inclusion of all affected communities in a public discussion on infrastructure and planning initiatives.

In this last section, we discuss the failed attempt to introduce the *débat public* (DP) in Italian legislation, which demonstrates a structural political difficulty in accepting negotiation and deliberation as tools of politics and the policy process (Citroni, 2024b).

The introduction of deliberative and participatory processes in policy-making processes started in Italy in the late 1990s and was recognized as a significant phenomenon by the mid-2000s (Bobbio, 2004). Initiatives were mostly taken at the local level, and concerned urban planning and, to a more limited extent, the planning of social services. Through the use of techniques such as open space technology meetings, public assemblies, participatory planning, and in some cases participatory budgeting processes, an increasing number of municipalities experimented with the engagement of individual citizens and organized groups in decision-making at a time when party politics was widely de-legitimized and struggled to maintain its hold on the composition of conflicts (Citroni, 2010).

The widespread experimentation of inclusive and deliberative processes occurred in a context of a complete lack of institutionalization: no legislation or regulation was in place to define when, how, and to what effect public authorities should or could engage in deliberation with stakeholders and citizens. The first attempt to regulate the matter came from regional legislation, first in Tuscany (2007), then

Apulia (2017), and Emilia Romagna (2018): a legislative framework was tested that regulated and supported local initiatives, stating general principles of inclusion and deliberation, providing funding, and defining the procedures to respond to citizens' and stakeholders' input. The law approved in Tuscany also introduced the "dibattito pubblico", forged on the model of the French *débat public*: a procedure that is set in motion whenever a large infrastructure project is planned, whereby the plan is made public in a complete, neutral and comprehensible report, and public assemblies, written observations, and any form of participation may be used to communicate and improve or reject the plan; the results are again made public, and the planners and authorities may decide whether to accept or ignore suggestions. However, in either case, they have to publicly justify their decision and will be held accountable for implementing it.

At the national level, the proposal to introduce the DP was first made in parliament in 2012 and supported by the then Minister for Infrastructure of the "technical" (non-partisan) cabinet led by Mario Monti. The political context, and especially the discussion concerning infrastructure, was heavily influenced by the recent resurgence of the conflict in Val di Susa, a valley in the Alps where a strong movement has fought the construction of a high-speed train line since 1995 (Della Porta & Piazza, 2008). Intense clashes in February and March proved that previous attempts to negotiate had failed, the media attention was high, and the government was keen to show it could expedite construction effectively (Leonardi, 2013). Proposals in parliament soon came from all sides of the political spectrum, except from the Lega Nord. They all cited the French model as a direct inspiration, but mostly framed the issue as a matter of effectiveness in the implementation of public works and made little mention of environmental issues (which were the leading frame of the French DP), or democratic empowerment of communities (which was the frame used by legislators in Tuscany).

Legislation introducing the DP was passed in 2016 in the context of a general reform of public contracts. The DP was inserted under the heading of "Transparency in the participation of stakeholders", but operational norms, including the definition of the rules and procedures, would be defined by a successive decree—which was only approved 2 years later. After the approval of this decree in 2018, another two-and-a-half years went by before the National Commission for Public Debate was established in 2021. Meanwhile, several cabinets had changed, a pandemic had hit the world, and the National Recovery and Resilience Plan under Next Generation EU, as well as the European Green Deal, envisaged unprecedented amounts of investment in infrastructure.

When the DP became operational in 2021, several limitations that experts already signaled were confirmed in practice. First of all, the above-mentioned Commission that is in charge of guaranteeing impartiality and compliance with the basic principles of participation and deliberation is not designed as an independent body but is instead hosted by the Ministry of Infrastructure—which is, in most cases, engaged in the process as a promoter of the project under discussion. Secondly, the Commission itself is heavily understaffed and underfinanced—for the first 2 years, during which almost twenty debates took place, the Commission had no budget. Thirdly, the law states that the "coordinator" of each DP, the person who designs and leads the activities, should be a manager from within the civil service. However, no such expertise exists in the civil service, and all coordinators had to be contracted out. Finally, a tendency to favor expedited procedures over articulated discussions is clearly visible in the very strict time frame that is imposed on DP processes: in the "ordinary" procedure, the Commission only has 15 days to react to the project dossier that will be used to inform the public, and can only reject it or make observations once; whenever projects are financed through Next Generation EU, this deadline is halved to 7.5 days. Similarly, the whole debate must only last 45 days regarding such projects.

A process of consolidation and institutionalization appeared to be taking place under the Draghi cabinet (again, a "technical", non-partisan one) and included substantial funding for the Commission, provided by law in early 2022. However, the whole system of the DP was all but dismantled by the end of the same year: the new right-wing Prime Minister, Giorgia Meloni, appointed the leader of the Lega—the only party who never supported DP—as Minister for Infrastructure; soon thereafter, a reform of the legislation on public contracts scraped the National Commission for Public Debate and left only the DP in place as an online consultation with organized stakeholders—thus excluding any form of participation by individual citizens.

8.6 Conclusions: The What, the When and the How of Participation in Large-scale Projects

The description of the complex decision-making process concerning the deposit of nuclear waste in Italy, and the analysis of the events that led to the institutionalization and later dismantling of DP in national legislation, contribute to an understanding of the state of public participation in Italy. While a comprehensive overview of the complex landscape of local initiatives is beyond the scope of this chapter, some concluding remarks can be made that relate more generally to the attitude of national political parties and governments towards public participation in large-scale projects. In the present context characterized by the energy transition and the implementation of Next Generation EU and the Green Deal, the national political and administrative framework and the way national actors go about planning infrastructure are highly relevant, not only to the "operational capacity" needed to accomplish defined targets, but also to the "analytical" and "political" capacity that is required to tackle complex new problems and territorial conflicts (Wu et al., 2015). A revived center-periphery cleavage looms over the energy transition, whereby rural, peripheral areas are subjected to hosting onshore wind and solar plants and other strategic infrastructures, the benefits of which will be concentrated in the more energy-intensive cities and industries: innovative, "entrepreneurial" policy-making is required to manage this specific type of mismatch between costs and benefits (Wilson, 1973).

The cases of the high-speed train in Val di Susa and of the nuclear waste deposit in Scanzano are paradigmatic examples of the difficulty in managing the center-periphery conflict between mountain and rural areas and strategic national decision-making. The attitude assumed in the Berlusconi era through the *Legge Obiettivo* was one of quasi-military centralization, as symbolized by the choice of an army general as special commissioner for the nuclear-waste deposit. This approach has certainly given way to a softer rhetoric in later years, when the nuclear issue was redesigned in legislation by including observations, seminars and negotiation, or when the DP was institutionalized as a deliberative tool. However, the rhetorical use of these terms was not matched by an adequate political investment in the substance of participation: extremely limited timeframes, the substantial exclusion of unorganized stakeholders, and the ultimate recourse to central authority are more consistent with the aim of the speedy conclusion of procedures than with the aim of building strong legitimacy and composing territorial conflicts in a sustainable and credible manner. The imprint of technical cabinets on the establishment of DP, and the fact that it was framed in the context of public works (as opposed, for example, to land management, environmental policy, or open government) seem to have contributed to this narrow view and limited long-lasting impact.

The limited impact of the institutionalization of the DP is also proven by the extremely limited public attention that was paid by the media and political actors when it was effectively dismantled. With the exclusion of a rather limited community of practitioners and direct stakeholders, there were no significant reactions. Indeed, the legal institutionalization had not been accompanied by a deeper process of social institutionalization in terms of acceptance and recognition by communities, trade unions, political parties and the media. This, in turn, makes it rather unlikely that a countermovement towards reinstating structured participatory processes will emerge any time soon.

References

Alford, J., & Head, B. W. (2017). Wicked and less wicked problems: A typology and a contingency framework. *Policy and Society, 36*(3), 397–413.

BASE. (2021). *Expert response to the report by the EU Commission's Joint Research Center "Technical assessment of nuclear energy with respect to the 'Do No Significant Harm' criteria in Regulation (EU) 2020/852, the 'Taxonomy Regulation'"*. Bundesamt für die Sicherheit der nuklearen Entsorgung—The Federal Office for the Safety of Nuclear Waste Management.

Bobbio, L. (2004). *A più voci. Amministrazioni pubbliche, imprese, associazioni e cittadini nei processi decisionali inclusivi*. Edizioni Scientifiche Italiane.

Brown, B., & Spiegel, S. J. (2019). Coal, climate justice, and the cultural politics of energy transition. *Global Environmental Politics, 19*(2), 149–168.

Brunnengräber, A., & Di Nucci, M. R. (2019). *Conflicts, participation and acceptability in nuclear waste governance. An international comparison* (Vol. 3, 1st ed.). Springer VS.

Brunnengräber, A., Di Nucci, M. R., Losada, A. M. I., Mez, L., & Schreurs, M. A. (2015). *Nuclear waste governance. An international comparison*. Springer VS.

Brunnengräber, A., Di Nucci, M. R., Losada, A. M. I., Mez, L., & Schreurs, M. A. (2018). *Challenges of nuclear waste governance: An international comparison* (Vol. 2, 1st ed.). Springer VS.

Citroni, G. (2010). *Mai più soli! Note sulla democrazia partecipativa*. Bonanno.
Citroni, G. (2024a). Deep rock is more stable than society: The siting of repositories for high-level nuclear waste in Italy, Germany and France. In A. Lippi & T. Tsekos (Eds.), *Policy, design, capacity and the sustainable development goals: Wicked problems in uncertain environments*. Emerald Publishing.
Citroni, G. (2024b). Arene e attori del policy dismantling. La parabola del Dibattito Pubblico in Italia. *Stato e mercato, 131*, 333–361.
Curli, B. (2022). *Il progetto nucleare italiano (1952–1964): Conversazioni con Felice Ippolito*. Rubbettino.
de Ruggieri, R. (2004). Il problema delle scorie radioattive: Il caso di Scanzano Jonico. *Economia della Cultura, 14*(1), 83–92.
Della Porta, D., & Piazza, G. (2008). *Le ragioni del no: Le campagne contro la TAV in Val di Susa e il Ponte sullo Stretto*. Feltrinelli.
El-Showk, S. (2022). Final resting place. *Science, 6583*, 806–810.
European Commission. (2017). *Report from the Commission to the Council and the European Parliament on progress of implementation of Council Directive 2011/70/EURATOM and an inventory of radioactive waste and spent fuel present in the Community's territory and the future prospects*. European Commission.
EU-TEG. (2020). *Taxonomy report: Technical annex. Updated methodology & updated technical screening criteria*. EU Technical Expert Group on Sustainable Finance.
EU-TEG. (2020). *Technical report. Taxonomy: Final report of the Technical Expert Group on Sustainable Finance*. EU Technical Expert Group on Sustainable Finance.
Fischer, F. (1993). Citizen participation and the democratization of policy expertise: From theoretical inquiry to practical cases. *Policy Sciences, 26*(3), 165–187.
Fischer, F. (1999). Technological deliberation in a democratic society: The case for participatory inquiry. *Science and Public Policy, 26*(5), 294–302.
Fouquet, D. (2022). The healing force of renewables calls for a nuclear free taxonomy in times of aggression. *Renewable Energy Law and Policy Review, 10*(3–4), 1–3.
Giliberto, J. (2021). Svelata la mappa del deposito nucleare. Da Nord a Sud, ecco le zone idonee. *Il Sole 24 Ore* (05.01).
Head, B. W. (2019). Forty years of wicked problems literature: Forging closer links to policy studies. *Policy and Society, 38*(2), 180–197.
Howlett, M., Mukherjee, I., & Woo, J. J. (2015). From tools to toolkits in policy design studies: The new design orientation towards policy formulation research. *Policy & Politics, 43*(2), 291–311.
JRC. (2021). Technical assessment of nuclear energy with respect to the 'do no significant harm' criteria of regulation (EU) 2020/852 ('Taxonomy Regulation'). In *JRC science for policy report*. Joint Research Center—European Commission/European Atomic Energy Community.
Koppenjan, J. F. M., & Klijn, E.-H. (2004). *Managing uncertainties in networks: A network approach to problem solving and decision making*. Routledge.
Kühne, O., Parush, D., Shmueli, D., & Jenal, C. (2022). Conflicted energy transition—Conception of a theoretical framework for its investigation. *Land, 11*(1), 116.
Leonardi, E. (2013). Foucault in the Susa Valley: The No TAV movement and struggles for subjectification. *Capitalism Nature Socialism, 24*(2), 27–40.
Levin, K., Cashore, B., Bernstein, S., & Auld, G. (2012). Overcoming the tragedy of super wicked problems: Constraining our future selves to ameliorate global climate change. *Policy Sciences, 45*(2), 123–152.
Lippi, A., & Tsekos, T. (2024). *Policy, design, capacity and the sustainable development goals: Wicked problems in uncertain environments*. Emerald Publishing.
NEA, & OECD. (2017). Communication on the safety case for a deep geological repository. In *Radioactive waste management*. Nuclear Energy Agency/Organisation for Economic Co-operation and Development.
Nucci, D., & Rosaria, M. (2006). The nuclear power option in the Italian energy policy. *Energy & Environment, 17*(3), 341–357.

Nucci, D., & Rosaria, M. (2015). Breaking the stalemate. The challenge of nuclear waste governance in Italy. In A. Brunnengräber, M. R. Di Nucci, A. M. I. Losada, L. Mez, & M. A. Schreurs (Eds.), *Nuclear waste governance. An international comparison* (pp. 300–322). Springer VS.
Rein, M., & Schön, D. (1996). Frame-critical policy analysis and frame-reflective policy practice. *Knowledge and Policy, 9*(1), 85–104.
Risoluti, P. (2014). *Il deposito italiano delle scorie radioattive: 18 anni di tentativi*. Armando Editore.
Rittel, H. W. J., & Webber, M. M. (1973). Dilemmas in a general theory of planning. *Policy Sciences, 4*(2), 155–169.
SCHEER. (2021). *SCHEER review of the JRC report on Technical assessment of nuclear energy with respect to the 'do no significant harm' criteria of Regulation (EU) 2020/852 ('Taxonomy Regulation')*. SCHEER—EU Scientific Committee on Health, Environmental and Emerging Risks.
SOGIN. (2003). *Deposito nazionale centralizzato per i rifiuti radioattivi*. Studio per la localizzazione di un sito di deposito. SOGIN Società Gestione Impianti Nucleari.
Sovacool, B. K. (2021). Who are the victims of low-carbon transitions? Towards a political ecology of climate change mitigation. *Energy Research & Social Science, 73*, 101916.
Stagl, S. (2020). *Does nuclear power comply with the DNSH criteria of the EU taxonomy for sustainable activities? A literature review*. BMK—Bundesministerium für Klimaschutz, Umwelt, Energie, Mobilität, Innovation und Technologie, Austrian Federal Ministry for Climate Action, Environment, Energy, Mobility, Innovation and Technology.
UNECE. (2020). The role of nuclear energy in sustainable development—Entry pathways. In *Draft report: Application of UNFC and UNRMS*. United Nations Economic Commission for Europe (UNECE).
van Bueren, E. M., Klijn, E.-H., & Koppenjan, J. F. M. (2003). Dealing with wicked problems in networks: Analyzing an environmental debate from a network perspective. *Journal of Public Administration Research and Theory, 13*(2), 193–212.
Wilson, J. Q. (1973). *Political organizations*. Basic Books.
Wu, X., Ramesh, M., & Howlett, M. (2015). Policy capacity: A conceptual framework for understanding policy competences and capabilities. *Policy and Society, 34*(3–4), 165–171.
Zeigermann, U., & Ettelt, S. (2023). Spanning the boundaries between policy, politics and science to solve wicked problems: Policy pilots, deliberation fora and policy labs. *Sustainability Science, 18*(2), 809–821.
Zinn, D. L. (2007a). Il caso di Scanzano: La ragione di stato e le ragioni di una ribellione. *Quaderni di Sociologia, 44*, 151–174.
Zinn, D. L. (2007b). I Quindici Giorni di Scanzano: Identity and social protest in the New South. *Journal of Modern Italian Studies, 12*(2), 189–206.

Chapter 9
Local Participation in Large-Scale Projects: The Various Ways of Influencing the Decision-Making Process in Switzerland

Erika Schläppi and Kelly Bishop

Abstract Large-scale projects typically address national or regional needs rather than local interests. These projects include public infrastructure for transport, energy, or large public facilities but may also be initiated by private stakeholders such as for industrial or tourist purposes. Switzerland's federal system involves multiple levels of authorities taking decisions in various phases of realizing projects such as in the design, in planning and implementation, or around public funding. The legal framework around spatial planning, public funding and construction permits creates arenas for local interests to be taken up at all stages of a large-scale project. The chapter aims to highlight how local participatory processes are shaped by national and cantonal frameworks and what arenas and processes exist for local interests to influence the decision-making on large-scale projects in Switzerland. The chapter concludes that in Switzerland local interests are not only playing a role in local governance processes but also regularly feed into political processes at higher levels. The participatory processes are perceived as relatively successful in bringing in new facts and clarity about the varying views and positions of different stakeholders, including those of locals, and allow for a more solid balancing of interests by the decision-makers at all levels.

Keywords Participation · Large-scale projects · Spatial planning · Infrastructure · Public funds · Local decision-making

9.1 Introduction

Large-scale projects are usually not initiated by local authorities to serve local interests and needs. They are shaped in a national, cantonal or at least regional logic—beyond the perspective of one municipality—to respond to identified public needs

E. Schläppi (✉) · K. Bishop
Ximpulse GmbH, Bern, Switzerland
e-mail: es@ximpulse.ch

K. Kössler, E. Schläppi (eds.), *Citizen Participation in Local Governance*, Local and Urban Governance, https://doi.org/10.1007/978-3-031-99824-9_9

and serve the interests of the larger constituency, such as building infrastructure for public transport (e.g. railroads, roads), energy production and distribution, big hospitals or universities. In other cases, large-scale projects are initiated by private stakeholders with the aim of, for example, constructing an industrial plant or a tourist infrastructure, based on a concession (a legal entitlement to use a public asset granted by a public authority), or just serving private economic interests, affecting the economic and social development interests of the region.

In Switzerland's federal system, the planning and the realization of large-scale projects involve decisions of public authorities at many levels and in different phases. The laws and regulations set the legal frame, and the spatial planning framework must be adequate and accommodate the project. Public funding must be ensured for the planning and implementation of public projects. The building permits must be issued. Finally, the construction phase must ensure its conformity with the legal and planning framework.

In the unique Swiss semi-direct democracy, the executive bodies, the parliaments, and the voters have specific roles in decision-making—contrary to the more common system of representative democracy where voters are limited to elect their representatives (Linder & Sean, 2017, 295). From the perspective of citizen participation, the local arena is important but not the only significant area of influence on the decision-making process within the Swiss system. The scope of local participatory processes is shaped by national and cantonal law and many decisions are not made locally. From the perspective of bringing in local interests in cantonal or federal decision-making processes, the active participation of municipalities is most relevant.

This chapter briefly sketches the variety of arenas and processes where local interests can come into play around decisions on large-scale projects in Switzerland, with some anecdotal examples.

9.2 Participation in Shaping Relevant Laws and Regulations

Large-scale projects are often based on national and cantonal needs and interests and framed by federal and cantonal legislation. For example, the road and railroad infrastructure, the use of water resources, and the energy supply is shaped by federal and cantonal laws. Thus, federal and cantonal laws set the scene for balancing different interests by providing rules on which interests are to be taken into account and how they are to be weighed. The cantonal laws shape the competences of local authorities, and sometimes even the distribution of roles between the local protagonists—between the local executive and the voters or local parliaments. Where there is no leeway and scope for local decision-makers, there might also be limited space for effective local participatory mechanisms.

On the other hand, local interests do find their way into the Swiss legislative processes. At all levels, the Swiss political system is based on multi-party governments, thus working towards consent and compromise. The system and its protagonists tend to identify and accommodate the views and interests of actors perceived as powerful in the political process as early as possible, with the aim of avoiding costs, minimizing risks and delays due to a possible veto vote against new or revised laws (Linder & Sean, 2017, 299). Thus, consultation processes on legislative proposals are common practice at all levels at an early stage, although with different set-ups and different participants. Federal and cantonal law reforms are then discussed and decided upon in the respective parliaments where different private, public, national, cantonal and local interests are represented and actively involved.

The recent revision of the Federal Spatial Planning Act[1] exemplifies how representative and direct democracy, and formal and informal participatory mechanisms are interlinked. The Federal Parliament has adopted in December 2023 a revised version of the Act after extensive and contested debates in both chambers over five years. The discussion was initiated by a popular initiative proposing to put a constitutional amendment to a popular vote, to strictly separate building zones from non-building zones and protect the non-building zones from construction activities.[2] The initiative was submitted by a consortium of various civil society organizations working for protecting the environment and nature conservation. The proposed constitutional amendment was expected to impact the possibility of building, for example, new roads, public transport or ski infrastructure in zones that are not set for construction. The new provisions in the revised Spatial Planning Act adopted by the parliament regulate construction outside the building zone, and strengthen the separation of building zones and non-building zones. However, contrary to the initiative's text, the new provision set the principle that land uses that are not tied to a specific zone should be possible anywhere in the country. This new version of the Spatial Planning Act was subject to an optional referendum—and citizens (organized by political parties and/or specific interest groups) could have asked for a popular vote. However, in this case, it seems that the initiating organizations were satisfied with the proposal and did not collect signatures to ask for a referendum. The popular initiative was withdrawn and not put to popular vote. The initiators argued that the new provisions of the Spatial Planning Act took up their main issues of concern and they agreed with the compromise.

9.3 Participation in Spatial Planning

The spatial planning framework is most relevant for decisions on construction projects. In many cases, public decisions are needed to adapt the spatial planning framework to the specific land use foreseen by a big infrastructure project. In Switzerland, the competences for spatial planning are shared between the national (federal),

[1] Systematic Compilation of Federal Legislation SR 700.

[2] https://www.landschaftsinitiative.ch/ (visited 28-11-2023).

cantonal and local levels. The Federal Act on Spatial Planning sets the principles and rules for land use and zoning for the cantonal planning authorities, including the principles for balancing the different public interests in land use. In addition to the general principles framing spatial planning, the federal authorities are also responsible for drawing up thematic policies and sectoral plans and ensuring that they are compatible with the spatial planning. They also work closely with the cantons, "informing them in good time of its policies, sectoral plans and building projects" (Article 13 Federal Spatial Planning Act). The purpose of thematic policies and sectoral plans (e.g. on traffic, transmission lines, deep geological repositories or military) is to ensure spatial coordination with other uses and to safeguard space for the various projects, by identifying the needs and by roughly determining their location or route. Where the federal authorities have the competence to build (and plan), for example in the case of national roads, the federal law foresees objection and complaint procedures, inviting the cantons, the municipalities, individuals and private organizations whose rights or duties are at stake to express their views.

According to the Spatial Planning Act, the main cantonal planning instrument is the structure plan (*Richtplan*), which is binding for local authorities. The structure plan is the hub for controlling spatial development and coordinating spatially effective planning and projects across all levels of government and subject areas. The cantonal structure plan is expected to bring together the interests of the planning authorities of the communes, the cantonal and federal government, and also incorporate the requirements of the various sectoral policies that are in force (e.g. agriculture, economic development, environmental policy). Weighing up and assessing the interests of land use is therefore one of the central tasks of the cantonal structure plan.[3] Projects with a significant impact on space and the environment must be included in the cantonal structure plans (Article 8(2) Federal Spatial Planning Act). The Federal Spatial Planning Act enshrines the principle of information and adequate participation in the planning process (Article 4 Federal Spatial Planning Act). The German terminology of *Mitwirkung* makes clear that this kind of participation is expected to be more than passive information but involves active involvement of participants (Hoffmann, 2021).

Cantonal rules differ with regard to the spatial planning regulations as well as the competence of municipalities in spatial planning. In the canton of Berne, the cantonal structure plan is perceived as a management instrument of the cantonal government, while regional conferences (consisting of municipalities in a certain geographical area) have duties and rights in the process of developing regional structure plans. Formal parliamentary participation is not foreseen. However, planning authorities must provide information to the public as early as possible. Public participation must be granted for the enactment, non-minor amendment and repeal of structure plans, building regulations and superstructure regulations, in different formats depending on the object and content of the proposal. The minutes of

[3] See also Schweizerische Kantonsplanerkonferenz, Broschüre Kantonaler Richtplan, 11, www.espacesuisse.ch (visited 23-5-2024).

hearings and summary reports of the views expressed are public (Article 58 of the Bernese Building Law).[4]

Informal discussions and political debates on large-scale investments often take place around the revisions of the structure plans. For example, in the recent formal consultation procedure to revise the cantonal structure plan of Berne to accommodate a project to expand the reservoir and construct a new hydropower plant in the Grimsel region, a variety of stakeholders raised their voice, including the regional conferences (consisting of the municipalities of a certain geographical area), individual municipalities, a neighboring canton, political parties, civil society organizations, and individual citizens. The question of how a municipality should position itself in this process is often hotly debated among local residents, providing an opportunity for individual citizens and local interest groups to raise their voice. The various amendment proposals to the structure plan are discussed in the consultation report by the cantonal government, explaining in detail why proposals are accepted or rejected by the planning authorities.[5] In this case, the consultation process and its results were widely discussed in public media, and political parties, as well as organizations, published their positions and statements.

In the framework of the cantonal structure plan and cantonal regulations and concepts, Bernese municipalities are responsible for the utilization plans (that specify the land use for each plot) and the superstructure regulations (*Überbauungsordnung*). However, the cantonal authorities can decide at cantonal level on superstructure and building regulations "to safeguard cantonal or regional interests", which can be the case of large-scale infrastructure projects (Article 102 of the Bernese Building Law). The cantonal law explicitly mentions this possibility for cantonal building regulations on a series of topics, such as public works and transportation facilities, industrial zones, landfill and material extraction sites, measures relating to the townscape, landscape and shoreline design, recreational areas, zones for public use, zones for sports and leisure facilities, green zones and protected areas.

With regard to spatial planning processes, information and formal consultation with the local residents are mandatory. Municipalities can even go beyond the cantonal rules allowing citizens and interested groups to raise objections and make suggestions in the planning process, and involve the residents of a certain neighborhood in the finding of adequate solutions in an early planning phase (Article 58 of the Bernese Building Law). When a first proposal is drafted, it is submitted to the cantonal authorities for a preliminary examination to check the conformity of the draft plan or regulations with cantonal and national law. Then, the municipality's proposal is made public. By analogy to the rules regarding construction permits, objections may be raised by residents that are "directly affected" by the proposal "in their own interests worthy of protection." Equally, private associations with

[4] Bernese Compilation of Legislation BSG 721.0.

[5] Richtplan Kanton Bern Mitwirkungsbericht Richtplananpassungen Trift/Grimsel/Oberaar, 28. November 2022, https://www.be.ch/de/start/dienstleistungen/medien/medienmitteilungen.html?newsID=d62a2154-049d-4404-ad24-140a75ac58de (visited 23-05-2024).

“non-material purposes” can also raise objections, but only in areas that have been the subject of their statutory purpose for at least ten years. While the elected municipal council (the executive) prepares the various draft proposals and leads the objection procedures, the final decision on the land use zoning and regulations is taken by the voters themselves in the municipal assembly or—where a municipal parliament exists—by the local parliament, mostly with the possibility of an optional referendum (Article 66 of the Bernese Building Law).

If a specific infrastructure project does not fit the municipal land use plan or the building regulations, the municipality may revise the plans and regulations to accommodate the project—in the frame of the national and cantonal structure and sectoral plans and in accordance with the above-mentioned participatory procedure, which usually takes time. Initiators of projects often invest considerable means and time in information and informal hearings from the beginning of their project planning to convince local residents that the project is in their interest—or at least compatible with their interests. They often adapt their proposals according to informal objections made and compromise on various issues that are raised by local residents. In the case of the regional railroad company BLS, a draft project for a new facility for maintenance and repair of trains was withdrawn in 2022 after many years of planning, due to the persisting resistance of local residents and environmental organizations. The local media titled its article on the issue with: “They brought the big BLS to its knees.”[6]

On the other hand, a big investment in a new tourism infrastructure, with two new ropeways in the valley of Grindelwald, was eventually successfully implemented, despite considerable resistance of local residents and environmental protection associations over many years. The project owner, a private railroad company, organized numerous round tables with authorities, federal and cantonal agencies and voters in the mountain communities and municipalities. In the municipal assembly, which finally approved the revised municipal plan in 2014, more local citizens gathered than ever before, and the discussions took several hours. The Wärgistal mountain community, a common land community which had to agree with selling the right to cross their land to the company, first rejected the project in 2014, before approving it in a second vote in 2015. The subsequent procedure for approving the detailed project had to deal with many objections and repeals, and getting the construction permits took almost 3 years. The new cableways were inaugurated in 2020—more than 10 years after the first public discussion.[7] The costs for the planning phase are estimated at 12 million CHF.

Importantly, within the given cantonal legal frame, the municipalities/communes can decide autonomously within their range of competence (Article 50 of the Swiss

---

[6] https://www.derbund.ch/sie-zwangen-die-grosse-bls-in-die-knie-923095871303 (visited 1-12-2023); https://www.bls.ch/de/unternehmen/medien/medienmitteilungen/2022/02-24-mm-planungsstopp-chliforst-nord (visited 1-12-2023).

[7] https://www.jungfrau.ch/de-ch/jungfraujoch-top-of-europe/v-bahn/ (visited 1-12-2023); Beat Kohler, Der lange Weg vom Y über V zum Bau, Jungfrauzeitung, 15.6.2018, https://www.jungfrauzeitung.ch/artikel/164023/ (visited 3-12-2023).

Constitution). The cantonal authorities do not have any right to overrule a municipal decision against an infrastructure project even if this serves cantonal interests. And in case cantonal authorities would do so, municipalities can challenge such decisions because municipalities are entitled to submit allegations of violations of autonomy to the Federal Supreme Court (Article 189(1)(e) of the Swiss Constitution), which refers to the cantonal laws to define the scope of the autonomy.

9.4 Participation in the Shaping of Infrastructure Programs

Public infrastructure projects are usually financed, at least partially, with public funds from the federal, cantonal or municipal budgets, depending on the distribution of competences. An example of close cooperation in and shared funding of infrastructure investment projects are the agglomeration programs which are drawn up by the cantons and municipalities (according to their rules and participatory procedures), and then examined and evaluated by the federal government. In the current fourth generation of the program, projects are co-funded by the federal level if they contribute to solving traffic problems, have a very good cost-benefit ratio and are ready for implementation. The cantons and municipalities then implement the individual projects on the basis of performance and financing agreements with the federal government.

National roads and railroads are in the competence of the federal level, and decisions on the pluri-annual commitments of funds for the development of national roads and railroads are discussed and taken by the federal parliament. Most often, specific cantonal and regional or even local interests are eagerly defended by parliamentarians representing their (local) constituency. In general, before submitting their proposals to the parliament, the federal government invites interested stakeholders to give their comments in a standardized consultation process based on federal law. The consultation procedure is applied for all federal projects of considerable political, financial, economic, ecological, social or cultural significance, to examine their factual accuracy, suitability for implementation and acceptance. For this purpose, the proposal is submitted to the cantons, the parties represented in the Federal Assembly, the umbrella organizations of the rural municipalities, the cities and mountain regions (which are promoted by specific federal investments), the umbrella organizations of the business community and other interested parties (Moeckli, 2017, 123; Ladner, 2019a, 2019b). In the case of the national road development program, for example, stakeholders and interest groups of different kinds, defending a diversity of public interests, and individuals have expressed their opinion on the pluri-annual programs, and the report of the consultation process explains in detail which arguments have been taken up or rejected in the revised proposal.[8] In

[8] Botschaft des Bundesrates vom 22. Februar 2022 zum Zahlungsrahmen Nationalstrassen 2024-2027, zum Ausbauschritt 2023 für die Nationalstrassen, zum Verpflichtungskredit und zur Änderung des Bundesbeschlusses über das Nationalstrassennetz, BBl 23.032, https://www.fedlex.admin.ch/eli/fga/2023/865/de (visited 15-8-2025).

addition, the debate and decision about the annual budget provides another opportunity for parliamentarians to influence the funding decisions of the executive.

9.5 Participation in Decisions on Public Funding

At the federal level there is no participatory mechanism to challenge funding decisions in the field of federal competence, and the federal parliament decides on the funding. But in most cantons, spending decisions above a certain threshold are submitted to an (optional) referendum. In the canton of Berne, for example, spending decisions for individual cantonal road projects that are beyond two million CHF, are submitted to the optional referendum, meaning that 10,000 signatures of persons entitled to vote and domiciled in the canton can ask for putting such decisions to a cantonal vote (Article 62 of the Bernese Constitution).

In the case of a widely discussed cantonal road project in the municipality of Aarwangen, there was a cantonal vote on the expenses for project planning in 2017, which was approved by 60.1% of the cantonal voters. The project was then elaborated and entered a public consultation process in 2020. In 2022, the road project plan was approved by the cantonal directorate responsible for building and transport, and several appeals against this decision are still pending. In the meantime, the cantonal expenses for construction have been approved by the cantonal parliament and then submitted to a cantonal vote in 2023. The cantonal result of the vote was narrowly positive (51.6% voting yes), with a low voter turnout: only 30.4% of the cantonal residents entitled to vote did effectively vote. In the municipality of Aarwangen, a clear majority of voters said yes (70.6%), with a relatively high voter turnout (57%), while the regional results were still positive but to a lesser extent (56%).[9]

Over all the years of preparation, the road project had been hotly debated in the municipality as well as in the region. A local and regional committee consisting of representatives from local enterprises, some political parties, municipalities of the concerned area, and public personalities promoted the project. They argued that it would end local congestion, improve local quality of life and increase road safety. Regional interests would be best served by the new road, and environmental protection had been taken into account. In the committee's view, the regional economic benefits would be great.[10] On the other hand, a variety of organizations, including farmers and environmentalists, campaigned against the project. They argued that the destruction of farmland and protected nature areas should be avoided, and they questioned the regional benefits of the project.[11] In their campaign they used

[9] https://www.bewas.sites.be.ch/2023/2023-03-12/ABSTIMMUNG/ergebnisse-abstimmung-de.html (visited 31-11-2023).

[10] https://verkehrssanierungen-ja.ch/verkehrssanierung-aarwangen/ (visited 31-11-2023).

[11] https://www.naturstattbeton.ch/ (visited 31-11-2023).

different arenas and means to mobilize political support, including events with dunning fires, media campaigns, or distributing earth and planting seeds in front of the cantonal parliament. After their defeat in the cantonal vote, they asserted that they would continue their opposition and challenge the lawfulness of the project in the still pending legal review. Many association members had lodged an objection to the road plan and later an appeal to the cantonal government.

This example generally shows that it is hard to say what local interests are—and who is a legitimate representative to bring them up. Local interests are often ambiguous and always heterogenous, conflicting or coinciding with the local interests of neighbors, the wider region or even national interest groups and, changing according to the chosen geographical parameters. It is an illusion to think that participatory processes per se are bringing the "right" answer to a conflict of interests—they can just aspire to make various views and interests more visible and evaluate the public support for the proposed solutions.

9.6 Participation in the Decision on the Building Permits

Large-scale infrastructure projects—like all construction projects—must have a building permit, according to cantonal law. For example, the project for the construction of a new cantonal road (as in the example above) is approved by the competent cantonal department, with the possibility of appeal to the cantonal government. However, in most construction projects, the municipalities are responsible for the permitting procedure.

The granting of individual permits is not subject to participatory decision-making. However, permitting decisions are subject to objection and complaint procedures that aim to protect the rights and interests of neighbors or other persons particularly affected by the construction project. This is about granting the right to be heard in a process where one's rights are at stake, not about participating in political decisions on the appropriateness of the project. In the case of large-scale projects, any application for a permit is published. As already mentioned for the objections to planning proposals, persons have the right to raise objections, if they are "directly affected by the construction project in their own interests worthy of protection" (Article 35(2)a) of the Bernese Building Law). Equally, private associations with "non-material purposes" can raise objections to the application but they can only raise arguments in areas that have been the subject of their statutory purpose for at least 10 years (Article 35c(3) of the Bernese Building Law). For objectors, the objection procedure is free of charge. The decision is then taken by the construction authorities. Decisions can be contested by lodging a building appeal to the cantonal authorities, by the applicant, the objectors, as well as the responsible municipal authority.

More general interests of environmental protection are addressed by the mechanism of environmental impact assessment that is enshrined in the Federal Act on the Protection of the Environment (Systematic Compilation of Federal Legislation SR

814.01). Before deciding on the planning, construction or modification of installations, an authority must assess their impact on the environment at the earliest possible stage. The environmental impact assessment must be carried out for installations that may significantly impact environmental areas. Any person who wishes to plan, construct, or modify an installation subject to an environmental impact assessment must submit an environmental impact report to the competent authority. The environmental protection agencies assess the preliminary investigation and the report and propose the required measures to the competent decision-making authority. The reports are publicly accessible (Articles 10a-10d Federal Act on the Protection of the Environment). These reports are often an important source of information and arguments for local opponents of such projects and are also useful in the political debate or in complaint procedures.

Environmental protection organizations have the right to appeal against rulings of the cantonal or federal authorities on projects for which an environmental impact assessment is required—this is certainly the case for many large-scale infrastructure projects. The right of appeal is only granted to organizations that work on a national basis—local activist groups are not able to use this right directly, except when allying with a national organization (Article 55 Federal Act on the Protection of the Environment). In addition, the environmental protection organizations are only accepted for complaints in "legal fields that have been subject to their statutory purpose for a minimum of 10 years" (Article 55(2) Federal Act on the Protection of the Environment, a formulation that was taken up by the Bernese Building Law as mentioned). In reality, citizens and local activists often closely cooperate with these associations and feed into these processes as well. The complaint mechanism is used relatively often: In 2024, 65 complaint procedures were closed, and 28 complaints were fully or partly successful.[12]

In terms of protecting "heritage landscapes and sites of local character, historical sites, and natural and cultural monuments", the federal authorities, the federal enterprises, and the cantons have a series of duties. They must ensure that landscapes, sites, and monuments are carefully managed and, where there is an overriding public interest, preserved undiminished. Authorities have to comply by suitably designing and maintaining their own buildings and installations, or by foregoing their construction altogether, by imposing conditions or requirements on the issue of licenses and authorizations, or refusing to issue them, and, finally, by restricting or refusing subsidies (Article 3 Federal Act on the Protection of Nature and Cultural Heritage; Systematic Compilation of Federal Legislation SR 451). Here again, organizations "concerned with nature protection, cultural heritage protection, monument preservation or related objectives" that are active throughout Switzerland have a right to appeal against cantonal and federal decisions, including on construction permits. The right to appeal is also granted to municipalities who can bring in the perspective of local interests.

[12] https://www.bafu.admin.ch/bafu/de/home/themen/recht/verbandsbeschwerderecht/statistik-und-evaluation-des-verbandsbeschwerderechts.html (visited 15-8-2025).

As mentioned in the case of the cantonal road project in Aarwangen, appeal procedures are often used to challenge projects not only from the perspective of legally protected private interests of neighbors but also for bringing in different views of public interests. Even if the complaints will be rejected in the end by the final instance authority, the delay in the construction process may be great and costly for the project owners. In many cases, they are eager to avoid these costs and show willingness to compromise, for example by negotiating and giving-in on some suggestions made by the complainants to make them withdraw the complaint. On the other hand, contrary to the objection procedure, the complaint procedures bear a considerable financial risk for complainers, as they are charged for the procedural costs in case of a negative outcome, and the costs for legal representation is often high, and increases with the complexity of the project at stake.

9.7 Participation in Monitoring the Implementation of a Project

It is often said that in Switzerland, participatory decision-making takes a long time but the gain is that the final decision is accepted, even by the groups and individuals whose opinions did not prevail. Participatory processes are expected to increase the legitimacy and credibility of a decision, and the approved projects tend to be less challenged in the implementation phase, for example, by informal opposition and resistance in "invented" spaces of protest. However, the example of "Westast Biel" shows the opposite: The road project for expanding the A5 national highways had been formally approved and was ready for implementation but in the end formally halted after many years of planning, many popular manifestations and actions of opposing residents, lengthy discussions, and several round tables.[13]

Once the project is approved, the municipal building police is responsible for taking necessary measures to supervise the compliance with the building regulations and the conditions and requirements of the building permit, in the construction phase and beyond. Neighbors or private associations with non-material purposes (environmental organizations, nature protection, or cultural heritage protection) that report shortcomings in the implementation of the project have the right to be constituted as a party in the proceedings to restore the lawful situation. In particular, if they constitute themselves as a party, they have the right to complain against any decision taken (Articles 45 and 46 of the Bernese Building Law). Environmental protection organizations often monitor the implementation of important projects and use their right to report misconducts by project owners. For example, in the case of the preparation of a World Cup ski slope on the glacier in Zermatt in 2023, several associations had reported that the work went beyond the building permit, and

[13] For the action taken see the website of the opponents, https://westast.ch/wordpress/facts/ (visited 2-12-2023).

the competent authorities immediately stopped the construction work, until the respect of the permit conditions was ensured.[14]

9.8 Conclusions: Potential and Challenges of Swiss Participatory Procedures

The previous sections have shown that in Switzerland a variety of participation procedures can be relevant in developing large-scale projects. More generally, the Swiss system of semi-direct democracy involves citizens at many levels, representing a political culture based on the importance of political compromise and power-sharing. With the widely used instrument of referenda, voters might have the last word in decision-making in many cases—so project initiators have some interest to factor in public opinion from the beginning.

The various procedures have different purposes and goals. In many cases, they serve the purpose of improving the factual basis for decision-making and assess the political opportunity of the decision at stake. The consultation and involvement procedures on the legal and planning framework are motivated by the idea of collecting basic information on the facts and the various (possibly conflicting) interests at stake, of possible alternatives to the chosen solutions, and of political support for the proposals. In fact, this helps the authorities assess the facts correctly and evaluate the prospects of success of their proposal (André et al., 2018). In general, the administrations are seen as relatively open to new insights and reflection, with less hierarchical attitudes and bureaucratic reflexes of resistance than in other European countries. This is at least partly due to the particularities of Swiss semi-direct democracy which has helped build a relatively high confidence and trust of the citizens in public authorities (Ladner, 2019a, 2019b).

While the trend to participatory procedures has become part of Swiss political culture, the idea of avoiding a referendum influences the assessment of the importance of expressed views, particularly in those cases where referenda are legally possible (Linder & Sean, 2017, 368) The opinion of political parties or groups that are well-organized, motivated and assessed as capable of organizing a referendum, will be taken more seriously than, for example, local interest groups which are not allied with cantonal or regional forces. As the governments (at national, cantonal and municipal levels) consist most often of representatives of different political parties, the consultation procedures may also help build a basis for the necessary compromise among the political decision-makers, putting a variety of interests on the table of the authorities from the beginning. The objection procedures to planning decisions follow the same logic, while objection procedures in construction permitting serve the objective of avoiding lengthy judicial procedures against the decision that might be initiated by neighbors or other specifically impacted parties and groups of interests. In the implementing phase of the project where the construction

[14] https://mountainwilderness.ch/bagger-auf-dem-gletscher-was-ist-da-los/ (visited 21-5-2024).

is taking place, the right to be constituted as a party to the proceedings and to have corresponding participatory rights is particularly important for associations that are committed to environmental protection or the conservation of nature or cultural heritage. These rights give them a certain weight in their monitoring of the construction phase which they often use, mobilizing public opinion in case of misconduct, or by formally reporting to the construction police authorities. In this sense, the participatory processes have an important accountability purpose.

Another question is who participates in the various consultation procedures. Large-scale projects are characterized by the fact that important decisions are taken at the cantonal level or even at the federal level (e.g. for the planning of national roads). However, the concrete impact of the decision, either positive or negative, is predominantly local. In the semi-direct democracy of Switzerland, participatory processes are taking place at all levels, legitimizing the cantonal and federal decision-making as well as the decisions at the local level. Thus, participation strengthens the legitimacy of cantonal and federal decisions on large-scale infrastructure, and decisions coming out of a participatory process might be more difficult to challenge at local level than purely administrative decisions. For cantonal projects (such as the road project in Aarwangen) or cantonal zoning decisions, the voices of the residents of the project location formally have the same weight as other cantonal residents, although they may make their voices heard in the political debate more prominently than residents from other regions. On the other hand, cantonal and regional interest groups, or well-organized environmental protection associations may have more weight and mobilization potential in cantonal processes than in local decision-making, where local residents might focus on defending their own personal interests in favor or against the plan or project at stake. Political science analysis confirms that the referendum system favors the building and strengthening of political parties and interest groups and their role in political decision-making (Vatter, 2020, 382).

Consultation procedures regarding planning decisions include the participation of all residents within the geographical scope, and local planning decisions are often taken by the local parliament, at local assembly and/or at the ballot box. When it comes to the individual construction permits, the participation to objection and complaint procedures requires a specifically protected individual interest, or the involvement of an association with "non-material" purpose and a proven long-term commitment to specific public interests such as environmental protection, nature or cultural heritage preservation.

It is important to keep in mind that local interests are not homogenous. As the examples show, local residents are not per se against a large-scale project. They may often also benefit considerably from a project, for example, in the case of economic benefits from a new touristic facility bringing new job opportunities, or in the case of a local road construction project reducing the risk of traffic jams, or even due to the expectations of higher tax income for the municipality. While the risk of an environmentally negative impact in terms of reduction of the local quality of life will motivate some residents to oppose the project, others will weigh local interests differently and be in favor of such projects.

A key aspect of participation is the question of who really participates in such "invited" spaces. The voting processes at the federal, cantonal, and municipal level generally allows only adult Swiss citizens to vote, formally excluding young people as well as more than one-quarter of Swiss residents who do not have a Swiss passport.[15] Particularly the younger generations are inventing their own ways of expressing their political views. And the right to participate is not used by all citizens on an equal footing. The empirical surveys of Swiss voting behavior shows that the system of semi-direct democracy does not guarantee that all groups are equally participating. Socially disadvantaged groups, less educated people, women and youth are participating less in popular votes and elections (Vatter, 2020, 554), with a trend of growing inequalities when complex issues or complicated procedures are at stake (Linder & Sean, 2017, 413). This might be even more true for more engaging participatory processes such as consultations and objection processes. In the case of a referendum relating to the public funding of a large-scale project, the complexity might not be as challenging as in the case of the objection procedure to cantonal structure plans where specific knowhow is needed to understand the issues at stake and make reasonable inputs.

It remains to be noted that, according to the views of several Swiss political scientists, the generally low voter turnout in elections and popular votes in Switzerland must be related to the high number of opportunities to participate in public decision-making and should not necessarily be considered as a sign of low quality of democratic processes (Vatter, 2020, 555). Compared to its European neighbors, Switzerland has the highest rates of satisfaction with the political system as well as a very high rate of trust in the government (Freitag, 2014).

More generally, participation comes with a relatively high cost for authorities, project owners, and participants, in terms of time and often also resources. The numerous participation processes require motivated and capable citizens, ready and available to study and digest planning documents, organize around common interests, invest in cooperation and coordination with other citizens and interest groups, participate in hearings, write position papers, take positions and raise their voice in procedural settings that are not always user-friendly. Local decision-making procedures—the municipal votes on zoning, or the objection procedures for construction permits—may be more accessible to local residents—but are not always the most important ones in the decision-making process. The necessary investment of time and resources is not only demanding on local residents defending their individual interests, but also on environmental protection groups that face the challenge of raising funds to invest in professional legal advice and communication, which may require a prioritization of processes that they are taking part in.

The complex participatory processes take time, contributing, together with other factors, to delays in the zoning and permitting processes. This is a key issue that is often discussed in Switzerland. For example, in the case of the cantonal road

[15] Bundesamt für Statistik, Switzerland's population in the year 2022, https://www.bfs.admin.ch/bfs/de/home/statistiken/bevoelkerung.assetdetail.28425364.html (visited 2-12-2023).

construction project in Aarwangen, it was argued that the design of the project is already outdated after the long preparation of over a decade, based on a needs assessment which is no longer accurate and does not consider new insights and strategies on how to manage local traffic congestions. In addition, the cost estimations for public projects might also be outdated requiring the revision of financial planning. For private owners, the costs for investment in long participatory processes are particularly high and often hindering investments in projects even if their necessity is not questioned by a big majority of voters and residents. The planning processes may take several years, and the construction permitting process and the judicial complaint procedures may often take another couple of years. In some cases, a large majority has approved a project in a local referendum, but then the project is delayed for years in a complaint procedure due to the overload of the courts. In the end, this means that an individual complainant does not necessarily have to have good arguments but must have enough money and be persistent in order to actually prevent a project that he/she does not approve of. After all, the impression that the long duration of Swiss procedures is generally hindering innovation has been questioned and even rejected by several surveys and political scientists (Vatter, 2020, 368; Linder & Sean, 2017).

Nevertheless, long procedures can have a serious impact on the quality of participation. Local residents may lose interest and patience due to the long duration or frustrated expectations—as the authorities remain competent in decision-making and will ponder the interests in their way in the end. Participants who are convinced of their own views and expect their voice to prevail are inevitably frustrated and often decide to withdraw from the participatory processes. This might be particularly the case if they feel manipulated by the authorities and the participatory process is seen as confirmation of decisions that are already taken (Drilling, 2021).

A key factor of successful participation in planning processes and decisions on project proposals is accurate information and communication. However, participation does not mean that information is only shared. The legal provisions emphasize the need for public information in the early phases of planning as well as when the project drafts are more concrete. Many authorities perceive information, transparency, and communication as a tool to collect necessary information and gain acceptance for their ideas, and project owners often proactively invest in information campaigns and leaflets, organization of site visits, informal public hearings, and roundtables. However, in practice, accurate information is not always easily accessible for potential participants. It is often communicated in a technical language which is difficult to understand for some. Digesting the information requires time that citizens might not have or are not ready to invest. Increasingly, electronic channels are used for public information, impacting how information is reaching out to different groups of citizens—and tending to privilege access to information for educated elites as well as the younger generations. In any case, as of today, digital communication and social media have become an integral part of the political process in terms of information, for shaping public opinion at all levels—and finally for opening space and news arenas for participation.

As demonstrated, with regard to large-scale projects, the national, cantonal and local arenas of participation are closely interlinked in Switzerland. The specific role of environmental protection organizations, nature preservation and cultural heritage preservation associations and the presence of political parties at all levels contribute to a coordinated use of participatory mechanisms at all levels. To be most effective, the associations play an important role in providing and distributing information on the projects, mobilizing public opinion, complementing the official views from a different perspective of public (environmental or cultural) interests. Together with their political role as potential organizers of referenda, which makes them relatively powerful players in politics, they also create spaces for more informal participation, such as national or local manifestations of different kinds, or public discussions and events. In this sense, the formal participatory processes and informal mechanisms are complementary, to a large extent. Even where spontaneous informal, often local movements to oppose large-scale projects are arising, the authorities often tend to integrate them in more formalized processes aimed at finding compromises around conflicting interests.

To sum up, in Switzerland local interests are not only playing a role in local governance processes but also feed into political processes at higher levels. The variety of participatory processes that are relevant for the planning and construction of large-scale projects involve different stakeholder. The participatory processes are perceived as relatively successful in bringing in new facts and clarity about the views and positions of different stakeholders, including locals, and allow for a solid balancing of interests by the decision-makers. However, to manage the expectations of participants, it must remain clear that the responsibility and accountability for decision-making on planning and construction permits remains with the competent authorities. At the local level, within the legal framework shaped by the federal level and the respective canton, some planning decisions are made by the voters. This enables—but does not guarantee—a public debate on the local issues at stake and increases the legitimacy of the planning decisions.

References

André, D., et al. (2018). In der Planung gehört die Zukunft den kooperativen Verfahren. In *Modellvorhaben, Nachhaltige Raumentwicklung, Lessons learned 2014–2018* (pp. 8–11). Bundesamt für Raumentwicklung.

Drilling, M. (2021). Die (Ohn-)Macht der Partizipation. Collage. *Zeitschrift für Raumentwicklung, 5*, 5–9.

Freitag, M. (2014). Politische Kultur. In P. Knöpfel, Y. Papadopoulos, P. Sciarin, A. Vatter, & S. H. Silja (Eds.), *Handbuch der Schweizer Politik*. Neue Zürcher Zeitung.

Hoffmann, K. (2021). *Kooperative Raumplanung: Handlungsformen und Verfahren*. Sui Generis.

Ladner, A. (2019a). *Der Schweizer Föderalismus im Wandel*. IDHEAP.

Ladner, A. (2019b). The organization and provision of public service. In A. Ladner, N. Soguel, Y. Emery, S. Weerts, & S. Nahrath (Eds.), *Swiss public administration, making the state work successfully* (pp. 21–42). Palgrave Macmillan.

Linder, W., & Sean, S. M. (2017). *Schweizerische Demokratie: Institutionen, Prozesse, Perspektiven* (4th ed.). Verlag Haupt.

Moeckli, S. (2017). *Das politische System der Schweiz verstehen, wie es funktioniert -wer partizipiert—was resultiert*. Kaufmännischer Lehrmittel Verlag.

Vatter, A. (2020). *Das politische System der Schweiz*. Nomos.

Part III
Participatory Budgeting

Chapter 10
A Comparative Overview of Participatory Budgeting in Italy

Mattia Bottino and Martina Trettel

Abstract The last two decades have seen a rapid diffusion of participatory governance in local budgeting. First crafted in Brazil, participatory budgeting (PB) represents one of the most prominent and institutionalized democratic innovations at the local level. Its introduction has been concomitant with the adoption of participatory legislation at the subnational level. This chapter engages in a comparative study of the most recent PB editions in three Italian municipalities, namely Bologna, Caltanissetta, and Malles Venosta. These cases showcase different patterns of development of PB, providing a picture of its pace of consolidation. The presence of strong traditions of municipal self-government, civic associationism, and progressive municipal governments are shown as crucial for the entrenchment of PB into local practices. Regional and local legislation on participation are proven to be key variables for the institutionalization of PB, making its implementation systemic rather than episodic. Notwithstanding the intrinsic differences among the cases (geographic, socio-economic, and political), this chapter emphasizes the exceptional role that PB plays in Italy as one of the most well-established settings of decentralized participatory decision-making. While fostering participation in budgeting processes, PB is conceived by the authors as a tool for expanding the scope of local self-government and fighting democratic disenchantment.

Keywords Participatory budgeting · Participatory democracy · Democratic innovations · Local government · Decentralization

M. Bottino
Dipartimento di Scienze Politiche e Sociali, University of Bologna, Bologna, Italy
e-mail: mattia.bottino3@unibo.it

M. Trettel (✉)
Institute for Comparative Federalism, Eurac Research, Bolzano, Italy
e-mail: martina.trettel@eurac.edu

K. Kössler, E. Schläppi (eds.), *Citizen Participation in Local Governance*, Local and Urban Governance, https://doi.org/10.1007/978-3-031-99824-9_10

10.1 Introduction

Participatory Budgeting (hereinafter PB) stands out as one of the most prominent tools within the realm of "participatory democracy" (Elstub, 2018). Over the past decade, there has been a significant global surge in the adoption of PB, particularly at the local level. Originating in the 1980s in Brazil, PB can be shortly defined as a democratic process in which community members collaboratively determine the allocation of a portion of public funds, employing consensus-driven and deliberative decision-making approaches (Ganuza & Francés, 2012; Röcke, 2014).

As elsewhere in the world, Italy has also embraced the practice of PB at all levels of government, especially at the local one. While all experiences of PB show common conceptual and design traits aimed at facilitating the deliberative engagement of non-elected citizens in public finance allocation, each experience remains unique due to diverse contextual factors, such as cultural, social, economic, political, and geographical conditions.

This chapter analyzes three distinct cases of PB that have unfolded in Italy at the local level, namely in Bologna, Caltanissetta, and Malles Venosta (in German, Mals).[1] These three case studies have been chosen because they represent very dissimilar realities: an industrialized metropolitan area in central-northern Italy (Bologna), a relatively poor medium-sized city in the southern island of Sicily (Caltanissetta), and a small and relatively wealthy rural municipality (Malles Venosta) located in a remote valley in South Tyrol, Italy's northernmost and predominantly German-speaking subnational unit.

The chapter will illustrate how the same participatory practice has developed in profoundly different contexts, trying to trace common trajectories, and drawing comparative lessons and insights. These will be built upon the analysis of the relative regional and municipal legislation on participation and PB. The peculiar socio-political and cultural landscape of each case-study will be considered, and a concise contextualization will be provided thereupon, as to grasp the most salient features of the three different PB experiences. Particular attention will be paid to the most recent PB editions. Before delving into the specifics of these three experiences (Sects. 10.3, 10.4 and 10.5), a preliminary section will outline the structure of PB – defining its essence, origins, and key characteristics (Sect. 10.2). Section 10.6 of final and comparative reflections will close the chapter.

10.2 Participatory Budgeting: Origins, Conceptualization and Functions

In recent years, representative democracy has encountered significant challenges across all levels of government, manifested through diminishing voter turnout and a prevailing disinterest in matters pertaining to society and citizenship. While the

[1] Malles Venosta, as much of rural and mountainous South Tyrol, is inhabited by a German-speaking population. For reasons of clarity, we will use hereafter the Italian name for the municipality (Malles Venosta).

established mechanisms of representative democracy, centered around elections, remain the cornerstone of democratic governance, participatory democracy provides pathways for the renewal of democracy at large. Carole Pateman, one of the leading scholars in the field of participatory democracy, states that "'participation' refers to (equal) participation in the making of decisions, and political equality refers to equality of power of determining the outcome of decisions" (Pateman, 1970, p. 43). However, conceptualizations of participatory democracy are often disputed, and agreement on its definition has not yet been achieved. This concept encapsulates an amalgamation of practices, tools, and procedures designed to facilitate active and substantive citizen involvement in the decision-making processes of public authorities (Allegretti, 2015; Allegretti & Herzberg, 2004). For this chapter, which takes into account one specific participatory institution, the notion of "democratic innovations" may be more suitable (Talpin, 2015; Trettel, 2015, p. 85). Elstub and Escobar (2019, p. 14) define democratic innovations as "processes or institutions that are new to a policy issue, policy role, or level of governance, and developed to reimagine and deepen the role of citizens in governance processes by increasing opportunities for participation, deliberation and influence". More radical interpretations of democratic innovations have placed emphasis on their creative and transformative implications, equating them to "processes of institutional creation" which entail "continuous social incidence over the public power and its administrative apparatus, and therefore also over the political system itself' (Gunza Lavalle & Isunza, 2010, p. 19). The underlying common rationale of these innovative policy-making tools is threefold: to bolster the legitimacy of political decisions, to enhance the quality of democratic policymaking, and ultimately, to amplify the efficacy of these decisions.

From its origins in Porto Alegre in the late 1980s, PB swiftly diffused throughout the rest of Brazil in subsequent years before permeating into other Latin American countries (Wampler & Goldfrank, 2022). The Brazilian roots of PB should not be overlooked. The context of its emergence is indeed unique. Before looking at its replicability, it is important to stress how PB is expression of the re-democratization and decentralization process, championed by social movements, union groups, and leftist parties in post-dictatorship Brazil (Avritzer, 2009; Wampler & Avritzer, 2005). Before arriving to Europe, the meaning and scope behind PB were profoundly shaped by the visions of its political proponents, such as the Workers' Party in Brazil (Baiocchi, 2005),[2] which in turn reflected the transformations of Latin American left in the 1970s–1980s (Fedozzi, 2015). Radical democratic understandings of democracy guided the original approach to PB, which was based on: (1) direct citizen participation in government decision-making process and control, (2) administrative and fiscal transparency, (3) concrete amelioration of urban infrastructure and services in favor or low-income classes, (4) political culture change, and cognizing of citizens as holders of democratic rights (Goldfrank, 2007, p. 95). Any assessment of PB must consider the early political rationale at the foundation of Brazilian PB, and the counterhegemonic role that PB was vested with in its early days (Baierle, 2007; Baiocchi, 2003).

[2] In Portuguese: *Partido dos Trabalhadores* (PT).

Deprived of its radical undertones, PB migrated to Europe in the 1990s, initially through pilot projects in Italy and Spain (de Vries et al., 2021). Since then, the number of municipalities adopting this process has constantly grown, including metropolitan cities such as Rome, Naples, Milan, and Bologna. In recent years, there has been a particular focus on promoting PB at the regional level, with some regions (e.g. Sicily) introducing legislation to support its implementation (Badia, 2022; Bassoli, 2012). As documented by the PB World Atlas, Italy is among the countries that have embraced PB more enthusiastically in Europe, which is in turn the continent with the most extensive utilization of this democratic engagement tool.[3] With nearly 5000 instances of PB recorded, the geographical distribution of its adoption stands as follows: 46% in Eastern Europe, 46% in Southern Europe, 5% in Western Europe, and 2–3% in Northern Europe. This distribution underscores the diverse regional uptake of participatory democracy, reflecting variations in political culture, governance traditions, and societal priorities.

Given such a far-reaching diffusion, PB constitutes a multifaceted phenomenon, and a polysemous concept. This has turned any encompassing classification of PB hardly doable. It follows that several analytical frames have been put forward to study PB. Goldfrank (2002, 2007) outlines four normative approaches to this tool (radical democratic, orthodox leftist, liberal, and conservative). A more institutional typification of PB in Europe has been proposed by Sintomer et al. (2008) who identify six ideal types. Evaluations of the diverse forms of participatory governance in budgeting have distinguished between partial PB and full PB, based on the consultative or binding character of decision-making powers (Baiocchi, 2011). Other studies differentiate PB varieties based on the effective degree of citizen participation, which is then linked to the notion of co-production of public policies, encompassing co-planning and co-designing (Barbera et al., 2016). Integrated approaches, drawing from public management and governance studies, have been elaborated to grasp the complex ensemble of PB manifestations (Manes-Rossi et al., 2023). Despite the lack of overarching and cross-national frameworks of analysis, the essence of PB is straightforward: instead of vesting decision-making authority exclusively in elected officials or public authorities, citizens are asked to participate in determining how a portion of the tax revenue is expended (Ryan, 2021; Wampler, 2012; Wampler et al., 2021). Moreover, PB does not lead to "yes-or-no" decisions but to a compromise outcome that represents a synthesis of the diversified interests of pluralist societies, and that aims at complementing traditional decision-making procedures (Floridia, 2014; Palermo & Kössler, 2017, p. 115). In this respect, PB is fashioned to pluralize decision-making and concretize public deliberation, being the convergence point between radical democracy and radical pluralist thought (Mouffe, 1992).

The comparative study of the PB experimentations in the three selected case-studies is developed against the background set above. The paradigmatic shift from early Brazilian radical democratic PB to European institutionalized PB adaptations is fundamental to contextualize PB in Italy. The following analysis should therefore be taken as a step towards the full understanding of how PB has taken roots in Italy,

[3] For a better overview of the PB across Europe see the following link: https://www.pbatlas.net/europe.html.

being adjusted to local contexts and politics, and embedded into the different traditions of local self-government.

10.3 The Case of Bologna

Bologna lies in the southern portion of the Po Valley, in the region of Emilia-Romagna, of which it is the regional capital. It has ca. 392,000 inhabitants (ISTAT 2024),[4] plus daily "users", namely workers and students. Bologna represents the paradigm of what has been called the "Emilian model" (De Maria, 2012, 2014), where social democratic policies are matched with administrative efficiency and government accountability and rely on a vibrant civil society. Just as much of central-northern Italy, Bologna is characterized by an old and solid tradition of local self-government, epitomized by the Medieval Italian *comune* (Hyde, 1973; Putnam, 1993). While feudalism and a vertical hierarchy of power prevailed in the rest of Europe, in Bologna a more horizontalized approach to governing emerged. Just as in the rest of Northern and Central Italy, this remains a vivid narrative, stuck in the collective memory, and often employed to explain the high levels of social capital and civic engagement (Tanzini, 2014). It is also in the light of such historical legacy that modern Italian municipalism and grassroot democracy—conceptually rooted in the constitutional principle of horizontal subsidiarity (Article 117)—could blossom (Ascheri, 2006).

As a forerunner of PB, Bologna demonstrates how the implementation of participatory devices is tightly related to the rescaling of decision-making processes at the subnational and local level, exposing interrelation between democratic innovations and decentralization (Alber & Valdesalici, 2015; Trettel, 2020). The activation of participatory mechanisms is complementary to the enlargement of the spaces of deliberation at the sub-municipal level, as posited by pluralized and radicalized understandings of democracy (Bookchin, 2006, 2015; Kohn, 2003). Here, neighborhood-level constituencies are involved in a series of participatory mechanisms. PB in Bologna resembles late 1980s Porto Alegre's PB, whose creation was directly connected to neighborhood movements' struggle for public goods and inclusive policies, as a means of participatory local self-government (Avritzer, 2002, 2010).

The introduction of the PB in Bologna has followed the application of Regional Law 3/2010 Norms on the Definition, Reorder and Promotion of the Procedures of Consultation and Participation to the Elaboration of Regional and Local Policies. This act has been substituted by Regional Law 15/2018 Law on the Participation to the Elaboration of Public Policies. Besides, the Municipal Council of Bologna was the first in Italy to approve a regulation on the commons,[5] offering a normative

[4] Data extracted from ISTAT (Istituto Nazionale di Statistica): http://dati.istat.it/index.aspx?datasetcode=dcis_popres1.

[5] More details can be accessed at Labsus (*Laboratorio per al sussidiarietà*) website: https://www.labsus.org/.

framework for the shared administration of common goods in Article 3 of the Municipal Statute (Salati, 2022, 2023). This paved the way for the implementation of other participatory devices.

In Article 4ter, the Municipal Statute defines PB as an instrument of direct democracy that involves the citizenry in the decision-making processes concerning the allocations of the resources that are part of the annually forecasted municipal expenditure. The same article specifies that a portion of each year's estimated budget must be used for the realization of PB, which will be implemented at the level of neighborhoods. In 2015, Bologna's Municipal Council approved a new regulation on decentralization, reshaping the size and functions of neighborhoods. Article 21bis(1) and Article 27decies of this regulation establish that neighborhoods' authorities are responsible for organizing PB every year. The activation of PB therefore falls within the responsibilities of the neighborhoods, that were reduced in number (from nine to six), but whose role was enhanced for what concerns the promotion of *active* citizenship. An ad hoc regulation on PB (hereafter PB regulation), adopted in 2016, further details how PB shall be managed. Article 5(2) of the latter states that municipal authorities entrust a third qualified subject with the tasks of supervision and methodological support to guarantee "impartiality" and "adequacy". The third qualified body which is responsible for these functions is the *Fondazione per l'Innovazione Urbana* (FIU).[6] FIU is a multi-disciplinary center that works on urban regeneration, social inclusion, and democratic innovations. It is the operational hub that rallies scientific know-how and manages the implementation of participatory processes such as PB (Allegrini & Paltrinieri, 2020b). It promotes patterns of coproduction of public policies via other innovative means such as the neighborhoods' laboratories,[7] which constitute the settings within which participatory mechanisms, such as PB, are enacted (Allegrini & Paltrinieri, 2018, 2020a, 2020b).

On a procedural level, PB is activated by the municipal government once it has heard the Conference of the Presidents of the Neighborhood Councils ("Conference") (Article 6(1)). The "Conference" monitors the implementation process and works with the municipal government to ensure that the PB achieves the best results (Article 6(2)). The neighborhoods' councils, which are directly elected representative bodies, adapt PB to territorial peculiarities (Article 6(3)). As provided for by Article 3 of the regulation on decentralization, the neighborhood council "represents the needs of the corresponding community … and favors and promotes the participation and involvement of citizens in the decision-making process cure and management of common goods". Municipal decentralization can be said to be the backbone of local self-government and participatory democracy.

Article 4 of the PB regulation lists the holders of participation rights: (1) citizens registered in the electoral lists of the municipality of Bologna; (2) people residing in Bologna who have already turned sixteen; (3) non-resident citizens who either work or study in Bologna; (4) foreigners and stateless individuals who either work or

[6] See http://www.fondazioneinnovazioneurbana.it/fondazione-innovazione-urbana-home.

[7] In Italian: *laboratori di quartiere*.

study in Bologna. The fields on which citizens can have a say through the PB are (Article 2(2)): extraordinary maintenance; requalification and reorganization of spaces; urban regeneration; urban equipment and furniture. Unlike in Caltanisetta, no explicit exclusion criterium is set regarding the right to participate in PB.

The PB is then articulated in four phases (Article 7(1)):

1. involvement of citizens, information, communication and hearing;
2. co-projecting of the proposals and verification of feasibility;
3. voting of admitted proposals and publication of results;
4. realization of the proposals.

The overall duration of phases one, two and three cannot exceed six months (Article 7(2)). Phase one of the PB is realized through the holding of public meetings and laboratories (Article 8(2)). The co-projecting of the proposals is then supported by facilitators and municipal experts (Article 9(4)). The proposals are then analyzed and verified by municipal technical boards that examine technical and economic issues as well as timing (Article 9(5)). The proposals admitted are those that positively pass this analysis. Phase two is concluded with the publicization of admitted proposals (Article 10(1)). After advertisement, citizens are called to vote (electronically), and thereby express their preference among the admitted proposals. Each citizen can vote for one proposal. The voting phase only lasts for 20 days, after which the results are published (Article 11). The selected projects are the most voted ones in each neighborhood (in total six citywide), within the limits of available resources (Article 12(1)). Once the selection process is over, the municipal authority is responsible for updating information about the state of the PB process and the implementation of the selected proposals (Article 13(1)).

Since the introduction of PB, this participatory mechanism has been enacted in 2017, 2018, 2019/2020, and 2023.[8] The overview of the salient figures of the four PB editions is illustrative to framing the main developments of this mechanism throughout the years.

For the first and second editions, the available budget was 150,000 EUR per neighborhood. In 2017, PB involved 1900 citizens. This figure decreased to 1800 in 2018. The PB process included a wide range of activities such as public meetings and consultations through which citizens and representatives of organized civil society could engage. Proposed projects were refined in a co-projecting phase with the aid of municipal technical staff. 27 and 33 projects proposals were admitted to the voting phase, in which 14,584 and 16,348 citizens participated in 2017 and 2018 respectively.

In the 2019/2020 PB edition, the funds made available by the city of Bologna doubled to two million EUR, allocated for two categories of proposals on which citizens could vote separately. 150,000 EUR were destined to the funding of projects of requalification at the level of neighborhoods, mainly targeting public buildings and infrastructure, public gardens and parks, public furniture and equipment.

[8] See the Bologna municipality website on participation http://partecipa.comune.bologna.it/bilancio-partecipativo/storico/ and the FIU website on PB http://www.fondazioneinnovazioneurbana.it/progetto/bilanciopartecipativo.

The remaining part of the funds was allocated to projects centered on sport, environment, culture and society, and economics. Six public assemblies were realized in the context of the new town-planning scheme (*Piano urbanistico generale del Comune di Bologna*) and 1000 citizens took part. 600 citizens participated in the second phase and designed 157 proposals. An additional 268 proposals were submitted online. Later, 22,247 citizens participated in the voting phase online which was delayed due to Covid-19 pandemic.

The ongoing fourth edition of PB has seen another increase in the budget reserved, which now amounts to 500,000 EUR per neighborhood. The six *laboratori di quartiere* and online form collected 385 proposals. 19,327 citizens participated in the voting phase. All the projects are to some extent related to the aims set by *Bologna Missione Clima*, according to which Bologna is committed to reach climate neutrality by 2030.

The winning projects in the four PB editions mainly regarded the requalification of public gardens, the renovation of public buildings, and the implementation of cycle paths, public art spaces, public furniture, urban greenery, and inclusive public spaces.

The pioneering role played by Bologna's PB experimentations can be confirmed for a variety of reasons. Allocated funds have been constantly rising, allowing for a diversification of the areas of public intervention. Citizen participation has followed the same upwards trend until 2020, after which the number of voters saw a decrease. Women have shown to be more inclined to participate. Throughout the four PB editions, they have always outnumbered men by a significant percentage: 58% in 2017, 56% in 2018, 54% in 2019/2020, and 57% in 2023.

All in all, PB experimentations in Bologna are certainly seen as reference cases. The engagement of citizens in the co-projecting and decision-making phases of PB is matched with institutional accountability and transparency and followed by the effective realization of the proposals – as regularly reported by the municipality's website. Although PB is spreading throughout Italy, Bologna represents an exceptional case when it comes to political participation. Its uniqueness within the Italian context is tantamount to that of Porto Alegre with respect to the rest of Brazil. PB can flourish more vigorously in those municipalities with a high rate of associative activity and popular militancy (Abers, 2000; Avritzer, 2003). The consolidation of PB is also part of the broader progressive posture of the current municipal government.

10.4 The Case of Caltanissetta

Caltanissetta is a municipality in the center of Sicily, an island, and the southernmost and biggest Italian region. It has a resident population of over 58,000 people (ISTAT 2024).[9] From a socioeconomic point of view, Caltanissetta is comparatively poor. In the province of Caltanissetta, the GDP per capita is around 18,100 EUR

[9] See http://dati.istat.it/index.aspx?datasetcode=dcis_popres1.

(2020),[10] which is below the Sicilian average, and by far below the Italian average of 30,136 EUR (2021), as well as that of the provinces of Bologna (43,500 EUR in 2020) and Bolzano (49,600 EUR in 2020), where Malles Venosta is located. The gap between Southern and Northern Italian regions and cities has characterized Italy's history since its unification in 1861. It is so deep that the post-pandemic Recovery and Resilience Plan is intended to tackle such social and territorial inequalities by dedicating 40% of the resources available to Italy's South.[11] Moreover, Caltanissetta, and the rest of the province, is still profoundly affected by the harmful repercussions of organized crime, i.e. the Sicilian mafia.

Highlighting the material poverty of the region, its economic stagnancy, and the deep rootedness of mafia organizations is crucial to fully grasp the meaning and impact that the introduction of democratic innovations entails in Caltanissetta. In addition, low levels of political participation, in terms of electoral turnout, deeply characterizes Caltanissetta, just as Sicily and the rest of Southern Italy. In the 2022 Italian elections, the voter turnout in Caltanissetta was around 55.7%, against a national average of around 64%.[12] In the 2022 Sicilian regional election, the voter turnout in the city of Caltanissetta was approximately 49%,[13] compared to Malles Venosta's 75.6%[14] and Bologna's almost 70% in similar subnational elections.[15] A first comparison among these figures may infer that Caltanissetta will show lower levels of civic involvement in participatory mechanisms, such as PB. From a general perspective, it is indeed against the background of citizens' disaffection towards the traditional forms of representative democracy that participatory democracy might offer new venues for the involvement of citizens in the local public and political life, augmenting the interest towards electoral moments as well.

PB has been used several times in Caltanissetta based on Regional Law 5/2014. This law establishes that all Sicilian municipalities must employ at least 2% of the financial transfers coming from the region in "forms of participatory democracy", by using the devices that engage the citizenry for the deliberation over actions of collective interest' (Article 6(1)), PB duly qualifies among the forms of such kind. To better regulate this field, the municipal government adopted in 2016 a regulation on civic participation. Article 50 of this regulation introduces PB in the municipality of Caltanissetta as a means for the "involvement of citizens" who can play an "active role" by sharing proposals with the local administration, and eventually voting the ones they prefer. According to this document, participation in PB is a right held by the "population of the community", meaning every citizen above sixteen years old

[10] See https://www.sisreg.it/index.php?option=com_content&view=article&id=102&Itemid=75.

[11] See https://www.istat.it/it/archivio/280052.

[12] See https://elezionistorico.interno.gov.it/index.php?tpel=C&dtel=25/09/2022&tpa=I&tpe=C&lev0=0&levsut0=0&lev1=24&levsut1=1&lev2=2&levsut2=2&lev3=1&levsut3=3&levsut4=4&ne1=24&ne2=242&ne3=2421&es0=S&es1=S&es2=S&es3=S&es4=N&ms=S&ne4=210180040&lev4=180040.

[13] See http://www.elezioni.regione.sicilia.it/regionali2022/rep_6/Caltanissetta/affluenzaProvinciale CL3.html.

[14] See https://civis.bz.it/vote/landtag2018/results/awf_li_vg.htm.

[15] See https://wwwservizi.regione.emilia-romagna.it/elezioni2020/Affluenza.aspx?prov=013.

in Caltanissetta. However, the regulation also outlines who must abstain from participating in the PB: elected officials at all levels of government; members of the administrative councils of any kind of body with public participation; members of the leading organs of political parties and unions; associations who are related to political factions; and public officers of the Caltanissetta municipality (Article 52). By minimizing the clout of organized groups and stakeholders on PB, the regulation tries to guarantee the actual emergence of citizens' needs. These criteria of exclusion intend to reduce the risks of neo-corporatism (Sintomer et al., 2012), and infringements on PB by interest groups (Cortes & Gugliano, 2010; Fedozzi & Martins, 2015).

The management of PB is entrusted to a working group formed by members of three municipal bodies, namely the general secretary (*Segreteria Generale*), the data processing center (*Centro Elaborazione Dati*) and the Office for Participation (Article 53). PB is articulated in six phases (Article 53):

1. Information. Citizens are informed about the thematic areas and resources allocated to the PB via a public call;
2. First voting phase. Citizens can vote only one thematic area;
3. Submission of the project proposals related to the three most voted thematic areas;
4. Feasibility evaluation of the proposals by an ad hoc commission;
5. Second voting phase. Feasible projects are put to a vote. The vote is telematic and citizens can only vote once for one project;
6. Publication of the results, and realization of the most voted projects.

PB was implemented every year since 2017. The resources allocated has been decreasing. Between 2017 and 2019 allocated resources amounted to 54,000 EUR with a decrease to 40,000 in 2020 and to 30,000 in 2023. To those figures further 90,000 and 50,000 EUR of capital expenditures were added in 2018 and 2019, respectively. Although implemented yearly, the material impact of the PB is diminished due to the reduction of the allocated budgets. For reasons of comparability, it is appropriate to focus on the last three PB editions.

In 2021 and 2022, with allocated resources amounting to 40,000 EUR, selected projects could not cost more than 8000 EUR. Citizens were called to vote for three of the seven thematic areas chosen by the municipal government: culture, integration and inclusion; environment and sustainability; conservation of the old town; sport; economic development; tourism; protection and wellbeing of animals. The most voted thematic areas were culture, sport, and conservation of the old town. Citizens submitted 23 proposals and the ad hoc Commission responsible for the admission of the proposals decided the feasibility of the projects on the basis of the following criteria: juridical and technical feasibility, estimated cost, estimated time of realization, compatibility with the thematic area, financial resources available, and ongoing public fields of intervention. Of the 23 proposals, 18 were admitted to vote. Of the five most voted projects—which covered the 40,000 EUR budget—two were related to sports, two to culture, and one to the conservation of the old town. The PB edition of 2022 did not differ from the previous edition. Citizens showed almost the same preferences concerning thematic areas, while proposed projects decreased to 20 of which 13 were deemed feasible.

In 2023, however, allocated resources fell to 30,000 EUR, which is 10,000 less than previously. Citizens have been duly informed on the PB phases via the municipality's channels of communication but also by local television named Tele Futura Nissa. The latter has also broadcasted two brief reports on the 2023 PB process in Caltanissetta on YouTube, thus allowing citizens to have access to the process by not-written means.

So far, projects included a wide variety of interventions such as the building of a mini-basket field, the realization of a social garden (for inclusive urban gardening activities), the promotion of sport activities to tackle socio-economic exclusion of children and teenagers from low-income families, the realization of networks of proximity to tackle social exclusion and loneliness, a talent show for the promotion of arts, the valorization of the city's historical-architectural patrimony via artistic and technological means and the production of short films for cultural and touristic promotion.

Altogether, the realization of PB in Caltanissetta is a significant achievement. The overall low socioeconomic indicators, the comparatively weaker participation of citizens in the elections, and the pervasive and longstanding presence of organized crime are certainly not conducive to the strengthening of democratic governance. However, in a context that displays comparatively higher levels of poverty such as Caltanissetta, PB, if duly implemented, can foster political inclusion and social equality (Abers, 1998; Wampler, 2015), constituting a tool of "redistributive democracy" (Fedozzi, 2000; Santos, 1998, 2002) or "affirmative democracy" (Navarro, 1998), just as evidenced in early Brazilian PB (Marquetti, 2000, 2003; Marquetti et al., 2008).

However, a proper evaluation of the impact of PB in Caltanissetta would require the in-depth examination of each single edition, as well as of the socio-demographic profile of participants and their satisfaction with the process at large. The simple fact that PB took root in a complex political environment such as that of Caltanissetta stands out in the context of Sicilian politics. For any evaluation of PB in comparatively poorer and politically apathic societies "should be valued more for its provision of citizenry […] rather than for the material gains it brings" (de Vries et al., 2021, p. 183).

10.5 The Case of Malles Venosta

Malles Venosta is a municipality in the autonomous province of Bolzano, located in the north-eastern part of Italy. As an autonomous province, Bolzano enjoys a significant degree of legislative, administrative and financial autonomy. Within its borders, multiple linguistic groups coexist, in particular the German-speaking, the Italian-speaking and the Ladin-speaking communities. A standout feature of the province of Bolzano is its remarkable economic prosperity, evidenced by its high GDP per capita. The South Tyrolean People's Party (Südtiroler Volkspartei/SVP) has played a pivotal role in the province's politics. In Malles Venosta, which is characterized by a strong predominance of the German language group (nearly 97% of the population), the SVP has ruled without interruption since 1948 (Alber, 2017; Larin & Röggla, 2019). Interestingly, this municipality spreads over a huge territory of 250 km^2, making it one of the larger municipalities in the region, and has a population of 5279 residents (ISTAT 2024).[16] The primary economic activities of Malles Venosta include farming, particularly apple orchards, and tourism, mainly driven by its alpine surroundings. All these characteristics make it very interesting to analyze how Malles Venosta decided to shape and implement PB (Trettel, 2021).

Noteworthily, the municipal government in office from 2009 to 2020, led by the mayor Ulrich Veith (SVP), strongly championed the participatory approach to public decision-making. His government invested a lot in direct and participatory democracy, specifically PB, which was carried out in 2016 and 2017. The interest of this municipal administration in democratic innovation is even more evident from the introduction in the municipal statute of a new Article 39 dedicated to citizen participation. Article 39(4) states that PB "is introduced as a public form of participation related to the development of the municipal budget and its priorities. Through this form of participation, the municipality promotes transparency and accountability for both the public expenditures as much as for the possibilities of savings". However, as the mayor changed in 2020 (even if coming from the same political party, the SVP) interest in PB also waned. In fact, after 2019 this form of participation was no longer implemented, although the statutory provision is still in place.

In this regard, it must be noted that PB processes—such as all democratic innovations—often strongly depend on the political will of the municipality (especially its mayor) to function and be carried out regularly. Hence, a change of the dominant political force or just the mayor in very small municipalities can interrupt a practice of participatory democracy if there is no national or regional obligation for the municipality to do so. This is an inherent limit of democratic innovations. Even if Malles Venosta went a step further by introducing PB in the Municipal Statute, thus granting this instrument a legal guarantee, the current local government could simply ignore this provision. The issue of the effectiveness of democratic innovations and their institutionalization in legal sources is very prominent in current literature (Bobbio, 2018; Papadopoulos & Philippe, 2007).

Regarding the functioning of PB in Malles, every resident of the municipality, both citizens and non-citizens, had the opportunity to submit up to three proposals for the allocation of a specific portion of the annual budget, determined by the municipality for each fiscal year. The proposals could be submitted online or by hand/post-delivering to the appropriate offices and were subsequently presented to fellow residents in specially organized assemblies facilitated by the municipality. After the submission and presentation stages, the municipality collaborated with a council of 15 randomly selected citizens to assess each project's legal, technical,

[16] See http://dati.istat.it/Index.aspx?QueryId=18959.

and financial feasibility. If a proposal was found unfeasible due to any of these reasons, a clear justification was provided.

The municipality of Malles Venosta has put in place a comprehensive set of regulations for PB. These regulations encompass a range of important guidelines:

1. Unrestricted citizen participation: All citizens are empowered to endorse and support proposals, ensuring inclusivity and open participation.
2. Exclusion of city council and committee members: City council and city committee members are expressly barred from submitting proposals, thus preventing potential conflicts of interest.
3. Diverse proposal scope: Proposals have the flexibility to cover investments within the municipality as well as measures aimed at economizing municipal finances, expanding the scope of potential initiatives.
4. Proposal alignment: Proposals sharing similar goals or objectives have the opportunity to be combined after consultation with involved participants, streamlining the process for projects with common aims.
5. Individual proposal submissions with collaborative support: While proposals must originate from individuals, they can be strengthened by garnering support from others through signatures, promoting collective input.
6. Exclusion of associations and interest groups: Proposals from organized associations and interest groups are not considered, emphasizing the direct involvement of individual citizens.
7. Transparent and non-anonymous process: Suggestions and ideas must be transparently attributed to individuals and are not accepted in anonymous forms, ensuring accountability and openness.
8. No legal obligations for submitted proposals: The submission of project proposals does not impose any legal obligations on the municipality, preserving flexibility in the decision-making process.
9. Stringent feasibility criteria: Proposals are rigorously assessed based on criteria that encompass legal, financial, and technical feasibility, guaranteeing responsible allocation of resources.

In the 2016 PB edition citizens submitted a total of 33 projects. Out of these, 10 were voted the most promising and received funding from the 200,000 EUR allocated for that year. Nine of these projects were successfully carried out in 2017, while one was implemented in 2018.

PB in Malles achieved its primary objective of involving citizens in the budgetary decision-making process. Moreover, the manageable population size of the municipality facilitates information dissemination and exchange, resulting in relatively higher engagement compared to larger urban areas. Also, the most popular ideas generated through PB have been translated into tangible actions by the local administration. Despite these positive outcomes, it is again important to underline that with the change of mayor, the willingness to continue this experience has been interrupted. Information on the past editions of the PB has been removed from the website. This demonstrates that legal provisions are meaningless if not accompanied by a strong political will and a deep knowledge of the functioning of participatory procedures. This phenomenon is even more prominent in other municipalities of the Province of Bolzano. In fact, participatory budgeting is also provided for in the municipal statutes of Selva di Gardena and Cortaccia sulla Strada del Vino. However, to date, these provisions have never been implemented (Alber, 2023).

Table 10.1 Comparative data on PB in the three case studies

	Bologna Emilia Romagna	Caltanissetta Sicily	Malles Venosta South Tyrol
Geographic setting	Center-North limit	Island/southern Italy	Northern/Alpine Arch
Population[a]	392,000 (+one million daily 'users')	58,000	5300
GDP per capita PPP[b]	43,500	18,100	49,600
Political party in power[c]	Center-left coalition	Center-left and center-right coalition	Big-tent regional party[d]
Last regional election voter turnout	70%	49%	75.6%
Total number PB editions	4 (+2024)	7 (+2024)	2
Current status of PB	Ongoing	Ongoing	Suspended
PB allocated funds per capita	7.65 EUR	0.51 EUR	37.7 EUR
PB institutionalization	Yes (by municipal statute)	Yes (by ad hoc municipal regulation only)	Yes (by municipal statute)
Regional/provincial law on participation	Yes	No	Yes
Participation rights' holders	Residents over 16—non-residents who work/study in Bologna	Residents above 16	Residents above 16
Number of voters[e]	(19,327)	(646)	n.a.
Actors involved in PB	Citizens and civic associations	Citizens and civic associations	Citizens and civic associations
Facilitators	Technicians and FIU proximity experts	No	No
PB devices	Neighborhoods' laboratories, public meetings, and hearings	Public meetings	Public meetings
Voting phases and forms	One; online	Two (on thematic area and on project); online	One
Bindingness of most voted proposals	Yes	Yes	Yes

[a] This figure refers to the last year of implementation of PB in each case-study
[b] Data refer to the entire Province. Respectively: Province of Bologna, Province of Caltanissetta, and Autonomous Province of Bolzano
[c] This refers to the all PB editions in each case-study
[d] SVP, the party of German- and Ladin-speaking minorities in South Tyrol
[e] Reference years are different: Bologna (2023), Caltanissetta (2022)

10.6 Conclusions

The popularity of democratic innovations has led to the proliferation of PB experimentations throughout many Italian municipalities in the last two decades. The introduction of participatory mechanisms and the engagement of citizens in the decision-making stages of public policymaking have been set up to respond to the unfading popular request for improved political participation. The three selected case studies display different patterns of development of PB, rooted in the socio-demographic, geo-cultural, and economic characteristics of the municipality (Ryan, 2019).

Each of the municipalities analyzed bears a different degree of social complexity, as well as distinct institutional histories and collective resourcefulness. In this respect, Bologna is a *unicum*, a paradigmatic case where civic engagement is extraordinarily deeply rooted (Carlone & Landi, 2020). The centuries-long legacy of local self-government, the predominance of progressive forces within local elected bodies, the vibrancy of civic, social, university, and union movements throughout the twentieth century, led to the development of a tight interrelation between an extremely dynamic citizenry, and very responsive local authorities. PB in Bologna discloses the complexity and impact of democratic innovations in metropolitan areas. The introduction of participatory mechanisms is indeed intertwined with the high degree of municipal decentralization (division in neighborhoods) and is aimed at tackling not only the involvement of citizens in public policymaking, but also political inclusion, social and territorial equality (Massarenti, 2017). In addition to its distinguished municipalist tradition, Bologna proves to be a fertile ground for democratic innovations, embedding forms of citizen participation in sub-municipal decentralization. This combination has been characteristic of the post-authoritarian and new left in both Latin America and Europe and aligns PB in Bologna with that of Porto Alegre (Goldfrank, 2015; Robinson, 1992).

The intranational comparative analysis outlined in this chapter deepens the understanding of PB when applied to different contexts within Italy. It unveils the noncorrelation between economic prosperity and the consolidation of democratic innovations at the municipal level. From a financial perspective, in Malles Venosta, the budget share per capita reserved for PB (in the last year of implementation) was proportionally higher than those of Bologna and Caltanissetta: 37.7 EUR in Malles Venosta, 7.65 EUR in Bologna and 0.51 EUR in Caltanissetta. Such a rough quantitative overview demonstrates that PB has no longer been implemented where fundings available are comparatively higher. In Caltanissetta, the least thriving municipality among the selected cases, PB seems to be a rather consolidated participatory institution. Indeed, PB in Caltanissetta has been uninterruptedly implemented since 2017, just as in Bologna, where PB was suspended only in 2021 and 2022 due to the Covid-19 pandemic. Apparently, the consolidation or institutionalization of PB is not exclusively dependent on one municipality's wealth, but it is rather a matter of political will and perseverant and participatory-minded elected authorities and public officers. Among the analyzed cases, Malles Venosta is the only municipality where PB, although institutionalized at the statutory level, has been *de facto* suspended. Still, only an in-depth ethnographic study of this predominantly German-speaking, socio-politically homogenous and prosperous alpine municipality could explain the reasons behind the decline of PB there (e.g. Talpin, 2012). On the contrary, PB in Caltanissetta resisted the change in power between center-left and center-right municipal governments.

PB can certainly be praised for promoting transparency and accountability when using public funds, which, besides citizen participation, is a crucial aspect of democratic governance. Nonetheless, comprehensive democratic accountability cannot be fully achieved through this means because of the limited share of local public spending covered by PB. As for the patterns of inclusion and representation generally associated with PB, no comparative analysis can be provided in this chapter, since only the municipality of Bologna provides access to some data on the profiles of participants.

Overall, the use of PB in Italy has proved to be a powerful tool for fostering democratic engagement, community empowerment and inclusive decision-making. Its successful implementation in metropolitan cities, medium-sized towns, and even small rural communities showcases the adaptability and effectiveness of this approach in diverse contexts. As Italy continues to embrace participatory practices, it holds the potential to strengthen the social fabric of its cities and towns, while also promoting active citizenship and collective responsibility among its citizens. In this perspective, PB represents a more recent manifestation of the inherent deliberative potential of local constituencies, intended as association of individuals, who happen to pronounce themselves on the matters they deem important for their community life. Further research is needed, however, to provide a more extensive assessment of citizen participation, inclusion, representation and the impact of PB throughout Italy.

References

Abers, R. (1998). From clientelism to cooperation: Local government, participatory policy, and civic organizing in Porto Alegre, Brazil. *Politics and Society, 26*(4), 511–537.

Abers, R. (2000). *Inventing local democracy: Grassroots politics in Brazil*. Lynne Rienner Publishers.

Alber, E. (2017). South Tyrol's negotiated autonomy. *Treatises and Documents: Journal of Ethnic Studies, 78*, 41–58.

Alber, E. (2023). Innovazioni democratiche in Alto Adige/Südtirol: Un primo bilancio e prospettive. *Federalismiit, 32*, 233–255.

Alber, E., & Valdesalici, A. (2015). Framing subnational 'institutional innovation' and 'participatory democracy' in Italy: Some findings on current structures, procedures and dynamics. In F. Palermo & E. Alber (Eds.), *Federalism as decision-making. Changes in structures, procedures and policies* (pp. 448–478). Brill Nijhoff.

Allegretti, U. (2015). Participatory democracy in multi-level states. In C. Fraenkel-Haeberle et al. (Eds.), *Citizen participation in multi-level democracies* (pp. 205–215). Brill Nijhoff.

Allegretti, U., & Herzberg, C. (2004). *Participatory budgets in Europe, between efficiency and growing local democracy*. Transnational Institute and the Centre for Democratic Policy-Making.

Allegrini, G., & Paltrinieri, R. (2018). Partecipazione e collaborazione negli interventi di comunità: l'esperienza dei laboratori di quartiere del Comune di Bologna. *Sociologia urbana e rurale, 116*, 29–44.

Allegrini, G., & Paltrinieri, R. (2020a). I Laboratori di Quartiere come spazi di ricostruzione delle comunità. In F. de Biase (Ed.), *Rimediare, Ri-mediare, saperi, tecnologie, comunità, persone* (pp. 242–254). FrancoAngeli.

Allegrini, G., & Paltrinieri, R. (2020b). *Partecipazione, processi di Immaginazione Civica e sfera pubblica. I Laboratori di Quartiere e il Bilancio Partecipativo a Bologna*. FrancoAngeli.

Ascheri, M. (2006). *Le città-stato. Le radici del municipalismo e del repubblicanesimo italiani*. Il Mulino.

Avritzer, L. (2002). Orçamento participativo: As experiências de Porto Alegre e Belo Horizonte. In E. Dagnino (Ed.), *Sociedade civil e espaços públicos no Brasil*. Paz & Terra.

Avritzer, L. (2003). O orçamento Participativo e a teoria democrática: Um balanço crítico. In L. Avritzer & Z. Navarro (Eds.), *A inovação democrática no Brasil: O orçamento participativo*. Editora Cortez.

Avritzer, L. (2009). *Participatory institutions in democratic Brazil*. Johns Hopkins University Press.

Avritzer, L. (2010). Living under a democracy. Participation and its impact on the living conditions of the poor. *Latin American Research Review, 45*(S1), 166–185.

Badia, F. (2022). Participatory budgeting in Italy: A phoenix rising from the ashes. In M. S. De Vries, J. Nemec, & D. Sp̌acĕk (Eds.), *International trends in participatory budgeting. Between trivial pursuits and best practices* (pp. 47–62). Palgrave Macmillan.

Baierle, S. (2007). *Lutas em Porto Alegre: Entre a revolução política e o transformismo*. Mapas.

Baiocchi, G. (2003). *Radicals in power: The Workers' Party (PT) and experiments in urban democracy in Brazil*. Zed Books.

Baiocchi, G. (2005). *Militants and citizens: Local democracy on a global stage in Porto Alegre*. Stanford University Press.

Baiocchi, G. (2011). *Bootstrapping democracy: Experiments in urban governance in Brazil*. Stanford University Press.

Barbera, C., Sicilia, M., & Steccolini, I. (2016). The participatory budgeting as a form of co-production. In M. Fugini, E. Bracci, & M. Sicilia (Eds.), *Co-production in the public sector: Experiences and challenges* (pp. 27–39). Springer.

Bassoli, M. (2012). Participatory budgeting in Italy. An analysis of (almost democratic) participatory governance arrangements. *International Journal of Urban and Regional Research, 36*, 1183–1203.

Bobbio, L. (2010). Designing effective public participation. *Policing and Society, 38*, 41–57.

Bookchin, M. (2006). *Social ecology and communalism*. AK Press.

Bookchin, M. (2015). *The next revolution: Popular assemblies & the promise of direct democracy*. Verso.

Carlone, T., & Landi, G. (2020). Quartieri e partecipazione a Bologna. In M. Castrignanò, M. Bergamaschi, & G. Pieretti (Eds.), *Policentrismo urbano e processi sociali emergente* (pp. 85–100). Rubbettino.

Cortes, S. V., & Gugliano, A. (2010). Entre neocorporativistas e deliberativos: Uma interpretação sobre os paradigmas de análise dos fóruns participativos no Brasil. *Sociologias, 12*(24), 44–75.

De Maria, C. (2012). *Bologna futuro: Il modello emiliano alla sfida del XXI secolo*. CLUEB.

De Maria, C. (2014). *Il "modelle emiliano" nella storia d'Italia. Tra culture politiche e pratiche di governo locale*. BraDypUS Communicating Cultural Heritage.

de Vries, S., Nemec, J., & Špaček, D. (2021). *International trends in participatory budgeting. Between trivial pursuits and best practices*. Palgrave Macmillan.

Elstub, S. (2018). Deliberative and participatory democracy. In A. Bächtiger, J. S. Dryzek, J. Mansbridge, & M. E. Warren (Eds.), *The Oxford handbook of deliberative democracy* (pp. 186–202). Oxford University Press.

Elstub, S., & Escobar, O. (2019). Defining and typologising democratic innovations. In S. Elstub & O. Escobar (Eds.), *Handbook of democratic innovation and governance* (pp. 11–31). Edward Elgar Publishing.

Fedozzi, L. (2000). *O poder da aldeia. Gênese e história do Orçamento Participativo de Porto Alegre*. Tomo Editorial.

Fedozzi, L. (2015). Porto Alegre: Participación contra-hegemónica, efecto-demostración y desconstrucción del modelo. In F. Carrion & S. P. Ponce (Eds.), *El giro a la izquierda: Los gobiernos locales de América Latina* (pp. 179–212). FLACSO.

Fedozzi, L., & Martins, A. L. B. (2015). Trajetória do orçamento participativo de Porto Alegre: Representação e elitização política. *Lua Nova: Revista de Cultura e Política, 95*, 181–224.

Floridia, A. (2014). Beyond participatory democracy, towards deliberative democracy: Elements of a possible theoretical genealogy. *Rivista Italiana di Politiche, 3*, 299–326.

Ganuza, E., & Francés, F. (2012). The deliberative turn in participation. The problem of inclusion and deliberative opportunities in participatory budgeting. *European Political Science Review, 4*(2), 283–302.

Goldfrank, B. (2002). *Urban experiments in citizen participation: Deepening democracy in Latin America*. University of California.

Goldfrank, B. (2007). Lessons from Latin American experience in participatory budgeting. In A. Shah (Ed.), *Participatory budgeting* (pp. 91–126). World Bank Institute, Public Sector Governance and Accountability Series.

Goldfrank, B. (2015). Reinventing the left in the Global South: The politics of the possible. *Cambridge Review of International Affairs, 28*(3), 516–520.

Gunza Lavalle, A., & Isunza, E. V. (2010). Precisiones conceptuales para el debate contemporáneo sobre la innovación democrática: Participación, controles sociales y representación. In A. G. Lavalle & E. V. Isunza (Eds.), *La innovación democrática en América Latina: Tramas y nudos de la representación, la participación y el control social* (pp. 17–82). CIESAS – Universidad Veracruzana.

https://demo.istat.it/app/?i=POS

Hyde, K. J. (1973). *Society and politics in medieval Italy; The evolution of the civil life, 1000–1350*. Palgreve-Macmillan.

Kohn, M. (2003). *Radical space: Building the house of the people*. Cornell University Press.

Larin, S. J., & Röggla. (2019). Participatory consociationalism? No, but South Tyrol's Autonomy Convention is evidence that power-sharing can transform conflicts. *Nations and Nationalism, 25*, 1018–1041.

Manes-Rossi, F., Brusca, I., Orelli, L., Lorson, R., Peter, C., & Haustein, E. (2023). Features and drivers of citizen participation: Insights from participatory budgeting in three European cities. *Public Management Review, 25*(2), 201–223.

Marquetti, A. (2000). Participatory budgeting in Porto Alegre. *Indicator South Africa, 17*, 71–78.

Marquetti, A. A. (2003). Participação e redistribuição: O Orçamento participativo em Porto Alegre. In L. Avritzer & Z. Navarro (Eds.), *A inovação democrática no Brasil: O orçamento participativo* (pp. 129–156). Cortez Editora.

Marquetti, A., Adriano, G., & Pires, R. (2008). *Democracia participativa e redistribuição: Análise de experiências de orçamento participativo*. Xamã Editora.

Massarenti, F. (2017). Le circoscrizioni di decentramento in Italia. L'evoluzione normativa, i fattori di crisi e le prospettive future. *Istituzioni del federalismo: Rivista di studi giuridici e politici, 1*, 251–282.

Mouffe, C. (1992). *Dimensions of radical democracy: Pluralism, citizenship, community*. Verso.

Navarro, Z. (1998). *Affirmative democracy and redistributive development: The case of "Participatory Budgeting" in Porto Alegre, Brazil [1989–1997]*. Programas Sociales, Pobreza y Participatión Ciudadana.

Palermo, F., & Kössler, K. (2017). *Comparative federalism: Constitutional arrangements and case law*. Hart Publishing.

Papadopoulos, Y., & Philippe, W. (2007). Are innovative, participatory and deliberative procedures in policy making democratic and effective? *European Journal of Political Research, 46*, 445–472.

Pateman, C. (1970). *Participation and democratic theory*. Cambridge University Press.

Putnam, D. R. (1993). *La tradizione civica nelle regioni italiane*. Mondadori Editore.

Robinson, W. (1992). The he Sao Paulo Forum: Is there a new Latin American left. *Monthly Review, 44*(7), 1–27.

Röcke, A. (2014). *Framing citizen participation. Participatory budgeting in France, Germany and the United Kingdom*. Palgrave Macmillan.

Ryan, M. (2019). Comparative approaches to the study of democratic innovation. In S. Elstub & O. Escobar (Eds.), *Handbook of democratic innovation and governance* (pp. 558–570). Edward Elgar Publishing.

Ryan, M. (2021). *Why citizen participation succeeds or fails. A comparative analysis of participatory budgeting*. Bristol University Press.

Salati, C. (2022). La libertà dei cittadini attivi oltre lo Stato: Prime considerazioni sull'amministrazione condivisa in Unione Europea. In F. Pizzolato, A. Scalone, G. Comazzetto, & F. Corvaja (Eds.), *La città oltre lo Stato* (pp. 83–94). Giappichelli.

Salati, C. (2023). *Towards a theoretical framework for civic participation through the commons in EU cities: The contribution of horizontal subsidiarity in Italian cities*. Università degli studi di Macerata.

Santos, B. S. (1998). Participatory budgeting in Porto Alegre: Toward a redistributive democracy. *Politics and Society, 26*(4), 461–510.

Santos, B. S. (2002). Orçamento participativo em Porto Alegre: Para uma democracia redistributiva. In B. S. Santos (Ed.), *Democratizar a democracia: Os caminhos da democracia participativa* (pp. 455–560). Civilização Brasileira.

Sintomer, Y., Herzberg, C., & Röcke, A. (2008). Participatory budgeting in Europe: Potentials and challenges. *International Journal of Urban and Regional Research, 32*(1), 164–178.

Sintomer, Y., Herzberg, C., Röcke, A., & Allegretti, G. (2012). Transnational models of citizen participation: The case of participatory budgeting. *The Journal of Public Health, 8*(2), 9.

Talpin, J. (2012). What can ethnography bring to the study of deliberative democracy? Evidence from a study on the impact of participation on actors. *Revista Internacional de Sociología, 70*(2), 143–163.

Talpin, J. (2015). Democratic innovations. In D. D. Porta & M. Diani (Eds.), *The Oxford handbook of social movements* (pp. 781–792). Oxford University Press.

Tanzini, L. (2014). *A consiglio. La vita politica nell'Italia dei comuni*. Edizioni Laterza.

Trettel, M. (2015). The politics of deliberative democracy. A comparative survey of the "Law in action" of citizen participation. *Revista de Derecho Político, 94*, 85–114.

Trettel, M. (2020). *La democrazia partecipativa negli ordinamenti composti: Studio di diritto comparato sull'incidenza della tradizione giuridica nelle democratic innovations*. Edizioni Scientifiche Italiane.

Trettel, M. (2021). Democratic innovations in (subnational) constitution-making. The institutionalized case(s) of the Italian Provinces of Trento and Bolzano. *Innovations, 34*(5), 782–802.

Wampler, B. (2015). *Activating democracy in Brazil: Popular participation, social justice, and interlocking institutions*. University of Notre Dame Press.

Wampler, B. (2012). Participatory budgeting. Core principles and key impacts. *The Journal of Public Health, 8*(2), 138.

Wampler, B., & Avritzer, L. (2005). The spread of participatory democracy in Brazil: From radical democracy to participatory good government. *Journal of Latin American Urban Studies, 135*, 737–752.

Wampler, B., & Goldfrank, B. (2022). *The rise, spread, and decline of Brazil's participatory budgeting. The arc of a democratic innovation*. Palgrave Macmillan.

Wampler, B., McNulty, S., & Touchton, M. (2021). *Participatory budgeting in global perspective*. Oxford University Press.

Chapter 11
Participatory Budgeting Through Budget Community Forums: The Practice of Macedonian Municipalities

Jelena Janevska

Abstract The process of decentralization, launched in 2001, strengthened local government's political, fiscal, and human capacities. The delegation of competences to municipalities brought the decision-making power closer to local communities and created instruments for citizens to influence decisions that affect their lives. Several reviews of the process of decentralization proved it had a positive impact on citizens' participation in decision-making at the local level. The Community Forums are the most massive and long-term mechanism of citizens' participation in Macedonian municipalities. There are four types of Community Forums: Project, Thematic, Inter-municipal and Budget. The subject of the Budget Forums is the municipal budget for the next year, and the result is an adopted municipal budget in consultation with citizens. This way, municipalities aim to increase citizens' understanding of the budgeting process, scarce resources and the need to prioritize, while at the same time increasing openness, transparency and accountability. Through six Budget Forum sessions, 60–100 citizens representing the municipality's diversity review the draft budget, discuss strategic priorities, budget programs, revenues, expenditures, and decide on the priority projects for the next year. After successful implementation from 2014–2017, 70 of the 80 municipalities institutionalized Community Forums as a tool for participatory budgeting.

Keywords Macedonia · Budget forums · ZELS · Community · Prioritization · Budget programs

---

J. Janevska (✉)
Network of Associations of Local Authorities of South-East Europe (NALAS), Skopje, Republic of North Macedonia
e-mail: janevska@nalas.eu

K. Kössler, E. Schläppi (eds.), *Citizen Participation in Local Governance*, Local and Urban Governance, https://doi.org/10.1007/978-3-031-99824-9_11

11.1 Introduction: The Process of Decentralization and Its Influence Over Participatory Budgeting

The process of decentralization in the Republic of Macedonia[1] started with the signing of the Ohrid Framework Agreement[2] in 2001. This agreement followed the ethnic conflict earlier that year, and provided for a set of political and institutional mechanisms to enable effective decentralization.

The process of decentralization aimed to reform local government, strengthening its political, fiscal, and human capacities and enabling it to provide high quality local services. With the delegation of competences at the local level, apart from increasing the efficiency and effectiveness of public services, one of the objectives of the decentralization was to bring the decision-making power closer to the local communities and create instruments for the citizens to influence decisions that affect the areas where they live.

The country has a single-tier system of state organization with 80 municipalities, both urban and rural, and the City of Skopje, with a special status. As of 2009, the country is divided in eight planning/development regions, which serve for statistical, economic and administrative purposes.

The Law on Local Self-Government[3] was adopted in January 2002, and is still effective today. In addition, Chapter IV (Articles 25–30) of the law focuses on the "direct participation of citizens in the decision-making of municipalities", and lists the forms of citizens participation, such as citizens' initiative, meeting of citizens, referendum, complains and proposals, public roundtables, surveys and proposals. Although this law does not specifically promote nor regulate participatory budgeting, its Article 42 on "Openness in the work of the municipal council", states that "during the discussion of the municipal budget, annual financial report and urban plans, the participation of citizens cannot be excluded". In practice, this means that citizen participation in managing municipal financial issues is not mandatory, but recommended, based on the principles of openness and transparency of local government.

Several reviews of the process of decentralization (Jovanova et al., 2014; Lessenski et al., 2006; Tedesco, 2008), as elaborated below, confirmed its *positive impact on citizens' participation in decision-making at the local level.* In addition, they have also noted a gradual increase of local practices and tools for citizens' participation in decision-making, especially concerning municipal priority activities and projects, but also related to the way local public resources are allocated, such as through an active role in the planning of the municipal budget, called participatory budgeting.

A review from 2006, conducted by the Institute for Regional and International Studies and the Institute for Democracy, Solidarity and Civil Society (Lessenski

[1] Now the Republic of North Macedonia.

[2] See https://www.osce.org/files/f/documents/2/8/100622.pdf.

[3] See https://aa.mk/WBStorage/Files/Zakon_lokalnata_samouprava.pdf.

et al., 2006) stated that citizens expect long-term benefits from the process of decentralization, such as their municipality providing more possibilities for civic participation, greater transparency and accountability, fairer allocation of local budgets, and in general for them to be in line with the European perspective of the country.

A review conducted in 2008 by the Organization for Security and Cooperation in Europe (OSCE) and the national Association of Local Self-Government Units (ZELS) (Tedesco, 2008) showed that 81% of the municipalities declared that they include citizens in the budgeting process, mostly through public debates for determining the financing priorities for the next year. Most of the municipalities that organized such debates (40%), held up to five such debates. Municipalities also organized meetings to present the annual financial reports and plans for the next year, which also contributes to openness and transparency. The dominant way of communication related to the municipal budget in this period were local media. However, the citizens included in this research did not share the same perception of municipal openness and transparency. Almost 86% of them stated that they have not met the mayor nor other people from the municipal administration to discuss municipal priorities for the next year. Most of the surveyed citizens showed a lack of understanding of the municipal budget with two-thirds stating that they do not know how the municipality is being financed.

A review conducted in 2014 by OSCE (Jovanova et al., 2014) indicated further progress in citizens' participation in local government issues, decision-making and participatory budgeting. All municipalities declared that citizens' participation represents an important tool in the process of local decision making. Still, the practices that this review evidenced were different. The review distinguished municipalities that used a systematic approach regarding citizen participation and participative budgeting, and municipalities that do so on ad hoc basis. Only two municipalities, Strumica and Bitola, were considered having a systematic approach in participative budgeting. In both cities there were functional neighborhood/village councils (84 such councils in Bitola and 30 in Strumica) that were included into the budget development process. In October of the current year, prior to an internal debate and prioritization, the councils submitted official budget plans to the municipality for their respective neighborhood, which become integral parts of the budget proposal, adopted by the Municipal Council by the end of the year. In both municipalities, this was a formal procedure, which institutionalized citizens participation in the creation of the municipal budget. The rest of the municipalities in the country were using an ad hoc approach to citizens' participation and participatory budgeting. Practices included: participatory development of municipal budgets, decisions about infrastructure investments, urban planning and strategic planning. The review concluded that the frequency of such activities depends on the involvement of donors or other supporters of citizens' participation.

This does not come as a surprise, considering that the international community, development donors and civil society organizations mobilized to support the process of decentralization, bring it closer to citizens and motivate them to be actively involved in local public life and decision-making. From all different tools used for citizen participation and participatory budgeting in particular, Community Forums stand out as the most systematic and comprehensive one, gradually expanding and being practiced by all municipalities in the country.

11.2 Community Forums: A Tool for Democratic Participation

The Community Forums Program was launched by the Swiss Development Cooperation (SDC) in 2006, in partnership with several local civil society organizations and with an active role of ZELS, after being successfully implemented in Switzerland and Bulgaria. The program was launched in three municipalities with the aim to support the decentralization process. This program set the basis for systematic citizens' participation in Macedonian municipalities, including participatory budgeting.

The Community Forums are considered a tool for the democratic participation of citizens in their local governments that aim to:

1. Increase cooperation of the municipality with its citizens,
2. Improve trust,
3. Increase citizens' awareness of the need to get involved in their municipalities and take responsibility for the decisions made,
4. Increase transparency of municipal work, and
5. Strengthen democratic processes.

The Community Forums are an institutionalized tool and platform that enables citizens to improve their lives with their own ideas and participation. For the local administration, this platform enables the practice of participative, accountable, and trust-building local governance (Hadzi-Vasileva et al., 2017). The Community Forums develop citizens' initiative and action, strengthen the community's project development skills, and reinforce advocacy capacities and partnership building. Ultimately, the Community Forums increase community's social capital and cohesion.

The Community Forums are organized to:

1. Publicly discuss and reach an agreement with the local public for proposed priorities in the documents for strategic local development,
2. Open public debates on the issues local communities face, their solutions, and priorities,
3. Discuss and plan the municipal budget,
4. Propose and select projects,
5. Develop projects of interest for the community.

A Community Forum can be *initiated by* the mayor, municipal council, any local institution or organization, as well as by an individual, by submitting an initiative addressed to the mayor, who decides upon it. So, the final decision for the organization of the Community Forum lies with the mayor, who also needs to make sure that the forum is consistently implemented, decisions are being made and that it is eventually processed through the municipal decision-making process.

In practice, *four types of Community Forums* were devised: Project (the traditional one, which was piloted first), Thematic, Inter-municipal and Budget. The objectives of each of the four types of Community Forums are listed below (Fig. 11.1).

The Community Forums, and particularly Budget Forums, evolved over the years, as did their organization, based on the lessons learnt. After nine meetings initially, the number of citizens' gatherings was later reduced to six in total. They are usually held once a month and in person. The sessions are moderated in a structured process, where the first four are used to elaborate on issues, provide solutions and give recommendations for solving local issues. The fifth session is for deciding, and the sixth session is an informative session that updates citizens on the impact of implemented solutions, based on the decision of the forum, after they have been put into practice (Fig. 11.2).

The Community Forums, including those dealing with municipal budgets, i.e. Budget Forums, are organized based on the following *principles* which were—in the absence of recognition of the forums by the Law on Local Self-Government—published in a ZELS guidebook and are, therefore, not legally binding (adapted from Hadzi-Vasileva et al., 2017):

1. *Open for all interested citizens*, including all ethnic groups and a minimum of 40% women.
2. Active participation of the *civil society organizations, business sector and the local decision-makers* (mayor, city councilors) and administration.

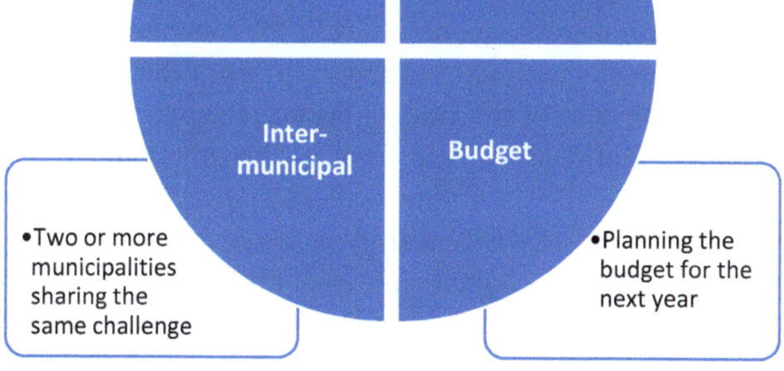

Fig. 11.1 Types of community forums

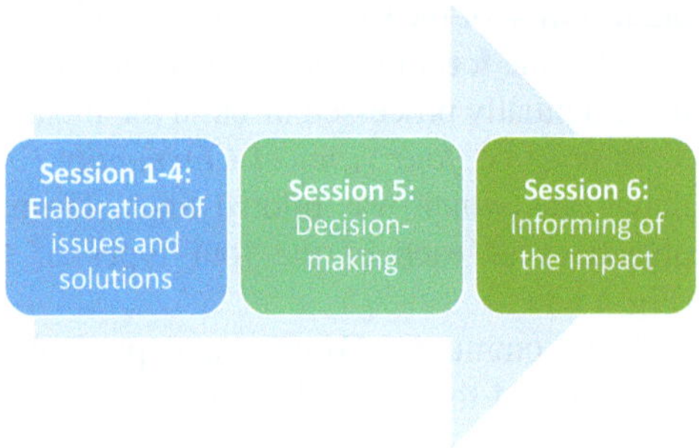

Fig. 11.2 Community forum's sessions

3. Taking place in a *neutral venue* in the community.
4. Structured discussions, based on a *pre-set agenda.*
5. The discussions are moderated by an *external, neutral, certified moderator*, supported by a co-moderator from the community and respected by the community, but not belonging to the local administration or municipal council.
6. Participants are assigned to groups, called *working tables*, based on their *social and economic interests*. The working tables reflect the *diversity* and needs of the municipality. Typical working tables include education, health, youth, unemployed, business sector, agriculture, etc. The working tables have a minimum of four participants and the average number of working tables is 10.
7. If a specific expertise is needed, *experts* outside the forum are invited to provide expertise to help the forum learn more and make informed decisions.
8. The working tables make the decisions collectively based on the principle "*one working table, one vote*". It is up to the working table how they decide on the one vote they have. Usually, it is based on consensus, which is built naturally through the Community Forum's sessions, as the understanding on the topic deepens and table cohesion grows. If the decision cannot be made by consensus, the group might decide by a majority vote, usually by raising hands.
9. The *local administration* sits at one of the working tables and has equal rights/vote as the other participants. Still, their information provision and clarification roles are very important, especially when it comes to municipal competences.
10. Municipal *councilors* can decide to join any of the working tables, form a separate one, or join the local administration table.
11. The *mayor* typically takes part in sessions one, five, and six to motivate active citizens' participation (session one), to hear the recommendations and commit to implementing them (session five) and to inform what has been implemented (session six). In the case of the Budget Forum, the mayor, as the one who proposes the budget and justifies it in front of the city council, takes part in all forum sessions.
12. The forums work out *solutions* and give *recommendations* to the municipal administration, municipal council, and local institutions.
13. The forums *build partnerships*, as different groups with the same or similar interests can work together.

14. The forum discussions lead to *results*-projects, recommendations, etc.
15. The forum projects are *implemented* with the resources of the municipality and/or other interested individuals or businesses. In the case of the Budget Forums, citizens have a say on what projects should be financed with the municipal budget, within the *budget programs*, as described below. Such projects range from several 1000 EUR to several 100,000 EUR, and in exceptional cases, for capital infrastructure investment projects, even more.

The Community Forums were expected to bring together a minimum of 40 citizens from small municipalities with less than 10,000 inhabitants, 60 citizens from those between 10,000–30,000 inhabitants and 80 citizens from municipalities with over 30,000 citizens. In practice, the number of citizens taking part in the forums was always higher than the requested minimum. The number of citizens involved certainly gives legitimacy. However, it also needs to be manageable, so practice showed that the number of citizens involved should range from 60 to 100, depending on the size of the municipality.

11.3 Budget Forums: Planning a Municipal Budget Tailored to Citizens' Needs

The Budget Forums were introduced a bit later than the Traditional/Project Forums, in the period 2008–2010, learning from the experience of the Project Forums, and once the municipalities entered the *second phase of the process of fiscal decentralization*, which enabled them to plan better and tailor their budgets based on the local needs. At the same time, the municipalities accumulated knowledge and experience in conducting the Community Forums and infused a habit of citizens' participation that were good preconditions for involving citizens in a transparent tailoring of the municipal budget.

The subject of the participatory decision-making process of the Budget Forums is *the municipal budget for the next year*, more specifically, the *budget programs*, and *the result* is the adopted municipal budget in consultations with citizens. This way, *municipalities aim* to increase citizens' understanding of the budgeting process, scarce resources, and the need to prioritize, while at the same time increasing openness, transparency, and accountability. Citizens contribute to the allocation of funds within the *budget programs*, which are linked to the key municipal competences, such as urban planning, local economic development, communal services, culture, environmental protection, social protection and protection of children, etc., as well as their subprograms. For illustration, the program Communal Services has several sub-programs, such as: maintenance of urban equipment, water supply, sewage, public lighting, public hygiene, roads and transport, etc. If the municipality has foreseen project funds, the Budget Forum is also a Project Forum. Citizens' contribution to the budget relates to the *development plans and capital investments* and does not tackle municipal operation costs. However, the whole budget is presented so that citizens get the whole picture.

At the first forum session, municipal administration informs the citizens about the *process of developing the municipal budget, budget objectives and principles* and explains the *structure of the budget*. During the next forum sessions, the draft *budget is reviewed in detail*, with concrete numbers and activities. Citizens discuss the strategic priorities, budget programs, revenues, expenditures, and potential projects to be implemented with external funding. Between forum sessions, the municipal administration reviews the proposals and provides inputs on their feasibility, alignment with national and local policies, technical documentation needed, procedures, etc. The discussions result with citizens' prioritization of projects that the municipality should implement within its annual budget. The proposals of the Budget Forum are then submitted to the mayor and become an integral part of the budget proposal submitted to the Municipal Council. It is then the Municipal Council that makes the final decision on the municipal budget, and although there is no legal obligation for it, as highlighted above, there is a practice that most of the proposals filed by the forums are being accepted and implemented.

All interested citizens are invited to take part in the Budget Forum, which is done via Municipal website, social media, local media, meetings with different civil society organizations, non-formal groups and community leaders, etc. There is no preselection of participants. Municipal administration, municipal council members and all local politicians and stakeholders are invited to participate in the Budget Forum. The work of the Budget Forum is organized through working tables, that are named based on the stakeholders they bring together, their occupation, interest or affiliation to one of the budget programs/municipal competences. There are, for example, tables on communal services, local economic development, education, etc.

The *timeline* of the Budget Forums is adjusted to the legal framework for the development and adoption of the municipal budget, i.e. the budget calendar, so the six sessions take place in *September–December* for planning the municipal budget for the next calendar year. In the end, at the last prioritizing and decision-making session, the Budget Forum forms a *working group for advocacy and monitoring* of the implementation of the forum's proposals, recommendations, and projects, which consists of representatives of all working tables. This group hands the recommendations to the mayor, signed by all forum participants, and takes part in the sessions of the municipal council and the relevant municipal committees, presenting and advocating for the proposals of the forum. The working group also *follows the implementation* of the selected projects. The group does not have any legal instruments to guarantee its work and influence but is considered a representative body of the Budget Forum that during the sixth, and last session of the forum informs about the *implementation of the budget*, in line with the recommendations made by the forum. This role guarantees the enforcement of the decisions, which has been confirmed by practice so far. The evaluation of the Budget Forums implemented in 2014–2017 showed that citizens prioritized almost 300 budgetary programs and around 900 projects. The municipalities adopted over 90% of citizens' proposals (Spirkovska, 2016).

11.3.1 The Practice of the Municipality of Bitola

The Municipality of Bitola[4] is one of the biggest urban centers, located in the Southwest of the country. Out of the 85,164 citizens, 69,287 live in the city and 15,877 in 65 villages. The Municipality of Bitola has a tradition of organizing Community Forums since 2008 and Budget Forums since 2022. From November until December 2023, the Municipality of Bitola organized a Budget Forum to solicit citizens' contribution to prioritizing the budget programs and projects as part of the municipal budget process for 2024.

In preparation of the Budget Forum sessions, the municipality shared a public call for all interested citizens to join the forum,[5] which was distributed via its website, social media, local media and announcement boards.

Also, in a pre-forum session, the mayor and the heads of the Municipal departments for Economic Development, Communal Affairs, Property and Legal Affairs and Finances, met with the presidents of neighborhood/village councils to present them with the idea of the planned budget forums and invite them to actively participate.[6] In order to raise awareness by all political parties, the mayor also invited their coordinators at this meeting.

The Budget Forum was organized in four sessions.

The first session, with the participation of 85 citizens, included:

1. An address by the mayor about the need for and importance of the Budget Forum process, from the perspective of the municipality, as part of its efforts for transparency and inclusion of citizens in creating and implementing local policies.
2. The moderator of the Budget Forum presented the process, objectives, methods, organizational structure, and rules of the forum.
3. The moderator of the Budget Forum presented the strategic priorities of the Municipality of Bitola for 2024, key strategic documents and explained the budget calendar.
4. In collaboration with the department on budget coordination, the moderator presented the municipal budget, including planned and executed revenues in 2023, proposed programs and related expenditures for 2024 and expected revenues for 2024.
5. A discussion on the structure of the Budget Forum/definition of working tables.
6. Discussion on the municipal revenues and proposals, ideas and recommendations for improving tax collection and increasing municipal revenues.
7. Selection of programs for discussion at the second and third forum session.

---

[4] See https://www.bitola.gov.mk/.

[5] See ПОКАНА ЗА УЧЕСТВО НА БУЏЕТСКИ ФОРУМ ЗА ПЛАНИРАЊЕ НА БУЏЕТОТ ЗА 2024 ГОДИНА | Општина Битола (bitola.gov.mk).

[6] See ПРЕТСЕДАТЕЛИТЕ НА УРБАНИТЕ И МЕСНИТЕ ЗАЕДНИЦИ НА СОСТАНОК СО ОПШТИНСКОТО РАКОВОДСТВО ПРЕД ФОРУМСКИТЕ СЕСИИ ЗА КРЕИРАЊЕ НА БУЏЕТОТ ЗА 2024 ГОДИНА | Општина Битола (bitola.gov.mk).

8. Evaluation of the session and definition of a timeframe for the second, third and fourth forum session.

It is noticeable that the number of participants was the highest during the first session of the Budget Forum. This was also the case in the previous year in Bitola and often in other municipalities too. Citizens are most curious at the beginning of the process, and their enthusiasm declines over time. This is an important message for the Budget Forums to intensify their work to motivate citizens to participate in all sessions.

The second Budget Forum session, with participation of 32 citizens, included:

1. Welcome, agenda, objectives and rules of the session, presented by the forum moderator.
2. Adoption of minutes from the first session.
3. Municipal administration presented, and citizens discussed the structure of the budget of the Bitola Municipality, planned and implemented revenues for 2023, until 30 September 2023, and projection of revenues for 2024.
4. Municipal administration presented the development priorities of the municipality for 2024, and clarified municipal competences related to policy making and decision-making.
5. The moderator presented the programs selected for review at the first forum session, as well as the work done between the two forum sessions, including new proposals received in a written form.
6. Participants discussed the relevance of the proposals received and elaborated a list of over 50 possible budget priorities to be discussed at the next forum sessions.
9. Next steps, information on the timeframe for the third forum session and evaluation of the forum session.

The third budget forum session, with participation of 38 citizens, included:

1. Welcome, agenda and objectives of the session, presented by the forum moderator.
2. Adoption of minutes from the second session.
3. Municipal administration presented the projected revenues and expenditures of the budget of the Municipality of Bitola for 2023, as well as part of the projects in the programs determined by the Budget Forum participants in the first forum session.
4. The moderator presented the work done by the municipal administration between the two forums. More than 150 potential projects have been reviewed and additional information provided to the forum, which then proceeded with the elaboration of the project ideas, from administrative, technical, legal and financial perspectives.
5. Evaluation of the session and definition of a timeframe for the fourth forum session.

The fourth and last Budget Forum session, with participation of 23 citizens, included:

1. Welcome, agenda and objectives of the session, presented by the forum moderator.
2. Adoption of minutes from the third session.
3. The moderator and municipal administration presented a report on the flow, organization and results of the forum process, including statistical data, the achievement of the objectives and lessons learnt from the process.
4. The moderator presented the work done between the sessions, based on citizens' proposals and a review of feasibility based on the input of the municipal administration.
5. The moderator presented the voting procedures and the forum working tables voted for their priorities of budget programs and projects.
6. The forum confirmed the voted priorities for a submission to the mayor.
7. The forum concluded with an evaluation of the session and forming a working group for following the implementation of forum's decisions.

The budget forum of the municipality of Bitola prioritized the following seven programs to be financed by the 2024 municipal budget:

1. Activities in sports and youth
2. Protection of environment and nature
3. Culture
4. Local economic development
5. Development plans
6. Social protection
7. Urban planning

Starting with more than 150 projects, the budget forum of the municipality of Bitola prioritized the following 14 projects for financing through the municipal budget.

1. Building a sports hall
2. Maintaining a bike park
3. Development of a culture strategy of the municipality
4. Support for the European Tennis Championship for children
5. Building a summer stage in the city park
6. Building beach volleyball court
7. Closing of the second walking zone in the Old Bazaar
8. Support for the reconstruction of a mountain hut
9. Increased financing for university sports in the municipality
10. River lighting in the area of the Old Bazaar
11. Electronic fences for supply vehicles in the Old Bazaar
12. Renovation of the old spa
13. Support to the women athletics night run
14. Organization of a competition for the best decorated window in the Old Bazaar

In addition to the voted priorities, the Budget Forum provided some 26 recommendations, compiled through the forum sessions, to be considered by the mayor: the reorganization of the work of schools, in one, instead of two school shifts; reuse of old, abandoned village schools as nature education centers; support for the production of organic and healthy food, etc.

The evaluation of the forum sessions revealed positive feedback. It demonstrated that the participants regard them as very useful, achieving the objectives and meeting the expectations concerning the forum process. The sessions have been evaluated with an average grade of 4.35 (on a scale from 1 to 5, with 5 being the best grade). With 4.6, the last forum session got the highest grade.

11.3.2 The Specificities of the Participatory Processes in Urban and Rural Contexts

Although the Budget Forums are open to all citizens, they need to reflect municipality's diversity, including participants with different backgrounds, such as social, age, ethnic, gender, professional, religious, etc. In the preparatory work before the forum, the mayors and local administration make sure that they reach out to all citizens, including those of remote, vulnerable and marginalized communities. This is done via traditional and social media, but also direct visits and meeting with these communities. In the cases of Bitola and Strumica, the municipalities, among other outreach mechanisms, used the neighborhood and village councils, which ensures that the whole territory of the municipality is invited. However, the experience of the forums has confirmed that due to limited human, financial and spatial capacities, the communication of the authorities with the citizens is still a challenge, especially in rural areas (Hadzi-Vasileva et al., 2017).

The Budget Forum working tables are different in different municipalities due to their specifics and needs. Rural municipalities that implemented the Community Forums had different compositions of working tables, including ones on agriculture, viticulture, animal husbandry, etc. When presenting the planned expenditures under the budget programs for the next year, the mayors provide a special overview on rural development. Also, the time when the forums take place has been adjusted based on the timing of agricultural works (Hadzi-Vasileva et al., 2017).

11.3.3 The Moderators/Process Managers

The moderator and co-moderator have a key role in implementing the Community Forums in general and the Budget Forums in particular. They are the promotors of local democracy, and help citizens become more active community actors and designers of local policies and local development.

The moderators ensure the flow of the forum process, its results and the active and constructive participation of citizens throughout the process. They have a key role in managing the discussions and debates, and guiding the forum to its decision. While the moderator is coming from outside the municipality for neutrality, the co-moderator is coming from the municipality. Since the beginning of the Community Forums Program, priority has been given to *training* both the moderator and the co-moderator of the forum. Initially, the training included lectures and practical work covering all the aspects of the role and tasks of the moderators, techniques for mobilization, moderation skills and processes for developing forum projects.

As the experience in implementing the forums grew, ZELS developed a *Certification Program for Forum Moderators* that started in 2013 and resulted in 62 certified moderators. The certificate is valid for 5 years, after which the moderator again participates in training, and takes a written and oral exam. The training today includes: legal framework, organizing and financing of local government, decentralization processes, forms of citizens' participation at the local level, types of Community Forums, steps in the implementation of forums, community mobilization, moderation, and facilitation.

11.3.4 Communicating with Citizens

The mobilization and motivation of citizens to join the Budget Forums and remain active throughout the process is an important task. Municipalities used several *outreach activities* to mobilize participants, such as meetings with neighborhood and village councils, visits to underrepresented or marginalized communities (like ethnic minorities or people living in rural and remote areas), meetings with citizens, meetings with local leaders, civil society organizations, informal groups, direct mailing, telephone calls, e-mails, etc.

Different *communication tools* like posters, bulletins, leaflets, blog posts, social media posts, traditional media coverage, statements, and interviews were used to inform and engage the citizens. The posters and leaflets informed of the upcoming forum sessions, while the bulletins provided an overview of the past sessions, decisions made, and citizens' experiences. The communication materials were distributed in the most visited locations in the community, such as municipal information boards, schools, shops, community centers, etc. The face-to-face contact, including a comprehensive explanation of the objectives and the process of the Budget Forums, proved to be the most effective tool for mobilizing participants.

11.3.5 Legislative and System Changes

Practice has demonstrated that Community Forums are very useful tool for citizens participation in the work of municipalities. However, since the Law on Local Self-Government does not recognize Community Forums, ZELS prepared *guidelines for municipalities* for changes in their statutes that introduced Community Forums as a tool for citizens participation in their municipalities, as well as a rulebook for organizing Community Forums in municipalities. Since adopting of these documents in 2010, 70 of the country's 80 municipalities have *institutionalized the Community Forums*.

As the importance of participatory budgeting increased in past decades, most municipalities have prepared so-called *Citizens' Budgets*[7] that aim to inform citizens on the municipal revenues and expenditures in an understandable way, educate them on local finances, increase their awareness on their role in the budgeting process, and increase active participation of citizens in planning and executing the municipal budget. The Citizens' Budgets raise citizens' awareness on the budgeting process and call for their active role, also serving as an invitation for their participation in the Budget Forums. During the Budget Forums, Citizens' Budgets are used as resource material, explaining the budget in an understandable way.

11.4 Conclusions

The Budget Forums, as a form of participatory budgeting, were introduced in Macedonian municipalities in the period 2008–2010, once the municipalities entered the second phase of the process of fiscal decentralization, which enabled them to plan better and tailor their budgets based on local needs.

The aim of the Budget Forums is to solicit citizens' opinions on the design of the municipal budget for the next year, more specifically, the prioritization of budget programs and the specific projects under these programs. Through the Budget Forums, municipalities increase citizens' understanding of the budgeting process, scarce resources, and the need to prioritize, while at the same time increasing openness, transparency, and accountability.

Through Budget Forum sessions, citizens discuss the priorities for the next year and decide on the specific priority budget programs and projects. Their decision is then submitted to the mayor and becomes an integral part of the budget proposal that goes for a review and adoption by the Municipal Council. Although there is no legal obligation, there is a practice that most of the proposals filed by the forums are accepted and implemented.

Budget Forums are open to all citizens. Still their composition needs to reflect municipality's diversity, including participants with different backgrounds, such as social, age, ethnic, gender, professional, religious, etc. In the preparatory work before the forum, the mayors and local administration make sure that they reach out to all citizens, including those of remote, vulnerable and marginalized communities.

[7] Example of citizens' budget for 2023 of the municipality of bitola: Microsoft Word - @0S0=A:8 1C_5B_°?HB8=0 8B>;0.docx (bitola.gov.mk).

There is no pre-selection of participants. People from the municipal administration, municipal council members and all local politicians and stakeholders are invited to participate in the Budget Forum. The work of the forum is organized through working tables, based on the principle “one table, one vote”, which limits the weight of individual interests and dominance.

Between forum sessions, the municipal administration reviews the proposals and provides inputs on their feasibility, their alignment with national and local policies, the technical documentation needed, procedures, etc. This is the only way in which the municipal administration influences citizens’ discussions and decisions.

The Budget Forums are organized as in-presence meetings. Some of the communication is done in a digital manner. However, the physical contact, including explanation of the objectives and the process of the Budget Forums, proved to be the most effective tool for mobilizing participants.

At the last prioritizing and decision-making session, the Budget Forum forms a working group for advocacy and monitoring of the implementation of forum’s proposals, recommendations, and projects. This group consists of representatives of all working tables. It submits the recommendations to the mayor and follows the implementation of the selected projects. Although the group does not have any legal instruments for enforcement, the expectation that it reports the results at the follow-up session of the Budget Forum gives it influence and guarantees the implementation of its recommendations. This has been confirmed by common practice so far.

The Budget Forum’s organization makes sure that needs of both urban and rural communities are considered. The municipalities, among other outreach mechanisms, use the neighborhood and village councils to ensure that the whole territory of the municipality is invited. The Budget Forum working tables are different in different municipalities to meet their specifics and needs. Rural municipalities had different compositions of working tables, including ones on agriculture, viticulture, animal husbandry, etc. When presenting the planned expenditures under the budget programs for the next year, the mayors provide a special overview on rural development. Also, the time of the forums has been adjusted based on the timing of agricultural works.

The Budget Forums brough a new dimension in citizens’ participation in Macedonian municipalities. Citizens got a mechanism to express their needs, have a say in determining municipal priorities for financing and learn more about the budgeting process. In the same time, the Budget Forums contributed to increasing responsiveness, openness, transparency, and accountability of municipalities. Practicing Budget Forums continuously will contribute to meeting citizens’ expectations for long-term benefits from the process of decentralization, related to active role of citizens, greater transparency and accountability, fairer allocation of local budgets, and policies and practices in line with the European perspective of the country.

References

Hadzi-Vasileva, K., Mehmeti, A. D., Angelov, G., Milenkova, S., Haziri, L., Sharkovski, B., Taseski, I., Shabani, F., Spirkovska, I., & Mihailov, D. G. (2017). *Community Forum in 11 steps*. ZELS.

Jovanova, K., Krstevska, M. L., Dalipi, L., & Dimovski, M. (2014). *Analytical report on the decentralization process*. OSCE Mission to Skopje.

Lessenski, M., Habova, A., & Shopov, V. (2006). *The process of decentralization in Macedonia: Prospects for ethnic conflict mitigation, enhanced representation, institutional efficiency and accountability*. Retrieved November 26, 2023, from https://idscs.org.mk/wp-content/uploads/2009/08/macedonia_decentralization.fullreport_appendix.pdf

Spirkovska, I. (2016). *Community Forums Program 2006-2016*. Community Forums Coordination Unit.

Tedesco, A. (2008). *Overview of decentralization for 2008*. OSCE Spillover Monitor Mission to Skopje.

Chapter 12
Participatory Budgeting in Poland

Anna Szustek

Abstract In Poland, participatory budgeting has been in use since 2011. The term "civic budget" is also used interchangeably. It is a form of participatory democracy. In the first 8 years, general acts on the territorial self-government units and provisions of local government law constituted the legal basis for participatory budgets. Since 2018, participatory budgets have had a statutory registered legal position. Civic budgets are developing primarily in municipalities. The creation of these budgets is specific to urban municipalities. In municipalities that are cities with county rights, it is mandatory to establish a civic budget. The regulations for civic budgets in counties and provinces are almost analogous to those for municipalities. In both cases, the civic budget is optional. The implementation of civic budgets to date is assessed positively. Lower marks are given to the formal and legal aspects of the budgets.

Keywords Participatory budget · Citizen budget · Participatory democracy · Socialization of administration processes · Local politics · Municipal governance processes

12.1 Introduction

This chapter aims to present participatory budgeting in Poland, its legal basis and how it works in practice. It is important to diagnose its qualities and weaknesses as an institution of participatory democracy, its role in building links in local communities and its importance in repairing of local government. The object of the study is to seek answers to the questions of how this form of deliberative democracy influences how local communities are animated, how participatory budgeting affects local interests and the quality of governance in local government units. The hypothesis comes down to the statement that the institution of participatory budgeting

A. Szustek (✉)
Faculty of Political Sciences and International Studies, University of Warsaw, Warsaw, Poland
e-mail: a.j.szustek@uw.edu.pl

K. Kössler, E. Schläppi (eds.), *Citizen Participation in Local Governance*, Local and Urban Governance, https://doi.org/10.1007/978-3-031-99824-9_12

requires further legal changes considering the experience to date. Moreover, for the instrument of participatory democracy to have a significant impact on improving relations between residents and local government authorities, it needs to be more widely promoted by local government units, third-sector organizations, local government associations (e.g., the Association of Polish Cities, the Union of Polish Metropolises), and local media. Support from the state factor (Chancellery of the President of the Republic of Poland, and the Minister of the Interior and Administration) would be important and desirable.

Among the numerous forms of urban activism, those that take an institutionalized form are particularly important. Spontaneous activism appears to be ad hoc, temporary and of short duration. If we want to involve local communities in public governance, their activity cannot be ephemeral.

Various forms of participatory democracy are used to shape an optimal relationship between public authorities and citizens. Nowadays, the essence of this democracy is the kind of citizen participation in urban governance that builds social capital in a wider perspective. Municipal governments use forms of participatory democracy such as consultations, the local initiative, and the participatory budget (Pytlik, 2017, pp. 104–106). Consultation works well in situations of acute conflict and can also help to prevent conflicts. The local initiative is useful for introducing new legislative solutions and was introduced in 2003 by the Act on Public Benefit Activity and Volunteerism. Residents submit an idea and declare their participation in its implementation which may include community service, in-kind or financial contributions. Consultations and local initiatives already have some practice. Participatory budgeting, in turn, is a relatively new institution in Poland's public life.

A key concept for the participatory budget is participation which "is one of the fundamental elements of citizenship. It thus defines the rights of citizens to participate fully and equally in the governance of the city or other local government units" (Błaszak, 2019, p. 203). Participatory processes can be looked at in traditional and modern ways. In the traditional view, what is important is "the participation of citizens in creating and implementing the policy, which has hitherto been reserved to the exclusive competence of local government and administration. Participation refers to involving residents who influence the decisions and actions of local government through their activity. These decisions can be taken by actors characterized by democratic legitimacy, i.e., those who exercise executive power (e.g., president, mayor, and councilors)" (Błaszak, 2019, pp. 203–204). In a modern view of public participation, "it should be defined not only as the participation of different groups of the local community in creating public policies (e.g., building development strategies), but should also be seen as their participation in the decision-making and implementation of tasks formulated jointly with the local government of these policies" (Błaszak, 2019, p. 204).

In Poland, the outlook on the institutions of participatory democracy is changing, as they are gaining increasing recognition. Until a few years ago, participatory democracy was deemed difficult to achieve in practice. Empirical studies have shown that "in social practice, participation is often illusory, it concerns matters of little importance, and citizens' opinions are only meant to legitimize decisions already taken" (Załęcki, 2018, p. 178). Residents have ample opportunities to get involved in various forms of participation. However, they do not feel that they have a say in the actions of the city government. The reason for this was considered to lie with the residents themselves, who show relatively little interest in public affairs in their town. But it was also highlighted that the passivity of residents is fostered by the "superficial nature of participatory solutions and procedures" (Załęcki, 2018, p. 178). In the conclusion of the empirical studies referred to, it was pointed out that participation is a great challenge for local governments in Poland: "Local government faces the important task of stimulating the social activity of its residents on the one hand and, on the other, of further improving and developing the various forms of participatory democracy" (Załęcki, 2018, p. 191).

In the theoretical view of participation, the real influence of citizens on decision-making is crucial. In practice, "due to the multi-faceted nature of the decision-making processes, the inclusion of citizens is unfortunately not obvious. There are many dilemmas of involving citizens in the co-governance process. Civic participation is an end in itself, but also a method of pursuing sustainable development" (Błaszak, 2019, p. 204).

The participatory budget is one of the most popular instruments of public participation in cities in Poland. The term *civic budget* is also used interchangeably. During the consultation of the 2018 draft law introducing participatory budgeting, representatives of the Association of Polish Cities pointed out that both terms should appear in the law. It was emphasized that "*civic budget* and *participatory budget* are currently used interchangeably. Both names have been in use for 6 years, variously in different local authorities, and residents are used to these terms, which are commonly used locally (many local government regulations sanction the operation of local affairs in a customary manner" (Association of Polish Cities, 2018). However, only one concept is left in the act. The act uses the term *civic budget*. The *participatory budget/civic budget* category is only just taking shape. There is an ongoing debate about this concept's semantic scope. In practice, the term *civic budget* has become more popular. This notion also prevails in the legal circuit, official circuit, and theoretical reflection. However, the term *participatory budget* is more widely recognized in the academic circuit. In the simplest terms, participatory budgeting can be defined as "a decision-making process in which citizens co-create the budget of a given city, thus co-determining the distribution of a specific pool of public funds" (Błaszak, 2019, p. 204). The theoretical approach emphasizes that the idea of participatory budgeting is part and parcel of a vision of civil society.

In Poland, participatory budgeting was implemented for the first time in 2011. The forerunner of participatory budgeting is the City of Sopot. The inspiration came from an informal group called the Sopot Development Initiative, which works for sustainable development and increased citizen participation in decisions affecting them. The city authorities have responded positively to this request. The budget planned to "subject to civic spending almost 1% of the total city budget expenditure, i.e., 5 million PLN" (Krasnowolski, 2020, p. 12) Residents submitted several hundred projects from among which a dozen were selected for each of the four wards and 22 city-wide projects. Out of over 32,000 residents entitled to vote, which included non-citizens, 2410 people did vote. Six projects were selected and implemented.

12.2 Legal Basis of the Participatory Budget

For the first 8 years from 2011, participatory budgets were created solely on the basis of the general statutory powers of the local authority concerned. It was assumed that the possibility to introduce a civic budget stems from Article 5a(1) of the Municipal Self-Government Act of 1990. In light of this provision, "the inhabitants of the municipality may be consulted in the cases provided for by the Act and on other matters of importance to the municipality." However, many objections have been raised about whether this is a sufficient legal basis for a participatory budget (Burski, 2016, p. 27). It was pointed out that treating participatory budgeting as a public consultation creates a contradiction. Public consultations "are not, in principle, binding for the authorities" since "as a result of them, only the opinion, wish or expectation of the residents as to how a matter within the authority's jurisdiction should be resolved is externalized. ... Even the fact of carrying out consultations in the form of a popular vote of the municipality's inhabitants, i.e., in a form similar to a referendum, and the solutions taken in resolutions or orders of bodies of units introducing the civic budget, which give the consultations a decisive dimension, will not change this nature. However, even in the absence of relevant provisions in local laws, giving the consultation a decisive dimension, the position that the consultation on the civic budget is de facto binding should be advocated. … In this case, the residents of the administrative unit in question act as the de facto decision-making entity, even though the budget resolution is formally adopted by the competent municipal authority" (Tykwińska-Rutkowska & Glejt, 2015, pp. 322–323).

Given the enigmatic statutory legal basis for the first 8 years, participatory budgets were implemented primarily on the basis of local acts. In matters of participatory budgets, separate resolutions of the city council were mostly adopted and implemented by an ordinance of the mayor or city president. Draft resolutions setting out the principles and procedures for consultation on participatory budgets were submitted for adoption by mayors and city presidents. Sometimes the executive body referred directly to the Municipal Self-Government Act. Less frequently, participatory budgets were created on the basis of mayor/city president ordinances based on the provisions for preparing and implementing the municipal budget. Most often, the initiative to set up participatory budgets came from the mayors and city presidents themselves, while Councilors were less active in this area. Occasionally, these budgets' have been initiated by social sector bodies such as the Municipal Council for Public Benefit.

Experience has shown the need for a more thorough statutory regulation of participatory budgets. Also in the literature, it was emphasized that "the budget's functioning should be based on a clearly and comprehensively defined procedure"

(Tykwińska-Rutkowska & Glejt, 2015, p. 321). The response to this was the enactment of an act in 2018 to increase citizen participation in the process of electing, functioning, and controlling certain self-government bodies. This law amended the Act on Municipal Self-Government of 1990, the Act on County Self-Government of 1998, the Act on Provincial Self-Government of 1998, the Act on the System of the Capital City of Warsaw of 2002 and the Act on Petitions of 2014. The most extensive regulation of municipal budgets is found in Article 5a of the Act on Municipal Self-Government. There are narrower regulations for county budgets and provincial budgets. In practice, participatory budgets are implemented primarily in municipalities. More specifically, creating these budgets is a characteristic of urban municipalities (Leśniewska-Napierała, 2019, p. 80, 90). Rural municipalities implement village budgets among the residents of the auxiliary units. "In municipalities that are cities with county rights, it is mandatory to establish a participatory budget." Under the provisions of the Act of 2018, the participatory budget "is a special form of public consultation. As part of the participatory budget, the residents decide on a portion of the municipal budget expenditure each year by direct vote. The tasks within the projects selected as part of the participatory budget are included in the municipal budget resolution. The municipal council, in the course of work on the draft budget resolution, may not remove or substantially change the tasks selected as part of the participatory budget."

The legislator has entrusted the municipal council with determining the requirements to be met by participatory budget projects. The municipal council shall determine by resolution:

1. The formal requirements for submitted projects.
2. The required number of signatures of residents who support the project. Here, a threshold is indicated, i.e., this number cannot be greater than 0.1% of the population of the area covered by the participatory budget pool in which the project is submitted.
3. Principles for evaluating the submitted projects. It was emphasized that the following criteria are mandatory when assessing projects: legal compliance, technical feasibility and meeting formal requirements.
4. An appeal procedure against a decision which does not allow a project to be voted on.
5. Procedural rules for the voting, the determination of results and their announcement. It is made clear that "the voting rules must ensure equality and directness of the vote".

In municipalities that are cities with county rights, the amount of the participatory budget must be at least 0.5% of the municipality's expenditure included in the last submitted budget report. The law allows for participatory budget funds to be divided into pools covering the entire municipality and parts of the municipality addressed to auxiliary units or groups of auxiliary units.

12.3 Operation of Participatory Budgets

In general, participatory processes aim, in my view, to improve the effectiveness of governance in local government units, work towards the benefit and subjectivity of residents and build civil society in local communities (Śwital, 2024, pp. 106–107). The participatory budget is intended to involve residents in co-designing the budget of the city in which they live or work (Dubicki, 2021, p. 103). From the perspective of the local authority in question, the objectives of participatory budgeting are defined, from the perspective of the local government, by residents' satisfaction with municipal governance. It is important to have a thorough understanding of the needs of local communities and for residents to be able to articulate these needs. The participatory budget is an instrument for building relationships between local government units and citizens and provides an opportunity to create new channels of communication. Based on empirical research, it can be concluded that "the scope of [participatory] budgets, the form of their organization, as well as the social and political dimensions look slightly different in different cities, even though they should look similar by design" (Błaszak, 2019, p. 205), as they use the same statutory basis. However, the details of participatory budgets are determined by the municipal councils by resolution.

Projects implemented as part of the participatory budget should be within the broad scope of the local authority's own tasks, both mandatory and optional (Gońda, 2017, pp. 175–176). However, in practice, it is not uncommon for local authorities to indicate top-down in which area projects can be submitted. Proposals for projects submitted for implementation as part of participatory budgets vary widely. Projects in the spheres of municipal services and environmental protection, culture and national heritage protection and education are frequent. Most often, they concern investments in small-scale renovations and innovations regarding facilities serving residents in the area they live in. Road, leisure, and sports infrastructure facilities are being constructed.

In participatory budgeting, the residents are the ones who propose projects for implementation. Which specific entities are entitled to submit proposals with projects is regulated by the resolutions on participatory budgets in each local authority in a given year. Different solutions are used. A popular solution is one where any resident (including minors) with permanent or temporary residence can submit a project if they collect, for example, 15 signatures in its support (the number of signatures in support varies greatly but is generally small). Sometimes an age censor was established, e.g., residents aged 16 and over. Another solution is the right to submit projects by those who have an active right to vote in city council elections and collect a certain number of signatures of support. Among the institutional actors able to submit projects were foundations, associations, housing cooperatives, housing communities, allotment gardens, school sports clubs, educational institutions, universities, urban movements, and informal groups. There is controversy around some of these entities as to whether their participation violates the essence of the civic budget, e.g., universities or educational institutions. First, those projects to be put to a popular vote are selected among the submitted proposals. This selection is made by groups comprising representatives of residents, social organizations and movements, politicians, councilors, and municipal officials. There is no standardized composition of such groups. The composition of these groups may be specified in the municipal council's resolution on the participatory budget. If it is not specified in the municipal council's resolution, such a group is formed by the municipal administration, the department that deals with implementing the participatory budget. Therefore, the composition may be different in each municipality in any given year. In a second step, the popular vote on projects is open to any resident with permanent or temporary residence. However, the detailed interpretation of this principle is set out in the resolution on the civic budget in the local authority in a particular year. In the early days of participatory budgets, it was assumed that residents who were at least 13, 16 or 18 years old and had at least limited legal capacity could vote. In recent years, solutions have sometimes been used where no lower age limit is adopted for voters so that, for example, even a pre-school children can vote. In other cases, the basis for participation in the vote was the possession of a PESEL number, a code that individuals are assigned within Poland's Universal Electronic System for the Registration of the Population (PESEL). It was also assumed that being on the electoral register for a local council election entitles a person to vote on civic budget projects. The above-mentioned 2018 Act specified that "the rules for the conduct of voting must ensure equality and directness of voting" (Article 5a(7)(4)). Equality means that everyone eligible to vote has the same number of votes. Different solutions are used (Radzioch, 2024, pp. 38–39). A popular solution is one where the voter can cast only one vote for one proposed projects. A formula is sometimes used whereby, for example, 10 projects take part in a poll and each voter has five votes to cast for any project of their choice. Directness is understood traditionally, i.e., for example, a parent cannot cast a vote in a minor's place.

Ultimately, the residents select the projects to be implemented by popular vote. To date, there has been no empirical research on citizens voting on projects from participatory budgets. We are therefore unable to say with any certainty from which social group or age range the people who actually take part in the vote are.

In local interests in Poland, political parties do not play the most important role, but they are not irrelevant. Local community leaders like lawyers, teachers or civil servants, who form their own electoral committees at election time, are also of great importance. This is because they are well-known, often communicate directly with people and enjoy authority. Their suggestions for projects in participatory budgeting are more easily accepted.

Clientelism plays a big role in local interests because participatory budget projects can help local leaders to win over voters. This phenomenon is also evident with participatory budgeting. In 2011, one municipality implemented a participatory budget, in 2012 there were five such municipalities, in 2013 there were 53 municipalities, in 2014 there were 146 municipalities, and in 2015 there were 136 municipalities. In the following years, the number of municipalities opting for participatory budgets decreased, and by the end of the second decade, this number had stabilized. The great interest in participatory budgeting between 2014 and 2015 is believed to have been linked to the local elections in November 2014: "Both groups vying for seats for their representatives and candidates for mayors and city presidents pledged to residents to implement participatory budgets in exchange for their support." (Krasnowolski, 2020, p. 13).

In Poland, formal and informal urban movements are gaining importance and influence. It is not uncommon for them to use the organizational and legal form of associations, and foundations (Brol & Derlukiewicz, 2023, pp. 40–41). Their aim is to increase the influence of residents on local government decisions, to enforce electoral promises and to shape local policy in line with the needs and interests of residents. They are a kind of vanguard in local politics. Urban movements are independent, with well-defined local interests. These social movements have names such as *Napraw sobie miasto* ("Fix yourself the city", e.g. in Warsaw, Katowice, Krakow, Bochnia, Rybnik, and Żory) and *Prawo do miasta* ("Right to the city", in Poznań), and they are closely linked to participatory budgeting: "All (...) urban movements and others like them provided a strong subsoil to support the functioning of citizen budgets" (Krasnowolski, 2020, p. 13). These social movements are a new urban activism with great prospects for growth.

The influence of national and regional interests on local decision-making depends on several factors. A significant impact can be observed in local government units where, for example, large investments are made, companies of particular importance are located, and facilities of strategic importance for national security are situated. Moreover, such impact will be substantial if the municipality is an important link in the region's development. In small, economically weak municipalities, national and regional interests only have a marginal role in local decision-making processes. In recent years, efforts have been made to equalize the development of different regions of the country. As a result of this policy, national and regional authorities are becoming more intensively involved in local politics in economically weak municipalities with investments and promotion.

In large cities, consultation districts are created to conduct a civic budget. They often coincide with neighborhoods although this has not always been the case (e.g. in Gdańsk in 2016). Citizens then vote for individual projects. In large cities, there are city-wide and neighborhood projects.

Voting for projects is usually done online. As a result, projects advocated by young people win more often. It cannot be said that older residents are excluded because of online voting, but their participation is definitely lower. Phone applications are also being used to allow people to cast their vote. This tool is well evaluated and recommended by experts. For those without internet access, there are sometimes information points, e.g., in shopping centers, where they can vote for a project of their choice. However, this form is used by very few people and the costs of organizing such information points are considerable. This method of voting is therefore considered not very forward-looking but is maintained to respect the principles of local democracy, according to which everyone should be able to participate in the vote, regardless of access to electronic communication tools.

To get citizens interested in the civic budget, local authorities carry out information campaigns (Leszkowicz-Baczyński, 2016, pp. 165–166). Different tools work well in promotional campaigns. First and foremost, meetings are held between local government representatives and residents, usually at the initial stage, before proposals are submitted. These are sometimes themed meetings on, for example, cultural, sporting, environmental, infrastructure, educational and senior citizens' issues. A creative solution is the institution of the Council of Civic Budget Ambassadors in the City of Kraków, which organizes meetings. Instructions on how to draw up applications and submit them are published, with a detailed list of the own tasks of the municipality and district in which projects may be proposed. Voting instructions are disseminated in various forms. Handing out flyers, putting up posters in high-traffic areas and using social media are popular. Especially, the cities' official websites play a major role. Spots on regional television appear less frequently and, if so, rather in large cities.

The civic budget projects are implemented effectively to a high degree. There are rarely conflicts between residents and local government units because of the implementation of civic budget projects. The evaluation of the implementation of participatory budgets is carried out by the community and by mixed bodies made up of residents' representatives and municipal representatives. A separate issue is the control exercised by state institutions and the supervision of the state. Local authorities are evaluating civic budget projects. Electronic tools created specifically for this purpose on local government websites are popular. The City of Gdańsk, for example, uses an evaluation questionnaire on the city's website and the City of Koszalin an online evaluation questionnaire and focus groups. How local authorities operate within the terms of participatory budgets is evaluated during local elections, especially in election campaigns, and at meetings between local government activists and residents.

An interesting solution is the establishment of entities such as the Civic Budget Council in the City of Kraków. The body was created by an order of the city's president. The council consists of representatives of NGOs (six people), the city president (11 people), the city council (four people), neighborhood councils and boards (10 people), civic budget applicants, and urban activists. The council "monitors the implementation of tasks on a monthly basis, especially major investment projects and their contractors. All tasks related to the civic budget are handled by the Municipal Centre for Supporting Social Initiatives" (Czaja-Hliniak, 2019, p. 53).

An important role is played by the local press and groups created on social media where discussions on projects are held, such as the "Przyjaciele Dolinki" ("Friends of Dolinka") group on Facebook (Warsaw). Social media has a special role when a local community does not want a particular project, causing conflict between the local authority and the residents. This was the case in Warsaw's Mokotow district, where residents protested against a project in the Dolina Służewiecka. In terms of procedures, the city-wide project was not objectionable. Residents of the "Służew nad Dolinka" housing cooperative did not want the investment because it was destroying a beautiful park with biologically preserved nature. Despite protests, the local authority went ahead with the project, claiming that it could not abandon its implementation, as this would result in the City of Warsaw's budget not being approved by the Regional Chamber of Auditors. Ultimately, the residents lost this case. The positive effect was effective organization and community integration.

Supervision is something different from control because it is broader. Control is fact-finding about how things are compared to how they should be by law. Supervision is fact-finding plus the ability to make changes. The supervision of the municipalities' activities with regard to participatory budgets in the first period of operation belonged to the provincial governors. Following the entry into force of the 2018 Act, this is dealt with by the regional chambers of auditors.

The implementation of participatory budgets is also of interest to the Supreme Audit Office. In 2019, for the first time, there was an audit of how local government units performed in the implementation of civic budgets. The audit covered 22 city councils, including cities with district rights from six provinces. In addition, a questionnaire survey was conducted among mayors of selected cities from 16 provinces on the functioning of civic budgets or reasons for not using this form of participatory democracy. The survey was addressed to 318 cities, including 58 cities with county rights. 262 local authorities responded, i.e., 82%. "The main objective of the audit was to answer the question: were civic budget projects implemented correctly and effectively?" (Supreme Audit Office, 2019, p. 59). The survey questions addressed "the legal basis creating the civic budget, its amount, voter turnout, the possible introduction of an age criterion for those eligible to participate in the consultations, the existence of difficulties or problems related to these consultations ... and the reasons for not implementing the civic budgets in some municipalities" (Supreme Audit Office, 2019, p. 60). The following questions were of particular interest:

1. "Were the resolutions of the municipal council and the orders of the mayor (commune leader, city president, mayor) regarding the operation of the civic budget correct?
2. Was the selection of citizens' projects carried out in accordance with the municipalities' internal laws?
3. Was the implementation of the tasks correct and as intended?" (Supreme Audit Office, 2019, p. 59).

According to the Supreme Audit Office (SAO), the resolutions of city councils and the orders of mayors and city presidents regarding civic budgets "were issued incorrectly, i.e. in violation of Articles 5a(1) and 5a(2) of the Municipal Self-Government Act. This was due to the right to participate in public consultations being subject to the completion of a certain age (in all local authorities), the imposition of an obligation to provide a PESEL number during the consultations (in 21 of the 22 controlled local authorities) and the extension of the circle of entities entitled to submit applications to, inter alia, housing communities and cooperatives, or non-governmental organizations (in four local authorities). In 12 cities, certain principles and elements of the consultation procedure were set out in orders of mayors and presidents, instead of in resolutions of city councils, which did not comply with Article 5a(2) of the above-mentioned Act" (Supreme Audit Office, 2019, p. 9).

Regarding the second question mentioned above, the SAO found that project selection "in 17 cities took place in accordance with internal regulations. In the remaining five cities, 42 of the 2643 projects considered in these units were found to have been unreliably verified, resulting in residents being allowed to vote on the selection of projects that did not meet the requirements adopted in the internal regulations" (Supreme Audit Office, 2019, p. 9).

In the cases covered by the third question above, the audit found that, of the 313 projects examined, 266 were implemented correctly and as intended. The irregularities concerned 47 projects and consisted of breaches of procurement law, internal regulations and payment for work not carried out, even though these irregularities often concern minor issues so that projects can still be implemented successfully in practice. While the SAO's assessment of the functioning of the participatory budget concerning some legal aspects was unsatisfactory, in general, it was concluded that "the effects achieved by the audited cities in the implementation of projects within the framework of civic budgets in 2016–2018 prove the effectiveness of this form of cooperation between the residents and the authorities of the local self-government units, even though the implementation did not always go well" (Supreme Audit Office, 2019, p. 9). The implementation of the participatory budget projects is being carried out correctly at around 85% of the time.

In Poland, participation in urban and rural self-governments has its own important specificities. This specificity is not conveyed by comparing the participatory budgets in urban municipalities and the village funds in rural municipalities. But it is worth briefly recalling that rural municipalities implement these funds in the auxiliary units they are composed of, which are the villages (*sołectwa*). The legal basis for the village fund is the Act of 2014 on the village fund. Its idea is similar to that of participatory budgeting in municipalities. In the light of legislation from 2014, "the fund's resources shall be allocated for the implementation of projects which, submitted in the application ... are the municipality's own tasks, serve to improve the living conditions of the residents and are in line with the municipality's development strategy".

Both the participatory budget in municipalities and the village fund in rural municipalities are established on the basis of a resolution of the municipal council. In municipalities that are cities with district rights, the participatory budget is mandatory. In rural municipalities, creating a village fund is not mandatory. The village fund appeared slightly earlier than the participatory budget in municipalities. The first law on the village fund was passed in 2009 and projects have been implemented since 2010. The village fund has been highly appreciated from the beginning and is much more popular than the participatory budget in municipalities. Already in the first years of operation of the village fund, more than 50% of municipalities that have a *sołectwo* established a village fund. In 2023, the village fund was in operation in 1522 municipalities, out of a total of 2173 municipalities where there are *sołectwo*, a rate of more than 70%. The village fund has a slightly different procedure for project applications. Applications can be made by the *sołtys* (village leader), the village council or 15 adult residents. The application is passed by the village assembly on the initiative of the *sołtys*. The *sołtys* forwards the proposal to the *wójt* (municipality head) for inclusion in the municipal budget proposal.

The specificity of participatory processes in urban and rural local government units is of a deeper nature. Its roots are to be found in the tradition of self-organization. The different quality of ties in rural local communities plays an important role. Rural communities are more integrated and have more common interests and needs in terms of daily life. Urban communities are more dispersed and diverse.

In conclusion, communities in rural municipalities have human capital better prepared for participatory processes. This is due to the civic self-organization tradition. The social sector in rural municipalities stands with two pillars: the rural women's clubs and the voluntary fire brigades. This is the cradle of staff for participatory processes. In contrast, a weakness in rural municipalities is local government units as partners in participatory processes, especially those with a conservative attitude towards modern civic activity. In terms of organizational and legal forms, urban participation is weaker than rural participation. Cities do not have a tradition of civic self-organization passed down from generation to generation. Therefore, the new instruments for civic activation require a greater commitment from local government units. Openness to modern participation is also required among local government activists and municipal officials.

12.4 Conclusions

Poland is experiencing a crisis of the self-government system. It manifests itself on many levels. The lack of efficiency in the functioning of self-government bodies is significant. However, the superficial nature of local democracy is primarily expressed in the lack of meaningful citizen influence on decisions and co-governance. Researchers of the local government system believe that an institutional order conducive to civic participation has not yet taken shape in Poland. Social dialogue and civic participation have relatively little practice: "Be it residents or local authorities, neither party have well-developed effective communication systems. It is still a weak relationship space. The changes that should take place must move from representative democracy towards deliberative democracy. Residents are turning away from local authorities because they do not see them as their credible representatives. Seeing the civic budget as a remedy for the crisis of self-governance seems like a good idea. ... This budget restores the residents' so-called 'right to the city'" (Błaszak, 2019, p. 215).

Therefore, there is a need to improve this instrument of participatory democracy (Reszel, 2022, pp. 158–159). It is necessary to standardize the procedures in the civic budget. This is a task for associations of local governments such as the Union of Polish Counties, and the Union of Polish Cities (Ostachowski, 2020, pp. 173–174). These associations play an important integrating role for local government units. As Jolanta Blicharz points out, "they are that organizational and legal form which is generally complementary to the activities of local self-government. They serve in a special way to support its ideas on such an important episode as the performance of public tasks" (Blicharz, 2017, p. 127). Action in this regard should also come from the state, i.e., the government, the parliament, and the president of Poland.

An important value of participatory budgeting is revitalizing and building links in the local community. This aspect has received less attention to date. In this respect, the potential of participatory budgeting in Poland is still under-exploited. A wider promotion of participatory budgeting is necessary. This is a role for schools, social sector actors, the public media, and local authorities themselves.

References

Association of Polish Cities. (2018). *Proposed amendments to the Municipal Government Act concerning the regulation of participatory budgets*. Retrieved from https://www.miasta.pl/uploads/attachment/file/2115/projekt_zmian_BOP.pdf

Błaszak, M. (2019). Budżet obywatelski w Polsce i dylematy z nim związane. *Ruch Prawniczy, Ekonomiczny i Socjologiczny R, 81*(3), 203–220.

Blicharz, J. (2017). Zagadnienie charakteru prawnego stowarzyszeń jednostek samorządu terytorialnego. *Przegląd Prawa Administracji, 109*, 115–127.

Brol, M., & Derlukiewicz, N. (2023). *Budżet obywatelski w największych polskich miastach – perspektywa urzędników i aktywistów*. Wydawnictwo Uniwersytetu Ekonomicznego we Wrocławiu.

Burski, K. (2016). Prawna problematyka budżetu obywatelskiego i obywatelskiej inicjatywy uchwałodawczej. *Kortowski Przegląd Prawniczy, 1*, 26–31.

Czaja-Hliniak, I. (2019). Wybrane aspekty budżetu obywatelskiego w mieście metropolitalnym. *Kwartalnik Prawno-Finansowy, 1*, 42–59.

Dubicki, P. (2021). Budżet obywatelski jako element partycypacji społecznej. *Studia z Polityki Publicznej, 8*(1), 91–105.

Gońda, E. (2017). Tak zwany budżet obywatelski jako instrument alokacji środków publicznych w jednostkach samorządu terytorialnego. *Prace Naukowe Uniwersytetu Ekonomicznego we Wrocławiu, 485*, 169–177.

Krasnowolski, A. (2020). *Budżety obywatelskie (partycypacyjne). Historia instytucji i jej funkcjonowania w polskich samorządach*. Chancellery of the Senate.

Leśniewska-Napierała, K. (2019). Budżet obywatelski jako nowy instrument partycypacji na obszarach wiejskich w Polsce. *Studia Obszarów Wiejskich, 53*, 77–93.

Leszkowicz-Baczyński, J. (2016). Budżet partycypacyjny jako szansa redukcji społecznych problemów miast. *Przegląd Socjologiczny, 65*, 147–168.

Ostachowski, P. (2020). Funkcjonowanie i wyzwania władz lokalnych związane z budżetem partycypacyjnym w Polsce na przykładzie największych miast. *Rocznik Administracji Publicznej, 6*, 162–176.

Pytlik, B. (2017). Budżet partycypacyjny w Polsce. Ewolucja i dylematy. *Studia z Polityki Publicznej, 1*(13), 103–122.

Radzioch, J. (2024). Różnice w realizacji budżetów obywatelskich w Polsce. *Przegląd Politologiczny, 4*, 31–42.

Reszel, M. (2022). Ograniczenia budżetów obywatelskich w miastach na prawach powiatu w Polsce. *Academy of Management, 6*(1), 148–161.

Supreme Audit Office. (2019). *Funkcjonowanie budżetów partycypacyjnych (obywatelskich). Informacja o wynikach kontroli*. Registration no. 20/2019/P/18/064/LGD.

Śwital, P. (2024). Budżet obywatelski—Jako forma partycypacji społecznej. *Gubernaculum et Administratio, 2*(30), 97–110.

Tykwińska-Rutkowska, D., & Glejt, P. (2015). Prawna regulacja budżetu obywatelskiego a jego praktyczna realizacja—Czyli o uspołecznianiu wykonywania zadań publicznych na przykładzie rozwiązań przyjętych w Trójmieście. *Gdańskie Studia Prawnicze, 34*, 317–332.

Załęcki, J. (2018). Demokracja partycypacyjna (na przykładzie Gdańska). *Miscellanea Anthropologica et Sociologica, 19*(1), 178–193.

Chapter 13
Local Governance and Public Participation in South Africa: An Urban-Rural Perspective

Michelle Rufaro Maziwisa and Curtly Stevens

Abstract This chapter examines the effectiveness of public participation mechanisms in South African local government, with a strong focus on the municipal budget process. It argues that despite South Africa having an impressive range of legislative instruments detailing public participation mechanisms, the implementation of these mechanisms still leaves many behind in the practice of public participation. The chapter establishes that although public participation in the budget at the local government level is a constitutional imperative, this constitutional imperative is yet to be fully realized due to several institutional impediments, resulting in citizens viewing public participation as a mere rubber-stamping exercise. It finds that communities, instead of using invited spaces such as ward committees, are increasingly resorting to participation in invented spaces through engaging in protests, some of which turn violent. The chapter calls for addressing the issue of capacity and skills shortage of ward committees. It argues that the adoption of alternative methods, such as online meetings, to promote public participation has limited the space for disadvantaged communities and vulnerable groups, such as women, children, and those living in informal settlements, to participate in the budget formation process and worsened the digital divide between urban and rural communities.

Keywords Municipalities · Participatory budgeting · Public participation · Local governance · Ward committees · Informality

---

M. R. Maziwisa (✉)
Centre for Human Rights, University of Pretoria, Pretoria, South Africa
e-mail: michelle.maziwisa@up.ac.za

C. Stevens
Dullah Omar Institute, University of the Western Cape, Bellville, South Africa
e-mail: cstevens@uwc.ac.za

K. Kössler, E. Schläppi (eds.), *Citizen Participation in Local Governance*, Local and Urban Governance, https://doi.org/10.1007/978-3-031-99824-9_13

13.1 Introduction

Public participation is a central part of democratic governance in modern societies as a means to ensure governance "of the people, by the people, for the people", drawing from the famous words of Abraham Lincoln's Gettysburg address "that these dead shall not have died in vain – that this nation, under God, shall have a new birth of freedom and that government of the people, by the people, for the people, shall not perish from the earth" (U.S. President Abraham Lincoln, 1863).

Although human rights are not the subject of this chapter, it is important to reflect on the rights which form the basis of the claim to public participation in South Africa to establish the context and also to stress their importance. Additionally, the historical context of exclusion during apartheid is a compelling reason to ensure public participation in South Africa, as historically, groups were denied participation in government in the form of voting, being elected, and accessing public services based on race.

Various instruments urge states to create mechanisms to encourage and implement public participation. Particularly, Article 13(4) and (5) of the African Charter on the Values and Principles of Decentralization, Local Governance and Local Development (African Charter on Decentralization) states that "[l]ocal public officials shall duly represent the interests of local communities and shall consult with their populations on an on-going and regular basis through clearly specified mechanisms and timeframes" and that "[c]entral governments shall adopt legislation and establish administrative and financial mechanisms and use ICTs to encourage local residents and communities to provide feedback to their locally elected representatives, and make their grievances heard, and seek redress".

Globally, mechanisms to realize participation have largely centered around elections and ensuring universal suffrage, which has, over the years, dismantled various barriers such as those related to race, gender, age, religion, culture, and economic and social status. This is also demonstrated in core human rights instruments, such as the Universal Declaration of Human Rights (UDHR) (United Nations, 1948), and the International Covenant on Civil and Political Rights, and these are mirrored in regional instruments, such as the African Charter on Human and People's Rights. For example, the UDHR states in Article 21 that:

1. Everyone has the right to take part in the government of his country, directly or through freely chosen representatives.
2. Everyone has the right of equal access to public service in his country.
3. The will of the people shall be the basis of the authority of government; this will shall be expressed in periodic and genuine elections, which shall be by universal and equal suffrage and shall be held by secret vote or by equivalent free voting procedures.

This provision is echoed in Article 25 of the International Covenant on Civil and Political Rights (ICCPR) and Article d of the African Charter. Article 25 of the ICCPR guarantees both the "right" and "opportunity", "without unreasonable restrictions" to participate in public affairs, "directly or through freely chosen representatives", to vote and be elected at periodic elections by universal and equal suffrage, by secret ballot, and to have equal access to public services. In the African Charter, we find similar sentiments, "[e]very citizen shall have the right to participate in the government of his country, either directly or through freely chosen representatives in accordance with the provision of the law." Article 13(2) and (3) also speak to the rights of equal access to public services, and public property on an equal basis.

Recognizing that decentralization can be a useful tool to facilitate public participation, Article 6(1) of the African Charter on the Values and Principles of Decentralization, Local Governance and Local Development (African Charter on Decentralization) calls on central governments to "create enabling conditions for decision-making, policy and program initiation, adoption, and implementation to take place at lower levels of government where local authorities offer a better guarantee of pertinence and efficacy". Article 13(3) of the African Charter on Decentralization speaks to the duty of the central government to ensure "democratic, free, fair, and transparent local government elections", and to establish mechanisms for the full participation of marginalized groups in local government elections.

The South African Constitution, apart from securing representative democracy, also aims to encourage and promote participatory democracy, particularly at the local government level. In addition, various legislative instruments have been enacted by the national government to facilitate public participation at the local level, including the Municipal Systems Act, Municipal Structures Act, Municipal Finance Management Act, and policy instruments, such as the White Paper on Local Government. Yet despite these numerous instruments, many are often left out of governance. This will be discussed further in this chapter, especially feelings among some community members that decisions are made by the municipal council prior to consultation, making public participation, for example, through community meetings, a mere rubber-stamping exercise.

This chapter examines the effectiveness of public participation mechanisms in South African local government, with a strong emphasis on the municipal budget process. It argues that while South Africa has an impressive range of legislative instruments detailing public participation mechanisms, and has made significant progress in the transitional era, the implementation of these mechanisms still leaves many behind in the practice of public participation.

The approach of the chapter will be as follows. Section 13.1 sets out the context and background for the chapter, while the following Sect. 13.2 will explore the concepts of "public participation" and "participatory budgeting" to frame its meaning within the context of local government in South Africa. This will be followed in Sect. 13.3 by an evaluation of the legal and policy framework on public participation in South Africa and then in Sect. 13.4 an analysis of the practice of public participation within the context of budget processes. Section 13.5 of the chapter will then draw conclusions and make recommendations.

13.2 Defining Public Participation

Public participation has multiple definitions, and according to Theron and Mchunu, public participation has become a buzzword and feel-good concept in South Africa (Theron & Mchunu, 2014, 113). While it is recognized as a key element of good governance, some scholars have warned that public participation should not be viewed as the panacea for all developmental problems (Cooke & Kothari, 2001). Notwithstanding this, the bulk of public participation definitions are similar. In particular, Malemane and Nel-Sanders refer to public participation as "democratic local governance," which "entails the involvement of local citizens in decision-making processes in the affairs of a city or town" (Malemane & Nel-Sanders, 2021). Public participation thus allows local citizens and their organizations, such as NGOs or ratepayers associations, to participate in decision-making on matters of local governance (Van der Waldt, 2014, 53).

Social scientists have put forward various models of public participation, drawing on the participation modalities developed by Arnstein in 1969 (Arnstein, 1969, 216–224; Rowe & Frewer, 2005, 251–290). These modalities, which the South African government endorsed in the 2007 National Framework on Public Participation, include consultations (i.e., the community is given information and asked to comment) and informing (i.e. municipality giving information to stakeholders), amongst others (Department of Provincial and Local Government, 2007; South African Local Government Association, 2013).

In the South African context, the scholarship on participation has also focused on participatory budgeting (United Nations Human Settlements Programme UN-HABITAT, 2008; Kraai et al., 2023, 63). Various conceptualizations of participatory budgeting exist. In particular, (Gilman, 2016) describes it as "an innovation where citizens and other local stakeholders have the right to participate in the elaboration of their municipal fiscal policy." Others conceptualized participatory budgeting by placing citizens at the centre of the budget process, distinguishing it from the traditional budgeting process which is primarily driven by the administration. They described participatory budgeting as a "co-managed process" that is open and brings together both state and non-state actors to identify priorities and allocate resources according to the community needs (Masiya et al., 2021, 4; Masiya & Makanza, 2009). In this chapter, public participation regarding budgeting is understood as an open process by which members of a selected community can share their perspectives to influence decision-making which enables government to direct its programs and budget priorities toward community needs (Mzimakwe, 2010, 501–519). This may take many forms, but as demonstrated below, the South African legal system places significant emphasis on consultation and information sharing as essential participatory instruments.

13.3 Public Participation in South Africa: Legal and Policy Framework

As noted in the introduction above, public participation carries particular importance in South Africa due to the history of apartheid, during which the majority black population, coloureds and Indians were prevented from participating in many governance processes. Indeed, the practice of engagement between citizens and government during apartheid was lacking and characterized as hierarchical, secretive, and deeply unfair to most people.

It is, therefore, no surprise that the new democratic government in the 1996 Constitution has taken a position to at least formally, facilitate and encourage the participation of communities and community organizations in matters of local governance, as one of local government's core developmental objectives (Section 152(1)(e) of the Constitution).

13.3.1 Objectives and Benefits of Public Participation in South Africa

At the municipal level, participatory budgeting as a form of participation aims to deepen democracy, promote good governance and increase the trust in government (Karner et al., 2019, 237). Indeed, the involvement of citizens in governance processes ensures that their experiential and grounded perspectives inform government of their needs and how they can best be addressed. Others have also defined the objective of public participation, particularly in the South African context, as a measure to counter service delivery protests (Mofolo, 2016, 230–245. Similarly, Mzimakwe (2010, 505) argues that participation aims to improve the quality of policymaking by providing an opportunity for government to tap into comprehensive sources of information, perspectives and potential solutions, creating space for greater and faster interaction between the public and governments, and fostering accountability and transparency, which improves representativeness and public confidence (thus, mitigating service delivery protests) (Mzimakwe, 2010, 501–519).

In the context of participatory budgeting at a municipal level, Masiya and Makanza identify several benefits (Masiya & Makanza, 2009). For example, they highlight that it creates trust between citizens and municipalities and increases efficiency ensuring that scarce resources reflect communities' priorities.

These benefits and objectives have also been expressed in the Constitution and various policies and legislative acts regulating local government. In particular, the Constitution tasks municipalities with the responsibility of creating platforms for public participation and calls on municipalities to structure their budgeting process to give priority to the basic needs of the community (Section 152(e) and 153 of the

Constitution). Moreover, the White Paper envisages local government working together with local communities as voters, consumers of public services, and partners in policy and financial processes including planning and budget and resource mobilization (Paragraph 3(3) of the White Paper on Local Government). The White Paper further emphasizes the importance of inclusive approaches to actively empower the most marginalized, while also acknowledging the barriers to participation such as lack of transport, personal safety, and household responsibilities concerning women's public participation (Paragraphs 1(3) and 3(1) of the White Paper on Local Government).

The Municipal Systems Act envisages a "culture of municipal governance that complements formal representative government with a system of participatory governance" (Section 16(1)), implying that these two forms of governance are complementary rather than substitutive. This is further supported by the National Policy Framework on Public Participation, which emphasizes the advantages of public participation as a mechanism for enhancing accountability, identifying needs more precisely, and thus, enhancing service provision (Department of Provincial and Local Government, 2007, 17). Therefore, it must be emphasized that local community participation does not amount to interference with the municipal council's right to govern and to exercise its executive and legislative authority. Public participation at a municipal level should also not be conflated with the idea that municipalities are bound by the views of the public. This was stressed by the Constitutional Court in *Merafong Demarcation Forum and Others* when it held that "being involved does not mean that one's views must necessarily prevail" (*Merafong Demarcation Forum and Others v President of the Republic of South Africa and Others*, 2008, ZACC 10 paragraph 50). The fact that public participation is intended to supplement and enhance government action, not replace or veto it is also clearly stated in the White Paper on Local Government. The White Paper envisions "empowered and capacitated municipalities to play a transformational and developmental role in building viable human settlements which meet the needs and aspirations of local communities" (Paragraph 1(2) of the White Paper on Local Government).

13.3.2 Participatory Rights of Local Communities

Public participation at a municipal level has also been entrenched as a statutory right and is not merely an ideal in the Constitution. Indeed, the Systems Act guarantees participatory decision-making in the budgetary process by recognising the right of members of a local community to contribute to the decision-making process of a municipality and to submit written or oral recommendations, representations, and complaints to the municipal council or another political structure (Section 5(1)(a)(i)(ii) of the Systems Act). Members of the community also have the right to be informed of council decisions that affect their rights, property, or reasonable expectations (Section 5(1)(c) of the Systems Act). The right of local communities to participate in the budgeting process is further strengthened in the Municipal Finance

Management Act, where municipalities are instructed to solicit the views of the local community on its draft budget (section 23(1)(a) of the Systems Act).

The statutory public participation rights and obligations at a municipal level are enforceable in a court of law. Indeed, Steytler and De Visser have long held that the reasonableness standard for review developed to assess public participation for national and provincial legislatures (*Doctors for Life International v Speaker of the National Assembly and Other* (CCT12/05) [2006] ZACC 11) is equally applicable to local government decisions (Steytler and De Visser 2016, 6–16). Moreover, in another case the court determined that municipal decisions are held to a more stringent standard of review (*Borbet South Africa (Pty) Ltd and Others v Nelson Mandela Bay Municipality* (3751/2011) [2014] ZAECPEHC 35). In addition, courts have also adopted a liberal position regarding the question of standing by allowing ratepayers' associations and members of a local community the right to initiate legal action against municipalities based on the desire for public participation (*Stellenbosch Ratepayers' Association v Stellenbosch Municipality* 2009, JOL 24616 (WCC) [17]; *Mnquma Local Municipality and Another v The Premier of the Eastern Cape and Others* 2009, (231/2009) [2009] ZAECBHC 14).

13.3.3 Duties of Municipalities to Promote Public Participation

Several legislative enactments have been authorized since 1994 to give effect to public participation at a municipal level. These include the Municipal Systems Act, Municipal Structures Act, and Municipal Finance Management Act.

The Systems Act, which has a dedicated chapter on "community participation" (Chapter 4, Sections 16–22), includes the local community as a constituent part of a municipality. The act broadly defines the local community as "the residents of the municipality; ratepayers of the municipality, any civic organizations and non-governmental, private sector or labour organizations or bodies which are involved in local affairs within the municipality; as well as visitors and other people residing outside of the municipality who, because of their presence in the municipality, make use of services or facilities provided by the municipality" (Section 1 of the Systems Act). In principle, this means that a municipality comprising a political structure (i.e. council and administration) must involve and consult its local community when making decisions affecting the rights or interests of its community. Indeed, as confirmed in the case of *Matatiele Municipality and Others v President of the Republic of South Africa and Others 2007*, elected officials cannot speak on behalf of the electorate to fulfil public participation requirements. Importantly, where a policy proposal or a specific budgetary proposal affects a group of a particular community, courts have required that municipalities make an extra effort to ensure that the affected group is consulted (*South African Property Owners Association v Council of the City of Johannesburg Metropolitan Municipality and Others* 2013, (1) BCLR

87 (SCA) paragraphs 35–37). Failure to comply with facilitating public participation has the effect of invalidating the decision.

The duty to consult the local community is explicit in a number of provisions in the Systems Act and Structures Act. For example, Section 19(3) of the Structures Act mandates each municipality to develop mechanisms to consult its local community and community organizations, and where necessary, consult traditional authorities.

Similarly, Section 16(1)(a) of the Systems Act specifically imposes a duty on municipalities to encourage and to create conditions for the community to participate in the affairs of the municipality relating to the review of the municipality's integrated development plan (IDP), setting key performance indicators for the municipality, the preparation of the budget, and participating in strategic decisions relating to the provision of municipal services. In line with the principle of subsidiarity, each municipality is enjoined to establish its mechanisms for public participation, but such mechanisms must comply with the minimum conditions set out in Section 17 of the Systems Act. Specifically, municipalities must ensure that there are mechanisms in place for:

1. receiving, processing and considering petitions and complaints
2. notifying the public
3. public comment
4. public meetings and hearings by the municipal council and other political structures and office bearers
5. consultative sessions with locally recognized community organizations and traditional authorities where relevant
6. report back to the local community.

Regarding inclusiveness, the Systems Act further requires that municipalities, when communicating with local communities, consider the special needs of people who cannot read or write and people with disabilities, women and other disadvantaged groups and language preferences (Section 17(2) of the Systems Act). This provision is critical considering the low literacy levels in rural areas compared to urban areas. Provisions are also made to allow municipalities to appoint one or more advisory committees comprising community members who are not municipal councillors to advise the council, and such committees must ensure gender representation (Section 17(4) of the Systems Act).

Another important aspect of public participation is communication. Notification of meetings and all communications from the municipal council to the general public must consider the language preferences of the local community (Section 19 of the Systems Act), in keeping with Section 6(3) of the Constitution, which instructs municipalities to take into account the language usage and preferences of their residents. In addition, communications through the media should be made in the local newspaper, a newspaper circulating in the area, or by way of radio broadcast covering the area of the municipality (Section 21(1) of the Systems Act). A copy of the notice must be published in the Provincial Gazette or the media and must be displayed at the municipal offices.

The Systems Act requires that councils notify the public in advance of any meeting, noting the date, venue, and time of the meeting for ordinary meetings, and in the case of special or urgent meetings, notice must be given unless it is not possible due to time constraints (Section 18(2) of the Systems Act). In general, council meetings (except executive committees and mayoral committees under certain circumstances) are open to the public, including the media. For certain matters, council and committee meetings may not be closed to the public. These include the tabling of a draft by-law, tabling of the municipal budget, tabling of the draft IDP, the tabling of the municipality's draft performance management system or amendments to such system, and any decision to enter into a service delivery agreement mentioned in Section 76(b), or any other matter specifically prescribed by regulation (Section 20(2) of the Systems Act). For matters where the municipal council requests public comment on the municipal budget, it must also notify the public in the invitation for comments that persons who cannot write may be assisted in person at the municipal offices by a municipal official who will transcribe their comments (Section 21(4) of the Systems Act). Similarly, if the municipality requires forms to be completed or payment of money to be made, then it must assist persons who cannot read or write (and by extension marginalized or otherwise disadvantaged groups) (Section 21(5) of the Systems Act).

These aims often require financial resources for implementation, hence Section 16(1)(b)(c) of the Systems Act further instructs municipalities to dedicate funds and build the capacity of local communities to enable them to participate in municipal affairs, having due regard to the municipality's financial and administrative capacity. Thus, public participation at a municipal level extends beyond formalities of making information available, but as confirmed in a court case, it requires municipalities "to build the capacity of communities to participate", and "allocate resources to the task" (*Borbet South Africa (Pty) Ltd and Others v Nelson Mandela Bay Municipality* (3751/2011) [2014] ZAECPEHC paragraphs 80–82).

13.3.4 Public Participation in Specific Processes: Participatory Budgeting

The participatory requirements in the Systems Act are not exhaustive but must be viewed alongside those provided in other legislative instruments, such as the Constitution, Municipal Finance Management Act, Structures Act and the White Paper on Local Government. Moreover, the minister responsible for local government may make regulations or issue guidelines establishing minimum standards or facilitating participation of the local community. Such regulations or guidelines may be staggered in terms of the dates on which certain provisions will become applicable. They may also apply generally to all municipalities, or differentiate between different categories of municipalities, or apply to only a specific category of municipalities (Section 22(1) and 4 of the Systems Act). This is especially important when considering mechanisms of participation that are more suitable to particular contexts such as large, urban metropolitan cities, compared to small, rural municipalities, as matters such as access to modern technologies, physical space for meetings, resources, timing of agricultural seasons and so forth, may come into play.

In this section, the focus is turned more specifically to participatory budgeting which Marzuki defines as "a decision-making process where citizens deliberate and negotiate over the distribution of public resources" (Marzuki, 2015; Masiya et al., 2021). Public participation in municipal budget processes is important because it can help to foster transparency, build trust, and legitimacy, give a voice to communities, and ensure better alignment between community needs and government's allocation of resources. As noted above, the South African approach to public participation is framed in a way to redress the ills of the apartheid era, including by ensuring inclusiveness regarding all citizens, including those at the grassroots level, in decision-making processes. The municipal budget process is intricately linked with the policy formulation processes within the framework of integrated development plans. The mechanisms for participatory budgeting rely significantly on the broader public participation framework and institutions, such as the use of ward committees as an intermediary between the municipal council and local communities in shaping municipal spending priorities.

A key area for policy formulation and the allocation of municipal financial resources in line with the development mandate (Section 152 and 153 of the Constitution) is the formulation and adoption of the municipal budget, which runs alongside the adoption of the IDP (every 5 years) or amendment of the IDP annually when necessary. The IDP process is not only a planning process, but is also a tool for participatory budgeting. According to Section 22–23 of the Municipal Finance Management Act (MFMA), both of these processes are earmarked for public engagement, given that municipalities are obligated to invite and consider public comments regarding their budget before its submission to and adoption by the council. Municipalities are required to publish all supporting documents accompanying the budget, which include any amendments to the IDP, rates and tariff increases, and to invite the public to make comments (Section 22(a)(i)(ii) of the MFMA).

The steps for adopting a municipal budget seek to create multiple opportunities for public participation. In October, the Municipal Manager (MM) and Chief Financial Officer (CFO), often the same person, request departmental budgets from the heads of the municipal divisions which should lay out the financial plan for each department and must be submitted to the CFO and also to the local community for consideration through the ward committees and *imbizos*, an institution based on traditional elders' councils, by November each year. In December, the CFO then consolidates the division budgets into one municipal budget, makes the necessary projections and amends to incorporate comments received through ward committees and *imbizos*, then meets with the MM and divisional heads to further amend the budget. The draft budget must be presented to the municipal council for consideration and an opportunity must be given for public participation in January through ward committees and imbizos where the views of the community must be taken into account and the necessary changes made to the draft budget. As such, ward committees comprising one municipal ward councillor (who sits as the chair of the ward committee), and 10 other persons who are not councillors, is an important mechanism through which communities can participate at the grassroots level to contribute or make submissions in relation to the municipal budget process (Section 73 of the Structures Act). Ward committee members are elected for the same period as municipal councils, and they are elected according to the individual municipality's rules. In terms of Section 73(3) municipalities must set these rules taking into account the need for the equitable representation of women, and diversity of interests to be represented. However, the South African Local Government Association (SALGA), which represents organised local government, also sets some guidelines for municipalities on the election of ward committee members in a model code of conduct. The ward councillor in turn relays the comments from the community to the municipal council and is required to also give the feedback from council back to the ward committee. Ward committees are sometimes used in conjunction with *imbizos* a concept drawn from the historic elders' councils called by the traditional monarchs in South Africa, in some ways akin to town hall meetings which invite ward committees, community members, municipal administration and council to discuss municipal issues such as budget proposals (Masiya et al., 2021).

In addition to ward committees' inputs and *imbizos*, the key points of the draft budget must be placed on a notice board at the municipal offices to allow for further public comment. Individual citizens may make written submissions to the municipal council and lodge these at the municipal council offices. After this consultation process, the council adjusts the draft budget to incorporate the views of the community and other stakeholders.

The council must review all budget-related submissions and the mayor must be allowed to comment on the submissions (Section 23(2) of the MFMA), although the language does not make it compulsory for the mayor to comment. The council is obligated to convene by May 30th to deliberate on the budget and thereafter approve it before the commencement of the new fiscal year on June 1st. Failure to do so will necessitate intervention by the provincial executive as guided by Section 139 of the Constitution, which may necessitate the dissolution of the municipal council, coupled with the appointment of an administrator and the adoption of a temporary budget.

The budget must also be submitted to the National Treasury and the Provincial Treasury in accordance with Section 22(b) of the MFMA. Some municipal councils also submit it to the provincial department of local government. In June the approved final budget is published in the newspaper circulating in that area. The budget speaks to municipal revenue, tariffs, rates, and municipal expenses among other things, and can be a useful tool to anticipate municipal expenditure and monitor corruption and mismanagement of funds.

13.4 Participatory Budgeting in Practice: Success and Challenges

South Africa has made ample legislative and policy provisions for inclusive and participatory governance that encourages engagement with local communities, supported by capacity building, mechanisms and spaces for participation in policy formulation, implementation and review through the IDP and performance review, as well as in budget and strategic decision-making processes. However, in spite of these statutory mechanisms, problems exist with participatory local governance in South Africa, in general, and specifically in the budgetary process.

For instance, in 2016, Mchunu, Theron, and Mubangizi while examining municipal participation contended that "the current structure of public participation provided for by local government legislation is largely inadequate for facilitating meaningful and inclusive expressions of voice, particularly for poor and marginalized grassroots beneficiaries" (Mchunu et al., 2016, 177). As stated by these authors, impoverished communities remain marginalized in local governance decision-making. Instead of using invited spaces such as ward committees, we have seen an increase in communities resorting to participation in invented spaces through engaging in protests, some of which turn violent (Malemane & Nel-Sanders, 2021, 2). The majority of protests are targeted towards local government, whether the matter is a local government competency or not, because local government is often perceived as the face of government and it is the sphere of government closest to the communities. However, protests are also targeted across the spheres of government indiscriminately, such as service delivery (local government competence) protests taking the form of burning down schools (education is a concurrent competence of national and provincial government). In this regard, the lack of participation has also become a source of violent service delivery protests.

Indeed, communities choose to utilize these invented places instead of ward committees for a variety of reasons. First, as ward committees have no formal powers, they are often bypassed during the decision-making process (Piper, 2011, 30–42). Second, earlier studies also revealed that councillors do not frequently attend ward committee meetings, and as a result, ward-related issues are not tabled in council (Mle, 2014, 56–68; Cameron & Milne, 2011, 28–44). On the other hand, where matters are presented before council, it has been established that ward councillors and municipal officials tend to not provide feedback on meetings and community issues (Molepo et al., 2015, 345–369). Third, the effectiveness of ward committees has also been undermined by politics. Piper confirms this in his observation that the ward committees have been taken over by politicians to advance their particular political interests (Piper, 2011, 33). This was also confirmed by Smith and De Visser in an earlier study which showed that youth and women are under-represented on ward committees (Smith & De Visser, 2009, 16–17). Other studies have also shown the lack of sufficient administrative and financial support are all factors that constrain the effectiveness of ward committees (Masango et al., 2013, 91–104).

Specifically, many of the general problems have also manifested themselves in the budgetary process. For example, case studies have revealed that ward committees lack technical expertise to address certain matters, among which is the draft municipal budget, indicating a need for its capacity development (Kraai et al., 2023, 77 and 88). The lack of understanding of the budget and its process has also been regarded as a reason for the lack of participation, highlighting the point that without an equipped citizenry, participatory budgeting will not be effective (Masiya et al., 2021, 10). There is also a perception among citizens that participatory budgeting is merely a formality to meet legal requirements, rather than actively seeking input from the local community (Masiya et al., 2021, 11).

Finally, during the Covid-19 pandemic, the legal framework for participatory budgeting faced significant challenges due to inflexibility and restrictions on in-person meetings for budget approval (De Visser & Chigwata, 2022, 113–119). The ban on in-person council meetings set into motion by the announcement of a national lockdown on March 23, 2020 sought to limit the transmission of the virus through stay-at-home orders, but had the effect of limiting the space for public engagement both in urban and rural spaces as it had blanket application. As noted above, this period is crucial for public participation in the budget formulation process as public comment is mostly obtained between February and May each year. Stay-at-home orders thus eliminated opportunities for ward committee meetings and *imbizos* to discuss the draft budget and priority areas and the prohibition of council meetings meant that participation in IDP amendment and budget processes was not possible during this period.

The ban ceded all executive authority to the mayor and municipal manager, removing the public and elected municipal councillors from the decision-making table during this period, including on budget-related matters. This changed when directives were issued, which allowed councils to hold online meetings to approve the budget retrospectively. On March 30, the National Treasury temporarily exempted municipal councils from compliance with the strict rules of the MFMA, including rules concerning public procurement, until the state of national disaster had passed, and only thereafter to take the relevant actions.

On May 7, 2020, when Direction 6.7.1 was issued, it directed municipalities to adopt their IDPs and budgets and re-commence public service delivery while complying with Covid-19 containment measures. This was facilitated by Direction 6.7.4(b), which allowed for several municipalities to adopt ICT enabled alternative mechanisms for in-person meetings such as community radio, messaging services, live streaming of meetings and the use of online meeting platforms. Municipalities were permitted to adopt special adjustments budgets by June 15, 2020 in order to legalize Covid-19 related expenditure. As municipalities did not have rules of order on the use of online council meetings, the South African Local Government Association (SALGA) drafted some guidelines.

However, this change brought the digital divide to the forefront. It acted as a barrier to inclusive public participation, especially for community members who do not have access to digital devices or those who do not have access to data (De Visser & Chigwata, 2022, 115–116). Consequently, the regime change limited the space for disadvantaged communities, and vulnerable groups within communities, such as women, children, and persons living in informal and rural spaces to participate in the budget formation process, as many did not have the resources to participate in the online processes. Not only did this Direction worsen the digital divide between urban and rural communities, but it also highlighted the infrastructure, finance and human resources gaps among municipalities themselves.

This phenomenon presented both an opportunity and a difficulty, particularly for rural municipalities, and especially for remote rural municipalities lacking sufficient essential telecommunications infrastructure. The differences among rural municipalities also demonstrated the resource inequalities among municipalities, as some more affluent municipal winelands in the Western Cape, such as Stellenbosch, would have likely had better municipal ICT infrastructure, compared to very remote lower income rural municipalities, and likewise their populations would have similar resource gaps. A second layer to this is that within the populations of both well-resourced municipalities and under-resourced municipalities, multiple intersectional layers of inequalities exist, such as structural socio-economic inequalities, race, and gender.

While virtual meetings facilitated public engagement for a more extensive audience, the blanket use of virtual meetings had the opposite effect of reserving public participation for a select few, excluding the majority who do not have access to internet services in rural areas.

13.5 Conclusions

Public participation in decision-making processes is an imperative that ought to bring citizens closer to local government and ensure that local communities' voices and concerns are heard by elected officials. It is also essential to ensure that public policies, programs and projects are tailor-made to meet the actual needs of local communities as defined by the communities themselves. As such, public participation is necessary for development. Concerning South Africa, this chapter establishes that a comprehensive legislative framework for public participation in a local government exists demonstrating the country's policy-level dedication to the importance of such engagement. Indeed, municipalities are required to consult and inform the public on a variety of policy areas, such as the formulation of the municipality's integrated development plan (and amendments) and budget.

The legislative framework thus creates ample opportunity for public participation on the face of it. However, in practice some challenges exist, such as how the general public understands and interacts with the budget, and whether the views of the public are in fact taken into account in formulating and finalising the budget. This tends to make civil society organisations (CSOs) an important stakeholder in that they can simplify the budget for grassroots communities. This may even include the use of infographics and local languages.

The chapter reveals that there is an urgent need to review the composition and functioning of ward committees and community meetings (invited spaces) and consider whether they are adequately resourced. The increase in service delivery protests and the distinctive difficulties arising from the Covid-19 pandemic (including the prohibition of in-person council meetings) further illustrated the importance of developing the legislative framework to enable a more flexible approach that allows municipalities to explore alternative methods for public engagement. The minister overseeing local government has the authority to promulgate regulations that establish distinct criteria and standards for public participation. This authority ought to be utilized to foster collaboration between urban and rural municipalities by considering the unique characteristics and resources of each type of municipality.

It is evident that various gaps are present among urban and rural municipalities, such as big budgets, infrastructure, human resource capacity, and distance from larger cities, as well as gaps between and within their populations, including various intersections of inequalities, such as ICT infrastructure, gender, access to financial resources for accessing data, access to digital devices and electricity to charge those devices on a regular basis, and access to information facilitated by access to ICTs. A lot must be done to ensure that in future emergencies, municipalities are better equipped to ensure some forms of public participation that can be customized to the municipal context, whether urban or rural, well-resourced or under-resourced, even in the face of national disasters. Lessons should be drawn from the Covid-19 experience, even as the world faces more imminently, the risks associated with climate change.

References

Arnstein, S. (1969). A ladder of citizen participation. *Journal of the American Planning Association, 35*(4), 216–224.

Cameron, R., & Milne, C. (2011). An analysis of metropolitan governance and institutional issues in South Africa. *African Journal of Public Affairs, 4*(3), 28–44.

Cooke, B., & Kothari, U. (2001). *Participation: The new tyranny?* Zed Books.

De Visser, J., & Chigwata, T. C. (2022). Municipal budgeting and planning during Covid-19. In M. R. Maziwisa & J. de Visser (Eds.), *Local government in South Africa: Responses to urban-rural challenges* (pp. 113–119). Zenodo. https://doi.org/10.5281/zenodo.5733466

Department of Provincial and Local Government. (2007). *National policy framework for public participation*. Retrieved December 31, 2023, from https://pmg.org.za/files/docs/070625pppolicy.doc

Gilman, H. (2016). *Engaging citizens: Participatory budgeting and the inclusive governance movement within the United States*. Retrieved April 16, 2024, from https://dash.harvard.edu/bitstream/handle/1/42372454/participatory-budgeting-paper.pdf?sequence=1

Karner, A., Brown, K. B., Marcantonio, R., & Alcorn, L. G. (2019). The view from the top of Arnstein's ladder: Participatory budgeting and the promise of community control. *Journal of the American Planning Association, 85*(3), 236–254.

Kraai, S., Ndevu, Z., & Matsiliza, N. (2023). Participatory budgeting to Foster inclusivity, transparency, and accountability in local government: A case study of the City of Ekurhuleni Metropolitan Municipality of South Africa. *African Journal of Public Affairs, 14*(1), 63–88.

Malemane, K., & Nel-Sanders, D. (2021). Strengthening participatory local governance for improved service delivery: The case of Khayelitsha. *Africa's Public Service Delivery and Performance Review, 9*(1), 500. https://doi.org/10.4102/apsdpr.v9i1.500

Marzuki, A. (2015). Challenges in the public participation and the decision making process. *Sociologija iprostor, 53*(1), 21–39.

Masango, R., Mfene, P., & Henna, T. (2013). An analysis of factors that negatively affect the performance of ward committees in the Buffalo City Municipality. *Africa Insight, 3*(1), 91–104.

Masiya, T., & Makanza, V. (2009). Participatory approaches to urban development in Zimbabwe: The case of participatory budgeting in Gweru. *Namibia Development Journal, 2*(1), 14–21.

Masiya, T., Mazenda, A., & Gwabeni, T. N. S. (2021). Participatory budgeting in a South African local municipality. *International Journal of Management Practice, 14*(3), 325–342.

Mchunu, N., Theron, F., & Mubangizi, B. (2016). Developmental local government and good governance—Facilitation from grassroots. In F. Theron & N. Mchunu (Eds.), *Development, change and the change agent: Facilitation at grassroots* (2nd ed., p. 177). Van Schaik.

Mle, T. R. (2014). Potential benefits of monitoring and evaluation as a tool in the South African local government spheres. *Africa's Public Service Delivery & Performance Review Journal, 2*(1), 56–68.

Mofolo, M. A. (2016). Intergovernmental relations system for public participation in the local sphere of government. *Journal of Public Administration, 51*(2), 230–245.

Molepo, J. N., Maleka, M. C., & Khalo, T. (2015). Public participation and service delivery: The case of the City of Tshwane. *Journal of Public Administration, 50*(2), 345–369.

Mzimakwe, T. (2010). Public participation and engagement in local governance: A South African perspective. *Journal of Public Administration., 45*(4), 501–519.

Piper, L. (2011). Not waiting for Jackie: Lessons for public participation advocacy in South Africa. *Africanus, 41*(1), 30–42.

Rowe, G., & Frewer, L. J. (2005). A typology of public engagement mechanisms. *Science, Technology, & Human Values, 30*(2), 251–290. https://doi.org/10.1177/0162243904271724

Smith, T., & De Visser, J. (2009). *The role of ward committees in South Africa*. Community Law Centre.

South African Local Government Association. (2013). *Effective public participation*. Retrieved December 31, 2023, from https://www.salga.org.za/Documents/Knowledge-products-per-theme/Governance%20n%20Intergovernmental%20Relations/Effective%20Public%20Participation.pdf

Steytler, N., & De Visser, J. (2016). *Local government law of South Africa*. Johannesburg.

Theron, F., & Mchunu, N. (2014). Public participation as a micro-level development strategy: The principles and context for authentic and empowering development. In I. Davids & F. Theron (Eds.), *Development, the state and civil society in South Africa* (3rd ed., p. 113). Van Schaik.

Universal Declaration of Human Rights, United Nations General Assembly (UNGA) Resolution 217A, Paris, adopted 10 December 1948.

United Nations Human Settlements Programme and Municipal Development Partnership for Eastern and Southern Africa. (2008). *Participatory budgeting in Africa: A training companion with cases from eastern and southern Africa Volime I: Concepts and principles*. Retrieved April 12, 2024, from https://internationalbudget.org/wp-content/uploads/Participatory-Budgeting-in-Africa-A-Training-Companion-with-Cases-from-Eastern-and-Southern-Africa.pdf

Van der Waldt, G. (2014). Municipal management: An orientation. In G. Van der Waldt (Ed.), *Municipal management: Serving the people* (2nd ed., p. 53). Juta Legal and Academic Publishers.

Part IV
Promises and Pitfalls of Digital Participation

Chapter 14
Digital Democratic Participation in Local Governance from an Urban-Rural Perspective

Marianne Kneuer, Maria A. Wimmer, and Giulia Bahms

Abstract With the advent of the Internet along with the vastly evolving digital tools and technologies, digital participation bears great potentials for better democratic participation and the inclusion of less active citizens and marginalized groups. In this chapter, we discuss digital participation at the municipal level from an urban-rural perspective. We outline the different circumstances for (successful) digital participation. Among the promises of digital participation in local governance are the empowerment of citizens, the enablement of new forms of citizen participation in political decision-making such as co-creation, and the Internet serving as a vehicle for revitalizing or reforming democracy. We also discuss whether the potential for better participation is more promising at the local level than at the national or global levels, and we identify the spatial scope as an important factor. Among the pitfalls and challenges of digital participation, we identify the lack of enduring leadership of participatory governance initiatives, the risk of triviality of non-electoral participatory initiatives that leads to disappointment of citizens, and the difficulties in assessing the impact of citizen participation initiatives. While technology is not the main factor of successful and impactful digital democratic participation, the challenge lays rather in how technology is embedded in the wider participatory governance process. The rise of innovative technologies such as artificial intelligence (AI) and machine learning (ML) offers new potentials of digital participation at the local level. However, further research is needed to thoroughly embed such technologies in the vastly dynamic environments of local governance.

Keywords Digital participation · Local governance · Democratic promises · Democratic pitfalls · Disruptive technologies

---

M. Kneuer (✉) · G. Bahms
Institute of Political Science, University of Technology Dresden and Center for Scalable Data Analytics and Artificial Intelligence (ScaDS.AI) Dresden/Leipzig, Dresden, Germany
e-mail: marianne.kneuer@tu-dresden.de; giulia.bahms@tu-dresden.de

M. A. Wimmer
Research Group E-Government, Faculty of Computer Science, University of Koblenz, Koblenz, Germany
e-mail: wimmer@uni-koblenz.de

K. Kössler, E. Schläppi (eds.), *Citizen Participation in Local Governance*, Local and Urban Governance, https://doi.org/10.1007/978-3-031-99824-9_14

14.1 Introduction

Digital participation (also called e-participation or online participation) has been at the forefront of scholarly and practical work since the emergence of the Internet, web 1.0, web 2.0 and following technological innovations. Since then, different cycles have unfolded, each of which addresses the potential of the new technological paths for broader and better participation opportunities, and the empowerment and inclusion of less active citizens. However, an initial optimistic phase has been followed by an increasingly negative and critical view of the potential of the new technologies. Meanwhile, it is common knowledge that the effects of digital participation are rather ambivalent and that the high normative expectations expressed in the 1990s often did not materialize in practice.

This chapter looks at digital democratic participation in local governance from an urban-rural perspective. Taking the local level as the point of departure for digital participation implies some specificities within the overall field of digital participation, which are connected to the different conditions that the small-scale nature of local level citizen participation entails. The aim of this chapter is to outline the different circumstances for (successful) digital participation and the conditions, objectives, and significance of participatory processes in local governance. We argue that digital participation encounters different operational conditions at the local level. In addition, we also discuss whether the potential for successful participation might be more promising at the local level than at the national or global level.

Various disciplines engage in studying digital participation in local governance: political science, law, administrative science, informatics and neighboring disciplines, geography, and urban development. It has become apparent that a multidisciplinary perspective is desirable, and maybe necessary, to capture and understand the complex fabric in which participatory processes are enmeshed. This chapter examines digital participation from multidisciplinary angles: political science, informatics, and public administration.

For doing so, Sect. 14.2 starts with defining digital participation. Then we discuss the promises of digital participation (Sect. 14.3). On the one hand, it can be expected that this will lead to greater inclusivity of marginalized citizens, more participation in decision-making processes and increased empowerment in local governance in both urban and rural communities. However, exemplary studies will also be used in Sect. 14.4 to highlight possible pitfalls of digital participation so that the needs of both urban and rural communities can be addressed. Section 14.4 will also take a closer look at the challenges of digital participation at the local level, such as the digital and participatory divide. Technological development continues to create a dynamic environment for digital participation opportunities. Hence, we will investigate the dynamic environment of digital participation along with emerging and disruptive technologies in Sect. 14.5. Finally, we conclude with a discussion and indication of future needs for research in Sect. 14.6, which continues to emerge along technological innovations to overcome pitfalls and challenges of online citizen participation, as well as to leverage the public value through local e-participation.

14.2 Definitions and Concepts

Digital participation can be embedded in the concept of e-democracy (also known as digital democracy or cyberdemocracy). E-democracy is a normatively guided concept, as it is primarily concerned with improving the quality of democracy (Kneuer, 2019a, 2). Accordingly, digital democratic participation opportunities should serve to expand and improve democratic activities. This is achieved through the possibility of top-down and bottom-up interaction. This dual nature of e-participation can be derived from the argument that it responds to the need for reform of the communicative arrangements between state actors and citizens—often also demanded by the latter—and therefore gives rise to initiatives that are planned, financed and maintained by state agencies and actors (Kneuer, 2019b, 326–327). Even if this is still regarded as government communication, the electronic variant offers opportunities for interactive exchange, which governments are interested in and use. Coleman and Blumler speak of "top-down e-participation" or "e-participation from above" (Coleman & Blumler, 2009, 91) as institutionally organized and administered public discussion, while the bottom-up variant ("e-participation from below") is defined as autonomous interaction beyond the state, between and within publics and counter-publics (Coleman & Blumler, 2009, 117). Thus, the first is a vertical mechanism where decision-makers provide offers to citizens to participate, while the latter implies a horizontal interaction. The greater practical challenge lies in how the results of this interaction beyond the state will then be channeled to government actors.

Both variants are equally based on the fact that citizens now have new opportunities to participate in democracy. For this reason, the variant of executive-based online participation also ties in the expectations of democratic theory, which are generally associated with e-participation: How can policy-makers reach and include previously marginalized citizens in the public discourse and decision-making processes? The aim is to make decision-making and opinion-forming processes more inclusive and thus have more legitimate democratic processes. Both in the definition and application to practical political aspects, the model presented by the United Nations (UN) is an important reference. The United Nations Department of Economic and Social Affairs (UNDESA) defines e-participation as "[t]he willingness, on the part of the government, to use ICT to provide high quality (explicit knowledge) and effective communication tools for the specific purpose of empowering people for able participation in consultations and decision-making, both in their capacity as consumers of public services and as citizens" (United Nations, 2003, 11). E-participation thus expands the range of tools available to reach and engage citizens (United Nations, 2014, 61).

According to the UN concept, which has become referential, digital participation encompasses three dimensions: *information* "enabling participation by providing citizens with public information and access to information without or upon demand", *consultation:* "engaging citizens in contributions to and deliberation on public policies and services", and *decision-making*: "empowering citizens through co-design of policy option and co-production of service components and delivery modalities" (UN, 2022, 200). Most recently, other subdimensions were added in order to reflect current trends and modalities on "how governments engage their people in public policy-making, implementation and evaluation" (UN, 2022, 200). Social media has brought about monitoring as a further function, as political and social actors can be observed and controlled via these platforms. It is assumed that information can not only be spread better and faster, but that citizens can also get involved to draw attention to grievances (Hindman, 2009, 136–138; Kneuer, 2016, 671).

Although this concept refers to the above mentioned top-down e-participation, citizens do play a crucial role by being part of democratic self-government, participating in public discourse and decision-making, and taking part in collaborative or deliberative processes, because "citizen participation is where the citizens are actively involved in decision-making processes to achieve more accountability and good governance" (Mkude et al., 2014, 2055; Ackerman, 2004). In order to ensure digital democratic participation in urban and rural communities, free and equal network access is a prerequisite. Also, a legal basis is required that includes Internet freedom. Both prerequisites are not self-evident, not only in regards to authoritarian or hybrid regimes where Internet freedom might not be in place, but also in terms of free and equal access to the net in democracies where e.g. rural areas or determined communities in urban areas have less connectivity and thus are not in the same conditions to participate (Mossberger et al., 2007).

Moreover, the legitimation dimensions (input, throughput, and output dimensions) also provide a framework for reviewing the successful implementation and use of digital participation tools. The input dimension enables people to formulate and contribute their own interests to the authorities, so they can influence political decisions. An early involvement of citizens at the local level in administrative, municipal, and city council decisions is desirable in order to ensure such influence. Throughput legitimacy is given when citizens feel transparently involved in decision-making processes. To achieve this, the decision-making processes must be transparent to everyone. Finally, output legitimacy comprises a satisfactory result after the participation process. Therefore, digital participation tools are successful if they fulfil the three legitimation dimensions. Above all, citizens need to have trust and an understanding in all the new measures for there to be a successful adoption and usage of new technologies in terms of e-participation (Wimmer & Spitzer, 2021, 80).

14.3 Promises of Digital Participation

The new information and communication technologies (ICTs), as well as the digitalization of communication, have nurtured an array of high expectations. Thus, the emergence of the Internet fueled euphoric—partially utopian—visions can be summarized as democratic promises. These promises ascribed to the new technology a democratizing potential for empowering citizens, establishing new forms of citizens' participation, and including more citizens in public debates and decision-making, especially previously marginalized and disadvantaged ones (Rheingold, 1993; Wilhelm, 2000; Bimber, 2003; Hindman, 2009). These promises experienced an additional boost when, at the turn of the millennium, web 2.0 technology made way for overall connectivity and real-time interactivity in the ubiquitous virtual space, proliferating social platforms and digital tools of various kinds. On a micro level, the technological advance of web 2.0 was considered as offering unprecedented tools for empowerment and online self-communication (van Dijck, 2013, 11), blurring the roles of producer and user and creating what is generally coined as produser or the citizen journalist. All of these different promises stirred by the Internet crystallize into two main bundles. One refers to the expectation of curing all those ills that the model of representative democracy, especially in the last two decades, has manifested—in a nutshell, the Internet as a vehicle for revitalizing or reforming democracy. The other bundle of promises refers to the transformation of the public sphere towards one that is globally networked, deterritorialized and decentralized. As already mentioned, the perspective on the local level offers a different theoretical and practical claim: if and why—under different spatial conditions, namely in the local context—digital tools might be more likely to incentivize citizens to engage and involve more citizens in public debates and decision-making than on the national or global level. The theoretical argument is that scale matters and that spatial dimension plays a role in making a difference in effective e-democracy processes (Kneuer & Datts, 2020), and empirical studies corroborate this argument (Saglie & Vabo, 2009).

Hence, the promises of digital participation refer to the expected benefits and positive results associated with the implementation of digital participation in political decision-making processes. On the one hand, the promises of digital participation include greater empowerment and engagement of citizens. E-participation aims to involve citizens more closely in political processes by providing digital participation tools. These enable citizens to express their opinions, provide feedback and participate in decision-making from home or while travelling. Above all, the expansion of participation opportunities through new ICTs enables a better exchange with citizens and the municipalities (Przeybilovicz et al., 2020, 4), which has raised high expectations and should lead to an improvement of quality in the relationship and trust of citizens (Kneuer & Datts, 2020, 1; Wimmer & Spitzer, 2021, 80). Thus,

ICTs permit timely feedback from citizens to political actors involved in local governance. Otherwise, it enables even faster responsiveness on the part of the actors, which in turn can be expected to result in faster and more efficient decision-making. Last but not least, the development of the Internet has already offered the promise of democracy, with new opportunities for participation and greater involvement.

To date, digital participation opportunities and the spatial scope of application at local, national, transnational and international levels have been considered independently of each other. This was based on the assumption of an equal degree of effectiveness at all levels. However, Kneuer and Datts argue that the spatial level of the democratic promise of the Internet and digital participation instruments must be considered in a more differentiated way. This means that more citizens could become involved under different spatial conditions (Kneuer & Datts, 2020, 1). Territorial-geographical and functional factors can play a favorable role here. The territorial-geographical condition enables more inclusive participation and involvement in political decision-making processes. Second, functional conditions include, for instance, being more affected by local issues, being better informed, and potentially having a greater influence on the political agenda, so that a higher level of interest, better accessibility and hence more engagement of citizens can be assumed on the local level. Overall, these arguments demonstrate why it is worth to further test if digital participation processes can fulfil the expectation of more inclusion and empowerment to a higher degree at the local level than at the national or global levels.

Digital participation tools also go hand in hand with the hope of reducing participation costs (Granier & Kudo, 2016, 65–66; Tolbert & McNeal, 2003) by removing spatial and temporal barriers to participation (Ertiö, 2013, 3). This is because the smartphone, which is easy to use, enables many things to be done in this way (Datts & Kneuer, 2022, 29). In addition, mobile applications can be used to overpass spatial distances (Spitzer & Wimmer, 2021, 415). Increased public Wi-Fi also makes access easier. Overall, this allows political projects of the municipality to be brought to the attention of citizens in order to generate broad involvement in decisions about their implementation. Regarding cities, there is a new era of citizen participation opportunities via mobile devices (Ertiö, 2013; Ertiö & Ruoppila, 2014; Höffken & Streich, 2013; Le Blanc, 2020, 12; Martin, 2014). To this end, more recent studies investigated the question of whether mobile participation opportunities in urban spaces fulfil democratic promises, such as the promise of greater mobilization of marginalized and historically less represented citizens (Granier & Kudo, 2016, 65; Kneuer & Datts, 2020; Mossberger et al., 2013; Mossberger & McDonald, 2008). They investigated whether app-based participation processes increase participation and whether barriers can be broken (Datts & Kneuer, 2022, 28; Wimmer et al., 2013). Due to the advantages mentioned, Datts and Kneuer assume a difference in participation via apps and stationary devices (Datts & Kneuer, 2022, 29). This assumption could not be confirmed on the basis of the survey results. The data indicate no difference in previous participatory barriers, meaning that the advantages of mobile participation has no effect on an increase in participation. At the same time, the open question is how much participation depends on how well the apps are tailored to reach and motivate citizens to participate.

In another study, the co-creation method is used for the development of a mobile app for citizens. This method especially involved elderly people in rural areas to find out their user needs for interacting with the digital mobility app (Wimmer & Spitzer, 2021, 78). Therefore, co-creation is another opportunity for citizens to get more involved in participatory processes, as they are in touch with the design of public services from the very beginning (Wimmer & Spitzer, 2021, 80–81).

In addition, broad participation is a prerequisite for the realization of smart city and smart region projects. Even if definitions of smart city may vary, a critical element of the smart city concept is the element of participatory governance (Caragliu et al., 2011). From the perspective of participation, smart governance includes the participation (opportunities) of citizens in the political process, the quality of public services and the transparency and efficiency of public administration. After the first euphoria about smart cities, which partially implied a technopolitical orientation, the participatory component is once again coming into focus insofar as it is claimed that the procedures for participation should also be developed with the involvement of citizens (as collaborative and co-creative procedures) (Smith & Martin, 2022).

The dehierarchization of politics in a networked public sphere represents a further promise of democratization, which can also be attributed to the digital technologies introduced since the turn of the millennium. This has weakened the role of elites, bypassed state actors and markets, and challenged traditional media channels (Castells, 2011, 22–25; Castells, 2012, 9–10; Hindman, 2009, 154–156; Shirky, 2011; Benkler, 2006). This development underlines the crucial position and role of citizens in the e-participation process at the local level against the background that the realization of local projects depends on citizen input.

Furthermore, it can be assumed that transparency is increased through online-based interaction, as more information can be retrieved. Above all, this promotes accountability and the inclusion of marginalized population groups. This also enables a more responsive dialogue between authorities and citizens. Likewise, social media produces a similar effect of influence by creating new opportunities for citizens to influence the public agenda (McCaughey & Ayers, 2003; van de Donk et al., 2004; Castells, 2012; Gerbaudo, 2012; Kneuer & Richter, 2015).

The digital democratic promises are linked to the concept of e-democracy. There is no standardized definition in this respect. However, there is a consensus that e-democracy contributes to improving democratic activities and structures by using information and communication technologies (Coleman & Norris, 2005; Shane, 2012, 7). Therefore, the promises of more participation, inclusion, transparency, and responsiveness through e-democracy and e-participation is a convincing concept at the local level. But to continue to implement e-participation effectively and therefore improve democratic activities, it needs to be adapted to local governance in order to maximize the accessibility and involvement of citizens in urban and rural communities. In addition, other factors such as user-friendliness, data security and challenges, such as the accessibility to marginalized citizens, must be considered to guarantee digital participation opportunities on mobile and stationary devices and to be able to completely fulfil the promises of digital e-participation.

14.4 Pitfalls of Digital Participation

While digital participation offers many promises and benefits to improve democracy and local governance (see previous Section), there are also a number of pitfalls and challenges as several studies indicate. For example, Fung argues that there are three major "challenges to deepening democracy through increased citizen participation" (Fung, 2015), which mostly do not directly result from the digital dimension of citizen participation but from the overall scope of collaborative governance and participatory innovation. These challenges, however, also impact digital participation substantially:

1. Leadership—successful, durable, and effective participatory innovation requires an enthusiastic champion that drives citizen participation in the beginning and sustains or expands participatory governance. Examples are, on the one hand, mayors committed to dialogue with citizens, leaders of ruling or opposition parties in municipal councils or municipal government managers with a strong interest in participatory governance. On the other hand, people from non-government organizations may have such a leadership role when constantly motivating citizens to engage in participatory governance processes. However, maintaining continued motivations for citizen engagement is extremely challenging.
2. "Lack of a broad popular articulation and agreement on the role of non-electoral public participation in contemporary democratic institutions", which is related to (1) and which makes the work of those champions much more difficult.
3. Triviality of participatory initiatives, which leads to the disappointment of citizens, as such participation does not happen on complex policy issues that would encompass real empowerment (see also Johnson et al., 2020).

Another challenge is to assess the impact of citizen participation initiatives. A study by Michels and Binnema (2018) develops a framework for analyzing the "impact of deliberative democratic initiatives at the local level", where the authors distinguish among instrumental, conceptual and strategic impacts that may be achieved on both political and societal levels. The authors identify five factors that are crucial in successful deliberative democratic participation and that may represent pitfalls of citizen participation in local policy discussions if not addressed properly:

1. institutional design,
2. the embeddedness in the political system,
3. the policy issue itself,
4. the connection with the existing civil society, and
5. the interaction between actors.

The authors apply the impact assessment framework to two local participation case studies in the Netherlands. Similarly, the study of Kleinhans and Falco (2022) identified the following as core challenges:

1. access and awareness,
2. sustaining user motivation,
3. expectation management,
4. re-establishing routines and practices, and
5. offline follow-up and decision-making.

However, the authors argued that technology is not the main factor of successful and impactful e-participation. Kleinhans and Falco (2022, 3) prove in their study that "the ways in which the technology is embedded in both the involved institutions and the actual participation process are more influential for the overall effectiveness of participation". Hence, the key issue is rather how technology is embedded in the wider participatory governance process and how the above challenges are addressed. While many studies evaluate success and impact of e-participation initiatives, there is no single approach to successful and sustained citizen participation. The factors put forward by Michels and Binnema (2018) and by Kleinhans and Falco (2022) have also been seen in combination with the three challenges spotted by Fung (2015) in order to generate a positive environment for impactful citizen participation in urban and rural communities. To overcome the above challenges, proper skills for designing citizen participation initiatives and participating through e-participation tools are further preconditions. However, particularly in smaller rural municipalities such skills are often not available at the local level when digital participation is implemented. This digital and participatory divide is also prevalent along the incorporation of inclusivity and representativeness of citizen online participation, as studies from German participatory initiatives evidence: "men participate more often than women", and the level of education plays a significant role in whether a citizen engages (Rottinghaus & Escher, 2020).

14.5 The Dynamic Environment of Digital Participation: Exploring Disruptive Technologies to Improve User Experience and Disruptive Events as Triggers

14.5.1 Disruptive Technologies

While technology is not the main factor of success in e-participation initiatives (Falco & Kleinhans, 2018; Kleinhans & Falco, 2022), online citizen participation has been shaped over the years by the evolution of new technological developments. In particular, the recent trends in the exploitation of innovative digital technologies create an extremely dynamic environment of digital participation. Among the emerging innovative technologies are artificial intelligence (AI)—in particular generative AI machine learning (ML), interactive displays (which build on digital twins and geolocation, and enable citizens to contribute their views in online deliberation, for instance, along urban planning procedures, see e.g. Luo et al., 2022), conversational agents and chatbots (which support citizens' communication with governments or other stakeholders in e-participation initiatives through automated interaction by applying AI-based techniques and NLP, see Segura-Tinoco et al., 2022), gamification, and augmented and virtual reality (AR/VR) (Wimmer et al., 2020). AI and ML enable the use of algorithms that establish human-like intelligent capabilities in digital agents, such as autonomous decisions and self-learning (Görz et al., 2010). AI can particularly support data-driven decision-making to generate knowledge from large data sets (e.g. statistical data, image data, geospatial data, large text files with substantial amounts of comments) and to visually present insights and lessons to citizens in participatory processes. AI and ML, in combination with natural language processing (NLP), can support in-text classifications and hate speech detection (Zhang et al., 2018; Liebeck et al., 2016). Sentiment analysis and stance detection, which are AI- and NLP-based computer techniques applied e.g. in social media and in online forums to analyse large textual data sets (ALDayel & Magdy, 2021), can automatically support the analysis of various positions in particular policy subjects (Hasan & Ng, 2013). Conversational agents, which are based on NLP and AI-based algorithms, can particularly support citizen engagements (Segura-Tinoco et al., 2022). Digital twins, enriched with interactive displays and gamification elements may serve as virtual representations of real environments upon which to deliberate and decide on e-participation initiatives (Luo et al., 2022; Hassan & Hamari, 2020). Augmented reality builds on such technologies and enables citizens to gather imaginations of virtual objects via smart glasses within real environments to better understand issues and potential solutions. The vast amount of examples of using disruptive technologies in e-participation create great user experiences, and citizens may be relieved from e-participation hindrances of triviality and complexity,[1] as they can contribute better informed discussions and the gamified user experience may motivate citizen engagement.

14.5.2 Disruptive Events as Triggers

Both the Covid-19 pandemic and the green transformation in the wake of climate change and decarbonization are two events that have a very concrete impact on the importance and design of digital participation, especially at the local level. The Covid-19 pandemic constituted a trigger for adopting and implementing new digital tools and using already existing ones. The restrictions on physical gatherings increased the demand for digital tools– as the mitigation measures in health services often were managed by the municipalities and cities—especially at the local level (Hovik & Giannoumis, 2022). However, neither the realization by some policymakers that the development of digital participation tools is lagging far behind (as is the case in Germany), nor the increased need for such tools, has automatically and

[1] See Sect. 14.4 above.

consistently led to their greater institutionalization. Rather, an asymmetrical development can be observed between ambitious cities with technology-savy residents, and rural areas where preferences and resources of the local governments might be different (Radtke, 2023, 19).

Moreover, municipalities are the focal points of the current and future green transformation processes that are being planned and decided at the national level, but which mostly have to be implemented and negotiated locally. For example, the German government identifies local authorities as the place where the transformation to sustainable development takes place in a concrete and tangible way and where the consequences of non-sustainable actions (ecological problems, social upheaval, and negative economic developments) can be seen as if under a magnifying glass (German Government, 2021). At the same time, local self-government is in a particularly good position to offer citizens the opportunity to help shape even difficult policy processes. Thus, the consequences of climate change will necessitate far-reaching infrastructural changes in cities and municipalities in the coming years, which cannot be implemented against the will and without the active participation of citizens (Nagorny-Koring, 2018; Radtke & Kersting, 2018). This points to the importance of formats that can bolster this kind of dialogue and collaboration between policy-makers, administration, stakeholders, and citizens.

14.6 Conclusions

The evolution of digital tools enabling citizen participation anytime and from anywhere has generated new cultures of online participation in local governance. Research on digital participation has vastly increased over the past two decades. In this chapter, we reviewed promises and pitfalls, and the dynamic environment of digital participation. Along with this, we focused on local governance from an urban rural perspective. We outlined different circumstances promoting or hampering citizen participation in local governance.

Among promoting factors of online participation in public discourse and empowerment in decision-making processes are: the inclusion of more and previously marginalized citizens overcoming digital and social divides, the interactive exchange and consultations along public policy formulation and decision-making involving both top-down and bottom-up participatory initiatives, achieving more accountability, trust and good governance in decision-making processes, and strengthening and reforming democracy overall. Nurtured by the fast evolution of digital and innovative technologies (e.g. AI, ML, NLP, conversational agents, sentiment analysis and stance detection, AR/VR, digital twins, and gamification) and based on the availability of a vast amount of digital data, the dynamic environments of digital participation further boost expectations. They contribute to a transformation of the public sphere toward a globally networked and reconfigured power distribution and deterritorialization. However, insights from our research indicate that citizens' online participation in democratic decision-making is more successful at the local level. Several smart city initiatives provide evidence for this.

While most scholarly work focuses on the promises and benefits of (local) online citizen engagement, hampering circumstances also need to be investigated. Pitfalls of successful participation in local governance, where digital tools are used to reach out to a wider constituency and particularly to marginalized groups, can be grouped into:

1. motivational and institutional factors, such as the lack of sustainable leadership and of institutional arrangements of non-electoral public participation to be integrated with the political system,
2. democratic and connectedness factors, such as triviality of participatory initiatives, where citizens are not enabled to contribute substantial policy inputs, leading to disappointed citizens and distrust in the political system; a lack of connection of rulemakers with the existing civil society in general and discontinued motivation of users,
3. difficulties in expectations management and expected impact of citizen participation in policy-making, no matter whether online or analogue,
4. procedural and usability factors, such as lack of practices of citizen (online) engagement and empowerment, badly designed user interfaces, and lack of transparent policy and decision-making procedures, along which the citizenry can engage, and
5. a lack of proper skills for designing and executing successful and durable online democratic participatory processes, particularly in small-scale local governance.

The current landscape of studies of scholarly work demonstrates that further research is needed on systematizing the success and the hindering factors for effective local e-participation.

Furthermore, participation needs to be conceptualized in its blended form of digital and analog application, in the linking of offline and online formats. As Radtke rightly argues, "the aim is … to use people's digital activities to make them interested in offline occurrences and planning processes affecting the (local) community" (Radtke, 2023, 18). Thus, a visit to the local council can be useful and, at the same time, citizens might find it also beneficial to follow the council's decision via online tools or access council members online etc. This kind of links and intersections have hardly been considered or taken advantage of (Radtke, 2023, 18) which should therefore be high on the agenda for scholars and local stakeholders. There is still work to do in terms of tackling the intersection between digital and analog participation and of real-world implementation.

Finally, another methodological desideratum is comparative work. Regarding the local level, there is a considerable amount of single case studies or small-n studies that compare cities in the same country or a sample of two or three cases in different countries. Such studies have limited explanatory power as they are very context-sensitive (the institutional setting of political systems, centralized or decentralized states, political cultures etc.) and might not be transferable to other countries or regions. On the other hand, the data base for large-n studies also has its limitations.

However, large-n studies can refer to the national data to get a more complete understanding of national disparities or to get a global perspective. Regarding the first, there are no such projects to our knowledge. The global perspective is better covered by the newly established Local Online Service Index (LOSI) created by the UN (United Nations, 2022).[2] This recently established data set covers five criteria (institutional framework, content provision, services provision, participation and engagement, and technology) broken down in 86 indicators. It constitutes a valuable data base for studies on local participation and allows a broad comparative perspective. Still, more comparison, especially cross-regional comparison, is needed to get a more complete picture of actors' motivations (be it policy-makers or citizens) to adopt, implement and institutionalize local digital participation tools and to get a better understanding of which conditions enhance or hinder online participation on the local level and thus account for the success or failure of attempts to better include citizens in decision-making.

References

Ackerman, J. (2004). Co-governance for accountability: Beyond 'Exit' and 'Voice'. *World Development, 32*(3), 447–463. https://doi.org/10.1016/j.worlddev.2003.06.015

ALDayel, A., & Magdy, W. (2021). Stance detection on social media: State of the art and trends. *Information Processing & Management, 58*(4), 102597. https://doi.org/10.1016/j.ipm.2021.102597

Benkler, Y. (2006). *The wealth of networks. How social production transforms markets and freedom*. Yale University Press.

Bimber, B. A. (2003). *Information and American democracy: Technology in the evolution of political power*. Cambridge University Press.

Caragliu, A., Del Bo, C., & Nijkamp, P. (2011). Smart cities in Europe. *Journal of Urban Technology, 18*, 65–82. https://doi.org/10.1080/10630732.2011.601117

Castells, M. (2011). *Communication power*. Oxford University Press.

Castells, M. (2012). *Networks of outrage and hope. Social movements in the Internet age*. Polity Press.

Coleman, S., & Norris, D. (2005). A new agenda for e-democracy. *OII Forum Discussion Paper, 4*, 1–36. https://doi.org/10.2139/ssrn.1325255

Coleman, S., & Blumler, J. G. (2009). *The internet and democratic citizenship: Theory, practice and policy*. Cambridge University Press.

Datts, M., & Kneuer, M. (2022). Mobile politische Beteiligung—Erneut nur die üblichen Verdächtigen? Eine empirische Analyse der Nutzung der Tübinger BürgerApp. *Stadtforschung und Statistik: Zeitschrift des Verbandes Deutscher Städtestatistiker, 35*(2), 28–35.

Ertiö, T. (2013). *M-participation: The emergence of participatory planning applications*. Turku Urban Research Programme. Retrieved February 22, 2024, from https://www.turku.fi/sites/default/files/atoms/files/tutkimuskatsauksia_2013-6b.pdf

[2] The first LOSI pilot study started in 2018 with the assessment of online portals of 40 cities. This was scaled extended to 100 cities in the 2020 edition. In the edition of LOSI 2022, the most populous cities from each of the 193 UN member states have been included in the study, increasing the number of cities assessed from 100 to 193.

Ertiö, T., & Ruoppila, S. (2014). Supporting 'participation' in mobile participation. *Innovation and the Public Sector, 21*, 3–12. https://doi.org/10.3233/978-1-61499-429-9-3

Falco, E., & Kleinhans, R. (2018). Beyond technology: Identifying local government challenges for using digital platforms for citizen engagement. *International Journal of Information Management, 40*, 17–20. https://doi.org/10.1016/j.ijinfomgt.2018.01.007

Fung, A. (2015). Putting the public back into governance—The challenges of citizen participation and its future. *Public Administration Review, 75*(4), 513–522. https://doi.org/10.1111/puar.12361

Gerbaudo, P. (2012). *Tweets and the streets. Social media and contemporary activism*. Pluto Press.

German Government/Bundesregierung. (2021). Kommunen als zentrale Akteure für eine nachhaltige Entwicklung. *Staatssekretärsausschuss für nachhaltige Entwicklung*. Beschluss vom 14. Juni 2021. Retrieved July 8, 2023, from https://www.dstgb.de/themen/klimaschutz-und-klimaanpassung/aktuelles/nachhaltige-entwicklung-kommunen-als-zentrale-akteure-dauerhaft-staerken/beschluss-sts-ausschuss-vom-21.06.21-und-sachstand-kommunen-nachhaltigkeit-23.09.21.pdf?cid=jjp

Görz, G., Rollinger, C.-R., & Schneeberger, J. (2010). *Handbuch der Künstlichen Intelligenz* (4th ed.). Oldenbourg Verlag.

Granier, B., & Kudo, H. (2016). How are citizens involved in smart cities? Analysing citizen participation in Japanese "Smart Communities". *Information Polity, 21*(1), 61–76. https://doi.org/10.3233/IP-150367

Hasan, K.-S., & Ng, V. (2013). Stance classification of ideological debates: Data, models, features, and constraints. In R. Mitkov & J. C. Park (Eds.), *Proceedings of the Sixth International Joint Conference on Natural Language Processing* (pp. 1348–1356). Asian Federation of Natural Language Processing.

Hassan, L., & Hamari, J. (2020). Gameful civic engagement: A review of the literature on gamification of e-participation. *Government Information Quarterly, 37*(3), 1–21. https://doi.org/10.1016/j.giq.2020.101461

Hindman, M. (2009). *The myth of digital democracy*. Princeton University Press.

Hovik, S., & Giannoumis, G. A. (2022). Linkages between citizen participation, digital technology, and urban development. In S. Hovik, G. A. Giannoumis, K. Reichborn-Kjennerud, J. M. Ruano, I. McShane, & S. Legard (Eds.), *Citizen participation in the information society* (pp. 1–23). Springer.

Höffken, S., & Streich, B. (2013). Mobile participation: Citizen engagement in urban planning via smartphones. In C. N. Silva (Ed.), *Citizen e-participation in urban governance. Crowdsourcing and collaborative creativity* (pp. 199–225). IGI Global.

Johnson, P., Robinson, P., & Philpot, S. (2020). Type, tweet, tap, and pass: How smart city technology is creating a transactional citizen. *Government Information Quarterly, 37*(1), 101414. https://doi.org/10.1016/j.giq.2019.101414

Kleinhans, R. J., & Falco, E. (2022). Digital participation in urban planning. A promising tool or technocratic obstacle to citizen engagement? In R. Rocco, G. Bracken, C. Newton, & M. Dabrowski (Eds.), *Teaching, learning & researching spatial planning* (pp. 70–81). TU Delft OPEN Publishing.

Kneuer, M. (2016). E-democracy: A new challenge for measuring democracy. In M. Kneuer, B. Geissel, & H.-J. Lauth (Eds.), *Measuring the quality of democracy* (pp. 666–678). Special Issue der International Political Science Review.

Kneuer, M. (2019a). E-democracy. In T. Klenk, F. Nullmeier, & W. Göttrik (Eds.), *Handbuch Digitalisierung in Staat und Verwaltung* (pp. 1–11). Springer Fachmedien Wiesbaden.

Kneuer, M. (2019b). E-Democracy: Theoretische Debattenlinien, empirische Erkenntnisse, Umsetzungsdimension. In W. J. Schünemann & M. Kneuer (Eds.), *E-Government und Netzpolitik im europäischen Vergleich* (pp. 321–356). Nomos Verlagsgesellschaft.

Kneuer, M., & Datts, M. (2020). E-democracy and the matter of scale. Revisiting the democratic promises of the internet in terms of the spatial dimension. *Politische Vierteljahresschrift, 61*(2), 285–308.

Kneuer, M., & Richter, S. (2015). *Soziale Medien in Protestbewegungen. Neue Wege für Diskurs, Organisation und Empörung?* Campus.

Le Blanc, D. (2020). E-participation: A quick overview of recent qualitative trends. *UN DESA Working Paper (163)*, 1–33. https://www.un.org/esa/desa/papers/2020/wp163_2020.pdf

Liebeck, M., Esau, K., & Conrad, S. (2016). What to do with an airport? Mining arguments in the German online participation project Tempelhofer Feld. In C. Reed (Ed.), *Proceedings of the Third Workshop on Argument Mining* (pp. 144–153). ArgMining.

Luo, J., Liu, P., & Cao, L. (2022). Coupling a physical replica with a digital twin: A comparison of participatory decision-making methods in an urban park environment. *International Journal of Geo-Information, 11*(8), 1–17. https://doi.org/10.3390/ijgi11080452

Martin, J. (2014). Mobile media and political participation: Defining and developing an emerging field. *Mobile Media & Communication, 2*(2), 173–195. https://doi.org/10.1177/2050157914520847

McCaughey, M., & Ayers, M. D. (2003). *Cyberactivism. Online activism in theory and practice.* Taylor and Francis.

Michels, A., & Binnema, H. (2018). Assessing the impact of deliberative democratic initiatives at the local level: A framework for analysis. *Administration & Society, 51*(5), 749–769. https://doi.org/10.1177/0095399718760588

Mkude, C. G., Perez-Espes, C., & Wimmer, M. A. (2014). Participatory budgeting: A framework to analyze the value-add of citizen participation. *IEEE*, 2054–2062. https://doi.org/10.1109/HICSS.2014.260

Mossberger, K., Tolbert, C. J., & McNeal, R. S. (2007). *Digital citizenship: The internet, society, and participation.* The MIT Press.

Mossberger, K., & McDonald, J. (2008). The benefits of society online: Civic engagement. In K. Mossberger, C. J. Tolbert, & R. S. McNeal (Eds.), *Digital citizenship. The internet, society, and participation* (pp. 47–66). MIT Press.

Mossberger, K., Tolbert, C. J., & Franko, W. (2013). *Digital cities: The internet and the geography of opportunity.* Oxford University Press.

Nagorny-Koring, N. C. (2018). The power-knowledge of best practice: Governing climate change in German municipalities. In *The politics of urban sustainability transitions* (pp. 67–87). Routledge.

Przeybilovicz, E., Cunha, M. A., Geertman, S., Leleux, C., Michels, A., Zsuzsanna Tomor, C., Webster, W. R., & Meijer, A. (2020). Citizen participation in the smart city: Findings from an international comparative study. *Local Government Studies, 48*(1), 23–47. https://doi.org/10.1080/03003930.2020.1851204

Radtke, J. (2023). E-participation in post-pandemic-times: A silver bullet for democracy in the twenty-first century? *RIFS Discussion Paper*, 1–27. https://doi.org/10.48481/rifs.2023.022

Radtke, J., & Kersting, N. (2018). Energiewende in Deutschland. Lokale, regionale und bundespolitische Perspektiven. In J. Radke & N. Kersting (Eds.), *Energiewende. Politikwissenschaftliche Perspektiven* (pp. 3–16). Springer VS. https://doi.org/10.1007/978-3-658-21561-3

Rheingold, H. (1993). *The virtual community: Homesteading at the electronic frontier.* Addison-Wesley Publishing Company.

Rottinghaus, B., & Escher, T. (2020). Mechanisms for inclusion and exclusion through digital political participation: Evidence from a comparative study of online consultations in three German cities. *Zeitschrift für Politikwissenschaft, 30*, 261–298. https://doi.org/10.1007/s41358-020-00222-7

Saglie, J., & Vabo, S. I. (2009). Size and e-democracy: Online participation in Norwegian local politics. *Scandinavia Political Studies, 32*(4), 382–401. https://doi.org/10.1111/j.1467-9477.2009.00235.x

Segura-Tinoco, A., et al. (2022). A conversational agent for argument-driven e-participation. In *Proceedings of DG.O 2022: The 23rd Annual International Conference on Digital Government Research* (pp. 191–205). https://doi.org/10.1145/3543434.3543447

Shane, P. (2012). Online consultation and political communication in the era of Obama. An introduction. In S. Coleman & P. M. Shane (Eds.), *Connecting democracy. Online consultation and the flow of political communication* (pp. 1–20). MIT Press.

Shirky, C. (2011). The political power of social media: Technology, the public sphere, and political change. *Foreign Affairs, 90*(1), 28–41.

Smith, A., & Martin, P. P. (2022). Going beyond the smart city? Implementing technopolitical platforms for urban democracy in Madrid and Barcelona. In L. Mora et al. (Eds.), *Sustainable smart city transitions* (pp. 280–299). Routledge.

Spitzer, V., & Wimmer, M. A. (2021). Conception of a digital mobility platform for citizens in rural areas. In *Proceedings of the 14th International Conference on Theory and Practice of Electronic Governance* (pp. 414–421).

Tolbert, C. J., & McNeal, R. S. (2003). Unraveling the effects of the internet on political participation? *Political Research Quarterly, 56*(2), 175–185. https://doi.org/10.1177/106591290305600206

United Nations. (2003). *Global E-government survey 2003*. Retrieved November 21, 2023, from https://publicadministration.un.org/egovkb/portals/egovkb/Documents/un/2003-Survey/unpan016066.pdf

United Nations. (2014). *E-government survey 2014: E-government for the future we want*. Retrieved November 21, 2023, from https://publicadministration.un.org/egovkb/Portals/egovkb/Documents/un/2014-Survey/E-Gov_Complete_Survey-2014.pdf

United Nations. (2022). *Local online service index (LOSI)*. Retrieved May 4, 2024, from https://publicadministration.un.org/egovkb/en-us/About/E-Government-at-Local-Level/Local-Online-Service-Index-LOSI

van de Donk, W., Loader, B., Nixon, P., & Rucht, D. (2004). *Cyberprotest. New media, citizens, and social movements*. Routledge.

van Dijck, J. (2013). *The culture of connectivity. A critical history of social media*. Oxford University Press.

Wilhelm, A. G. (2000). *Democracy in the digital age. Challenges to political life in cyberspace*. Routledge.

Wimmer, M. A., Grimm, R., Jahn, N., & Hampe, J. F. (2013). Mobile participation: Exploring mobile tools in e-participation. In D. Hutchison, T. Kanade, J. Kittler, J. M. Kleinberg, F. Mattern, J. C. Mitchell, M. Naor, O. Nierstrasz, C. Pandu Rangan, B. Steffen, M. Sudan, D. Terzopoulos, D. Tygar, M. Y. Vardi, G. Weikum, M. A. Wimmer, E. Tambouris, & A. Macintosh (Eds.), *Electronic participation*. Lecture Notes in Computer Science (Vol. 8075, pp. 1–13). Springer.

Wimmer, M. A., & Spitzer, V. (2021). User needs for a mobility app to support living in rural areas. *International Conference on Electronic Participation*, 77–89. https://doi.org/10.1007/978-3-030-82824-0_7

Wimmer, M. A., Pereira, G. V., Ronzhyn, A., & Spitzer, V. (2020). Transforming government by leveraging disruptive technologies: Identification of research and training needs. *eJournal of eDemocracy and Open Government, 12*(1), 87–113. https://doi.org/10.29379/jedem.v12i1.594

Zhang, Z., Robinson, D., & Tepper, J. (2018). Detecting hate speech on twitter using a convolution-GRU based deep neural network. *European Semantic Web Conference*, 745–760. https://doi.org/10.1007/978-3-319-93417-4_48

Chapter 15
An Overview of Participatory Practices in the Digital Transformation of Italian Municipalities

Martina Trettel and Stefania Paolazzi

Abstract The intersection of participatory democracy and digitalization in Italy is a promising avenue for enhancing civic engagement and democratic practices at the local level. Leveraging digital tools underscores a commitment to fostering transparent, inclusive, and responsive governance. This chapter explores how Italian municipalities are embracing digital platforms to bridge the gap between citizens and institutions, enabling active participation in decision-making processes. Through the deployment of digital platforms and innovative methods like crowdsourcing and Urban Digital Twins, local governments are creating opportunities for citizens to voice their opinions, propose ideas, and contribute to policy development. However, challenges such as digital literacy, the digital divide, data privacy, and ethics must be addressed to ensure equitable participation. This study delves into three specific approaches to digital citizen engagement in Italian municipalities: Digital Participatory Platforms, innovative digital methods, and the use of Urban Digital Twins. It highlights the importance of balancing online and offline engagement, fostering partnerships for civic technologies, embracing multidisciplinary approaches, and ensuring sustainability and civic impact. By examining diverse examples, this chapter aims to stimulate reflection on the integration of democratic procedures with digital tools in the context of local government.

Keywords Participatory democracy · Digitalization · Civic engagement · Italian municipalities · Digital platforms · Urban digital twins

---

M. Trettel (✉)
Institute for Comparative Federalism, Eurac Research, Bolzano/Bozen, Italy
e-mail: martina.trettel@eurac.edu

S. Paolazzi
Policy Advisor at the City of Bologna, Bologna, Italy
e-mail: stefania.paolazzi@comune.bologna.it

K. Kössler, E. Schläppi (eds.), *Citizen Participation in Local Governance*, Local and Urban Governance, https://doi.org/10.1007/978-3-031-99824-9_15

15.1 Introduction

In recent years, the concept of participatory democracy has gained significant traction worldwide as a means to strengthen citizen engagement in decision-making processes (Trettel, 2015, 87). Globally, efforts have been made to enhance democratic practices in the context of policy-making and promote greater inclusion at all levels of government, especially at the local level. With the rapid advancement of digital technologies, public authorities and promoters of participatory practices are leveraging the potential of digitalization to foster participatory governance and empower citizens. In the same way, the processes of digitalization and technological development of cities are increasingly coupled with processes of civic engagement, with the aim of pursuing more transparent, inclusive, and democratic local development strategies (Margheri, 2010).

In fact, it has been widely acknowledged that the digital realm, particularly the Internet, stands as a catalyst to foster citizen participation, leading to a novel form of civic engagement that has the potential to fortify democracy. This perspective is crucial, given the pressing need for innovative methods and tools in today's democratic landscape, especially considering that a significant portion of citizens have disengaged from voting for several decades, and citizens often perceive that their requests go unheard. Therefore, the Internet emerges as a fundamental element for democratic renewal, potentially even representing a shift in the democratic paradigm capable of challenging or adapting systems of representative democracy in favor of participatory models (Côme & Rouet, 2023).

All this considered, this chapter will delve into the intersection of local participatory democracy and digitalization in Italy. It explores how Italian municipalities are embracing digital tools and platforms to bridge the gap between citizens and institutions, enabling them to actively contribute to the decision-making processes that affect their daily lives. By analyzing diverse examples, the authors will shed light on the different possibilities that technology offers for facilitating civic engagement and shaping the future of democracy.

Through the deployment of digital platforms and mobile applications, local governments are creating opportunities for citizens to voice their opinions, propose ideas, and contribute to policy development. These channels of communication allow for broader representation but also promote transparency and accountability in decision-making (European Committee on Democracy and Governance, 2021, 4), while at the same time prompt the need of reflecting on who is included and who tends to be excluded from virtual communication. Moreover, the digitalization of local democracy in Italy has witnessed the emergence of novel deliberative processes, such as online forums and virtual town halls. These platforms serve as virtual meeting spaces where citizens can engage in dialogue with their elected representatives. By transcending geographical limitations and time constraints, digital tools have the potential to overcome traditional barriers to participation and encourage diverse perspectives (Hovik & Giannoumis, 2022).

Digital participatory democracy also presents significant challenges. Concerns surrounding digital literacy, the digital divide, data privacy, and ethics must be addressed to ensure that participatory governance remains accessible and equitable for all citizens. Furthermore, questions regarding the balance between online and offline engagement, and the potential exclusion of marginalized communities, warrant careful consideration in the pursuit of an inclusive digital democracy (Russon Gilman & Cerneiro Peixoto, 2019).

This chapter exclusively addresses methods of citizen inclusion in the adoption of public authority decisions, drawing upon the concepts of participatory democracy and democratic innovations (Elstub, 2018; Elstub & Escobar, 2019). As a matter of fact, the chapter will provide an overview of different experiences trying to exemplify and categorize the many cases of participation through digital means that are employed by Italian municipalities. Due to length limitations, the authors cannot provide an exhaustive compilation of the digital modes of participation nor go into detail about each specific example. This chapter's main aim is to stimulate a deeper reflection on the many possibilities for integrating democratic procedures with digital tools in the context of local government.

As to the structure, the chapter will concentrate on three specific approaches to digital citizen engagement in Italian local entities: firstly, Digital Participatory Platforms (DPPs) (Sect. 15.2), secondly, strategies employing innovative digital methods such as crowdsourcing, citizens science, immersive technologies and gaming to involve citizens in local decision-making processes (Sect. 15.3), and finally the newest frontier of local digital transformation, *i.e* the Digital Twin, to explore if and eventually how this cutting-edge tool can accommodate citizen democratic participation (Sect. 15.4). The authors will provide examples for each of these approaches from selected Italian municipalities. The chapter will conclude with a final reflection on the analyzed experiences in Sect. 15.5.

15.2 Digital Participatory Platforms

A Digital Participatory Platform (DPP) refers to a web-based or software-driven environment designed to facilitate and enhance civic engagement, collaboration, and interaction among individuals, groups, or organizations in the digital realm. These platforms serve as dynamic spaces where individuals can contribute to decision-making processes, express their opinions, and actively engage in shaping policies that impact their communities. These digital tools empower citizens to voice their perspectives on issues ranging from local governance to national policies. The accessibility and convenience of these platforms facilitate a more inclusive and widespread participation, enabling individuals from various demographics and geographic locations to contribute to policy-making. DPPs can encompass a wide range of applications, from online surveys, public forums to collaborative idea-sharing platforms and social media networks to crowd-sourcing initiatives, virtual town halls, and e-democracy platforms, all aimed at fostering inclusive, transparent, and accessible avenues for citizen involvement and democratic decision-making (Falco & Kleinhans, 2018).

In the last decades, the use of DPPs at the local level has witnessed a remarkable surge. Through these digital channels, individuals can voice their opinions, propose initiatives, and collaborate with local authorities on various matters such as urban planning, public services, and environmental concerns. The ease of access and user-friendly interfaces have enabled a broader and more diverse spectrum of citizens to participate, bridging the gap between government and the governed (De Blasio & Selva, 2019). In many instances, DPPs serve as valuable complements to traditional offline participatory processes, offering enhanced opportunities for involvement, especially for individuals facing difficulties in attending physical gatherings, like for example people with disabilities or with physical limitations or those individuals who work specific hours and would typically struggle to participate in participatory processes designed solely for in-person engagement. By bridging the gap between online and offline realms, these platforms cater to the needs of those who may encounter barriers, such as geographical constraints or time limitations, enabling a more diverse and representative range of voices to participate in shaping community initiatives and policies (Grönlund et al., 2009).

The landscape of digital civic participation is characterized by diverse typologies of platforms showcased by the diversity of DPPs that Italian municipalities have employed. Hereafter, varied cases are presented to see how these digital tools offer distinct participatory opportunities to citizens who live in municipalities that are different in size, geographical location, and socio-cultural background.

First of all, open-source civic participation platforms have become one of the main ways Italian municipalities have implemented DPPs. To this extent, the platform ParteciPA, developed by Formez, a training and consulting center for the public administration, is the most widely used tool in this context.[1] ParteciPA has been in operation for several years, with its inception dating back to 2011 when Formez initiated its development to encourage participation and collaboration in public administration projects. The ParteciPA platform comprises three main components: (1) Ideario, a space where users can share and discuss ideas, proposals, or visions related to a particular topic or project; (2) Commentario, a feature for commenting and providing feedback on ideas, proposals, or experiences; (3) Esperienze where one can provide case studies, success stories, challenges faced, lessons learned, or best practices, allowing others to learn from past experiences and apply them in their own context.[2] Essentially, it incorporates technical and functional features akin to social media and social networks, aiming to facilitate interaction, sharing, and the creation of relevant information for the community. ParteciPA is a reusable platform

[1] Formez supports professional development, efficiency, and effectiveness in the public sector, and is involved in various projects to modernize and improve public services. See https://www.formez.it/

[2] See https://partecipa.gov.it/

that any public administration can adopt. In 2021, as part of a project called "Opengov: Methods and Tools for Open Administration" Formez began assisting regional and local public administrations interested in utilizing the software Decidim. In fact, ParteciPA relies on Decidim, an open-source software for developing DPPs that has recently become very popular. Decidim, firstly developed for the City of Barcelona, is built on open-source software, and can be modified and adapted by municipalities to suit their specific participation needs. This adaptability enables local governments to customize the platform to address unique local challenges and involve citizens in a more tailored manner (Aragón et al., 2017; Borge et al., 2023).

Many Italian municipalities, with distinct demographic, geographic, and socio-cultural characteristics, have employed the Decidim software to develop digital platforms for citizen participation in local policy-making. Among these is Milan, a metropolitan city in Lombardy; Prato, a medium-sized city in Tuscany; and Zola Predosa, a small municipality in Emilia-Romagna. The DPPs that they developed are, respectively, Milano Partecipa,[3] ParteciPO[4] and #ZolaPartecipa.[5] Through these platforms, citizens can actively engage in various experiences, such as consultations, debates, and meetings. They can evaluate proposals, express their opinions, and stay informed about ongoing and upcoming initiatives, thereby enhancing the effectiveness of their dialogue with municipal authorities. This proves how Decidim can be easily adapted to diverse local needs. Open-source platforms, such as Decidim, emphasize transparency, accessibility, and community-driven development, allowing citizens to actively contribute to the platform's evolution and improvement. Moreover, they offer various participatory tools and features, such as polls, debates, and collaborative decision-making mechanisms, facilitating more inclusive and democratic discussions among citizens.

DPPs based on open-source software are the most widespread example at the local level due to the ease in implementing and developing these platforms. However, this is not the only instance of DPP through which citizens can contribute to policy-making at the local level. In fact, many platforms are developed and managed directly by local administrations. These types of platforms often provide a structured and regulated environment for citizens to participate in decision-making processes and offer a certain level of reliability and government backing.

Again, different examples come to the fore. We have chosen three to showcase the variations among locally developed DPPs in different Italian Regions. The first example is the case of the Municipality of Lecce, which recently developed a purpose-built digital platform that is aimed at involving the community in the renewal of the General Urban Plan (*Piano Urbanistico Generale*).[6] The interactive pages published on the platform aim to not only collect structured proposals and observations from the citizens but also document their experiences related to

[3] See https://partecipazione.comune.milano.it/pages/milanopartecipa-presentazione?locale=en

[4] See https://www.pratodigitalcity.it/it/partecipo/pagina1900.html

[5] See https://zolapredosa.fondazionercm.it/

[6] See https://www.puglecce.it/

specific locations and neighborhoods. The website facilitates the identification of strategic thematic areas within the city through maps, presenting key data about the municipal territory through visual representations and providing accessible information.

Another noteworthy example can be highlighted in the Puglia region, where the municipality of Lecce is situated.[7] We are talking about the participatory platform *Puglia partecipa* which was developed by the region with the purpose of promoting digital and hybrid participatory processes at the regional and local levels. This platform provides the opportunity for municipalities in this region to leverage their support for local participatory processes. At the moment of writing this chapter, 83 local participatory processes have been initiated through this platform, a significant indicator that attests to the widespread use of this service by local authorities.

Another example is provided by the municipality of Terni, where we find a digital platform developed by the municipality and designed to provide the citizens with different possibilities of interaction with the local authority.[8] This example replicates that of many other Italian municipalities, developing an area of the institutional website that is dedicated to the highly interactive services made available by the municipality. In this case, on the interactive portal we find some possibilities that are granted to citizens to interact with the municipal administration, even if very limited in terms of participation.

We then find “ProponiTi”, a platform developed by the Municipality of Genoa through which citizens can propose to activate Collaborations Pacts with the city.[9] Collaborations Pacts are specific agreements in which both the citizens and the local administration agree on the cooperation for the shared administration of common goods (the so-called “commons”).[10] The commons in this regulation are intended as material spaces, such as public squares, green areas, or schools, but also immaterial commons, such as education and social inclusion and digital commons like applications and digital alphabetization (Arena, 2014). So, in this case, the City of Genoa decided to develop a dedicated participatory digital platform to offer citizens the opportunity to propose and manage Collaboration Pacts through a digital channel.

Against the background of this diverse and widespread experimentation with DPPs in Italian municipalities, we can now consider the pros and cons of these widely used tools. On the one hand, DPPs have the potential to significantly enhance political engagement by providing accessible channels for citizens to voice their opinions, contribute to decision-making processes, and actively participate in civic affairs. The ease of access to information and the ability to express opinions in a digital space can potentially break down geographical and social barriers, enabling a more inclusive and diverse range of voices to be heard. Also, these offer a

[7] See https://partecipazione.regione.puglia.it/processes_groups/4

[8] See https://www.comune.terni.it/servizi-online

[9] See https://proponiti.comune.genova.it/

[10] See Chap. 4 in this volume.

convenient avenue for citizens to stay informed about political events, policies, and promote a more informed citizenship (Secinaro et al., 2021).

On the other hand, the utilization of DPPs introduces a challenge. There is a potential risk that administrations may proclaim a fulfillment of requirements for more citizens involvement merely by engaging in digital initiatives, to the exclusion of participation in person, even though digital participation is either constrained or lacks the deliberative elements that should underlie such endeavors. This raises concerns about the adequacy and authenticity of participatory practices in the digital sphere. For instance, the mere presence of online surveys or feedback forms on a municipal website may be cited as evidence of participatory efforts. However, the substantive nature of participation, characterized by meaningful dialogue, incorporation of diverse perspectives, and the influence of citizen input on decision-making is absent in such instances. In this way, the proliferation of digital tools, while offering new avenues for engagement, necessitates a critical evaluation of the quality and depth of participatory processes to ensure that they align with the principles of genuine deliberation and inclusivity (De Blasio & Selva, 2019).

Moreover, there are concerns that individuals who make use of DPPs are primarily exposed to information that aligns with their existing beliefs. This can lead to polarization and limit exposure to diverse perspectives, potentially hindering the beneficial effects of a participatory process (De Blasio, 2019; Falco & Kleinhans, 2018).

15.3 Citizen's Engagement Through Innovative Digital Strategies

Innovative digital tools leveraging methods such as gamification or immersive technologies also have a revolutionary potential with regard to democratic innovations. In fact, engaging citizens through game-like elements and mechanisms to incentivize and motivate individuals to participate actively in civic processes can bring about the development of participatory policy-making in which citizens can be truly active actors (Christodoulou et al., 2018). To this extent, we can mention with regard to Italian municipalities, some examples of how these innovative methodologies have been used.

One example is the use of crowdsourcing applications that transform data collection into an engaging and enjoyable experience for citizens. In Italy, such experiences have emerged in different municipalities, among which we can mention Udine, Genoa, and Venice, where citizens can report service disruptions to the relevant authorities through web portals. Through these web-based tools, citizens become an integral part of the urban problem-solving process, and administrations benefit from their engagement. In particular, in Udine, an online reporting service is active through the municipal portal, allowing citizens to communicate issues and service disruptions within the territory and automatically transmit them to the relevant offices.[11] Users can also monitor the progress and resolution of these issues through the website. The Municipality of Venice offers a similar capability, enabling citizens to report issues related to urban aspects and track them until their resolution.[12] Since the service's launch in May 2008, the City of Venice has received nearly 6700 reports, with over a third being marked as successfully concluded. A similar service is provided by the Local Public Services Authority of the Municipality of Genoa, allowing citizens to report service disruptions and malfunctions after authenticating on the city website[13]. These issues pertain to municipal services managed by the municipality and the associated companies. The authority manages these reports and communicates the outcomes to the interested users.

Another very interesting experience worth mentioning is the Air-Break Ferrara project, which has emerged as a pioneering initiative aimed at raising awareness about air quality issues and fostering community involvement in the co-creation and experimentation of innovative solutions to enhance livability.[14] With a bold objective to reduce air pollution by 25% in environmentally stressed areas within a three-year timeframe, the project has implemented a multifaceted approach. Through immersive technologies, the project has conducted numerous workshops, involved over 90 entities, and obtained contributions from more than 1000 citizens. The collaborative efforts have led to the activation of 12 monitoring stations across the urban area since September 2021, providing valuable insights into the city's ecosystem. Through these co-creation activities and community-driven initiatives, citizens can actively contribute to shaping innovative solutions, fostering a sense of shared responsibility for environmental well-being. This inclusive model not only enhances the accuracy of air quality data with the deployment of monitoring stations and sensors but also fosters a stronger connection between the community and the project, ensuring a sustainable and collective effort to reduce air pollution and improve the overall quality of life in the city.[15]

The consortium of Trentino municipalities (*Consorzio dei Comuni Trentini*) has also embraced an innovative digital approach to citizen participation through the SensoRcivico project.[16] This platform empowers municipalities to actively engage with citizens, gathering suggestions, observations, and reports on various aspects of community life. Covering diverse aspects of local life such as traffic, public works, tourism, environment, and waste management, the platform offers a versatile tool to municipalities in Trentino. By capturing the community's perspective, SensoRcivico enables administrators to assess and address needs effectively. Moreover, the platform supports collaborative idea generation by allowing administrators to work

[11] See https://segnalazioni.comune.udine.it/

[12] See http://iris.comune.venezia.it/

[13] See http://www.asplgenova.it/segnalazioni

[14] See https://airbreakferrara.net/

[15] See https://www.unife.it/it/notizie/2021/scienza-cultura-e-ricerca/airbreak

[16] See https://www.comunitrentini.it/archivio/Aree-e-Uffici/Innovazione/Servizi-offerti/SensoRcivico

with the community in formulating new proposals. Accessible directly from the official municipal website, this system is designed to transparently collect citizen reports, which can be forwarded to relevant authorities for issue resolution or shared publicly to spark inclusive discussions and community-driven proposals. Active in various municipalities, SensoRcivico stands as evidence of the transformative potential of digital platforms in fostering dynamic citizen-administration collaboration.[17]

Another successful application of gamification in civic participation occurs through challenge-based initiatives. Governments or organizations can introduce competitions or challenges that invite citizens to propose innovative solutions to specific problems. This is the case of the Municipality of Salorno in the Province of Bolzano, which initiated a participatory process (*Officina dei giovani di Salorno*) in which, through its website, asked young people of the municipality to propose ideas for improving civic life.[18] In this case the three ideas most voted for by the citizens of the municipality were awarded a cash prize. This triggered the effect of using competition to stimulate youth creativity. In the first edition, among the various proposals were the ideas of developing an app that would make the city's monuments known in a light and user-friendly way, developing a book exchange point, and the idea of extending the local bike path.

These are just a few of the many examples that can be ascribed to the category of democratic innovations that make use of innovative digital strategies to activate citizens' engagement in policy-making. The combination of these experiences highlights a new focus by administrations on utilizing digital tools not only for broad and general consultation processes but also for addressing specific issues related to daily life and the quality of public services. On the one hand, administrations engage in a collaborative and shared process with their users, aiming to resolve urban problems and ensure institutional accountability. On the other hand, citizens become active participants in managing and improving public services. Very often these kinds of experiences are brought to the local administration by projects funded by the European Union (such as Horizon Europe) and whose development is supported by consortia of research institutions and universities (Mäkinen, 2017). This element must be considered when evaluating such experiences since innovations in digital participation (with more or less well-known methods) are often brought by actors outside the administrative structure and are then difficult to sustain when the project activity is concluded. One example is the case of the *Officina dei giovani* process implemented by the Municipality of Salorno with the support of the GaYA project (Governance and Youth in the Alps) financed through the Alpine space funding framework.[19]

[17] The municipalities in which SensoR civico is active are Trento, Arco, Castello-Molina di Fiemme, Castel Ivano, Predaia, Riva, Storo, and Ville d'Anaunia.

[18] See https://www.comune.salorno.bz.it/it/Il_paese/Informazioni_utili/GaYa_-_Officina_Giovani

[19] See https://www.alpine-space.eu/project/gaya/

15.4 From Smart Cities Initiatives to Urban Digital Twin: The Challenge to Engage Citizens in Advanced Technological Tools for Urban Planning and Policy-Making

The concept of "Digital Twin" (DT) was born about two decades ago in the field of industrial development and has been present in the literature ever since. From a technical perspective, Digital Twins are composed of different technological layers combining, among others, innovations such as data spaces, digital platforms, algorithms, artificial intelligence, machine learning, 3D reproductions, and data visualization. Whereas the evident consensus is that a Digital Twin is a digital representation of a physical object (Saeed et al., 2022), to date, there is no single, unambiguous definition of DT, as it varies depending on its scope, the subject area, the scale of the physical component to be replicated and other possible variables.

In particular, the concept and application of DT on a city scale is still in its first experiments. Bolton et al. define Digital Twins as "realistic digital representations of physical things" (assets, systems, processes) that "unlock value by enabling insights that support better decisions" (Bolton et al., 2018).

Several scholars identify a multi-disciplinary approach, capable of taking into account the complexity of overlapping urban systems, as the key factor in taking advantage of the potential of Urban Digital Twins, moving from a smart city model oriented towards controlling the physical dynamics of the city to a broader concept encompassing physical, social and knowledge infrastructures (Tomko & Stephan, 2019) and integrating different domains such as governance, political context, people and community, economy, and natural environment (Chourabi et al., 2012).

Nochta et al. (2021) emphasize how the adoption of a socio-technical perspective to the design of Urban Digital Twins should be geared towards enhancing certain aspects, which can be traced back to three main domains:

1. Enabling technology to be harnessed for public value production purposes, fostering a participatory design of the Digital Twin model capable of informing technology directly with socio-political needs;
2. Inform customization processes of the solution and thus sustainability for the communities that will use that solution;
3. Consider capacity-building processes as integrated aspects in the development of the Digital Twin and not as "access costs" for urban Digital Twin users.

Thus, one of the biggest and most interesting challenges for the development of Local Digital Twins is for sure the possibility of interacting with users and citizens and incorporating the social component of urban systems into them, representing both their collective behavior (by collecting data about them) and their preferences (by collecting data provided by the users themselves) (Ye et al., 2023; Bononi et al., 2022).

In Italy, the concept of Urban Digital Twin is experiencing a phase of great popularity. Together with the private and the research sectors, public administrations are investing resources and competencies to better understand and scale up already existing technologies in order to develop Digital Twins for better managing their mobility systems, cultural heritage, building, and energy management.

In Italy, Bologna and Matera are becoming interesting laboratories for the integration of the socio-political dimension in Urban Digital Twins. While Urban DT vision can also apply to other social contexts, specifically rural areas, the adoption is still very limited in these areas regarding both scope and ambition due to factors such as poor infrastructure for connectivity and scarcity of data. In Italy, there are currently no cases of strategies for the adoption of urban digital twin models in rural areas, despite the presence of cases of Smart Villages supported as part of European and national strategies for the development and adoption of even digital solutions to improve services and livability in rural areas.[20]

The City of Bologna considers its Digital Twin[21] as a new civic infrastructure, supporting and guiding data-driven decision-making processes and being able to effectively involve citizens and decision-makers in urban transformation processes. To implement this vision, the City of Bologna promoted a public consortium,[22] thus equipping the project with sociological, service design, active participation and human-computer interaction skills and mixing research and development competences.

By placing the values of inclusion and democratic participation at the center of its design, the Bologna Digital Twin is supported by a stakeholder and citizen engagement strategy according to the Quintuple Helix approach,[23] which will accompany the technological development in all its phases. Territorial actors will be involved according to different levels of active involvement through specific service design methodologies, civic participation, and citizen science.

These activities will see the active involvement of different target stakeholders in the different phases of use-case development, according to a scheme that focuses on the public sector and public services in the first year of the project, then opening up to organized civil society and citizenship during the second year and to the diversity of urban stakeholders, including private actors, during the third year.

In this scenario, Bologna Digital Twin will be supported by research and experimentation processes of capacity-building to prepare the cultural, social, and material conditions for an increasingly integrated and advanced involvement of territorial actors within the Digital Twin project once it is fully operational.

[20] See the case of Ostana, in Cuneo province: https://www.smartrural21.eu/villages/ostana_it/

[21] See https://www.comune.bologna.it/notizie/gemello-digitale

[22] Bologna Digital Twin partners are: Municipality of BolognaUniversity of Bologna, CINECA, Foundation for Urban Innovation, and Fondazione Bruno Kessler.

[23] This approach envisages five areas - government, industry, academia, civil society and environment - in which to group the possible actors involved in a given project. The interaction between these five areas, or helixes, promotes the exchange of knowledge and resources, promoting innovative and sustainable solutions. With reference to the quintuple helix, the stakeholders include citizens, who will be involved in the construction of the GDB through different methodologies and tools, such as citizen science. This approach is open and inclusive and implies the involvement of citizenship, at different levels, in the co-production of scientific knowledge, from the sharing of simple environmental surveys to the collaborative construction of research questions. See Carayannis et al. (2012).

The City of Matera is the pilot case within a R&D project promoted in the framework of the national initiative "Casa delle Tecnologie emergenti"[24] implemented in collaboration with the Centro Nazionale Ricerche (CNR), between other partners.

Matera's project aims to develop an Urban Digital Twin to effectively support the governance of urban systems, overcome sectoral and functionalist approaches typical of the smart city, and integrate a participatory approach within it (Malvezzi & Castelli, 2022). The project aims to identify processes, tools, and technologies for resilient urban development within the Digital Twin approach, developing a prototype of a collaborative approach with stakeholders and local communities from the earliest project stages.

In particular, starting in April 2022, Matera's Digital Twin project implemented two main areas of complementary participatory activities:

1. Focus Groups and codesign: Five focus groups have been launched to initiate discussions with local association networks on the uses of the Digital Twin and focus on the topics of accessibility of the city, use of urban spaces, management of cultural heritage, promotion of cultural activities and events, and the impact of tourism. Based on the results achieved, co-design tables have been activated with interested local ecosystem actors, to deepen the functionalities of the Digital Twin currently under development, as well as to imagine further functionalities on which to receive active support and to set up operational collaborations for the Digital Twin development and use.
2. Crowd-mapping: Different crowd-mapping activities were activated to build shared knowledge of the places and experiences of the city and to feed the data flow underlying Matera's Digital Twin. A questionnaire was developed and disseminated to the local community and participatory mapping activities (named "Teen maps Matera") were activated in seven secondary schools to involve the younger segments of the population.
3. Information and dissemination activities: In addition to institutional communication activities, a physical space called "Digital Twin Lab" was set up to promote greater visibility of the project in the city and to promote moments of exchange between experts and the local community on the subjects of urban development and Matera's Digital Twin.

Other participatory activities are currently being developed and implemented.

15.5 Conclusions

In conclusion, the intersection of participatory democracy and digitalization in Italy presents a promising avenue for enhancing civic engagement and democratic practices at the local level. The surge in efforts to leverage digital tools underscores a commitment to fostering transparent, inclusive, and responsive governance. As we

[24] The initiative "Casa delle tecnologie emergenti" in Matera is realized under the MISE - Ministero delle imprese e del Made Italy program to support 5G emerging technologies. See https://www.ctematera.it/

navigate this multifaceted landscape, ranging from DPPs to the incorporation of advanced technological tools like Urban Digital Twins, it becomes evident that technology holds transformative potential in shaping the future of democracy.

Section 15.2 of this chapter showed the dynamic landscape of DPPs in Italian municipalities, reflecting the many possibilities for engaging citizens in decision-making processes. The surge in the use of DPPs, particularly at the local level, has transformed civic engagement, providing inclusive and accessible avenues for individuals to contribute to policymaking. The variety of platforms, ranging from open-source initiatives like Decidim to locally developed solutions such as the purpose-built platforms experimented in Lecce and Genova, showcases the adaptability and customization potential of DPPs even if challenges arise concerning the adequacy of digital platforms in developing appropriate contexts for meaningful engagement.

Section 15.3 shed light on how innovative digital strategies, such as gamification and crowdsourcing, have further revolutionized civic participation by encouraging interactive and purposeful engagement. It has been seen how crowdsourcing applications can transform data collection into an engaging experience, enabling citizens to contribute to urban problem-solving. The Air-Break Ferrara project is a good example for exemplifying the potential of immersive technologies to raise awareness and engage communities in co-creating solutions for environmental challenges.

Finally, Sect. 15.4 focused on the advent of Urban Digital Twins, illustrated by initiatives in cities like Bologna and Matera. These experiments go beyond technical considerations, emphasizing a socio-technical perspective that integrates the complexities of urban systems. Bologna's ambitious Digital Twin project prioritizes stakeholder and citizen engagement throughout its development. The participatory approach in Matera seeks to create a social infrastructure for the city, encompassing diverse participatory activities and the use of geo-referenced community surveys. While the potential of Urban Digital Twins is still in its early stages, their success hinges on the active involvement of stakeholders, the customization of solutions to meet local needs, and the integration of capacity-building processes.

As mentioned in the introduction, this chapter does not set out to analyze in detail the technological domain and its relationship to civic participation. However, from the reading of the reported experiences of Italian municipalities, some elements emerge that we consider important to point out, hoping to inform future research spaces:

- *On- and offline civic participation*: Digital participation does not seem to replace in-person participation. Instead, the two modes seem to combine and, in some cases, feed off each other, as it is possible to see from the in-depth study of numerous experiences mentioned in the previous paragraphs. A profound reflection is required on the effective integration between digital tools for participation and in-person moments of participatory discussion. Striking a balance between these approaches is vital for the success of participatory democracy, emphasizing the ongoing need for a nuanced and adaptive approach.
- *Partnerships for "civic technologies"*: The digitalization of participatory democracy unfolds across a broad spectrum, ranging from conventional tools like digital platforms to sophisticated innovations such as the Digital Twin. Local public

administrations can find themselves lost in the management of technological innovation processes, or unable to focus on the opportunities presented by digital technologies for their territories and citizens. Research agencies can sometimes play a role of mediation, and are capable of triggering processes of administrative learning and innovation. Experiences with projects financed through EU funds and complex technologies, like Urban Digital Twins, highlight the pivotal role of these partnerships. These collaborations can prioritize the social and civic dimensions essential for the meaningful development of these technologies. On the contrary, the relationship between these initiatives and tech companies is still unclear. The delicate nature of this relationship raises important questions regarding the sustainability of these initiatives in the long term. While this topic is sensitive, it could potentially be explored as a future research avenue. This delicate balance underscores the need for a cautious and strategic approach in navigating cooperation with tech companies, ensuring that such partnerships align with the goals and capabilities of public administrations.

- *Urban-rural alliances*: A comparison with digitization practices, particularly the more advanced ones such as the local Digital Twins, clearly shows an imbalance between rural and urban areas in digital transformation processes. Future research efforts could focus on analyzing the conditions and opportunities for creating urban-rural alliances for the dissemination of practices, tools and processes for capacitating administrations that are less able to benefit from digital transformation.
- *Multi-disciplinary approaches for more inclusive technologies*: Researching and developing technologies is no longer considered an exclusive domain for technical disciplines. At the same time, a compartmentalized approach to technologies is not sufficient anymore. Challenges, such as defining the scope of Digital Twins on a city scale and ensuring inclusivity underscore the importance of a holistic and multi-disciplinary approach. The relationship between technology and democracy is not only a theoretical question but it is often determined by technical elements and choices, by the governance designed to develop and scale technologies, etc. The ongoing discourse on technologies with far-reaching effects, such as artificial intelligence, necessitates a continued deepening of reflections on civic participation within the realm of technological innovation.
- *Sustainability and civic impact*: Some of the reported experiences currently appear to be isolated and sporadic endeavors. For example, it is unclear whether the increase in data available to public administrations from crowdsourcing initiatives actually triggers virtuous processes in its use. Our research identified specific projects and initiatives, yet stable administrative practices in this direction seem to struggle to emerge, suggesting challenges in initiating lasting administrative learning processes and digital maturity. At the same time, it still seems difficult to understand and measure the specific impacts of civic engagement initiatives in technological development over the long term.

References

Aragón, P., Kaltenbrunner, A., Calleja-López, A., Pereira, A., Monterde, A., Barandiaran, X. E., & Gómez, V. (2017). Deliberative platform design: The case study of the online discussions in Decidim Barcelona. In C. G. Luca, M. Afra, & Y. Taha (Eds.), *Social informatics. Lecture Notes in Computer Science* (pp. 277–287). Springer.

Arena, G. (2014). *Un regolamento per la cura condivisa dei beni comuni*. Labsus, Laboratorio per la sussidiarietà.

Barricelli, B. R., & Fogli, D. (2022). Digital twins in human-computer interaction: A systematic review. *International Journal of Human-Computer Interaction*, 1–19.

Bolton, A., Butler, L., Dabson, I., Enzer, M., Evans, M., Fenemore, T., Harradence, F., Keaney, E., Kemp, A., Luck, A., Pawsey, N., Saville, S., Schooling, J., Sharp, M., Smith, T., Tennison, J., Whyte, J., Wilson, A., Makri, C. (2018). *Gemini principles (Report)*. CDBB. https://doi.org/10.17863/CAM.32260

Bononi, L., Donatiello, L., Longo, D., Massari, M., Montori, F., Stacchio, L., & Marfia, G. (2022). Digital twin collaborative platforms: Applications to humans-in-the-loop crafting of urban areas. *IEEE Consumer Electronics Magazine, 12*(6), 38–46.

Borge, R., Balcells, J., & Padró-Solanet, A. (2023). Democratic disruption or continuity? Analysis of the Decidim platform in Catalan municipalities. *American Behavioral Scientist, 67*(7), 926–939.

Bua, A., & Escobar, O. (2018). Participatory-deliberative processes and public policy agendas. Lessons for policy and practice. *Policy Design and Practice, 1*, 126–140.

Carayannis, E. G., Barth, T. D., & Campbell, D. F. (2012). The Quintuple Helix innovation model: Global warming as a challenge and driver for innovation. *Journal of Innovation and Entrepreneurship, 1*, 1–12.

Chourabi, H., Nam, T., Walker, S., Ramon Gil-Garcia, J., Mellouli, S. (2012). Understanding smart cities: An integrative framework. In *45th Hawaii International Conference on System Sciences*, 2289–2297.

Côme, T., & Rouet, G. (2023). Introduction: Local participatory democracy, discourses, and practices. In T. Côme & G. Rouet (Eds.), *Participatory and digital democracy at the local level* (pp. 1–9). Springer.

Christodoulou, N., Papallas, A., Kostic, Z., & Nacke, L. E. (2018). Information visualization, gamification and immersive technologies in participatory planning. *Extended Abstracts of the 2018 CHI Conference* (pp. 1–4).

De Blasio, E. (2019). *E-democracy*. Mondadori Università.

De Blasio, E., & Selva, D. (2019). Le piattaforme di partecipazione tra tecnologia e governance. I modelli di sviluppo in Italia, Spagna e Regno Unito. *Rivista italiana di politiche pubbliche, 3*, 349–382.

European Committee on Democracy and Governance. (2021). *Study on the impact of digital transformation on democracy and good governance*.

Falco, E., & Kleinhans, R. (2018). Beyond technology: Identifying local government challenges for using digital platforms for citizen engagement. *International Journal of Information Management, 40*, 17–20.

Elstub, S. (2018). Deliberative and participatory democracy. In A. Bächtiger, J. S. Dryzek, J. Mansbridge, & M. E. Warren (Eds.), *The Oxford handbook of deliberative democracy* (pp. 186–202). Oxford University Press.

Elstub, S., & Escobar, O. (2019). Defining and typologizing democratic innovations. In S. Elstub & O. Escobar (Eds.), *Handbook of democratic innovation and governance* (pp. 11–31). Edward Elgar Publishing.

Grönlund, K., Strandberg, K., & Himmelroos, S. (2009). The challenge of deliberative democracy online—A comparison of face-to-face and virtual experiments in citizen deliberation. *IP Information Polity, 14*, 187–201.

Hovik, S., & Anthony Giannoumis, G. (2022). Linkages between citizen participation, digital technology, and urban development. In G. Sissel Hovik, A. Giannoumis, K. Reichborn-Kjennerud, J. M. Ruano, I. McShane, & S. Legard (Eds.), *Citizen participation in the information society. Comparing participatory channels in urban development* (pp. 1–23). Palgrave Macmillan.

Mäkinen, K. (2017). All about doing democracy? Participation and citizenship in EU projects. In C. Wiesner, A. Björk, H.-M. Kivistö, & K. Mäkinen (Eds.), *Shaping citizenship: A political concept in theory, debate and practice* (pp. 190–205). Routledge.

Malvezzi, R., & Castelli, G. (2022). Gemelli Digitali Urbani per lo sviluppo di comunità partecipanti: il caso di Matera. In C. Belingardi, G. E. De Vita, L. Lieto, G. Papparlardo, & L. Saija (Eds.), *Agire collettivo e rapporto tra attori nel governo del territorio* (Atti XXIV Conferenza Nazionale Siu) (Vol. 5). Planum Publisher e Società Italiana degli Urbanisti.

Margheri, A. (2010). L'e-democracy nelle regioni e negli enti locali. *Informator, 17*(4), 9–13.

Nochta, T., Wan, L., Schooling, J. M., & Parlikad, A. K. (2021). A socio-technical perspective on urban analytics: The case of city-scale digital twins. *Journal of Urban Technology, 18*(1–2), 263–287.

Russon Gilman, H., & Carneiro Peixoto, T. (2019). Digital participation. In S. Elstub & O. Escobar (Eds.), *Handbook of democratic innovation and governance* (pp. 105–118). Edward Elgar Publishing.

Saeed, Z. O., Mancini, F., Glusac, T., & Izadpanahi, P. (2022). Future city, digital twinning and the urban realm: A systematic literature review. *Buildings, 12*(5), 685.

Secinaro, S., Brescia, V., Iannaci, D., & Jonathan, G. M. (2021). Does citizen involvement feed on digital platforms? *International Journal of Public Administration, 45*, 708–725.

Tomko, M., & Stephan, W. (2019). Beyond digital twins—A commentary. *Environment and Planning B: Urban Analytics and City Science, 46*, 395–399.

Trettel, M. (2015). The politics of deliberative democracy. A comparative survey of the "Law in action" of citizen participation. *Derecho Politico, 1*, 86–114.

Ye, X., Jiaxin, D., Han, Y., Newman, G., Retchless, D., Zou, L., & Zhenhang, C. (2023). Developing human-centerd urban digital twins for community infrastructure resilience: A research agenda. *Journal of Planning Literature, 38*(2), 187–199.

Chapter 16
Public Participation, Municipal Websites, and Transparency in Procurement in South Africa

Tinashe Chigwata and Jaap de Visser

Abstract South Africa has a well-developed system of local government which is anchored on public publication. This chapter examines the basic features of the legal and policy framework for public participation and assess to what extent e-participation has taken root in municipalities to augment traditional forms of participation. It highlights transparency as a precondition for public participation. The chapter establishes that the legal and policy framework for public participation in South Africa provides vast opportunities for democratic participation that go beyond just voter representation. However, communities do not always make use of public participation mechanisms created by municipalities. Often times, they invent their own spaces to voice their concerns. Furthermore, municipalities do not always make information publicly available in a way easily understandable by their communities to enable effective public participation. Whereas the law requires every municipality to establish and maintain a website to enhance digital participation, the chapter presents empirical evidence which show that municipal websites are not yet an effective mechanism of fostering public participation due to a number of reasons. The evidence also suggests that there is culture of lack of transparency particularly with regards to the publication of municipal procurement information which is inhibiting public publication.

Keywords Local government · Public participation · Municipal websites · Transparency · Procurement · South Africa

---

T. Chigwata (✉) · J. de Visser
Dullah Omar Institute, University of the Western Cape, Bellville, South Africa
e-mail: tchigwata@uwc.ac.za; jdevisser@uwc.ac.za

K. Kössler, E. Schläppi (eds.), *Citizen Participation in Local Governance*, Local and Urban Governance, https://doi.org/10.1007/978-3-031-99824-9_16

16.1 Introduction

The Constitution of South Africa is committed to public participation. It commits not only to representative democracy, but also to participatory democracy. For local government, it lists a specific objective "to encourage the involvement of communities and community organizations in the matters of local government" (Section 152(1)(e) Constitution). Furthermore, in its values and principles for public service, the Constitution instructs public administrations to be responsive: "People's needs must be responded to, and the public must be encouraged to participate in policy-making." (Section 195(1)(e) Constitution). These instructions are more than ambitions. The Constitutional Court and the lower courts regularly review and set aside decisions of national, provincial or local governments which failed to make a reasonable effort to facilitate public participation (*Doctors for Life International v Speaker of the National Assembly and Others* 2006 (12) BCLR 1399 (CC)); Steytler & De Visser, 2007, 6–15).

This chapter focuses on local government. It examines the basic features of the legal and policy framework for public participation and assesses to what extent e-participation has taken root in municipalities to augment traditional forms of participation. It highlights transparency as a precondition for public participation and argues that social auditing can be an effective mechanism for collaborative public participation. It then examines one specific area in which transparency is critically important to make social auditing possible: municipal procurement of goods and services. It presents and analyzes empirical evidence on how municipalities utilize their websites to facilitate transparency in procurement. The inquiry begins with an overview of the policy and legislative framework for public participation.

16.2 Policy and Legislative Framework for Public Participation

The law, policy and practice in South Africa on public participation in local governments can be divided into four conceptual levels, with the first being the "lightest" and the fourth being the "most intense" form of public participation (Steytler & De Visser, 2007, 6–9).

16.2.1 Transparency

The first level of public participation is transparency. Local governments are expected (and also instructed by law) to be transparent about what they do. This is because participatory democracy and accountable governance are not possible when local governments do not share critical information with the public (Nyawo, 2017). This relates to information about:

1. governance (e.g. council meetings, minutes, policies, by-laws etc.);
2. finance (e.g. budget, financial statements, costs of services); and
3. administration (e.g. what goods and services have been procured, where/how to get hold of officials to raise service delivery issues).

Municipalities in South Africa must maintain a website (Section 21B Systems Act). Municipalities generally also use social media, and some even developed apps dedicated to keeping the public informed. The national government-run eTender Portal is available for municipalities to inform companies and the general public about the available procurement opportunities. But they must also display information in accessible places such as municipal notice boards, libraries and municipal offices so as to not disadvantage those with limited access to the internet (Section 21A Systems Act). South Africa has 12 official languages. Using the correct language is important: municipalities must assess the language preferences in their area and decide which language(s) to use when communicating with the public (Strijdom, 1999).

This is the "lightest" form of public participation because it is generally "one-way traffic": the municipality makes information available (Steytler & De Visser, 2007, 6–9). The next level is complaints, petitions and demonstrations.

16.2.2 Advocacy Through Complaints, Petitions and Demonstrations

Residents and communities will not always be content with the municipality. They may have grievances or complaints, big or small. The Constitution recognizes everyone's right to peacefully demonstrate, picket and petition (Section 17 Constitution). The right to demonstrate is also an important element of public participation. The municipality plays an important role in facilitating this right (Ntliziywana, 2011).

It is important that there are avenues for the public to air these grievances (Steytler & De Visser, 2007, 6–12). First, residents will feel unheard if there are no avenues, and tensions may boil over. Second, grievances and complaints may contain information that assists the municipality to do better. Municipalities in South Africa offer these avenues in the form of complaints boxes, anonymous hotlines to report fraud or corruption, etc. The question is whether online methods are used by communities to air, and by municipalities to collect, grievances.

The key message of a demonstration is often contained in a petition. This usually involves a serious complaint, often made to public officials. For example, a group of residents may officially "hand over" a petition to the mayor or the municipal manager. Municipalities must develop procedures to receive and process petitions (Section 17(2)(a) Systems Act). Many have a council committee dedicated to dealing with petitions. There is little evidence of municipalities actively facilitating e-participation at this level. However, communities and residents are increasingly using online methods to air their grievances. Increasingly, petitions take the form of online petitions, managed by non-governmental organisations or platforms. For example, *Amandla Mobi* is an NGO that hosts social justice campaigns, often targeted at municipalities. On its website (amandla.mobi), it uses the slogan: “turning every cell phone into a democracy building tool”.

While this form of public participation is more intense than the mere publication of information under the first theme, the municipality is still only required to “receive” information (Steytler & De Visser, 2007). The next theme, namely consultation, requires more engagement by the municipality.

16.2.3 Consultation

This third level is about the municipality opening up opportunities for public input in the decision-making process. Again, a key question is whether e-participation is common with regard to this level of participation. The municipality must consult communities, communicate with them, and provide feedback. Unlike the first two themes, this is no longer passive; the municipality must actively seek the public’s input or comments and establish two-way communication on those comments (Steytler & De Visser, 2007, 6–12(1)). The principle is that the municipality must consult communities about any decision that will affect them.

At a basic level, this requires that municipalities publish draft decisions, and invite the public to comment. However, inviting and receiving written comments on a draft by-law, budget, policy, or project is not enough. The municipality must analyze the comments and provide feedback to communities. Also, it may be necessary to support communities in providing comments. For example, it may be appropriate to convene community meetings, provide transport, translation, and/or assist people who cannot read or write (*Mogale and Others v Speaker of the National Assembly and Others 2023 (9) BCLR 1099 (CC)* paras 68–80). There are two major municipal decisions in which municipalities are expected to make a special effort to involve residents. These are the integrated development plan (Chapter 5 Municipal Systems Act) and the budget. The integrated development plan (IDP) is a 5-year strategic plan for the municipality. It sets out how the municipality, in collaboration with national and provincial governments, will deliver services and facilitate development. The IDP is not just a plan without resources. It must be accompanied by a 3-year financial plan. Therefore, if a project is included in the IDP, the municipality’s financial plan must make provision for it (unless it is funded by another level of government). Each year, the municipality adopts a budget based on the IDP. It gives the municipality permission to incur the expenditure associated with the strategies and projects identified in the IDP. It also determines how the municipality's plan will be funded, i.e. through municipal taxes, fees for services, funding from other governments, loans, etc. While preparing the budget (based on the IDP), the municipality must again reach out to residents and communities and ask for their input into the draft budget.

Municipalities are slowly starting to manage the invitations and management of public comments through online platforms. For example, the City of Cape Town has integrated a public comments webpage into its online interface with citizens. When municipal residents visit its CityConnect interface to pay an account, apply for a job, or request a service, the same webpage invites comments on draft policies, by-laws and initiatives. However, Okeke-Uzodike and Dlamini report that, in general, "the concept of e-participation remains untapped at the local municipal levels of government in South Africa" (Okeke-Uzodike & Dlamini, 2019, 465).

16.2.4 Collaboration

The fourth level of public participation is co-production or collaboration. This is when the municipality partners with residents, communities and/or community organizations. This form of public participation is no longer about the municipality "presenting a draft decision" for the public to comment on. Rather, it is about the municipality collaborating with residents, communities and/or community organizations in a more organized, regular, or institutionalized way. The policy and legal framework for local government contains a range of mechanisms for this.

One of the most prominent mechanisms is the ward committee, regulated in sections 72–80 of the Municipal Structures Act. Each municipality is divided into a number of wards (constituencies). Each ward is represented by a ward councilor who is elected by the voters in that ward. The ward committee is then a group of ten community members from that ward who assist the ward councilor. Each of the ten community members is selected from a specific sector, such as business, churches, civic organizations, youth organizations, etc. The ten community members assist the ward councilor with identifying issues in that ward that must be addressed by the municipality (Naidu, 2012). So, while a politician heads the committee, he or she must work together with members of the public. There are about 4400 wards in South Africa, all of which have a ward committee. This means that, via the ward committee system, more than 40,000 members of the public can play an active role in the affairs of their municipalities.

A second example is social auditing. Berthin (2011) defines a social audit as an "accountability mechanism where citizens organize and mobilize to evaluate or audit government's performance and policy decisions". At the local level, residents audit the quality of municipal services. *Asivikelane*, a civil society initiative coordinated by the International Budget Partnership South Africa (IBP-SA), is an example of social auditing (IBP-SA, 2023). This initiative aims to improve the delivery of basic services in informal settlements. *Asivikelane* identifies residents in informal settlements to participate in the campaign. They anonymously complete monthly online surveys on the accessibility and quality of basic services in their area, such as water, sanitation, and refuse removal. *Asivikelane* also collects details of their experience with each service, and often, photos and videos are submitted. IBP-South Africa collates the information, analyzes it and allocates the responses to the relevant municipality. Municipalities are then rated with a 'traffic light' rating on the accessibility and quality of the services. The results are shared with the municipality. This assists the municipality with improving service delivery. More detailed results are provided, with comments from the community members being sent to the relevant municipalities so they can act on these needs. In this way, *asivikelane* creates a channel between municipal governments and informal settlements. The results are also made public in a short, accessible document which is disseminated via email lists and social media.

Social auditing, such as *asivikelane,* is an innovative and effective way to involve residents in local government affairs and make municipalities more responsive to their needs. It has the potential to facilitate accountability for service delivery failures. The critical question is whether "citizens have the skills, capacity and tools to effectively monitor and evaluate their governments and decision-makers" (Berthin, 2011). Without transparency, social auditing cannot be effective. In addition, auditing always occurs against a standard, and if the public is not made aware of the standard and how the delivery is organized, social auditing occurs in a vacuum. That is why the issue of transparency, highlighted in Sect. 16.2.1, is critically important and takes center stage in the remainder of this chapter.

16.2.5 Reflection

The legal and policy framework for public participation in South Africa provides vast opportunities for democratic participation beyond just voter representation (Palmer et al., 2017, 34). Residents and communities have access to more than just elections as an instrument to take part in municipal affairs. (Smith & De Visser, 2009). Sometimes, this includes access to online mechanisms to submit petitions and comments even though most municipalities continue to rely on traditional methods of public participation.

There are practical challenges with this framework, and in particular with the way it is practiced (Nyawo, 2017). Often, a distinction is made between "invited spaces" for public participation and "invented spaces" for public participation. The "invited spaces" are those spaces that the municipality creates, and "invites" residents to participate in (Naidu, 2012). Examples are the invitation for public comment, including limited online mechanisms, ward committees and IDP hearings. The "created spaces" are spaces for public participation that residents and communities create with their own initiative (Naidu, 2012). (Online) petitions, marches, and demonstrations are examples of that. The reality of participation in local government in South Africa is that, often, residents prefer "invented spaces" (such as protests and marches) over "invited spaces". This is because too many of the structures created by the municipality for public participation, such as ward committees, have become politicized (Smith & De Visser, 2009; Naidu, 2012). It is tempting to argue that marginalized residents (such as the youth, persons living in informal settlements etc.) prefer "created spaces" and the well-to-do (such as suburban dwellers) prefer "invented spaces". However, the reality is more complex. For example, groups of suburban residents in some municipalities have resorted to withholding payments to the municipality and using the funds to organize their own services in a "Robin Hood" type of protest against poor service delivery (Sefoloko, 2023). They are thus "creating" an (unlawful) space of contestation with the municipality.

Furthermore, the fact that the law directs municipalities to consult the public at every turn has encouraged a "tick box" mentality where municipalities conduct public participation for the sake of compliance, rather than to benefit from the inputs (Nyawo, 2017). Also, these structures are too often "unfriendly" to residents. For example, youth movements concerned about unemployment, or the lack of opportunities are not easily convinced that submitting written comments to a draft budget, or participating in ward committee meetings, will make a difference. They will be more inclined to join an online petition. Service delivery protests are a common occurrence in municipalities. For example, as shown in Fig. 16.1 below, in 2018 a total number of 237 protests were recorded. There was a significant decrease in the number of protests in 2020 (102) and 2021 (121), which can be attributed to the COVID-19 pandemic and the lockdown. With the relaxation of the lockdown and the containment of the COVID-19 pandemic, the number of protests rose to 193 in 2022. Access to electricity was the main driver of service delivery protests in the same year (Municipal IQ, 2023). A significant percentage of those protests were violent. Nyawo (2017) argues that the increase in service delivery protests indicates a lack of citizen participation, transparency and accountability.

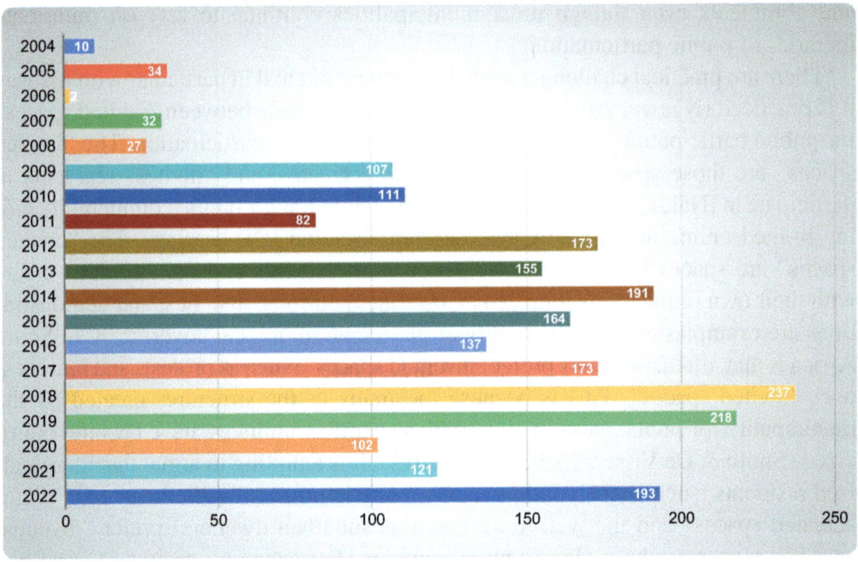

Fig. 16.1 Major service delivery protests by year (2004–2022). (Source: Own creation with data provided by Municipal IQ (2023))

Social auditing is a mode of public participation that straddles the divide between invited and invented spaces. However, as indicated earlier, transparency is essential for social auditing to work effectively. This is why this chapter examines transparency as a mode of public participation, with a specific focus on municipal procurement and the use of municipal websites to increase transparency.

16.3 Transparency in Municipal Procurement

As stated above, public participation and accountability cannot be effective without transparency (Nyawo, 2017). The key question is: are municipalities in South Africa transparent? We address the question by examining the state of transparency in local government with a particular focus on procurement and the use of municipal websites. The discussion is based on findings from two surveys of municipal websites to assess whether municipalities are transparent about the goods and services they procure. The first survey was conducted in 2020 and targeted 34 municipalities. The second survey, conducted in 2021, expanded the sample to 49 municipalities. This included municipalities across all nine provinces, in all three municipal categories, as well as across all the subcategories used by the National Treasury, namely:

1. A—metropolitan municipalities or metros;
2. B1—secondary cities, local municipalities with the largest budgets;
3. B2—local municipalities with a large town as the core;
4. B3—local municipalities with small towns, with a relatively small population and significant urban population but with no large town as the core;
5. B4—local municipalities that are mainly rural with communal tenure and with, at most, one or two small towns in their area;
6. C1—district municipalities that are not water services authorities; and
7. C2—district municipalities that are water services authorities.

Table 16.1 below lists the municipalities in the sample according to the three municipal categories.

Table 16.1 Surveyed municipalities

Category A: metropolitan municipalities (Metros)	Category B: local municipalities (LMs)		Category C: district municipalities (DMs)
City of Tshwane	Emfuleni	The Big 5 False Bay	Ugu
Ekurhuleni	Polokwane	Msukaligwa	Mopani
Buffalo City	Rustenburg	Thabazimbi	Namakwa
City of eThekwini	Thulamela	Stellenbosch	Ngaka Modiri
Nelson Mandela Bay	Greater Taung	Dr. Beyers Naudé	West Coast
Mangaung	Nkomazi	Amahlathi	
City of Johannesburg	Msunduzi	Tswelopele	
City of Cape Town	Okhahlamba	Setsoto	
	Makana	Metsimaholo	
	Nkomazi	Dihlabeng	
	Emalahleni	Msinga	
	Dawid Kruiper Joe	Tswaing	
	Morolong	Ventersdorp	
	Mossel Bay	Randfontein	
	Knysna	Albert Luthuli	
	Inxuba Yethemba	Pixley Ka Seme	
	Matjhabeng	Sol Plaatjie	
	Moqhaka		
	Indaka		

Before discussing the findings, we will briefly discuss why it is important for municipalities to publish procurement information on their websites. In South Africa, municipalities are responsible for the delivery of basic services. Section 1 of the Municipal Systems Act defines basic services as those services that if not provided will jeopardize public health or safely. Municipalities do not always produce these services. In many instances, they rely on private companies whom they contract to deliver these services. The services include refuse removal, cleaning of public places, road maintenance, the clearing of storm water drainage systems, and the delivery of water to underservices areas. There is, however, "very limited or no public engagement by communities in the public procurement of outsourced basic services, from the actual tender process to the delivery and monitoring of the delivery of the services" (IBP-SA, 2018). This is mainly due to the fact that municipalities do not make procurement information easily available for public scrutiny. The procurement of these services is generally regarded as a matter between the municipality and service providers. As a result, while communities are the ultimate beneficiaries of these services, they are unable to scrutinise a municipality's procurement decisions which affects them. It is argued that local democracy dictates that communities should have say on how local decisions are made, including the procurement of services (Dullah Omar Institute (DOI) and International Budget Partnership-South Africa (IBP-SA, 2020) Hence, municipal procurement must not be inward-focused, or oriented only towards service providers. Rather, municipalities must work with local communities, and ensure that the procurement of goods and services, particularly essential services like water and sanitation, is transparent (De Visser & Chigwata, 2020).

Section 21B(3) of the Municipal Systems Act imposes two obligations on municipalities which are crucial for transparency and citizen participation in local governance. First, municipalities must establish a municipal website. Second, municipalities have an obligation to regularly update their respective websites with information. The National Treasury (2013) has further issued guidelines to municipalities which specifies the information that must be published on these websites. The information includes, tender notices and prices of contracts, among other forms of procurement information. Citizens' access to this information on the municipal website enables communities to know exactly what should be delivered, who is responsible, and how often it should be delivered (IBP-SA, 2018). With the assistance of civil society initiatives, such as *asivikelane*,[1] they can conduct social auditing on those services and contribute to improved service delivery. If communities are not happy with the state of services delivered by the service provider they can raise their concerns with the municipality for redress. Thus, municipal websites are an important vehicle for enabling citizen participation in the modern world. The question is whether municipalities are complying with the requirement to (1) establish a municipal website and (2) to publish procurement information on them regularly?

With regards to the first requirement, the 2021 survey established that the sampled municipalities had functional websites with the exception of Inxuba Yethemba Local Municipality and Ventersdorp Local Municipality (DOI and IBP-SA, 2020, 2021). The 2021 assessment further established that while three municipalities; Indaka,

[1] See Sect. 16.2.4 above.

Greater Taung and Setsoto; had functional websites, they either did not publish procurement information on their respective websites or their websites contained old information. The assessment also found that procurement information on Joe Morolong and Dawid Kruiper municipalities was not updated during the survey period (DOI and IBP-SA, 2021). Besides the issue of functionality of municipal websites and the available of procurement information, both the 2020 and 2021 surveys established that municipal websites presents other challenges for effective citizen participation. While some municipalities had functional websites with regularly updated procurement pages, it was difficult to access this information. For instance, the procurement information of eThekwini Metropolitan Municipality and City of Johannesburg Metropolitan Municipality was buried under the "Resources" and "Work in Joburg" pages, respectively. Moqhaka Local Municipality had fully functional website with a dedicated procurement page but procurement information was only accessed under the "Quick links" function of the website (DOI and IBP-SA, 2021). Lastly, the two surveys found that the City of Cape Town restrict access to procurement information by requiring registration upfront. The registration involves the provision of company details, among other information. Thus, companies and other related actors that bids for tenders, rather than ordinary members of the public, are the primary target audience of the City's procurement page. The requirement for registration does not augur well for transparency, citizen participation and accountability (DOI and IBP-SA, 2020).

Coming to the second requirement, we assessed the availability of a variety of procurement information namely tender notices, tender specifications, tender prices and service level agreements. Once a municipality has decided to procure goods and services, it must publish a tender notice (also known as a tender advertisement), alerting service providers to submit bids for the delivery of goods and service identified in the notice. The publication of this notice is the first signal to service providers and the community that the procurement of the identified goods and services has begun as well as how the procurement process will proceed (IBP-SA, 2018). One of the questions which surveys sought to investigate was whether municipalities publish tender notices on their websites for easy of access, not only by service providers, but also by members of the general public interested in this information. The 2021 survey results show that 26 of the 45 municipalities with a functional website published a list of tender notices that appeared to be complete (DOI and IBP-SA, 2021). Another group of municipalities (15) published tender notices on their websites but the list of tender notices was incomplete. Lastly, four municipalities namely, Joe Morolong, Greater Taung, Ehlanzeni, and Metsimaholo did not publish tender notices on their websites at all. This means that key information necessary for informed citizen participation was not made available through an accessible platform. As with the 2020 survey, the 2021 survey also established that poor performing municipalities are found in all municipal (sub)categories, as defined above (DOI and IBP-SA, 2020, 2021).

A tender notice is often accompanied by tender specifications or an indication of where the tender specifications can be accessed. Tender specifications "contain details such as the exact nature of the request, technical specifications, the volume of the goods or scope of the services required, and the timing of the delivery" (DOI and IBP-SA, 2021). The procurement contract often builds on these tender specifications. The publication of tender specifications "enable community members to assess what was specified against what is delivered in practice, and demand accountability in cases of poor or non-performance" (DOI and IBP-SA, 2021). This is why the National Treasury's MFMA Circular 62 of 2013 imposes an obligation on municipalities to publish them. Regrettably, the 2021 survey established that only nine of the 45 municipalities with functional websites published tender specifications on their website which are downloadable free of charge. Thus, communities in these nine municipalities were able to easily access information which they need to audit the delivery of various services, procured by their respective municipalities, in their respective areas. A further nine municipalities published some tender specifications on their websites while the bulk of the specifications were only made available at the municipal offices, often at a fee. The remaining large group of municipalities (27) did not publish tender specifications on their respective municipal websites. This worked against transparency and citizen participation in the area of municipal procurement.

Once a municipality has completed the bid adjudication, it identifies the top bidder with whom it may enter into a contract to deliver the identified goods and services. The surveys also sought to establish whether municipalities do publish the names of these successful bidders. This is against the background that section 23(c) of the Municipal Supply Chain Management Regulations and the MFMA Circular 62 requires municipalities to publish the names and details of successful bidders, of bids over R200,000, on their websites. The publication of the details of successful bidders "informs a community of which contractor(s) has/have been awarded the contract to provide a service, as well as the duration of the contract (including when the delivery of the service is supposed to start)" (IBP-SA, 2018). The publication thus enhances transparency and enables the community to enforce accountability in cases of service delivery failures (DOI and IBP-SA, 2021). Majority of the sampled municipalities performed dismally on this aspect. While six of the 45 municipalities with functional websites published details of successful bidders regularly, it was unclear whether they met the 5 days rule (DOI and IBP-SA, 2021). The exception is Dawid Kruiper Municipality which complied with this rule religiously. However, we were able to verify that 20 municipalities published the names of successful bidders but did not comply with the 5 day rule. Municipalities in this category published details of successful bids on a monthly, quarterly or annual basis (DOI and IBP-SA, 2021). We could not find evidence suggesting that the remaining 19 municipalities with functional websites published names of successful bidders on their respective websites. Once again, poor performance transcends municipal (sub)categories with high capacity municipalities, such as metros, equally underperforming like some of the poor or small local municipalities (DOI and IBP-SA, 2021). Similar performance patterns where established by the 2020 survey as well. Thus, details of successful bidders are some of the procurement information which municipalities generally keep in secrecy or are published but not within the required timeframe. This practice contradicts the law, as stated above.

Lastly, the surveys also assessed whether municipalities publish project implementation information, such as service delivery agreements and implementation plans. These documents usually provide the name of the service provider and sub-contractors (where applicable), the timelines for service delivery, where services will be provided or goods delivered, and the quantity of goods and services, among other details. The publication of this information "enable communities to know exactly who is responsible for delivering a service in their area and the exact frequency and days of the week the service should be delivered" (IBP-SA, 2018). It is therefore an important initiative to enable social audits of service delivery in communities. Results of both the 2020 and 2021 surveys reveals that the sampled municipalities performed the worst on this metric. Knysna Municipality is the only municipality of the 45 municipalities with functional websites, which published service level agreements on its website (DOI and IBP-SA, 2021). However, we could not find evidence suggesting that the Municipality publishes its service level agreements regularly and consistently. Without the service level agreements and other project implementation documents, communities in the 44 municipalities lack some of the key information they need to hold private service providers and the municipality accountable (DOI and IBP-SA, 2021).

16.4 Conclusions

The Constitution, legislation, and the policy framework for local government all place a high premium on transparency. Municipalities are required to establish municipal websites, and regularly publish information on them. In addition, they may make use of other publication platforms such as municipal notice boards, and the national government's eTender portal. This is in recognition of the fact that transparency is a precondition for effective public participation. Despite improvements in information technology, digital participation remains largely unexplored by municipalities. The use of traditional mediums of participation continues to dominate due to varying reasons, including capacity limitations. Communities, however, do not always use these invited spaces. Transparency is particularly important in the case of procurement. Social auditing of basic municipal services is an effective form of public participation. However, it is only possible with transparency in the procurement process. Access to the various types of procurement information is necessary for communities to be aware of the benchmarks against which they can evaluate service levels.

The results of the 2020 and 2021 surveys on procurement transparency in local government reveal a lack of transparency. Some municipalities do not have functional websites. Those that have, do not regularly publish all relevant procurement information. Procurement information on some municipal websites can only be accessed upon registration, with requirements for company details. This suggests procurement information on these platforms, is published for the benefit of private service providers rather than ordinary citizens. The impact of this lack of transparency is that communities are not able to effectively participate in local government and hold the municipality, and the private service providers that it has appointed, accountable for the quality of municipal services.

The culture of secrecy transcends municipal categories and subcategories. Both high capacity municipalities (such as metros) and low capacity municipalities (often locals and districts) are not transparent. This suggest that the lack of transparency may have little to do with capacity limitations particularly in high capacity municipalities. While the intent to publish procurement information might be there for some municipalities, the internal organization or capacity to make this happen might be lacking in poor or small municipalities. It is thus concluded that, wittingly or unwittingly, a culture of secrecy around procurement has taken hold of local government. Municipalities seem to prefer to undertake procurement away from the public eye.

References

Berthin, G. (2011). *A practical guide to social audit as a participatory tool to strengthen democratic governance, transparency, and accountability*. UNDP Regional Center. https://www.undp.org/sites/g/files/zskgke326/files/migration/latinamerica/Practical-Guide-to-Social-Audit.pdf

De Visser, J., & Chigwata, T. (2020, August 16). The devil is in the detail—Transparent procurement leaves thieves with nowhere to hide. *The Daily Maverick*. Retrieved November 10, 2023, from https://www.dailymaverick.co.za/article/2020-08-16-the-devil-is-in-the-detail-transparent-procurement-leaves-thieves-with-nowhere-to-hide/

Dullah Omar Institute and International Budget Partnership-South Africa. (2020). *How transparent are municipal websites about the goods and services that municipalities procure?* Dullah Omar Institute.

Dullah Omar Institute and International Budget Partnership-South Africa. (2021). *How transparent is municipal procurement?* Dullah Omar Institute.

International Budget Partnership-South Africa. (2018). *Which procurement information should we publish?* IBP. Retrieved November 10, 2023, from https://internationalbudget.org/wp-content/uploads/which-procurement-information-should-metro-municipalities-in-south-africa-publish-ibp-2018.pdf

International Budget Partnership-South Africa. (2023). *Asivikelane*. Retrieved November 7, 2023, from https://asivikelane.org/about/

Municipal IQ. (2023, January 31). *Protest numbers for 2022 bounce back to pre-Covid numbers*. Municipal IQ. Retrieved November 10, 2023, from https://www.municipaliq.co.za/publications/press/202302011028353438.doc

Naidu, R. (2012). Subduing local voice-public participation and ward committees. In S. Booysen (Ed.), *Local elections in South Africa; Parties, people, politics* (pp. 279–293). Sun Media.

National Treasury. (2013). *MFMA Circular 63: Supply chain management: Enhancing compliance and accountability*. National Treasury.

Ntliziywana, P. (2011). The municipality's role in implementing the Gatherings Act. *Local Government Bulletin, 13*(3).

Nyawo, J. (2017). Public participation and accountability in local government with particular reference to Jozini municipality. *Journal of Human Ecology, 57*(1,2), 60–69.

Okeke-Uzodike, O. E., & Dlamini, B. (2019). Citizen's e-participation at local municipal government in South Africa. *Journal of Review on Global Economics, 8*, 458–468.

Palmer, I., Moodley, N., & Parnell, S. (2017). *Building a capable state*. Zed Books.

Sefoloko, T. (2023, August 8). Durban homeowners withhold payments to protest rates hike. *Groundup*.

Smith, T., & De Visser, J. (2009). *The role of ward committees in South Africa: Evidence from six case studies*. Community Law Center.

Steytler, N., & De Visser, J. (2007). *Local government law of South Africa*. LexisNexis.

Strijdom, H. (1999). Facing the language challenge. *Local Government Bulletin, 1*(4), 6–8.

Chapter 17
Promises and Pitfalls of Digital Participation in Spain

Moneyba González-Medina

Abstract The digital transformation has changed expectations about governments, leading to the emergence of new opportunities for participation through ICTs. In this chapter we firstly address the notion of digital participation, defined as the engagement and interaction between citizens and state actors through electronic means in decision-making and/or policy or service implementation. Secondly, we explore its application at local level in Spain, one of the leading countries in developing this digital transformation. We conduct a qualitative analysis of five initiatives focused on the local level, namely the platform Decide Madrid (2015–), the National Plan of Smart Cities (2015–2017), the National Plan of Smart Territories (2017–2023), the Smart Rural 21 project in the village of Ansó (2019–2022), and the Smart Rural initiative launched by the Basque Country (2020–2022). The analysis shows how supralocal governments are more oriented towards providing digital infrastructure and fostering the engagement of economic stakeholders to enhance service provision and business, while local-led initiatives are more aimed to engage citizens in decision-making. Besides, the cases provide an overview of how digital transformation impacts in local contexts, uncovering its promises and pitfalls in the case of Spain.

Keywords Digital participation · E-governance · E-democracy · Smart cities · Smart territories

17.1 Introduction

Digital transformation refers to the process of adopting electronic tools and methods by an organization (Observatory of Public Sector Innovation, 2024). This transformation has changed expectations about governments in terms of greater openness and the creation of spaces and mechanisms where citizens and businesses can voice

M. González-Medina (✉)
Institute of Local Law and Government, Universidad Autónoma de Madrid, Madrid, Spain
e-mail: moneyba.gonzalez@uam.es

K. Kössler, E. Schläppi (eds.), *Citizen Participation in Local Governance*, Local and Urban Governance, https://doi.org/10.1007/978-3-031-99824-9_17

their needs. In this chapter, we explore the notion of digital participation and its application at the local level in Spain, one of the leading countries in digitalization (OECD, 2009; 2010) in the European Union (EU).

To understand the notion of digital participation, we need to first clarify other related concepts such as e-governance, which refers to the use of information communication technologies (ICTs) to engage citizens and non-governmental stakeholders in policy-making processes to deliver improved services, reliable information, and greater knowledge (UN, 2002, 54–55). E-governance can be split into three distinct areas, namely: e-administration, e-government, and e-democracy. All of them are characterized by using ICTs, but each one of them is oriented to different goals or outputs. First, e-administration aims to transform information systems and internal processes, improving its internal functioning and service delivery. This is considered a precondition for developing e-government and e-democracy (Neudecker, 2018, 8).

Second, e-government (also referred to as digital government) uses ICTs to improve the accountability and transparency of public administration by establishing proper information provision to enhance the quality, efficiency, and efficacy of public service delivery. It is considered a thematic area of 'open government',[1] defined by the OECD as "a culture of governance based on innovative and sustainable public policies and practices inspired by the principles of transparency, accountability, and participation that fosters democracy and inclusive growth" (2016, 3). It reconciles thus the divergent paths of digital democracy and e-government by improving government performance through three dimensions, namely transparency, participation, and collaboration (Harrison et al., 2011; Ricciardi et al., 2015).

Finally, e-democracy (also referred to as digital democracy) seeks to increase the engagement of citizens in public decisions and actions and to make representatives more responsive to citizens' views. It can be divided into two specific areas: e-voting and e-participation (Macintosh, 2004; Neudecker, 2018, 8–9). Ricciardi et al. (2015) highlight that e-government is more focused on the administrative sphere (improvement of efficiency and quality of service delivery), while digital democracy consists of all electronic means of communication that enable/empower citizens to hold rulers/politicians accountable for their actions in the public realm, employing different techniques such as: (1) increasing the transparency of the political process; (2) enhancing the direct involvement and participation of citizens; and (3) improving the quality of opinion formation by opening new spaces of information and deliberation (Kies et al., 2003, 3).

In comparison, Seifert and Rössel (2019) suggest that digital participation is about active involvement in digital society using ICTs. This participation includes

[1] It is important to note that the use of ICTs is not a necessary attribute of open government initiatives, even if frequently present in them. Examples of open government initiatives are open data, data sets and hackathons; open budget and participatory budgeting; open parliament; open contracting; public procurement; public sector innovation; public financial management; civil service/human resource management; town hall meetings; innovation labs and open science; asset disclosure and management of conflicts of interests; and whistle-blower protection (OECD, 2016, 3).

access to not only the Internet but also various online services and content. In this definition the access to ICT would be thus the crucial attribute of digital participation. GIZ (2020) provides another insight into digital participation, highlighting that citizens, civil society and state actors interact via social networks, in virtual discussion forums or within the scope of public services provided in digital form. These formats, which enable a new scope for action, networking, and decision-making via ICT of state and non-state actors, are collectively referred to as digital participation (GIZ, 2020, 1). In this definition, the main attribute of digital participation is the interaction between state and non-state actors using ICT.

The interesting point here is that none of these definitions differentiate between decision-making, policy implementation or service delivery as specific areas. Moreover, the Netwerk Democratie considers examples of digital participation in a variety of instruments, such as petition platforms, tools to establish the political agenda, online co-creation of bills, voting apps, participatory budget tools, online discussion platforms, interactive notification, and information systems (Netwerk Democratie, 2020, 17). As a result, we have adopted an working definition of digital participation that embraces the engagement and interaction between citizens and state actors through electronic means in decision-making and/or policy or service implementation.

Further, we have adopted a territorial approach to digital participation, which implies considering e-governance initiatives in specific territorial contexts. In their study, Peart and Ramos (2007) founded out that in Spain the most robust examples of e-democracy appeared on the very local level, and that they mainly consist of the provision of an online political platform for citizens to propose and debate new policies or to participate in government activities such as draft the budget. However, it is important to note that the local level is extremely varied. In fact, one of the interviewees declared the following: “I think that participation at rural level is different. It is more ‘on site’ and direct”. This suggests that the difference between rural and urban may be relevant in terms of digital participation. Another term that needs to be considered is that of “smart”, which is frequently related to the use of ICTs in specific territories (e.g., smart cities, smart villages, or smart territories).

The adoption of this territorial approach to digital participation has led us to select five initiatives where citizen participation (or collaboration), ICTs and territory are explicitly related to decision-making or production of policies and services. To this end, we have analyzed secondary data (statistical information related to the information society and grey literature on the matter) and primary data obtained through semi-structured interviews conducted in the framework of the project “Local Government and the Changing Urban-Rural Interplay project (LoGov)”.[2] As a result, beyond gaining a better understanding of digital participation in theoretical and empirical terms, we try to uncover the promises and pitfalls that face digital participation in Spain.

This chapter is structured in five sections. In this introduction we have presented the conceptual framework which allows us to adopt an analytical definition of

[2] See https://www.logov-rise.eu/

digital participation and the methodology. In the next section, we conduct a literature review about the benefits and risks of digital participation. In section three, we provide an overview of the digitalization policy in Spain with the aim to contextualize the analysis. In section four, we present the five initiatives we have analyzed. Finally, we reflect on the results and provide a general conclusion.

17.2 Promises and Pitfalls of Digital Participation

In the era of digital transformation, ICTs have been presented as an opportunity to strengthen democratic legitimacy. In the case of Spain, where the two primary challenges to democracy are a decreasing confidence in political parties and participation in elections, the promise of e-democracy emerges to ameliorate this undesirable situation (Peart & Diaz, 2007, 27–28). However, positions vary from the deepest optimism to strong suspicion regarding the supposed benefits of technological advances (Barber, 2006).

On the one hand, those favorable to the use of ICTs in the public sphere maintain that a good use of digital participation (1) improves communication and interaction between authorities and citizens; (2) ensures deliberation and community building, and (3) increases the participation and influence of citizens in public decision-making (Netwerk Democratie, 2020, 17). This is because they can offer greater access to *information* for citizens, the possibility of *consulting* citizens, fluid *feedback* between rulers and citizens, and greater *accountability* (Araya Moreno, 2007).

On the other hand, the literature remarks some obstacles and pitfalls of digital participation. In the 1990s, the digital divide debate was about *access* to the Internet and the material conditions that made it possible. However, this debate has evolved towards the *skills* necessary to develop more active participation (Webler & Tuler, 2000; Pizzi et al., 2023), and the attitudes and *motivation* to participate digitally. According to van Deursen and van Dijk (2020), the Internet can strengthen traditional kinds of inequality rather than ameliorate them. Moreover, they highlight that it is wrong to assume that physical access[3] to computers and the Internet automatically entails all benefits associated with their use. In fact, Spain is an example of this.

Bobbio (1991) was also very sceptical about what he called "computercracy" and warned of the possible effect of political saturation and the increase of electoral apathy. The fact is that digital participation is rather low. In fact, Cruickshank et al. (2009) consider that 1% participation in any e-participation initiative is a success. Ferro and Molinari (2010) concluded that only 3 to 5% of the population participate in electronic consultations. Other data show that 90% of internet users are "lurkers" (Lange et al., 2008), and 9% contribute a small extent (Nielsen, 2006; Oliveira &

[3] Physical access is not equal to material access. Material access includes all costs related to the use of computers, connections, peripheral equipment, software, and services (van Deursen & van Dijk, 2020).

Garcia, 2019). Moreover, the protection of privacy, data security and individual data sovereignty, the new forms of manipulation and propaganda, as well as questions about respecting democratic rights and freedoms in the digital arena are some other pitfalls pointed out by GIZ (2020).

Based on these considerations, we propose an analytical framework to assess digital participation initiatives split in two dimensions: the one focused on the benefits or promises (Araya Moreno, 2007) and the other one focused on the risks or pitfalls (GIZ, 2020). Regarding the first dimension, we also consider the intensity of participation (GIZ, 2020) and, in the second, the issue of the digital divide going beyond the physical and material access to internet (van Deursen & van Dijk, 2020) (Table 17.1).

17.3 An Overview of Digitalization Policy in Spain

Spain is an interesting case to explore digital participation. Since 2017,[4] it has ranked among the leading countries in digitalization according to the Digital Economy and Society Index (DESI), standing ahead of the EU average, especially in the categories of digital public services and connectivity. Furthermore, Spain is gradually improving in areas where it has showed greater weakness, such as knowledge and advanced use of digital technologies by citizens (Fundación Telefónica, 2023). In 2022, Spain ranked fifth in the category "Digital Public Services" (Fig. 17.1), which includes a specific sub-dimension labelled e-government, but which refers to a set of indicators related to: e-government users, pre-filled forms, digital public services for citizens, digital public services for businesses, and open data. However, the DESI does not include any indicator regarding digital

Table 17.1 Analytical framework to assess digital participation initiatives

Benefits	Levels of participation	Risks	Digital divide
Greater access to information	Information	Lack of digital infrastructure	Physical and material access
Possibility of consulting	Consultation	Manipulation and propaganda	Motivations
Fluid feedback between rulers and citizens	Cooperation	Lack of digital skills	Internet skills
Greater accountability	Co-creation	Threats to privacy, data security and individual data sovereignty	Usage of internet

Source: Own elaboration

[4] The Digital Economy and Society Index (DESI) summarizes indicators on Europe's digital performance and tracks the progress of EU countries from 2014 to 2022. Since 2023, the DESI has been integrated into the State of the Digital Decade report and used to monitor progress towards the digital targets. This has changed the methodology in terms of information available on the specific components of this composite index, therefore we use data from 2022.

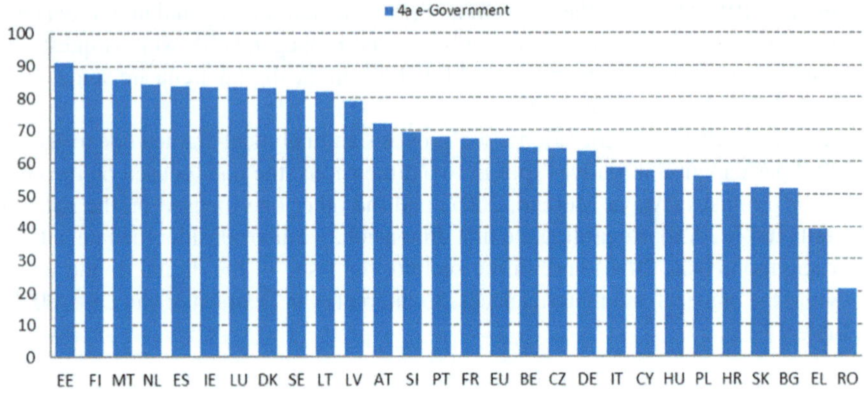

Fig. 17.1 Digital Public Services: ranking of European countries (2022). Source: European Commission (DESI Index 2022), licensed under CC-BY 4.0

participation in decision-making processes. Most indicators refer to administrative performance or infrastructural attributes.

This position results from stable digitalization policies whose basis can be situated in 1999, when the Government of Spain approved the Strategic Initiative for Development of the Information Society "Info XXI". The policy was supported by an organic structure that remains until today: Red.es,[5] created in 2002 to promote the implementation of the digital agenda in the country.

In 2013, the "Digital Agenda for Spain" (2013–2015) (DA) was approved, which was promoted jointly by the Ministry of Energy, Tourism and Digital Agenda and by the Ministry of Finance and Public Function and was in line with the European digital agenda. The DA was a roadmap to modernize the Spanish economy and society through the efficient and intensive use of ICTs by citizens, businesses, and public administration (Government of Spain, 2013, 4). In operational terms, it adopted a concept of digital participation circumscribed to the use of electronic administration by the population. Further, although the DA stated that it would promote transparency in the public administration through (1) access to the information and results of administrative activity; (2) citizen participation in the decisions of the administration, allowing for the collection of suggestions, comments and criticisms; and (3) collaboration with citizens, businesses and public administration bodies in the design, implementation and delivery of digital services (Government of Spain, 2013, 33); it should be noted that no indicators were explicitly assigned to assess citizen participation and collaboration.

The DA was developed through 11 plans, two of which had a territorial approach to digitalization, namely: the National Smart Cities Plan (2015–2017) and the National Plan for Smart Territories (2017–2023), which was based on the experience accumulated during the implementation of the previous Smart Cities Plan. Of note, the second plan adopts a broader definition of territories which includes rural areas. However, the approach is like that of smart cities.

[5] See https://www.red.es/es

In July 2020, the "Digital Spain 2025" strategy was launched. Two out of ten of its goals were related to digital participation, in particular: promoting the digitalization of public administrations (2025 goal: 50% of public services available on mobile apps) and guaranteeing citizens' rights in the new digital environment (2025 goal: a national charter of digital rights) (Government of Spain, 2020, 8). In line with this, the Charter of Digital Rights was approved in 2021. It explicitly recognizes the right to citizen participation through digital means as follows: digital environments shall be fostered in order to contribute to the right to effective access to public information, transparency, and accountability, as well as to individuals' right to propose and participate in actions of the public administrations in their respective scopes of authority, in accordance with the Spanish Constitution (Government of Spain, 2021).

The approval of the Spanish Recovery Plan (Reconstruction and Resilience Fund, NextGenerationEU) in July 2021 gave new momentum to the digital agenda. The plan allocated an unprecedented volume of resources to invest in digitalization, reinforcing the implementation of the Digital Spain 2025. The strategy was supported by eight sector-specific digitalization plans (e.g., digital skills, artificial intelligence, cybersecurity, etc.). However, the Plan for the Digitalization of Spain's Public Administration (2021–2025) only mentions citizen participation in relation to one measure, that of "GobTechLab": a laboratory for citizen-government experience innovation in a bid to enhance the experience of using digital public services by tapping citizen participation, co-creation and innovation in public services.

In sum, digitalization policy in Spain has shown great stability and continuity over time. The commitment to the development of ICT infrastructures and e-government is strong and it has been reinforced with a lot of economic resources. However, despite these high levels of digitalization (e.g. households that have internet access as a percentage of total households is 96.1% in 2022[6]), Spain has lower levels of knowledge and advanced use of digital technologies by citizens (Fundación Telefónica, 2023). Moreover, the promotion of digital participation in the frame of the Digital Agenda is still limited. To delve into this reality, we adopt a territorial approach to digitalization that led us to focus on experiences at the local level, where citizen engagement, ICTs and territory dimensions are interwoven.

17.4 Exploring Digital Participation in Spain in Local Contexts

In this section, we present and conduct a qualitative analysis of five initiatives carried out in Spain and focused on the local level, namely the platform *Decide Madrid* (2015–), the National Plan of Smart Cities (2015–2017), the National Plan of Smart Territories (2017–2023), the Smart Rural 21 project in the village of Ansó (2019–2022), and the Smart Rural initiative launched by the Basque Country (2020–2022) (Table 17.2).

[6] Date retrieved from ONTSI, based on Eurostat and the National Institute of Statistics.

Table 17.2 Initiatives selected to explore digital participation in Spain

Concept	Objectives of DP	Territorial scope of DP (local level)	Case of DP	Promoter
Digital Participation	Decision-making	Urban	*Decide Madrid* (2015–)	City of Madrid
	Production of policies and/or services		National Plan of Smart Cities (2015–2017)	Government of Spain
		Rural	National Plan of Smart Territories (2017–2023)	Government of Spain
			Smart rural 21. The Smart Village of Ansó (Aragon) (2019–2022)	European Commission
			Smart Rural Programme (2020–2022)	Basque Country

Source: Own elaboration

17.4.1 Decide Madrid (2015–)

Decide Madrid[7] is an online platform based on CONSUL,[8] an open-source digital democracy platform. The initiative was launched by the city council of Madrid in 2015 to facilitate public participation in decision-making. It was conceived as a "one-stop shop" for all open governance processes in the municipality, including issues of transparency, open data, and participation (Observatory of Public Sector Innovation OPSI, 2024).

The platform enables citizens to (1) propose ideas for new regulations (citizen initiatives) that can be voted by residents once they have reached the minimum threshold,[9] (2) partake in the participatory budget and (3) participate in debates and consultations. Therefore, participation is more oriented towards single citizens than towards organizations like NGOs. As Madrid's CEO for Citizen Participation put it, "citizens' decisions are mandatory for the local council/administration. We were permanently monitoring the level of accomplishment of the project. The responsible areas were accountable for it. However, we identified that in some cases, area managers paid more attention to their own initiatives compared to those proposed by citizens. To overcome this problem, there was a clear instruction from the mayor: proposals selected in the frame of citizen participatory processes must be prioritized."[10] However, it is important to specify that decisions resulting from

[7] See https://decide.madrid.es/

[8] See https://foundation.consuldemocracy.org/

[9] The proposals gather support for 12 months. Once they reach the minimum 1% of support from citizens over 16 years registered in Madrid, they can be voted by citizens. The proposals voted are analyzed by the City Council, which prepares a technical report on their legality, feasibility, competences and economic cost.

[10] Interview with Madrid's CEO for Citizen Participation 2015–2019.

consultation are mandatory only once they have succeeded "technical filters" (i.e. legality, feasibility, competences and economic cost).[11]

The great strength of *Decide Madrid* is that a "high number of public decisions (more than 1,000) were taken. They were pertinent, useful, and balanced in terms of cost-benefit analysis".[12] However, *Decide Madrid* faces many challenges, such as how to interrelate and merge a large number of similar citizen proposals. In this vein, artificial intelligence (AI)-based tools could be helpful. Another challenge is related to participation. It has been detected that "residents of right-wing districts tend to vote less through our tool compared to left-wing districts, that value positively participatory tools".[13] In fact, according to the media, the right-wing government led by mayor Martínez-Almeida let the platform die. In 2023, the number of visits hit an all-time low.[14] Moreover, *Decide Madrid* is not used by everybody (e.g., elderly, and young people).[15] Finally, it has been recently reported that *Decide Madrid* faces other challenges (Cheyaden, 2021), such as decreasing citizens' interest, lack of transparency about the internal working of the city council, lack of feedback, lack of moderation or other mechanisms to organize debates and proposals, and concerns about the security of the platform and verification processes.

17.4.2 National Plan of Smart Cities (2015–2017)

There are several notions of smart cities. Meijer and Rodríguez Bolívar (2016) identified three ideal-typical definitions as cities (1) using smart technologies, (2) with smart people, and (3) with smart collaboration (2016, 396). A smart city is a place-based ecosystem where ICTs are used to provide a better quality of public service and citizen welfare. The collection and analysis of data interactions with (and usage of) public infrastructure allows for improved service delivery and user experience. In this urban ecosystem, citizens engage and interact through mobile devices and connected vehicles and buildings (The Welding Institute, 2024). For the European

[11] It is important to note that *Decide Madrid* was an emblematic project of Mayor Manuela Carmena. Once the local government changed (with the new Mayor José Luis Martínez-Almeida), this practice changed as well. For instance, more than 200 projects selected through the participatory budgeting were cancelled by Martínez-Almeida and the court had to annul his decision. See https://www.europapress.es/madrid/noticia-tribunal-anula-decision-gobierno-almeida-declarar-inviables-232-proyectos-presupuestos-participativos-20220913112041.html

[12] Interview with Madrid's CEO for Citizen Participation 2015–2019.

[13] Interview with Madrid's CEO for Citizen Participation 2015–2019. It is important to note that *Decide Madrid* was created under a left-wing government. Since May 2019, the Popular Party (right-wing oriented) is ruling the city.

[14] See https://elpais.com/espana/madrid/2023-07-26/decide-madrid-la-plataforma-de-participacion-ciudadana-que-el-gobierno-de-almeida-dejo-morir.html

[15] Interview to the Director General of Citizen Participation, Municipality of Madrid.

Commission,[16] a smart city means regarding services smarter urban transport networks, upgraded water supply and waste disposal facilities and more efficient ways to light and heat buildings. In comparison, concerning policies it means a more interactive and responsive city administration, safer public spaces and meeting the population's needs.

Spain has been committed for years to the promotion of smart cities (Orejon-Sanchez et al., 2022) and ranks as the country (together with Italy) in Europe with the most "smart city" projects (21 out of 196[17]). The creation of a Spanish Smart Cities Network (RECI) in 2011 and the launching of the National Plan of Smart Cities[18] in 2015 have led to the consolidation of a "Spanish Model of Smart Cities" (Ministry of Energy, Tourism and Digital Agenda, 2017). The plan was focused on three areas: standardization (UNE standards), industry support and (corporate) governance to favor the development of innovative solutions. It was conceived as a strategy to enhance economic and industrial development, especially in the field of tourism. Participation here aims to encourage cooperation between companies, local authorities, and related networks (RECI, red.es, and Spanish Federation of Municipalities and Provinces), promote economic development and channel public funding. The plan neither explicitly mentions citizen participation nor includes specific measures related to it.

17.4.3 National Plan of Smart Territories (2017–2023)

This national strategy continues the model promoted by the former National Plan of Smart Cities. However, one significative change is that the plan expands its scope to smart rural territories, which emerge as a new niche for developing ICTs-based solutions for specific rural needs: "It is about maximizing the possibilities of the "city platforms" to provide better public services in cities and rural world" (Government of Spain, 2017, 12). The plan[19] channels financing for Smart Tourist Destinations and Internal City Objects (i.e. buildings, stations, ports and airports). It aims to improve the tourist experience and the management of information coming from the internal objects of the city (buildings, airports, stations, ports, etc.) to optimize municipal services.

However, there is no innovation in terms of digital participation. The governance approach is based on the participation of the business sector, local authorities, and other corporate stakeholders (mainly networks, foundations, and the

[16] See https://commission.europa.eu/eu-regional-and-urban-development/topics/cities-and-urban-development/city-initiatives/smart-cities_en

[17] See https://smart-cities-marketplace.ec.europa.eu/projects-and-sites/cities?f%5B0%5D=country%3ASpain

[18] See https://plantl.mineco.gob.es/planes-actuaciones/Paginas/plan-nacional-ciudades-inteligentes.aspx

[19] See https://www.red.es/es/iniciativas/proyectos/plan-nacional-de-territorios-inteligentes

standardization body UNE). All these actors must be integrated into a Smart Territories Forum. Again, even if in this plan mentions citizen participation (even if just once), no specific requirements or measures have been included.

17.4.4 Smart Rural 21: The Smart Village Strategy of Ansó (2019–2022)

The Smart Village is a relatively new concept that the European Commission has promoted to reduce disparities between rural and urban realities after the Cork Declaration on Rural Development and Agriculture (2016). It is conceived as a community-led local, territorial development instrument, that is, a participatory approach to develop and implement strategies to improve economic, social, and environmental conditions by promoting innovation and mobilizing solutions offered by digital technologies. Here, the term "smart" means using innovative solutions, including digital technology, that involve and benefit the local community. In other words, digitalization is a tool but not an end itself (Smart Rural 21 2023, 4–5).

The assumption is that the implementation of ICTs in rural areas can bring solutions in the fields of business (e-commerce), health (eHealth), (remote) education, transportation and smart mobility, etc. In the field of e-government, they can bring the public authorities closer to the villagers, improve collaboration networks between different stakeholders or territories, and more agile public procedures, such as e-voting (García Fernández & Peek, 2023, 6–7).

As a result, the Preparatory Action on Smart Rural Areas in the Twenty-First Century (Smart Rural 21[20]), aimed at developing smart village approaches across Europe, started in December 2019 and concluded in November 2022. Twenty-one villages were selected to put into practice this approach. Ansó, a small village in Aragon (405 inhabitants), was the only Spanish municipality to be selected. The project was built according to its website upon citizen engagement and provided a digital solution to a placed-based problem: "The concern in our village about ever fewer inhabitants and the lack of housing for young people and newcomers has led us to start creating the best possible environment for teleworkers and new businesses. We are working on creating housing for letting to residents, refurbishing municipal buildings for startups and teleworkers and we're upgrading our internet connection. Additionally, we would like to run a media campaign to change people's perception of what living in a village can be like, now that technology makes the dream of living and working close to nature a reality."[21]

Unlike the case of smart cities, here, citizen participation emerges as a central element of this territorial development approach, although not in terms of digital participation. However, technology is presented as an element that provides

[20] See https://www.smartrural21.eu/smart-rural-21-project/ab

[21] See https://www.smartrural21.eu/villages/anso_es/

solutions to place-based problems and lays the foundation for further development of digital participation.

17.4.5 Smart Rural: Smart and Competitive Rural Environments (2020–2022)

The Smart Rural project[22] was launched by the Basque Country (Euskadi) Government in 2020 and ended in 2022. It is a case of policy transfer (Dolowitz & Marsh, 2002) since it adapted the initiative described in Sect. 17.4.4 to the specific context of the region. It was managed by the Association for the Progress of Rural Development (MENDINET), which is the Local Action Group (GAL) responsible for managing the LEADER program in the Basque Country. The result was the development of seven smart strategies. The project adopted the "Key Stages in the Digital Transformation of Rural Areas conceptualized by the European Network for Rural Development (Table 17.3).

Table 17.3 Key Stages in the Digital Transformation of Rural Areas

Stages	Digital attributes
Excluded village	Poor or no broadband Low or no digital skills Low or no public or private digital services Low or no digital inclusion
Connected village	Basic broadband Development of elementary digital skills Basic level of digital literacy and inclusion The population is involved in identifying priority actions
Committed village	Widespread use of digital services and full digital literacy Local access to training, education, public and digital business services Contribution by the population to the design, implementation and monitoring of service
Experienced village	Fibre optic broadband Entrepreneurial and citizen capacity to exploit digital innovation Partners in the digital transformation of the territory Access to digital services equivalent to that in metropolitan areas
Actor village	Comprehensive technical, economic and social capacity to innovate and contribute to a digital and sustainable economy and society The people are co-owners of their data and the added value of the resources created They become partners for the development of new producers and services

Source: Smart Network for Rural Development (See https://ec.europa.eu/enrd/sites/default/files/enrd_publications/smart_villages_briefs-smart_villages_and_rural_digital_transformation-v07.pdf)

[22] See https://www.mendinet.org/smart-rural-2/

17.5 Conclusions

In this chapter, we have explored the notion of digital participation and its application in Spain, one of the leading countries in digitalization in the EU but where there is greater weakness regarding knowledge and advanced use of digital technologies by citizens (Fundación Telefónica, 2023). This divide is interesting since the digitalization policy of Spain has been (and still is) a national priority over the years. It has been developed beyond partisan positions and endowed with a large amount of funding. The point is that the policy's success is measured in terms of ICT infrastructures, internet and digital devices users, and availability of digital services, not in terms of citizen engagement through electronic means in decision-making.

To delve into this paradox, we have adopted a territorial approach to digital participation and conducted a qualitative analysis, adopting a broad definition of digital participation that embraces the engagement and interaction between citizens and state actors through electronic means in decision-making and/or policy or service implementation. We have selected five initiatives where citizen engagement, use of ICTs and local territory were related to decision-making or production of policies and services. We decided to focus on the local level-related initiatives because research pointed out that in Spain, the most robust examples of e-democracy appeared on the very local level (Peart & Ramos, 2007).

In the literature, local e-government has been defined as the use of ICTs to offer to individuals and businesses in a given territory the services and conditions for the promotion of democracy and quality of life, relating the political power and local public administration with the citizen and the companies, resorting to information exchange of electronic base (Gouveia, 2004, 25). This concept presents a differentiating factor, that is, the territorial proximity to the individual is reinforced by building a closer digital relationship with the local community (Gouveia, 2004, 24).

The cases show, however, that there is great variation in terms of digital participation in practice. First, the platform *Decide Madrid* emerges as a paradigmatic case of an e-democracy tool that allows high levels of participation (consultation and even co-creation). It provides information, the possibility of consulting and to accounting. However, the increasing lack of interest, and the participation divide related to age and party affiliation threaten the positive impact of this internationally renowned tool.

Second, the Smart Cities and Smart Territories Plans emerge as e-government and businesses-oriented framework based on standardization, and the support of industry and governance to favor the development of innovative solutions. However, even if initiatives of digital participation are mentioned in these cases, they are rather conceived as a strategy to enhance economic and industrial development, especially in the field of tourism. Participation here is aimed at encouraging cooperation between companies, local authorities, and related networks, while citizen participation is rather limited to the provision of data and use of services. The digital divide is mainly formulated in terms of physical and material access to the internet and electronic devices.

Third, the Smart Rural initiatives, both in the case of Ansó and the Basque Country, show significant differences between the governance approach adopted by the smart cities/territories initiative (more business and corporate oriented) and that of smart villages (more community-led). Here, citizen engagement is at the centre, even if it is more "on site" participation and regarding digital solutions, the implementation of solutions and the community-led approach lay the foundation of digital participation in the future according to the Key Stages in the Digital Transformation of Rural Areas scheme. Based on this, we expect that as digitalization takes hold, the digital divide is narrowing, and levels of digital participation are potentially rising in the territory. In this vein, the "actor village" is the stage where the people are co-owners of their data and the added value of the resources created, and they become partners for the development of new products and services.

Finally, the analysis confirms that the difference between rural and urban is relevant in terms of digital participation. However, the recent adoption of the Charter of Digital Rights (2021), which recognizes the right to citizen participation through digital means and the implementation of initiatives such as GobTechLab mentioned above, could be pointing to a future paradigm shift at national level. Today, institutionalized e-democracy initiatives are few (and more rooted at local level), while the institutionalization of the provision of e-services, open data and a "Spanish model of smart cities" is more widespread and given a strategic role. Rural areas emerge as an interesting field for experimentation that has attracted the attention of institutions and the business sector, but with the risk of replicating the smart city model where citizen engagement is more focused on their collaboration in the provision of their own data instead of in decision-making. In this vein, although Spain has emerged as a leading country in terms of digital transformation, going beyond these technocratic practices towards greater institutional commitment for a more inclusive digital participation is still a challenge.

References

Araya Moreno, E. (2007). Problemas y perspectivas de la democracia en América Latina: Las posibilidades de la democracia electrónica en el ámbito local. *Elecciones, 7*, 67–115.

Barber, B. R. (2006). Hasta qué punto son democráticas las nuevas tecnologías de la telecomunicación. *Revista de Internet, Derecho y Política, 3*, 17–27.

Bobbio, N. (1991). *El futuro de la democracia*. Fondo de Cultura Económica.

Cheyaden, S. (2021). *Case study: Digital Democracy at the local level in Spain—Decide Madrid*. Medium. Retrieved November 2, 2023, from https://medium.com/updating-democracy-rebooting-the-state/case-study-digital-democracy-at-the-local-level-in-spain-decide-madrid-5ff910df773e

Cruickshank, P., Edelmann, N., & Smith, C. (2009). Signing an e-petition as a transition from lurking to participation. In J.-L. Chapellet, O. Glassey, M. Janssen, A. Macintosh, H. J. Scholl, E. Tambouris, & M. A. Wimmer (Eds.), *Electronic government and electronic participation* (pp. 275–282). Trauner Verlag.

Dolowitz, D. P., & Marsh, D. (2002). Learning from abroad: The role of policy transfer in contemporary policy-making. *Governance, 13*(1), 5–23.

Ferro, E., & Molinari, F. (2010). Making sense of Gov 2.0 strategies: No citizens, no party. *JeDEM-eJournal of eDemocracy and Open Government, 2*(1), 56–68.

Fundación Telefónica. (2023). *Informe Sociedad digital en España 2023*. Retrieved November 2, 2023, from https://www.fundaciontelefonica.com/cultura-digital/sociedad-de-la-informacion/2023/

García Fernández, C., & Peek, D. (2023). Connecting the smart village: A switch towards smart and sustainable rural-urban linkages in Spain. *Land, 12*, 822. https://doi.org/10.3390/land12040822

GIZ, Gesellschaft für Internationale Zusammenarbeit. (2020). *Position paper_public participation in the digital age*. Retrieved November 2, 2023, from https://www.giz.de/fachexpertise/downloads/GIZ_Position%20Paper_Public%20Participation%20in%20the%20Digital%20Age_2020.pdf

Gouveia, L. B. (2004). *Local e-government—A governação digital na autarquia*. Sociedade Portuguesa de Inovação.

Government of Spain. (2013). *Digital agenda for Spain*. Retrieved November 2, 2023, from https://plantl.mineco.gob.es/digital-agenda/Documents/digital-agenda-for-spain.pdf.

Government of Spain. (2017). *National plan of smart territories (2017–2023)*. Retrieved November 2, 2023, from https://avancedigital.mineco.gob.es/es-es/Novedades/Documents/Plan_Nacional_Territorios_Inteligentes.pdf

Government of Spain. (2020). *Digital Spain 2025*. Retrieved November 2, 2023, from https://espanadigital.gob.es/sites/agendadigital/files/2022-01/Digital-Spain-2025.pdf

Government of Spain. (2021). *Charter of digital rights*. Retrieved November 2, 2023, from https://www.lamoncloa.gob.es/presidente/actividades/Documents/2021/140721-Carta_Derechos_Digitales_RedEs.pdf

Harrison, T. M., Guerrero, S., Brian Burke, G., Cook, M., Cresswell, A., Helbig, N., Hrdinová, J., & Pardo, T. (2011). Open government and e-government: Democratic challenges from a public value perspective. In *The Proceedings of the 12th Annual International Digital Government Research Conference, June 12–15, College Park, MD, USA*. Retrieved November 2, 2023, from https://www.ctg.albany.edu/media/pubs/pdfs/dgo2011_opengov.pdf

Kies, R., Mendez, F., Schmitter, P. C., & Trechsel, A. H. (2003). Evaluation of the use of new technologies in order to facilitate democracy in Europe. *E-democratizing the parliaments and parties in Europe*. Retrieved November 12, 2023, from https://www.europarl.europa.eu/thinktank/en/document/IPOL-JOIN_ET(2003)471583

Lange, A., Mitchell, S., Stewart-Weeks, M., & Vila, J. (2008). *The connected republic and the power of social networks*. The Cisco Internet Business Solutions Group.

Macintosh, A. (2004). Characterizing e-participation in policy-making. In *37th Annual Hawaii International Conference on System Sciences, 2004. Proceedings of the Big Island, HI, USA* (p. 10). https://doi.org/10.1109/HICSS.2004.1265300

Meijer, A., & Rodríguez Bolívar, M. P. (2016). Governing the smart city: A review of the literature on smart urban governance. *International Review of Administrative Sciences, 82*(2), 392–408. https://doi.org/10.1177/0020852314564308

Ministry of Energy, Tourism and Digital Agenda. (2017). *Spanish smart cities model*. Retrieved November 2, 2023, from https://plantl.mineco.gob.es/digital-agenda/Documents/Spanish-Smart-Cities-Model.pdf

Netwerk Democratie. (2020). *A guide on local practices of digital participation*. Retrieved November 2, 2023, from https://northsearegion.eu/media/12392/digital-democracy-guide.pdf

Neudecker, M. (2018). *Citizen participation in the Digital Age. Theoretical and practical opportunities and challenges for e-participation in modern democracies*. Master Thesis. Paris Lodron University of Salzburg and Vrije Universiteit Brussel.

Nielsen, J. (2006). Participation inequality: Encouraging more users to contribute. *Quaderns De Filologia Estudis Literaris, 2688*, 11–25.

Observatory of Public Sector Innovation. (2024). *Digital transformation*. Retrieved November 2, 2023, from https://oecd-opsi.org/guide/digital-transformation/

OECD, Organization for Economic Co-operation and Development. (2009). *Information society strategies: From design to implementation. The case of Spain's Plan Avanza*. Working paper. Retrieved November 12, 2023, from https://www.oecd.org/gov/44242867.pdf

OECD, Organization for Economic Co-operation and Development. (2010). *Good governance for digital policies: How to get the most out of ICTS. The case of Spain's Plan Avanza*. Retrieved November 12, 2023, from https://www.oecd-ilibrary.org/governance/good-governance-for-digital-policies-how-to-get-the-most-out-of-ICTs_9789264031104-en

OECD, Organization for Economic Co-operation and Development. (2016). *Open government. The global context and the way forward*. Retrieved November 12, 2023, from https://www.oecd.org/gov/open-gov-way-forward-highlights.pdf

Oliveira, C., & Garcia, A. C. B. (2019). Citizens' electronic participation: A systematic review of their challenges and how to overcome them. *International Journal of Web Based Communities, 15*(2), 123–150.

Orejon-Sanchez, R. D., Crespo-Garcia, D., Andres-Diaz, J. R., & Gago-Calderon, A. (2022). Smart cities' development in Spain: A comparison of technical and social indicators with reference to European cities. *Sustainable Cities and Society, 81*. https://doi.org/10.1016/j.scs.2022.103828

Peart, M. N., & Diaz, J. R. (2007). *Comparative project on local e-democracy initiatives in Europe and North America*. e-Democracy Center Research Centre on Direct Democracy Faculty of Law University of Geneva Switzerland. Retrieved November 12, 2023, from http://www.ict-21.ch/com-ict/IMG/pdf/comparativeprojectsonlocaledemocracy.pdf

Pizzi, A., Pecourt, J., & Rius-Ulldemolins, J. (2023). De la "brecha digital" al control de internet. Usos, actitudes y participación digital en España. *Revista Española de Sociología, 32*(3), a178. https://doi.org/10.22325/fes/res.2023.178

Ricciardi, F., Labaqui, I., & Schenoni, L. L. (2015). *Estudio comparado de democracia y participación digital en América Latina y Europa*. Colección Estudios n° 12. Serie Análisis. Área Institucionalidad Democrática. Retrieved November 12, 2023, from https://sia.eurosocial-ii.eu/files/docs/1427453943-Estudio_Federico%20Ricciardi(ESPANOL)(F).pdf

Seifert, A., & Rössel, J. (2019). Digital participation. In D. Gu (Ed.), *Encyclopedia of gerontology and population aging*. Springer Nature. https://doi.org/10.1007/978-3-319-69892-2_1017-1

The Welding Institute. (2024). *What is a smart city?* Retrieved November 12, 2023, from https://www.twi-global.com/technical-knowledge/faqs/what-is-a-smart-city

United Nations. (2002). *Benchmarking e-government: A global perspective, assessing the progress of the UN member states*. United Nations DPEPA—Division for Public Economics and Public Administration and ASPA—American Society for Public Administration.

van Deursen, A., & van Dijk, J. (2020). *The digital divide. An introduction*. University of Twente. Retrieved November 12, 2023, from https://www.utwente.nl/en/centrefordigitalinclusion/Blog/02-Digitale_Kloof/

Webler, T., & Tuler, S. (2000). Fairness and competence in citizen participation: Theoretical reflections from a case study. *Administration & Society, 32*(5), 566–595.

Chapter 18
Comparative Conclusions

Karl Kössler, Erika Schläppi, and Kelly Bishop

Abstract Given the current crisis of representative democracy and the risk of political disenchantment turning into (sometimes violent) political protests, we raised the question of "alternatives to the brick and the ballot" in the introduction to this book. This volume has covered a broad range of such alternatives regarding four crucial areas for local governments in both urban and rural contexts: (1) people's involvement in local development and planning, (2) them having a say on large-scale projects, (3) participatory budgeting and (4) digital participation. This chapter brings together insights from the case studies included in the book based on seven guiding questions that the contributors were asked to bear in mind: (1) the aims of the analyzed participatory processes, (2), the issues that they address, (3) the people they include/exclude, (4) their way of organizing competing local (and other) interests, (5) the format of the participatory processes, (6) their specificities in urban and rural contexts, as well as (7) their actual impact on local decision-making.

Keywords Citizen participation · Local governance · Local development and planning · Large-scale projects · Participatory budgeting · Digital participation

Given the current crisis of representative democracy and the risk of political disenchantment turning into (sometimes violent) political protests, we raised the question of "alternatives to the brick and the ballot" in the introduction to this book. This volume has covered a broad range of such alternatives regarding four crucial areas

K. Kössler (✉)
Institute for Comparative Federalism, Eurac Research, Bolzano/Bozen, Italy
e-mail: karl.koessler@eurac.edu

E. Schläppi · K. Bishop
Ximpulse GmbH, Bern, Switzerland
e-mail: es@ximpulse.ch

K. Kössler, E. Schläppi (eds.), *Citizen Participation in Local Governance*, Local and Urban Governance, https://doi.org/10.1007/978-3-031-99824-9_18

for local governments in both urban and rural contexts: (1) people's involvement in local development and planning, (2) them having a say on large-scale projects, (3) participatory budgeting and (4) digital participation. Importantly, as explained in the introduction, we opted for using the term "citizen participation" concerning all these participatory processes without, however, understanding "citizen" in a limited formal-legal sense. Thus, in line with this broader notion of "citizen" many of the mechanisms covered in this book do not restrict participation to passport-holders with the right to vote. Quite often they also involve, for instance, foreign residents or minors. What all of these mechanisms have in common is that they may be analyzed, based on the guiding questions for the chapters of this volume, according to their aims, the issue that they address, the people they include/exclude, their way of organizing competing interests, their format, specificities in urban and rural contexts, as well as their actual impact as participatory processes on the outcome of political decisions at the local government level.

18.1 The Aims of Participatory Processes

For *local development and planning*, all presented cases in this volume highlight the importance of participation in enhancing democratic processes, improving decision-making quality, and fostering trust and collaboration between citizens and governments. However, upon closer examination there are considerable variations. While in several cases, the participatory processes are expected to improve decision-making processes, the Italian chapter on the "model of shared administration" (MSA) names quite ambitious substantive goals, highlighting the aim to develop, manage and reuse common space and goods through collaboration, ultimately fostering, reimagining and deepening the role of citizens and social movements in governance processes with the overall goal to make societies resilient and institutions sustainable. On the other hand, Argentina's Government Goal Plan aims at increasing transparency and accountability of governance which are expected to build dialogue and trust between the local government and the public. However, in practice, the process seems to primarily serve as a one-way information mechanism. In the case of Germany and Spain, the aim of the described participation processes is mainly to increase quality and acceptance of the local development plans and planning and include different needs and views into the authorities' mandatory process of "balancing of interests". In addition, the German petition system, although not a specific instrument for participating in the local development and planning, aims to strengthen direct democracy by giving citizens the opportunity to shape public policy on the local level. A successful petition leads to a referendum, which, if successful, replaces a binding decision of the municipal council regarding local development and planning.

The cases discussed show similar objectives of *participation in large-scale projects*. While all three cases display general aims of legitimizing the decisions that governments make and improving the quality of justification of decisions, the transparency or the (local) acceptance of large-scale projects, they also demonstrate that the aim of participation changes over time according to the stages of a large-scale project. While in the initial stages, participation aims at identifying (and balancing) the needs and interests at stake, during the implementation stage, participation often aims to block the initially proposed plans.

In the case of Argentina, indigenous communities have a formal right to negotiate the terms of extraction of lithium in their territories. Thus, participation is aimed at balancing economic and social benefits and burdens, alongside environmental challenges, cultural values and protection of other economic and social activities at the local level. Participation aiming at balancing and coordinating the various stakeholders' interests and needs at the design stage of large-scale projects is also common in Germany and Switzerland. In the Swiss case, the spatial planning framework along with the structure plan (*Richtplan*) ensures that cantons, municipalities, individuals and private organizations whose rights or duties are at stake express their views on the project early on. Moreover, cantonal and local decisions on funding large-scale projects are subject to an (optional) referendum.

In the phase of implementing, informal participatory methods mainly aim at blocking large-scale projects, as shown in the cases of Argentina, Germany ("Stuttgart 21") and Italy, in various forms such as roadblocks, demonstrations and sit-ins. At least in the Argentinian and the Italian cases, this seems to be linked to the fact that communities have not been sufficiently included in the decision-making process in the development phase of a project. In many cases the informal methods are supplemented by formal objections and complaint procedures against project decisions, mainly for those individuals and groups whose rights are particularly concerned by the project. For example, in the case of Switzerland with regard to building permits, and by legal action through court procedures, as seen in the case of Argentina, provided those avenues exist.

Regarding the aims of processes of *participatory budgeting*, there is considerable similarity among the cases examined in this volume. Typical objectives such as transparency, accountability responsiveness of policymakers, the quality of decisions and democratic empowerment are prevalent. However, the countries covered reveal additional specific goals for which two contextual factors seem to be important: the time when this tool of participation was introduced and the socio-economic conditions in the country where it operates. In some countries analyzed in this volume, it only took roots in the wake of a process of political transformation, albeit not always upon initiative from policymakers. In Poland, for instance, an informal citizen-led group dedicated to sustainable development in the City of Sopot inspired the first process of participatory budgeting in 2011. In the light of the country's history, it is interesting to see that participation is not only aimed at effective governance but also at building an active civil society in local communities, something absent in its communist past. In the North Macedonian case, this tool was similarly not among the first instruments of citizens' involvement in the aftermath of post-communist transformation, even if the seminal local government reform in 2002 enabled participation regarding the adoption of the municipal budget. It was only in 2008 that so-called budget forums were introduced, which enable citizens to influence what local governments prioritize in their annual budgets. Importantly, these forums were introduced during a second phase of fiscal decentralization in North Macedonia with the specific aims to increase people's awareness of the budgeting process and involve them regarding the prioritization of the (frequently scarce) resources available. It is hardly surprising, given the country's history and socio-economic conditions, that a similar rationale is behind participatory budgeting in South Africa. As the authors point out, this tool seeks—like other participatory processes—to redress the ills of the apartheid era. Thus, there is a strong focus on inclusiveness and the alignment of scarce resources with the needs of all local communities, with the latter also contributing to the aim of preventing service delivery protests.

As for the aims of *digital participation*, it is important to first get a sense of how this rather specific form of citizen involvement can be defined. Although the chapters in this book demonstrate the immense variety of such participation in practice, they also point out, albeit differently, that it is embedded in several concepts about the use of information and communication technologies in political and administrative processes. At the broadest level, digital participation can be put, as the chapter on Spain emphasizes, under the umbrella of e-governance. More specifically, it forms part of a specific subcategory of such governance, namely e-democracy, which seeks to involve citizens in political decisions and to make their elected representatives more responsive. While e-democracy goes beyond e-voting to include also e-participation, it is in any of these varieties a normative concept that ultimately aims at enhancing the quality of democracy.

Digital participation can achieve this through different instruments and with regard to different aspects of democracy. As for the latter, it seeks to make decision-making more democratic by enhancing inclusiveness, transparency, accountability and legitimacy. The instruments that digital participation has at its disposal can be, just as those of offline participation, more or less far-reaching. It is thus useful to categorize them, as the chapter on South Africa does, according to the level of involvement which they ensure. Instruments can be aimed merely at transparency, at advocacy (e.g. through petitions), at consultation or even at co-production, where local governments and their citizens become real partners in decision-making. To the extent that the instruments of digital participation analyzed in this book are more or less far-reaching, ranging from the transparency level to the highest level of co-production, they thus also pursue different specific objectives. At one end of the spectrum, it is—like in South Africa—"only" about transparency in online processes of public procurement because it is less time-consuming and less costly for citizens to retrieve relevant information. At the other end, the specific objective pursued with various digital participatory platform in Italy and Spain, for instance, is the effective involvement of people in decision-making.

All the cases show that, to be effective, participatory processes need to be designed according to the objectives at stake, targeting various groups of citizens, involving a variety of formats and forms in the various stages of administrative and political processes.

18.2 The Issues Addressed Through Participatory Processes

The chapters on *local development and planning* focus predominantly on administrative and political decisions in planning and development of urban areas, although some of the participation models can also be used in rural areas, as seen by the use of the model of shared administration (MSA) in a rural area of Italy. The Argentina case refers to the concrete Government Goals Plan, an instrument that in practice serves as an information tool for local governments about their plans in relation to urban infrastructure and spatial planning. The Italian MSA also shows a variety of issues that can be addressed through the view on shared administration of common goods. The topics here range from social and welfare issues, health, cultural initiatives, sport activities, innovation, education, agriculture, environment, inclusion, spatial planning, and urban regeneration. While the Italian example shows one way to incorporate grassroot social movements and somehow institutionalize such engagement, the German and Spanish cases refer to a more institutionalized participation model to influence administrative decisions on local planning and development, that are in the competence of the local authorities. While some processes address the balance among various public interests—by listening to the arguments of national and local stakeholders or giving a say to local residents that are particularly concerned (the German "petition for referendum")—other processes focus on the protection of legal rights of residents or landowners and their private interests in specific planning decisions.

The cases concerning *participation in large-scale projects* demonstrate that the projects typically address national or regional needs, such as infrastructure for public transport in the case of Germany, or industrial purposes (and even global interests) such as in the case of Lithium mining in Argentina or a safe nuclear waste disposal in Italy. Hence, large-scale projects are situated between development interests and benefits of national significance and the socio-economic challenges or expected negative impacts typically manifesting themselves at the local level, or towards specific (indigenous) communities. The participatory processes typically address the identification and distribution of socio-economic benefits and burdens as well as environmental challenges linked to the projects. In Argentina the conditions for lithium extraction, environmental and socio-economic burdens for local communities are at stake, while in Germany "Stuttgart 21" infrastructure for public transport was challenged with a set of more general arguments around the protection of environment that are currently also used against renewable energy projects. The case of Italy analyses the 30-year long—and still unaccomplished—debate over the siting of a disposal facility for high-level nuclear waste from a participatory perspective. The chapter on Switzerland shows how large-scale projects are obliged to address challenges in relation to environmental protection in a participatory way from the beginning, as the legal framework gives (national) environmental organizations the right to appeal against rulings of the cantonal and federal authorities on projects for which an environmental impact assessment is required.

As for the subjects of *participatory budgeting*, the cases compared in this volume reveal some variety. In South Africa, people's involvement in the allocation of municipal funds means a legal obligation for the entire draft budget to be submitted to a consultation process enabling written or oral recommendations in mandatorily public council and committee meetings. Like other instruments of participation in that country, a lack of compliance is enforceable in a court of law. Neither this mechanism nor the budget forums in the North Macedonian case are institutions of participatory budgeting in a strict sense, as they both allow for *advice* regarding the whole local budget but not for the *decision* about the allocation of a certain portion of it. As demonstrated in this volume by the example of the municipality of Bitola, these forums prioritize broad financing programs such as urban planning, culture, etc., then select concrete projects for financing through the local budget and, beyond that, provide further funding recommendations for the mayor to consider. Examples of participatory budgeting in a strict sense are the two European cases, with the Polish city of Sopot reserving around 1% of its budget to projects proposed and selected by citizens, which is quite impressive when compared to Bologna's 0.2%. Interestingly, a regional law in Sicily does not refer to a certain percentage of the total local budget but instead makes at least 2% of all financial transfers from the region the subject of participatory budgeting. While the concrete projects proposed by citizens for implementation varies immensely, some municipalities have chosen to group them. In Bologna, for example, citizens can vote for two different categories of projects: those focusing on sport, environment, culture and society, on the one hand, and on infrastructure development, on the other. A quite specific characteristic of the South African case is that the participatory allocation of the annual local budget is intertwined with and based on a municipality's Integrated Development Plan (IDP) which is adopted every 5 years similarly through a process mandatorily requiring public engagement.

Instruments of *digital participation* lend themselves to involve citizens on a number of different subjects. This is particularly evident from the Italy chapter which offers a broad panorama of how local governments apply tools of such participation. Very often they serve decision-making on how to use public spaces and other common good, illustrated, for example, by an online platform of the City of Genoa through which citizens can initiate Collaboration Pacts.[1] However, digital participation is also used in some Italian cities to make the local administration more responsive to public service disruptions (e.g. Venice) or to reduce air pollution (e.g. Ferrara). Still other local governments have started to experiment with digital twins of, i.e. virtual replicas of cities, that they use for simulations and developing different scenarios regarding spatial planning but also other issues such as mobility infrastructure and energy management. The Spanish chapter demonstrates that digital participation platforms can be surprisingly versatile. Rather than being geared towards a single issue, the online platform *Decide Madrid*[2] has been used during its

[1] See on these pacts, Chap. 4 in this volume.

[2] https://decide.madrid.es/

decade-long existence as a "one-stop shop" for involving citizens in such diverse processes as citizen initiatives for new local regulations, consultations, participatory budgeting and activities to improve transparency of local governments. The latter is also at the core of the chapter on digital participation in South Africa. It is pointed out that participation is key, in particular, concerning the five-year integrated development plan (IDP) of municipalities and the annual budget adopted based on this plan and that financial transparency is obviously of major importance for accountability regarding the budget's implementation. Due to the delicate nature of some projects and the substantial amount of funds involved, publishing information about procurement processes of municipalities is a key subject for digital participation and local governments are in this regard under several legal obligations. As the authors point out, nearly all municipalities have functional websites and most of them consistently publish tender notices. Worryingly, however, more specific information about the companies awarded contracts or about the contract price and implementation is only provided by few local governments and in a cumbersome manner. The lack of easily accessibility of such crucial information certainly hinders citizens' participation and monitoring with regard to large projects.

18.3 The People Included/Excluded in Participatory Processes

Depending on the aims and the design of the process, the inclusion and exclusion of different groups in processes of *local development and planning* can vary significantly in practice, although in most cases the participatory processes are formally targeting all "citizens" or "residents" of a certain geographical area.

For example, public hearings on the Government Goals Plan in Argentina mainly involve representatives from Non-Governmental Organizations (NGOs), Neighborhood Associations, and other groups such as professional associations, business chambers, universities, and political parties. However, individuals of the general public are less likely to participate. Instead, the hearings tend to attract small, voluntary social associations composed of middle-class professionals with specific advocacy goals. One possible reason for this mentioned in the chapter is the complexity of the information and documents and the limited timeframe for reviewing them and making submissions, all together requiring a considerable investment in time and professional resources for making adequate contributions. Similarly in the case of the Italian model of shared administration (MSA) of commons, there is a certain professionalism due to the requirements and format of the collaboration pacts. This brings with it the additional challenge that the shared administration of commons can sometimes be used to pursue particular private interests. Collaboration pacts, while undeniably requiring some degree of professionalism due to the complexity of the process and therefore showing some exclusionary aspect, can at the same time address inclusion within their substantive content. The example in this volume highlights an MSA initiative focusing on a marginalized group, namely foreign migrant workers in rural areas in Italy, and thus provides an example on how the collaboration pact itself can at least partly mitigate the potential exclusionary procedural aspects.

In Germany, the circle of eligible participants varies according to the aim and object of the process. On the one hand, at the beginning stages of the planning process a wide participation circle is addressed, ensuring a diversity of inputs for identifying and balancing the interests at stake. The public includes residents, non-residents, and NGOs, with specific amendments to include children and teenagers. Despite this inclusive legal framework, actual participation tends to be skewed towards better-educated, middle-aged males, civil servants and NGO representatives. Conversely, groups like women, foreigners and low-income workers are less likely to participate. On the other hand, the right to petition (e.g. to terminate a planning process) is limited to a smaller group (e.g. to residents of set municipality that is concerned by a planning process) with a legally binding and thus more impactful result. Similarly, a distinction between the general public and more closely affected individuals is made when landowners get individualized notification about and invitation to the hearing process in the case of participation in local planning in Spain.

The cases on *participation in large-scale projects* also show inclusion and exclusion of different groups and people. The chapters in this volume show that formal recognition of different interest groups generally has a positive effect on their inclusion in the participation process regarding large-scale projects. This is seen in the case of Argentina, where the rules and the dynamics on inclusion and exclusion in participation in large-scale projects in relation to lithium extraction vary significantly across different provinces. The Jujuy province legally recognized the rights of indigenous communities living near lithium production sites according to international and national standards such as the ILO Convention 169, including legal recognition as indigenous communities and their communal property rights, constituting these groups into legal actors who must be consulted before any intervention in their territories. On the other hand, Salta and Catamarca provinces did not. A broader formal inclusion of different groups was highlighted in the case of "Stuttgart 21". A general legal rule of (early) public participation in large-scale includes a public sphere beyond usual "citizen" participation, as it also includes interest groups, associations and non-EU foreigners. Moreover, on municipal level, EU foreigners are also entitled to vote in citizens' petitions and referenda, broadening the participation possibilities even further to groups traditionally excluded from similar decision-making processes. In contrast to this, in the case of Italy the opportunity for participation regarding decisions on nuclear waste deposits is envisaged in a "national seminar" that only includes public authorities and major interest organizations but excludes individual citizens or grassroot organizations. In the Italian case, recent political changes have further minimized the space for participation to an online consultation with organized stakeholders, excluding individual citizens completely.

Even with formal recognition of previously (and historically) excluded groups such as in the case of indigenous communities in Argentina and mandatory public involvement in large-scale projects in the case of Germany, the examples have highlighted additional challenges for the inclusiveness of the participation processes. The example on mining projects in Argentina highlights that corporate influence of the mining company in local politics and the economy can lead to manipulation and exploitation of divisions within communities and co-opting of key community members, with a negative impact on the transparency of the consultation process and the private and public interest at stake. In addition, formal recognition and the possibility to participate does not automatically result in effective inclusion and representative participation in practice. The German chapter highlights that middle- and upper-class citizens are generally overrepresented in local politics in general as well as in participatory processes regarding large-scale projects in particular. Even petitions such as in the case of Germany require a certain amount of organization and resources to collect the signatures and run the campaign. This tends to favor existing networks and organizations and groups that are self-confident and can invest time and resources. Looking at the example of Stuttgart 21, activists tended to be well-educated, wealthier and have a history of civic engagement, which potentially marginalized underprivileged neighborhoods and other groups facing additional barriers to participation, such as intersectional discrimination based on gender, socio-economic status, age or nationality. The Swiss chapter draws further attention to the fact that not all groups are equally participating. Namely, socially disadvantaged groups, less-educated people, women and youth participate less in popular votes and elections, especially when complex issues or complicated procedures are at stake. With greater complexity of issues regarding large-scale projects, participation of these groups might be even more challenged leading to underrepresentation and exclusion of their interests even when they are formally allowed to participate in the decision-making process.

A key issue concerning *participatory budgeting* is who is eligible to take part in the process and who, amongst these people potentially involved, actually participates. It is noteworthy that in the South African case the "local community" which the municipality is legally obliged to involve in the budget process is defined very broadly and, beyond residents, encompasses ratepayers of the municipality, other non-residents making use of services provided by the local government and even non-governmental organizations involved in local affairs within the municipality. Furthermore, local authorities must foster inclusiveness and give particular consideration to the needs of people from disadvantaged groups, among them illiterate people which is especially important in rural municipalities. North Macedonia's budget forums place a similar emphasis on inclusiveness, as municipalities are called upon to mobilize participants both generally and, more specifically, among marginalized communities. The definition of people eligible for participatory budgeting is similarly quite broad in the Polish case. In principle, the popular vote is open to anyone with permanent or temporary residence which also includes the non-adult population. Resolutions of city councils that interpreted participation in a narrow way and subjected it to certain age thresholds were recently found inconsistent with the country's law on municipal self-government. This contrasts with many other cases in which participation is limited to adults or, as in the Sicilian town of Caltanissetta, to people above the age of 16. The comparison of Italian municipalities reveals a variety of rules also with regard to citizenship and residence requirements. Whereas some local governments limit involvement to Italian nationals with residence, the City of Bologna, for instance, includes anyone working or studying there and has, interestingly, attracted considerably more female participants than men in each edition of participatory budgeting so far. When it comes to questions of eligibility, the definition of who is excluded is as important as that of who is included. In one of the Italian municipalities analyzed, the right to submit proposals under the participatory budgeting process is granted to every resident, with the notable exception of city council members. Another one additionally excludes people in leadership positions in political parties and unions or associations related to political factions. The reasoning behind these more or less far-reaching rules is evidently to prevent conflicts of interest and identify the authentic preferences of the local community.

When it comes to inclusion and exclusion of people, *digital participation* is faced with certain specific issues. As the chapter on Spain highlights, early debates in the 1990s about the digital divide were focused on the access to the Internet. But this has been replaced or at least complemented in many countries by a discussion on the necessary skills and motivation to actively engage in digital participation. The merely relative importance of online access is emphasized in several chapters which puts the expectation into perspective that the widespread use of smartphones would remove spatial and temporal barriers to digital participation. At the same time, one needs to bear in mind that the above-mentioned motivation to get involved online is not something which depends exclusively on citizens themselves. Apps also need to be designed in way that encourages the motivation for digital participation. Whether people are interested in getting involved presupposes, of course, that they have the *possibility* to get involved in a participatory process. As the Italy chapter points out, digital participation may be more inclusive towards individuals with problems in attending physical gatherings, provided that they are sufficiently skilled and motivated. Regarding the effective participation of *citizens*, the case study on Spain paints two different pictures depending on the urban or rural contexts. While the country's concept of "smart cities" is criticized for its focus on business actors, the more recently notion of "smart villages" leaves more room for citizens to get involved.

18.4 The Organization of Local (and Other) Interests Participatory Processes

The interests and views that stakeholders express in (local) participatory processes are often far from homogenous. The various cases have shown that local interests in processes of *local development and planning* are more effectively taken up when they are expressed and organized through NGOs, local interest associations or other more professionalized groups and stakeholders. In Argentina the limited timeframe between the publication of the Government Goals Plans and submissions for input at the hearing, make it crucial to organize local interests through a certain degree of professionalization (albeit still on a voluntary basis). This is also true in other contexts, such as Germany and Switzerland, where NGOs can participate in the statutory participation process to help authorities identify and balance the diversity of public interests.

On the other hand, the discussion in this volume shows that the adaptability to local interests depends also on the capacity of local governments and their understanding of the usefulness of the participatory tools in their local context. For instance, in relation to the model of shared administration (MSA) in Italy the collaboration pacts show significant possibility to adapt to the diversity of local issues. Originally developed in Bologna, the regulation serves as a prototype for various other regions that have adopted the regulation and used it to take up and address a variety of local interests. The author however also highlights that the adaptability of the MSA is largely dependent on how well local authorities understand the instrument and its potential for collaboration. Another example provides the Government Goals Plan in Argentina, which allows for the adaptation of local plans and taking up of local interests in a relatively informal manner. In the case of gender issues, where arguably local grassroot organizations were able to form a larger national debate, the topic was on occasion taken up by local governments and included in the Government Goals Plan.

The organized expression of local interests regarding *participation in large-scale projects* takes up different forms and depends on various factors. The examples show that the forms depend firstly on the arenas and frameworks in place to take up local interests. Where decision-making processes are centralized such as in the case of Italy regarding nuclear waste disposals, local interests are more difficult to organize effectively, without linking up to national level organizations. In Italy the instrument of "national seminar" allows namely for affected local authorities and the Association of Municipalities to examine the possible project and provide their views, but without decision making power (which is still by decree of the President). In contrast, in the cases of Germany and Switzerland local interests can influence government decision making on various levels (national, cantonal and also municipal) and can be organized within various formats such as the consultation of organized interest groups, or petitions or referenda within the planning and construction framework, with changing alliances among the participating groups across the levels.

Secondly, the legal recognition of (local) interest groups is another influencing factor. The case of Argentina demonstrated that the recognition of indigenous communities by local authorities constitute these groups into legal actors who based on the framework in place must be consulted before any intervention in their territories. This special legal recognition can also apply to other interest groups such as (well-established) environmental organizations mentioned in the case of Switzerland. Therefore, it depends on how well local interests are represented by or overlap with the interests of specialized organizations at the national level such as organizations concerned with environmental protection or cultural heritage, NGOs or local business associations. Another factor relates to how local interests are defined and whether they are considered legitimate to influence the decision. Without a legal framework in place, the case of Argentina has shown that local interests can feed into the process through negotiating directly with the private mining companies reaching ad hoc agreements. These case-by-case agreements, while allowing the company to quickly solve problems and commence mining and providing for some guidelines on job creation or environmental protection, lack the broader legitimacy of more formal public consultation processes and can show limits to what interests are taken up, potentially excluding marginalized local interests or voices.

The issue of how different interests are organized and represented in a process of *participatory budgeting* is crucial for it to really reflect the preferences of local communities. As mentioned above, Italian municipalities therefore exclude—to various extents—people with influence in local politics. It is curious that North Macedonian budget forums seem to follow quite a different logic, as one of their guiding principles is exactly the active participation of local business and local policymakers such as the mayor, city councillors and public officials. While the mere presence of these stakeholders does not necessarily mean interference with the process, the chapter on Poland noted that local authorities sometimes indicate, in a top-down manner, in which thematic areas, like infrastructure or environmental protection, projects can be submitted. Another interesting link in the Polish case between local politics and participatory budgeting is the use of the latter as a tool of political campaigning. Indeed, an increase in municipalities' interest in involving people in the financial planning process has been attributed to local politicians offering to implement participatory budgets in exchange for electoral support. Yet, it cannot be said that local policymakers dominate or even capture these processes (at least in cities), as urban civic movements with names such as "Fix your City" and "Right to the City" arguably contribute a lot the actual functioning of participatory budgeting. Another issue is the degree to which the interests of higher-level governments, i.e. the national government and, if they exist, subnational entities, play a role in processes of participatory budgeting and perhaps even capture them. Overall, the chapters in this book suggest that the effective influence of national and regional interests depends on several factors which make this more or less likely. In some countries, such influence has been observed in municipalities where large investments are at stake, private businesses of particular importance are based or projects with relevance for the development of the wider region are the subject of participatory budgeting.

18.5 Formats of Participatory Processes

In *local development and planning* the examples in this book show variation particularly in regard to their mode of initiation, adaptability and legal nature. The case of the Italian model of shared administration (MSA) shows the most bottom-up and collaborative format of participation. The collaboration between the authorities and different stakeholders can be initiated either by the public or the authorities and is set in a collaboration pact, which determines the mode of collaboration, but in case of dispute in the monitoring phase it can be challenged and remains non-binding. In contrast, the Government Goals Plan in Argentina is less collaborative and more driven by passive information of citizens. It ultimately serves as a reporting tool for the local government to which participants can comment and make statements during a physical public hearing. Although public hearings are not a binding mechanism, they are adaptable to various contexts and can become an important instrument, if governments are open and invite public participation to raise their own ideas or become aware of certain issues, or if governments choose to justify the decisions that citizens had objected to.

The examples from Spain and Germany show that participation formats can vary throughout the planning process. While at the beginning of planning the formats are quite open and informal, with concretization of the planning process and time, the circle of allowed participants becomes smaller and the results become more formal and legally binding. In Spain, the Citizen Participation Programs/Plans at the beginning of a planning process allow many different ways of participation such as presenting formal written observations but also more informal formats such as meetings and questionnaires. Once the planning instrument is preliminary approved, participation becomes more formal with more detailed requirements on how authorities need to plan and inform the public, with an additional obligation to notify concerned landowners individually. In this phase, the public information procedure becomes mandatory. This cascade of formalization of participation is also shown in the context of the German case, where for example the stage of final draft(s) of the proposed plan triggers the second (and main) stage of public participation, where the statutory requirements for participation are more detailed and have been further specified by an extensive body of jurisprudence. Finally, petitions are mostly used to lawfully pursue the blocking of an ongoing planning process, a process that shows an even more formalized format, with a clearly defined (smaller) circle of participants, with a legally binding outcome.

Participation in large-scale projects includes a range of formats varying from formal to informal avenues and designs. Although all four cases know formalized participation procedures, the authorities' adherence to them varies greatly across the different country examples in this book. In the case of Italy, coming from a centralized format of participation in large-scale projects, with limited opportunities for genuine public engagement, a law was passed in 2001 to expedite strategic infrastructure projects by simplifying decision-making procedures and further centralizing executive powers. When formal arenas are not effectively in place, the discussion in this volume demonstrates that informal avenues become increasingly used. In Argentina for instance, when national and provincial governments failed to activate consultative procedures, local communities felt compelled to organize themselves informally. In some cases, this has led the government to respond with repression. The lack of formal participation avenues and the environment of repression drew communities to seek alternative, informal methods of advocacy and negotiation and "invent" spaces of participation. The Italian case shows that the failure in adapting an adequate and acceptable decision-making process (participatory or not) may block the realization of projects for decades. In the German case, the same insight from the "Stuttgart 21" project, a significant urban development initiative, led to the establishment of early public participation rules in administrative procedures, ensuring that public input is considered from the initial stages. This legal framework includes various forms of public participation, such as planning approval processes and construction planning. Citizen petitions and referenda are additional tools available to the public, allowing them to influence local and state-level decisions. In general, the "Stuttgart 21" case illustrates how public protests and legal challenges can lead to significant procedural reforms and institutional changes, fostering a more participatory approach to large-scale projects. The case of Switzerland also demonstrates the interlinkage between and complementarity of various formats of participation. While national and cantonal laws enshrine formal participatory procedures in planning large-scale projects, these frameworks are subject to (optional) referendums allowing for public participation in shaping relevant laws and regulations as well as in taking decisions on projects. Other formal participation arenas are provided for, through citizens' involvement in decisions on public funding of projects or within the design of spatial plans. Formal appeal procedures regarding large-scale projects which can challenge and significantly delay projects even after a formal decision to go ahead with them by the authorities, provide incentives to constructive dialog and compromise in the decision-making stages by the authorities. This highlights that strong formal participation mechanisms in the developing stages do not avoid but mitigate the risk of encountering protests and other informal formats later on during the implementation stage. In the end, the time spared on more formal participatory processes might not pay off, as the year-long stillstand of Italy's high-speed train project in Val di Susa and the blockage of the high-level nuclear waste disposal projects illustrate.

As for the concrete formats that are used by *participatory budgeting*, a first question is who initiates and manages the process. Typically, participatory budgeting does not need to be "activated" specifically because there is usually an obligation under ordinary legislation or municipal bylaws to subject a certain amount of the local budget to this process. Things are quite different with North Macedonia's budget forums which can be initiated by the mayor, the municipal council, other local organizations or an individual, but must be approved in any case by the mayor who ultimately makes the final decision. Another specific trait of these forums is that they are led by an external and neutral moderator, usually trained in certification programs organized by the country's local government association ZELS, together with a co-moderator from the local community. While some of the Italian local governments compared, concerning the management of participatory budgeting exclusively, rely on municipality staff, the City of Bologna also to some degree externalizes this task. Indeed, municipal authorities entrust a foundation with several key tasks like methodological support, supervision, etc. with the explicit aim to ensure both impartiality and adequacy.

Diversity within Italy is also evident regarding the stages of the process. While the basic steps are more or less similar, the town of Caltanissetta involves a vote to identify the three most popular thematic areas to only then select single projects related to these areas. The small municipality of Malles Venosta stands out for a provision that allows it to merge proposals with similar goals after consultation with the participants involved. Diversity of procedures across municipalities is also a feature of the other countries compared in this volume and of course results not least from considerable local autonomy in determining these procedures. Indeed, Polish ordinary legislation, for example, empowers the municipal councils to make such determinations within rather broadly defined parameters and that of South Africa similarly only established minimum conditions, leaving the more detailed framing of people's participation in budget formulation to local governments based on an explicit reference to the principle of subsidiarity. In any case, this involves consultation of the ward committees, i.e. an elected intermediary body between the municipal council and local communities, which sometimes acts in conjunction with *imbizos*, an institution based on traditional elders' councils. In the North Macedonian case, the budget forums are not recognized by the Law on Local Self-Government so that the ten organizing principles do not have a legal basis. Instead, they were published in a guidebook by the country's local government association and are not binding, yet still widely followed.

Problems regarding the formats of participatory budgeting are as varied as the details of the individual procedures. In Poland, the usual practice of online voting on the single projects proposed is said to result in older people being disadvantaged, with voting via phone and information points being inadequate alternatives with a view to cost-benefit calculations. A similar issue with a digital divide, albeit one in socio-economic terms, is reported in the South African chapter. In the wake of Covid-related restrictions on in-person meetings, participation in the formulation of municipal budgets was shifted online, which did not give everyone the same chances to have their voices heard. Indeed, the authors point out that impoverished communities sometimes resort to "invented spaces" like (sometimes violent) protest instead of "invited spaces" such as the ward committees, because the latter are deemed ineffective for several reasons. Among these are their frequent lack of administrative and financial support, of formal powers and of technical expertise regarding the intricacies of the draft municipal budget.

The chapters in this book revealed that *digital participation* appears in a great variety of formats. Digital participatory platforms that are web-based or software-driven spaces seem to be particularly popular because they are easily available and not very difficult to use, even for local governments with limited technical skills and experience. As mentioned above, these platforms are sometimes dedicated to quite specific issues and used as a more general tool in other cases. But irrespective of the subject they focus on, the formats that they can potentially encompass are very diverse and range, from crowdsourcing initiatives to virtual town halls. From a comparative perspective, it is interesting to see that concerning the development of digital participatory platforms, a lot of exchange and learning occurs between local governments both within one country and across countries. Within Italy, this is facilitated by the fact that ParteciPA,[3] the most common platform, has been developed by a training center for the public administration. But this very same platform also demonstrates international exchange, since it is based on *Decidim*,[4] an open-source software for digital participatory platforms that was initially developed for the City of Barcelona. *Consul*, a similar software used by the City of Madrid is even more widespread on a global scale and used by local governments of 35 countries on different continents.[5] Other innovative formats analyzed in this volume are workshops using immersive technologies, which give participants a sense of being physically immersed in a non-physical environment through computer-generated simulations. Yet another format of digital participation are activities that make use of gamification by incentivizing people to get involved through challenge-based initiatives. Particularly intriguing formats of digital participation are those involving digital twins, i.e. virtual replicas of cities. This is because they do not only factor in collective behavior through data about citizens but also people's preferences by gathering data provided by individuals themselves.

18.6 Specificities of Local Participation in Urban and Rural Contexts

As for the urban-rural dimension of participation in *local development and planning* three issues are highlighted in this volume. Firstly, the practices discussed show an overwhelming focus on more recent models of participation in development and planning in urban contexts. The chapter on Spain focuses entirely on planning in urban areas, the chapter on Argentina likewise looks at the Government Goals Plan in the City of Cordoba and Italy's "management of shared administration" (MSA) with its collaboration pacts started in Bologna and has since been adopted in other largely urban municipalities (see namely Trento, Genova, Lucca, Gubbio, Viterbo, Palmi, Livorno, Ferrara, Latina, Bari, Empoli, Milano, Potenza, Torino, Bologna, Roma, Padova). This is contrasted by the German example, where the framework on statutory participation does not allow for participation in the planning process in already developed areas, which in practice often is the case in urban areas. In those cases, building permits can be granted without a previous planning process and the only way forward lies in a costly administrative suit against the building permit by directly affected third parties.

Secondly, the volume highlights some challenges for the transformation of these practices from urban to rural areas, especially of newer approaches to participation

[3] https://partecipa.gov.it/

[4] https://decidim.org/

[5] https://foundation.consuldemocracy.org/

in local development and planning, namely: the more limited financial resources of local governments (mentioned in the chapter on Spain) as well as the limited organizational capacity such as preparing necessary meeting documents, publication of quality information), the complexity (mentioned in the German chapter) or the lack of understanding on how to adapt the participatory arenas to the local context rather than copy-paste the same approach, an issue mentioned in the Italian chapter on collaboration pacts.

Thirdly, the possibility of urban-rural coordination and collaboration is mentioned as well. For instance, the chapter on Argentina mentions that the Government Goals Plan, in particular, and participation mechanisms, in general, do not promote cooperation between rural and urban local governments—an issue that is particularly important in times of growing mobility between urban and rural areas. In practice, the Government Goals Plan does not favor the interaction between the city and other areas, because the goals are circumscribed exclusively within the limits of its respective territory. A more promising approach for collaboration between rural and urban areas can be detected with respect to the collaboration pacts. The "governance of commons" may require a more functional approach and the involvement of different offices and levels of government, contributing to new of inter- and intra-organizational arrangements, including between different municipalities in urban and rural areas.

Urban-rural dimensions of *participation in large-scale projects* are notable in the chapters, particularly in the distribution of benefits, burdens and risks. Common themes highlighted in the different cases include the variations in the organizational capacity of urban and rural communities, the impact of geographic and economic factors, and the geographical differences in costs and benefits of large-scale projects concerning infrastructure (railways stations in Germany or national highways in Switzerland) or energy (wind turbines, nuclear waste disposal in Italy). However, each country exhibits unique aspects shaped by its specific contexts. In Argentina, the distinction between rural and urban areas significantly influences community participation in response to lithium mining activities. Urban communities, due to their proximity to transport hubs and higher population density, tend to have better organizational capacities and are more likely to mobilize effectively for their perceived interests. For instance, in Jujuy, the proximity to an essential international highway allowed the concerned communities to exert substantial economic pressure, making their mobilization efforts more impactful. In contrast, remote rural areas like Catamarca, with their isolated and dispersed populations, face greater challenges in organizing and articulating their interests. In Germany, urban areas see more frequent use of citizens' petitions and referenda compared to rural areas. Urban areas tend to have greater financial resources and higher economic activity, which translates into more large-scale transport and construction projects that invite public participation. Additionally, the political dynamics in urban municipal councils, with higher party politicization, also promote civic engagement through petitions for enhancing political profiles. The expansion of renewable energy infrastructure in rural areas might shift this dynamic, as rural communities might become more involved in such projects. This is the case in Italy, where a certain center-periphery divide influences participation in the context of energy transition projects. Rural and peripheral areas are often chosen for hosting wind and solar plants as well as nuclear waste disposals while the benefits of these projects are largely reaped by urban, energy-intensive regions. The perception of taking on a burden for the benefit of distant urban centers can fuel resistance and necessitate greater engagement and negotiation with rural stakeholders to ensure fair and equitable development processes.

As for the urban-rural dimension of *participatory budgeting*, the chapters assembled in this volume revealed several notable differences. One of them concerns the territorial scope of application, since large cities (understandably) organize such processes at the neighborhood level rather than regarding the city as a whole. This ensures a small scale which avoids the involvement of too many people and leads to a focus on truly local projects. Therefore, it hardly comes as a surprise that a city like Bologna deliberately linked in 2015 participatory budgeting with a process of urban decentralization. The chapter on Poland points to a similar trend, as the country's large urban municipalities often opt to conduct what is called a civic budget in specific districts alongside such processes at the city level. Interestingly, these districts do not always coincide with the administrative boundaries of neighborhoods. Another important insight concerning the Polish case is that, while participatory budgeting is open to all municipalities, it is in practice mainly carried out by urban local governments. If such a process is implemented in a rural context it usually differs significantly. As the chapter on North Macedonia emphasizes, budget forums in villages are highly distinctive regarding both the topics prioritized and the composition of the working tables. The authors exploring the South African case similarly underline the significant differences between various categories of municipalities with small rural ones being disadvantaged regarding such as access to modern technology and meeting infrastructure. Consequently, they call on the minister responsible for local government to use their power to issue regulations in such a way that these particularities are taken into account and that collaboration between urban and rural municipalities is promoted.

While the chapters in this volume agree that the local government level is the place of particularly robust examples of *digital participation*, this does not necessarily mean equal conditions in urban and rural contexts. To be sure, the Covid-19 pandemic has acted in both contexts as a catalyst for both the adoption of new tools and the actual use of existing ones. Thus, there has been the expectation that digital participation would not only be a merely temporary emergency solution but become a permanent complement to traditional offline participation and thereby have the benefit of increasing the number of potential participants overall involved.[6] Yet, as the chapters in this book confirm, the realization of this vision is hampered by a persisting digital divide that often exists not only in social terms, among groups

[6] "Ensuring the respect of the European Charter of Local Self-Government in major crisis situations", report and recommendations for the Congress of Local and Regional Authorities of the Council of Europe, 2021, https://bia.unibz.it/esploro/outputs/report/Ensuring-the-respect-of-the-European/991006160003301241, Para 67.

within a municipality, but also in territorial terms between urban and rural municipalities.[7]

Even though, as mentioned above, the focus of the digital divide debates arguably shifted from access to skills and motivation, this does not mean that the former has become totally irrelevant for all communities. In fact, people in remote areas often do not have, according to the chapters in this book, equal network access which would be a prerequisite for digital participation in the same conditions as city dwellers. But access to the Internet is not the only reason for a territory-based digital divide. Another one could be differences concerning the financial and technical resources of the local administration which are essential to implement more complex and costly participatory processes such as, in particular, those involving digital twin and immersive technologies. Moreover, the demographics of the local population also seem to play a role since people in cities are often younger and more technology-savvy than their counterparts in rural areas, which certainly facilitates digital participation. That overall, such participation seems to be more common in urban contexts may also result from some formats just being not needed in a rural environment. For instance, the crowdsourcing applications through which people may report public service disruptions in several Italian cities appear to be dispensable in a village because closer contact with authorities makes it easier there to report such issues directly. As far as digital participatory platforms are concerned, these especially widespread tools are in Italy not limited to urban environments. Indeed, as the chapter points out there are relevant examples from huge metropolitan cities to small municipalities with less than 20,000 inhabitants. Similar to these online platforms, the transparency procedures concerning procurement information, which the South African chapter examines, are arguably something that is (almost) as easily to implement for small rural local governments as for urban ones, since they do not seem to be overly cumbersome or expensive. While the analysis reveals that there are no remarkable urban-rural differences concerning the sometimes considerable levels of intransparency, this result is, as the authors emphasize, probably more alarming with regard to metropolitan municipalities, given their much higher share in the total procurement undertaken by local governments.

As several chapters point out, digital participation is potentially also linked to the concepts of "smart cities" and, more recently, "smart villages". Contributors to this volume concur that concepts of smart cities may vary a lot, but still acknowledge that they are essentially about both service provision and a more responsive local administration through participatory governance. According to the chapter on Spain, the notion of smart cities has become rather business-oriented, whereas the relatively new concept of smart villages is focused on territorial development to diminish urban-rural disparities which are community-led and based on participation, albeit not necessarily digital participation. The chapter specifically analyses

[7] "Ensuring the respect of the European Charter of Local Self-Government in major crisis situations", report and recommendations for the Congress of Local and Regional Authorities of the Council of Europe, 2021, https://bia.unibz.it/esploro/outputs/report/Ensuring-the-respect-of-the-European/991006160003301241, Para 21

the case of Ansó, a small Spanish village selected for the EU Preparatory Action on Smart Rural Areas in the Twenty-First Century. It concludes that rural areas have emerged as interesting places for experimentation. But the author also adds the caveat that they run the risk of eventually emulating the smart city model where participation by citizens (as opposed to business actors) is largely absent.

18.7 The Actual Impact of Participation on Local Decision-Making

Participatory processes may have intended results related to the set objectives mentioned above or non-intended results. The chapters in this volume show a mixed picture of results. It is not easy to establish clear outcomes of a certain procedure due to many contextual variables. However, some general factors of success can be identified.

In the chapters on *local development and planning* all contributions highlight that ultimately local governments and their behaviour play a key role in facilitating successful participatory approaches. The Italian example shows that the role of local governments is crucial, as catalysts in creating environments conducive of participation and collaboration between local institutions and social movements. Without the political commitment of municipalities, the often non-binding results of participatory processes have very limited effect, with a negative impact on the legitimacy of local governments as well as the citizens' motivation to public participation in the future. The Government Goal Plan of Argentina hinges on this aspect as public hearings are non-binding and the administration has no obligation to respond or incorporate public feedback on the plan. Similarly, the author in the chapter on Spain highlights that in the advanced phase of planning, participation is often limited to a "formality" with a limited capacity of citizens to question plans or propose new aspects. The limited impact of the statutory participation in Germany is also seen as linked to its non-binding legal nature. Statutory participation will only be effective in case the local government engages transparently and openly with the statements and concerns brought forward. The German chapter highlights the negative consequences on trust and confidence, when participants might not feel like their arguments are heard and taken seriously, and they may take their arguments outside of the structured participation process. Additional possibilities such as petitions to termination of planning or possible judicial intervention can motivate the local authorities to take the non-binding processes (mainly at the beginning of a planning process) more seriously. The impact of participatory processes, thus, does not only depend on their legal nature (binding/non-binding).

However, the impact does also depend on more practical organizational matters, such as the capacity of stakeholders to participate in the various fora, the capacities of local governments to respond and the political culture determining the attitudes and relationship between political actors. Challenges mentioned in this volume are time constraints of citizens and authorities (the chapters on Argentina particularly highlight this problem) and technical challenges and knowledge gaps, especially when it comes to highly technical planning issues. The complexity of the planning process also affects local authorities, especially in rural areas, which influences the quality and impact of participation processes greatly. Lastly, namely the example of Italy has shown that new approaches can have a positive impact on local development and planning. The use of the MSA tool in numerous other municipalities and its adaptability to different contexts has proven the discussion to have moved beyond the dichotomy of invented/invited spaces.

The chapters with respect to *participation in large-scale projects* show that participation impacts the dynamics between governmental authorities, communities and other stakeholders greatly. The case of the mining projects in Argentina reveals a complex interplay between (private and public) economic interests, governmental policies and responsibilities, and community rights. It shows the critical role of governmental responsiveness in conflict resolution. The administration's disregard for the local communities' views and expressed needs and interests led to protests and finally police repression. It also shows that when a formal framework for participation is missing, mining companies negotiate informally with individual communities (or with the powerful parts of them), which further complicates the situation. The case of Argentina also highlights how support by environmental lawyers and (national and regional) NGOs as well as international treaties and networks can leverage the possibilities and effectiveness of local communities to advocate for their rights and inclusion in the decision-making process, especially when local participation forums do not exist or are not effective.

In Germany, the "Stuttgart 21" project serves as a symbol of both mobilizing protest in informal spaces and the evolving discourse on more formal participation in large-scale projects. The substantial public outcry against the urban development project spurred significant political and legal reforms, such as the adoption of Section 25(3) of the Administrative Procedure Act, aimed at improving participatory processes. The case exemplifies how large-scale projects can also act as catalysts and motivation for legislative changes and may elevate public participation to a critical component of urban development policies. In Italy, however, the history of the design of participatory processes for siting nuclear waste disposal seems to indicate a political preference for expeditious project completion over genuine participatory engagement. The minimal reaction to the recent dismantling of the institutionalized participatory processes on large-scale projects highlights the lack of faith in these mechanisms and the failure to embed participatory processes more deeply within the societal and political fabric. Thus, Italy's experience reveals the challenges of fostering genuine community involvement without substantial political investment and commitment. Switzerland's semi-direct democracy presents a contrasting model where participatory procedures are integral to the institutional set-up and part of political culture. The extensive use of referenda and the involvement of citizens at various levels foster a high degree of trust and confidence in public authorities and a relatively transparent behavior of the latter towards the public. The chapter on Swiss participatory processes shows how participation processes serve to gather information and assess political support but also to build compromises among diverse political interests. This approach may take time but helps mitigate conflicts, demonstrating how robust participatory frameworks can enhance the legitimacy and long-term success of large-scale projects.

As for the impact of *participatory budgeting*, it is evident that successful examples trigger emulation by other local authorities. In North Macedonia, citizens' involvement in budget processes has arguably been on the rise. In the latter case, this has been true, in particular, for the period since 2010 and is also attributed to an active role played by the country's local government association. In comparison, the author analyzing the Polish case is rather cautious regarding her assessment and feels that the potential of participatory budgeting is still underexploited. Especially in the early stages, it has arguably been too often a top-down initiative that gained little traction with the local population so more promotion of the instrument is recommended by local government associations, the media, schools and other institutions.

Beyond the wide diffusion of participatory budgeting across many municipalities, another issue is then whether decisions made through such processes are effectively implemented. The Italy chapter has certainly affirmed this for the case of Bologna where the successful realization of the selected projects arguably contributes significantly to the city being considered a pioneer. The chapter also argues, however, that an assessment of the impact must be context-specific, as the mere survival of participatory budgeting in a more challenging political environment like that of Caltanissetta should be appreciated as a positive effect. The chapter on Poland is characterized by a consistently favorable assessment of the impact, since conflicts between local populations and authorities about project implementation seem to be rare.

Yet, the chapters in this volume point to several obstacles to the successful realization of projects. One obvious hindrance is an insufficient allocation of funds, which was namely discussed in the chapter on South Africa. Legislation and court rulings instruct local governments to earmark sufficient funds for participation, but with due regard to a municipality's financial capacity which does not always allow for appropriate means being dedicated. The problem of underfunding was also discussed in the chapter on Italy, for instance, for the town of Caltanissetta a clear link between decreased finances for and a decreased impact of the projects selected was observed. However, in this municipality, participatory budgeting is at least still practiced, albeit with fewer resources, while another Italian local government, namely Malles Venosta, has given up on it. The latter case demonstrates that the availability of financial resources is not all-important, as the budget share per capita dedicated to participatory budgeting was the highest, more than 70 times higher than that of Caltanissetta. Yet, the process was eventually discontinued due to another frequent impediment to implementation, i.e. an excessive reliance on the commitment of the mayor. Such personal leadership had introduced participatory budgeting in the small municipality of Malles Venosta. But the lack of such leadership after the mayor's resignation led to a stop, even though the relevant provisions in the municipal statute are still in place and the successor belonged to the same party. In Madrid, by contrast, it was the change from a left-wing to a right-wing government that led to a marginalization of *Decide Madrid*. This is because the new local administration, hostile to this online platform, moved to cancel several projects adopted through this participatory process. Finally, a key issue for the impact of participatory budgeting anywhere is the monitoring of the implementation of the projects selected. In the case of North Macedonia's budget forums, the last stage of the process foresees the formation of a working group for follow up. The chapter on Poland emphasizes that an assessment of implementation is done through a range of different tools. Examples are questionnaires, focus groups, the Supreme Audit Office and—in the City of Kraków—a special body with mixed representation of citizens and politicians which meets as often as once a month to monitor implementation. Such elaborate post-decision procedures seem well-suited to ensure the actual impact of participatory budgeting.

As far as the impact of *digital participation* is concerned, none of the chapters in this book considers it a panacea that shall replace participatory processes in person. Instead, they rather argue for blending these two different ways of involving people in democratic decision-making and them complementary. If a balance is struck between them, digital and face-to-face processes can jointly contribute to strengthening citizen participation, whether the latter is "merely" a political imperative or, as in the South African case, a legal obligation that is regularly reviewed and enforced by the judiciary. Yet. The authors of the South African chapter caution against expecting too much from such legal obligations. The acknowledge that these duties have also encouraged a "tick box" mentality with municipalities conducting participatory processes more for the sake of compliance with the law than to really benefit from people's inputs.

Overall, the chapters in this volume also alluded to certain risks, both specific ones for digital participation and more general ones. First, there is the concern that the involvement of people online often does not have a participatory quality that is equivalent to face-to-face processes, especially when it comes to the consideration of diverse perspectives in a process of meaningful deliberation. Secondly, not least because of this (perceived) lack of equivalence, digital participation may serve politicians as a fig leaf. They may declare the duty to involve citizens, whether it is political or legal, to be fulfilled without resorting to the often more onerous alternative of in-person processes, which again demonstrates the need for online and offline processes to be complementary. Thirdly, there is a concern that digital participation frequently tends to be applied to trivial issues rather than significant ones that entail real empowerment. The ensuing risk of mounting frustration among citizens about their rather ineffective involvement is in line with broad agreement across the chapters in this book that we are well beyond the (perhaps overly) optimistic period, from the 1990s onwards, regarding the potential of digital processes for a renewal of democracy. Even one of the more positive examples of digital participation, the platform *Decide Madrid*, is a mixed bag. On the one hand, it is lauded for the high number of decisions in which people have been involved through consultation and even co-creation. On the other hand, the platform is faced with several challenges such as generally decreasing interest, asymmetrical participation depending on factors like age and ideology, concerns about moderation and feedback, as well as security issues of the platform.

When we turn our attention from the present to the future, there are at least three major factors that this volume identified as crucial for the success or failure of online participation. First, the chapter on Italy, in particular, pointed to the new possibilities of artificial intelligence (AI). Whereas it seems indeed true that the generation of big data sets, the effective illustration of scenarios through virtual reality and other innovations have the potential to enhance the quality of people's involvement in decision-making, it is probably impossible at this stage to gauge whether the net effect of AI on digital participation will turn out to be positive or negative. Secondly, the green transformation which has been set in motion in a number of countries is another factor that is certain to become critically important in the near future. Indeed, many of the big investments that come with this change concern projects such as new infrastructure that needs to be implemented at the local level and municipalities would be well advised not to act in this regard against the will and without meaningful participation of local populations. Overall, the green transformation also offers an opportunity because digitalization is high on the agenda and tools for online participation, especially sophisticated ones such as the digital twin technology mentioned in the chapter on Italy, are costly concerning both equipment and expertise. The latter obviously requires the cooperation of local authorities not only with other levels of government but also with partnerships beyond the public sector with research institutions, private companies, etc. In any case, as some examples in this volume demonstrate, such collaboration and the implementation of digital participation more generally need continuous funding. This is to avoid a situation in which participatory processes are only carried by project-related ad hoc financing so that they fail to take root among citizens. Sustainability beyond merely temporary knock-on financing is key.

Index

K. Kössler, E. Schläppi (eds.), *Citizen Participation in Local Governance*, Local and Urban Governance, https://doi.org/10.1007/978-3-031-99824-9

MIX
Papier aus verantwortungsvollen Quellen
Paper from responsible sources
FSC® C105338

If you have any concerns about our products,
you can contact us on
ProductSafety@springernature.com

In case Publisher is established outside the EU,
the EU authorized representative is:
Springer Nature Customer Service Center GmbH
Europaplatz 3, 69115 Heidelberg, Germany

Printed by Libri Plureos GmbH
in Hamburg, Germany